INSIGHT GUIDES

UTAH

APA PUBLICATIONS

L

Part of the Langenscheidt Publishing Group

INSIGHT GUIDE
UTAH

ABOUT THIS BOOK

Editorial
Editor
John Gattuso
Editorial Director
Brian Bell

Distribution
United States
Langenscheidt Publishers, Inc.
36–36 33rd Street 4th Floor
Long Island City, NY 11106
Fax: 1 (718) 784 0640

UK & Ireland
GeoCenter International Ltd
Meridian House, Churchill Way West
Basingstoke, Hampshire RG21 6YR
Fax: (44) 1256 817988

Australia
Universal Publishers
1 Waterloo Road
Macquarie Park, NSW 2113
Fax: (61) 2 9888 9074

New Zealand
Hema Maps New Zealand Ltd (HNZ)
Unit D, 24 Ra ORA Drive
East Tamaki, Auckland
Fax: (64) 9 273 6479

Worldwide
**Apa Publications GmbH & Co.
Verlag KG (Singapore branch)**
38 Joo Koon Road, Singapore 628990
Tel: (65) 6865 1600. Fax: (65) 6861 6438

Printing
Insight Print Services (Pte) Ltd
38 Joo Koon Road, Singapore 628990
Tel: (65) 6865 1600. Fax: (65) 6861 6438

©2007 Apa Publications GmbH & Co.
Verlag KG (Singapore branch)
All Rights Reserved
First Edition 2005
Reprinted 2007

CONTACTING THE EDITORS
We would appreciate it if readers
would alert us to errors or out-
dated information by writing to:
**Insight Guides, P.O. Box 7910,
London SE1 1WE, England.
Fax: (44) 20 7403 0290.
insight@apaguide.co.uk**

www.insightguides.com
In North America:
www.insighttravelguides.com

The first Insight Guide pioneered the use of creative full-color photography in travel guides in 1970. Since then, we have expanded our range to cater for our readers' need not only for reliable information about their chosen destination but also for a real understanding of the culture and workings of that destination. Now, when the internet can supply inexhaustible (but not always reliable) facts, our books marry text and pictures to provide those much more elusive qualities: knowledge and discernment. To achieve this, they rely heavily on the authority of locally based writers and photographers.

Insight Guide: Utah is structured to convey an understanding of the state and its people as well as to guide readers through its attractions:

♦ The **Features** section, indicated by a yellow bar at the top of each page, covers the natural and cultural history of Utah as well as the state's wide array of recreational opportunities in a series of informative essays.

♦ The main **Places** section, indicated by a blue bar, is a complete guide to all the sights and areas worth visiting. Places of special interest are coordinated by number with the maps.

♦ The **Travel Tips** listings section, with an orange bar, provides full information on transportation, accommodations, restaurants, sports, the arts, adventure travel, and more. An easy-to-find contents list for Travel Tips is printed on the back flap, which also serves as a bookmark.

ABOVE: skiers on the slopes at The Canyons, a Park City ski resort.

The contributors

This book was produced by **John Gattuso** of Stone Creek Publications in Milford, New Jersey, a veteran of more than a dozen Insight Guides and editor of the Discovery Travel Adventures, a series for travelers with special interests such as bird-watching, skiing and scuba diving.

John worked closely with Santa Fe writer **Nicky Leach**, a regular contributor to Insight Guides since 1994. Nicky's connection to Utah has deep family roots. Ancestors on her mother's side converted to Mormonism in Britain, migrated to Ohio, and were among the first Mormon pioneers to reach the Salt Lake Valley in 1847. Her 20 years of cov-ering the American Southwest have led her into every corner of Utah and resulted in award-winning books on the state's spectacular parks, including several titles on Zion National Park. In this guide, she wrote about locations throughout southern and central Utah as well as the state's varied social makeup, natural history, American Indian cultures, Mormon culture, and more.

Utah's northern and western expanse was covered by veteran travel writer **Richard Harris**. The author of numerous guidebooks on the American West, Richard wrote about the greater Salt Lake City area, including Park City, Ogden and Provo, as well as the vast and lightly populated Great Basin region. He also gives readers an overview of Utah's world-class ski areas and outlines possibilities for such warm-weather adventures as river rafting, mountain biking, backpacking and rock climbing. When not traveling, he lives in Santa Fe, New Mexico, where he is president of the New Mexico Book Association and publisher of *Southwest Book Views*.

With more than 30 years experience as a news editor in the New York area, **Edward A. Jardim** knows how to transform a complex story into a concise narrative. Here he condenses three centuries of history into an engaging chronicle of Utah's development, from the Mormon exodus to the growth of modern-day Salt Lake City.

Stephen Trimble and **Tom Till** were the principal photographers. The book was indexed by **Elizabeth Cook**.

Map Legend

– – – –	State Boundary
–•–•–	National Park/Reserve
✈ ✈	Airport: International/Regional
🚌	Bus Station
❶	Tourist Information
✉	Post Office
✝ ✝ ✝	Church/Ruins
✝	Monastery
☾	Mosque
✡	Synagogue
🏰	Castle/Ruins
⌂	Mansion/Stately home
∴	Archeological Site
⋒	Cave
⌇	Statue/Monument
★	Place of Interest

The main places of interest in the Places section are coordinated by number with a full-color map (e.g. ❶), and a symbol at the top of every right-hand page tells you where to find the map.

INSIGHT GUIDE
UTAH

CONTENTS

LEFT: a hiker scales a sandstone formation known as the Vortex near Moab in southern Utah.

Travel Tips

Information panels

Places

THE BEST OF UTAH

From rafting rivers and hiking red-rock canyons in southern Utah's national parks to visiting the world headquarters of the Church of Jesus Christ of Latter-day Saints in Salt Lake City, travelers to the Beehive State have plenty to keep them busy

TOP SCENERY

● **Zion National Park** One of the state's top destinations. A new visitor center, history museum and tram system from Springdale make viewing the canyon and accessing summer hiking trails a snap. *See page 201.*

● **Grand Staircase-Escalante National Monument** Utah's hottest new wilderness destination has paved and four-wheel-drive backroads, slot canyon hiking and inspired small visitor centers. *See page 227.*

● **Island in the Sky, Canyonlands National Park** Hundred-mile views of canyons and a host of outdoor pursuits, from river running to hiking, biking and Jeeping. *See page 265.*

● **Bryce Canyon National Park** Hundreds of colorful, carved rock "hoodoos" clustered along the eastern edge of the Paunsaugunt Plateau give this high-country park a fanciful appearance. *See page 217.*

● **Alpine Loop** Closed by snow in winter, this dramatic drive through the Wasatch Mountains is best in fall when changing foliage in the aspen forests splashes color across Uinta National Forest. *See page 148.*

TOP FAMILY ATTRACTIONS

● **Wall of Bones at Dinosaur National Monument** A Disney-like tram ride, ranger talks and partially excavated dinosaur skeletons. *See page 159.*

● **Arches National Park** Thousands of sandstone arches, a pretty campground and lots of easy day hikes. It's a short drive from family-friendly Moab. *See page 273.*

● **The San Juan River** Easy paddling, great scenery, ancient Indian rock art, wildlife, swimming beaches and access to the adjoining Navajo Reservation. *See page 291.*

● **Monument Valley Navajo Tribal Park** Take an open-air Jeep tour or horseback ride through the West's most famous scenery. *See page 298.*

● **McCurdy Historical Doll Museum, Provo** Remarkable collection of more than 4,000 dolls created by an early 20th-century teacher. *See page 147.*

● **American West Heritage Center** Stay overnight in a teepee in this Wellsville living-history center or learn how to grow fruits and vegetables at the adjoining Jensen Historical Farm, a re-creation of a Mormon farm. *See page 129.*

ABOVE: Arches National Park. **LEFT:** San Juan River rafting

SPECTACULAR GAME VIEWING

● **Flaming Gorge National Recreational Area**
Every August and September, thousands of bright-red kokanee salmon spawn in Sheep Creek and may be viewed, along with bighorn sheep, bears and other wildlife, on Sheep Creek-Spirit Lake Scenic Byway Loop. *See page 157.*

● **Antelope Island State Park**
Home to herds of free-roaming bison, prong-horn and bighorn sheep, and thousands of shorebirds attracted to the lakeshore by brine flies in summer and fall. *See page 121.*

● **Hardware Ranch**
You can take a snowmobile or wagon ride to view the 600 elk who calve here in spring. *See page 129.*

● **Zion National Park**
Mule deer and wild turkeys wander road-sides while peregrine falcons, red-tailed hawks, and California condors nest on cliffs towering 2,000 ft (600 meters) above the Virgin River. *See page 201.*

ABOVE: ancient Pueblo ruin known as Hovenweep Castle.

ABOVE: a mountain lion

HISTORY AND CULTURE

● **Temple Square, Salt Lake City**
Home to the Church of Jesus Christ of Latter-day Saints. *See page 133.*

● **Highway 89 Scenic Byway, Sanpete and Sevier Valleys**
Scandinavian archi-tecture, artist studios and mining ghost towns. *See page 181.*

● **Donner-Reed Museum, Grantsville**
The possessions of the ill-fated Donner Party abandoned during their disastrous crossing of the Great Salt Lake

Desert. *See page 190.*

● **Nine Mile Canyon, Castle Country**
Contains the world's biggest outdoor museum of Fremont Indian rock art and other artifacts. *See page 173.*

● **Museum of People and Cultures, Brigham Young University**
Artifacts from Utah and other parts of the world that relate to Mormon history. *See page 146.*

RIGHT: Temple Square

OFF THE BEATEN TRACK

● **Pipe Spring National Monument**
Set in the lonesome Arizona Strip, between Grand Canyon and Zion National Parks, little-known Pipe Spring preserves an 1870s fortified Mormon ranch built atop a former Ancestral Pueblo village and surrounded by the Kaibab Paiute Reservation, all interpreted in the monument's excellent new cultural museum. *See page 209.*

● **Cleveland-Lloyd Dinosaur Quarry**
Getting there is half the fun for dinosaur lovers drawn to one of the world's biggest dinosaur die-off sites in the San Rafael Desert, east of Price. *See page 174.*

● **Trail of the Ancients**
The state's best Ancestral Pueblo ruins, working trading posts, the San Juan River, Lake Powell and the carved rocks of Monu-ment Valley, crown jewel of the Navajo Nation. *See page 289*

● **Outlaw Trail**
Follow in the footsteps of Butch Cassidy and the Wild Bunch, from Robbers Roost in Canyonlands north through the Uinta Basin to Brown's Park, their refuge on the Wyoming border. *See page 163.*

● **Range Creek**
Fly from Green River to a ranch atop Tavaputs Plateau for a chance to view some of Utah's best-preserved Fremont Indian artifacts along Range Creek before floating back on the Green River. *See page 177.*

OUTDOOR ADVENTURE

● **Slickrock Trail, Moab**
A favorite with fat-tire enthusiasts who come to Moab to challenge themselves on this hot and dusty but highly scenic desert bike trail. *See page 281.*

● **Cataract Canyon, Canyonlands National Park**
River runners vie for a chance to "Waltz the Cat" on the last 14 miles (23 km) of whitewater on the Colorado River before it enters Lake Powell. *See page 265.*

● **West Rim Trail, Zion National Park**
This overnight trail across Zion's Kolob Plateau offers a chance to hike a part of the Zion backcountry few visitors experience. *See page 208.*

● **Escalante Canyons**
Follow the Escalante River through its deep canyons on foot, horseback, or leading a pack llama to view Fremont Indian granaries and rock art as well as lush side canyons filled with arches, waterfalls, wildlife and historic cabins. *See page 231.*

● **Ride a Bobsled at Olympic Park**
Pay big bucks to hop aboard a four-man bobsled steered by a certified driver and reach 80 mph (130km/h) at Utah Olympic Park, where you can also learn Nordic skiing and luge racing. *See page 100.*

● **Best Snow on Earth**
Skiers and snow-boarders have their choice of world-class ski resorts, most within an hour or two of Salt Lake City. Nature has endowed northern Utah with some of the finest and most abundant powder in the West. Expanded and modern-ized for the 2002 Winter Olympics, the facilities at Snowbasin, Alta and Park City have never been more inviting. *See page 99–102.*

ABOVE: biking the Slickrock Trail outside Moab.

BEST FOR BIRDWATCHING

● **Bear River Migratory Bird Refuge**
Attracts hundreds of species of migratory and resident waterfowl. *See page 129.*

● **Fish Springs National Wildlife Refuge**
Mineral-laden, saline warm springs are home to over 5,000 wintering birds in this remote area off the Pony Express Trail. *See page 86.*

● **Scott Matheson Wetlands Preserve**
Next to downtown Moab, it provides quick access to the Colorado River to view a huge variety of bird species as well as other riparian wildlife. *See page 283.*

● **Ouray National Wildlife Refuge**
This Uinta Basin sanctuary is one of the best places in eastern Utah to view hundreds of birds attracted to wetlands. *See page 163.*

● **Dinosaur National Monument**
Harpers Corner Scenic Drive, in the Canyons section, is an excellent place to see eagles, hawks and other soaring raptors as well as sage grouse in spring. *See page 158.*

LEFT: a snowboarder slices through Utah powder

WINING AND DINING

● **Backroad Organics, Capitol Reef Country** Free-range meats, organic veggies and award-winning desserts adorn the menus of several restaurants off US 12. *See page 259.*

● **Center Cafe, Moab** Gourmet haven in a town bustling with breweries, bakeries, rib and steak joints, breakfast-only cafes, and Mexican fare catering to the outdoors crowd. *See page 323.*

● **Bit and Spur Mexican Restaurant, Springdale** This casual but hip restaurant near Zion National Park com-bines billiards with bar and elegant patio dining on specialties from sweet potato tamales to snapper. *See page 320.*

● **Ruth's Diner, Salt Lake City** Consistently voted the best breakfast spot in town. *See page 317.*

● **The Tree Room, Sundance Resort** This five-star restaurant is one of the big après-ski draws of actor Robert Redford's Sundance Resort in northern Utah. For culinary daring and romantic atmosphere, it has few equals in Utah. *See page 318.*

ABOVE: golden eagles patrol the skies.

ABOVE: Salt Lake City's award-winning library

CONTEMPORARY CULTURE

● **Sundance International Film Festival** The granddaddy of American Indie movie events, this weeklong celluloid celebration has become the biggest event of the year in Park City. *See page 153.*

● **Salt Lake City Public Library** The award-winning new Salt Lake City Library is one of Utah's top three attractions. *See page 136.*

● **Gallivan Center** Salt Lake's cultural center hosts a popular farmers market, concerts, folkloric dance festivals and a giant chess board. *See page 136.*

● **Delta Center** Home of the NBA's Utah Jazz, this 20,000-seat arena is also the place to see rodeos, circuses, pop concerts and other big events. *See page 137.*

● **Golf Mecca** St George, in southern Utah, has 10 golf courses and perfect playing weather year-round. *See page 211.*

MONEY-SAVING TIPS

● **Free Tours of Mormon Sites** All Mormon-owned sites in Utah, including the popular Mormon Tabernacle, Cove Fort and Jacob Hamblin House, offer free admission and tours.

● **Annual National Park Pass** The $50 National Park Pass offers unlimited admission for one year to all units of the National Park System – a huge savings and an essential investment. Buy at a park entrance station and all proceeds benefit the park.

● **Primitive Camping on Public Lands** Hike and camp for free on all undeveloped Bureau of Land Management and U.S. Forest Service lands. Many adjoin developed national parks where payment is required. All that's needed is a spirit of adventure and a well-stocked vehicle.

● **Free Wine and Movies on the Colorado River** Historic Red Cliffs Lodge, a ranch and resort on the Colorado River outside Moab, offers free wine tastings and self-guided tours of its vineyard as well as a free on-site museum containing memorabilia from the many movies filmed here, including *Rio Grande*, *Wagon Masters*, *Thelma and Louise* and *City Slickers*.

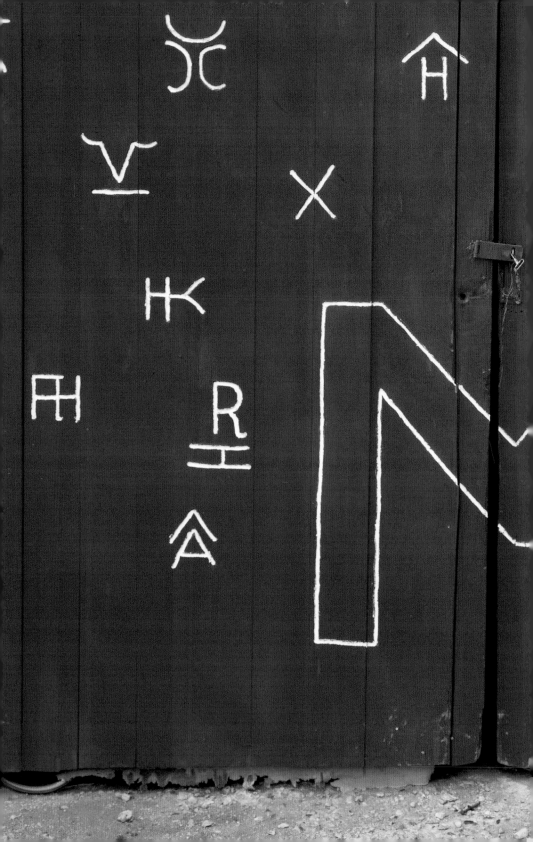

THE BEEHIVE STATE

Utah attracts visitors with beguiling landscapes,
world-class skiing and a rich history as America's Zion

Driving into southern Utah, one can't help but be struck by the otherworldly nature of the landscape. Here the ruddy sandstone of the Colorado Plateau has been sculpted by water, wind and ice into a fantasia of arches, spires, balancing rocks, "hoodoos," goosenecks and other bizarre formations. In few places are the Earth's geologic bones so beautifully exposed yet shrouded in such mystery, their shape and texture more akin to the whorls of living tissue than cold stone. This is the backdrop of such beloved national parks as Zion, Arches, Bryce Canyon, Capitol Reef and Canyonlands, and thousands of square miles of other public lands – a vast and wild playground enjoyed by hikers, mountain bikers, canyoneers and other outdoor enthusiasts as well as conventional automobile tourists.

The picture is altogether different in the northern tier of the state, which tends to be greener and more urban. The Wasatch Range runs like a spine down the center of the region, separating the forested peaks of northeastern Utah – justly renowned for some of the finest and most abundant snow in the West – from the sun-scorched flats of the Great Basin, where the Great Salt Lake shimmers under the desert sun like an empty promise. The lake is a vast but virtually sterile sea, too salty to sustain much more than algae and brine shrimp.

Thrust upon the world stage by the 2002 Winter Olympics, Salt Lake City has taken its place alongside Denver, Colorado, and Phoenix, Arizona, as one of the up-and-coming cities of the New West. Headquarters of the Church of Jesus Christ of Latter-day Saints, whose members settled the Salt Lake Valley under the leadership of Brigham Young more than 150 years ago, Salt Lake City has matured into an urbane, dynamic and fast-growing metropolitan center with cultural and commercial assets rivaling those of any American city of similar size. Unlike most cities, however, Salt Lake City is perfectly situated for lovers of the outdoors, who within an hour from downtown can be biking among wildflowers in the Wasatch Range, flying through mounds of fluffy powder at a world-class ski resort, or hiking a cool mountain trail shaded by pine and aspen. About 30 miles (50 km) west of Salt Lake City is Park City, a busted-out mining town that has been reborn as a winter sports mecca and hub of the prestigious Sundance Film Festival.

As if that weren't enough, Utah offers many other delights, ranging from the quiet pleasures of restaurants, museums and historic sites to the thrill of exploring dinosaur quarries, shooting the rapids in red-rock canyons and driving spectacular backcountry roads. Above all, there is the lure of the outdoors. Because of all of Utah's blessings – and they are many – surely the richest is a landscape unlike any other in the world. ❑

PRECEDING PAGES: the Mormon Tabernacle Choir, Temple Square, Salt Lake City; a cowboy at Pack Creek Ranch near Moab; a skier takes to the air at Snowbird.
LEFT: Delicate Arch in Arches National Park has come to symbolize the otherworldly beauty of Utah's red-rock country.

Decisive Dates

Prehistoric Cultures

ca 10,000 BC: A nomadic lifestyle is the cultural norm for the people who inhabit the region that includes present-day Utah.

ca AD 500: Anasazi, or Ancestral Puebloans, settle in villages in southern Utah, growing crops and flourishing as one of the main cultures of the Colorado Plateau.

ca 1300: Anasazi and Fremont cultures decline as their people are compelled to uproot themselves by a protracted drought.

European Arrivals

1540: Explorers from the groundbreaking Coronado mission cross into present-day Utah.

1776: The first comprehensive exploration of Utah by outsiders is carried out under two Franciscan priests, Silvestre Velez de Escalante and Francisco Atanasio Dominguez, searching for a route between the missions of New Mexico and California.

ca 1812: A trading route known as the Old Spanish Trail stretches from Santa Fe to California via Utah.

1819: Spain and the United States agree to a treaty recognizing the region that includes present-day Utah as Spanish-owned. Two years later, Mexico breaks away from Spain, declares itself a republic, and inherits Utah.

1824: Mountain man Jim Bridger encounters the Great Salt Lake. Meanwhile, an annual rendezvous system for trappers and traders gets under way in Utah.

1826: Utah is traversed as part of the first overland journey to California by an American, the fur trapper Jedediah S. Smith.

1830: Joseph Smith founds the Church of Jesus Christ of Latter-day Saints in Palmyra, New York. Its "Mormon" adherents later settle in Utah.

1833: Fur trader and explorer Joseph Walker travels across the northwest corner of Utah to California, encountering the Great Salt Lake and blazing a trail for surveyors and emigrants.

Wave of Emigrants

1844: Joseph Smith and his brother Hyrum are shot to death by a mob in Carthage, Illinois, and their co-religionists decide to seek sanctuary in the American West. Meanwhile, trader Miles Goodyear establishes Utah's first Anglo-American settlement, Fort Buenaventura, which gives rise to the town of Ogden.

1847: Mormon pioneers led by Brigham Young arrive in the Salt Lake Valley after a 1,200-mile (1,900-km) journey from Nauvoo, Illinois.

1848: The land that includes the future Utah Territory is ceded by Mexico to the United States.

1850: Congress rejects a Mormon proposal for a State of Deseret and instead establishes the Territory of Utah, population 11,390.

1851: Brigham Young is appointed by President Millard Fillmore as governor of Utah Territory.

1853: Tensions between Ute natives and settlers result in the Walker War in Utah Valley. Meanwhile, Captain John W. Gunnison and several of his men are killed in a Paiute attack.

1857: Disapproval of Mormon separateness, aggravated by the practice of polygamy, cause President James Buchanan to send an Army expedition to oust Brigham Young. Meanwhile, a massacre of non-Mormon emigrants at Mountain Meadows causes a national outcry.

1862: Congress restricts the practice of polygamy.

1863: Silver and lead are found in Bingham Canyon in the Oquirrh Mountains.

1864: Friction caused by encroachment on native lands sparks the Black Hawk War in central Utah.

1869: America's first transcontinental railway is completed at Promontory Point north of the Great Salt Lake. Meanwhile, Major John Wesley Powell begins his breakthrough explorations of the Green and Colorado Rivers.

1870: Women are granted voting rights by the

Utah legislature, the first such action in America.
1877: Mormon elder John D. Lee is executed for his role in the Mountain Meadows Massacre.
1877: Brigham Young dies at age 76.
1884: First prosecutions of Utah residents for polygamy are carried out under the Edmunds Law.
1890: Mormon leaders forsake the doctrine of plural marriage, clearing the way for presidential pardons and statehood.

Joining the Union

1896: Utah becomes the 45th state of the Union.
1897: The outlaws Butch Cassidy and The Sundance Kid make off with $9,000 in a daring rob-

1924: An explosion at the Castle Gate mine kills 171 miners.
1942: Nine months after the devastating attack at Pearl Harbor, an internment camp for Japanese-Americans is opened in central Utah.
1952: Uranium is discovered near Moab.
1962: Utah enters into an agreement for development of the Columbia River.
1972: The federal government offers to turn over all operations to the Navajo tribe within its reservation in Utah, New Mexico and Arizona.
1977: Convicted murderer Gary Gilmore is executed in state prison after intense national publicity.
1978: A long-held Mormon policy whereby African-

bery at a coal mining company in Castlegate, Utah.
1898: The worst fire in Utah history destroys much of Park City.
1900: More than 200 men and boys die in an explosion at the Winter Quarters coal mine.
1915: Spurning international protest, Utah executes militant union organizer Joe Hill for the murder of two Salt Lake City grocers. Hill becomes legendary as a martyr of the labor movement.
1917: Utah voters for the first time elect a non-Mormon to the governorship – Simon Bamberger.

PRECEDING PAGES: Mormon handcart pioneers.
LEFT: Pictograph House is an ancient Pueblo structure.
ABOVE: a family of Mormon settlers outside a log cabin.

Americans are denied priesthood status in the Church is ended as the result of a revelation announced by its leader, Spencer W. Kimball.
1979: The NBA New Orleans Jazz makes itself over as the Utah Jazz, and by 1991 key performers Karl Malone and John Stockton are packing a new 20,000-seat arena in Salt Lake City.
1996: A proclamation by President Bill Clinton sets aside 1.7 million acres (690,000 hectares) as Grand Staircase-Escalante National Monument.
2000: Utah's population totals 2,233,169, more than double the figure reported 30 years earlier.
2002: Salt Lake City plays host to the Winter Olympic Games. The global TV audience is an estimated 2.1 billion viewers. ❏

Chief A Tchee

NATIVE HERITAGE

From Ice Age hunters and ancient Pueblo civilizations to modern Indian tribes, Utah's indigenous people have left a singular mark on the land, and are still doing so

In 1990, the Utah Democratic party nominated an all American Indian slate for elected offices in San Juan County – a first in American history. The campaign was led by San Juan County Commissioner Mark Maryboy, a young Navajo who, just four years earlier, had succeeded in becoming the first American Indian to hold an elected position in Utah. With the exception of Maryboy, all the candidates were defeated. But the campaign drew widespread media attention, resulting in a surge in voter registration on Indian reservations in San Juan County.

For the first time, the 7,500 American Indians living in southeastern Utah (54 percent of the county's population) had entered mainstream politics. Statewide, the 25,000 members of Utah's Navajo, Southern Paiute, Northwestern Shoshone, Northern Ute, White Mesa Ute, and Goshute tribes, concentrated in southeastern Utah, the Uintah Basin and the Salt Lake City area, were showing their political strength after centuries of marginalization on their own lands. The Navajo slogan for the campaign: *Niha Whool Zhiizh,* or "It's Our Turn."

Ancient roots

As in neighboring Colorado, all of the tribes now living in Utah arrived there less than a thousand years ago, comparatively late in the human occupation of the Southwest. They moved onto lands that, for millennia, had been used by Ancestral Pueblo and Fremont Indian farmers, who built hundreds of villages, or pueblos, in southeastern Utah and the adjoining Four Corners that have been beautifully preserved on mesas and in canyons.

For the first humans on the North American continent at the end of the last Ice Age, 10,000 years ago, Utah's newly emerging grasslands and lakes and the wealth of big game must have seemed like the Promised Land. Paleo-Indian hunters crossed the Bering Land Bridge from

Mongolia to modern-day Alaska, then traveled south in family groups. The hunters moved with herds of oversized animals such as woolly mastodons, camels, giant bison and ground sloths that required strength and agility to bring down with spears. They slept in cave shelters, where they created stone tools and butchered

big game, and left behind bones, stone flakes and beautiful chert spear points. These people were known as the Clovis and Folsom, after the towns in northeastern New Mexico where their spear points were first uncovered.

The Pleistocene climate continued to warm and dry, and thousands of new plant species appeared. As the lakes and grasslands disappeared and desert conditions took their place, the big game herds died out, doomed perhaps by the changing environment and overhunting. People in Utah adopted a new lifestyle: that of hunter-gatherers. They hunted smaller game, such as modern bison and bighorn sheep, but also harvested wild plants. These people,

LEFT: Ute chief Atchee.
RIGHT: Ancestral Puebloan ruins, Grand Gulch.

dubbed the Archaic culture, fitted themselves gracefully into their surroundings and thrived for at least 6,000 years.

Knife blades, projectile points, milling stones and firepits have been found in rock shelters at Danger, Smith Creek and Deer Creek Caves near the margins of lakes and water sources and offer the first clear archaeological evidence of human activity in Utah during the early Archaic period (9000–7500 BC). By the Middle Archaic (7500–4000 BC), people were using a greater variety of ecological zones, from mountains to desert, and inventing new technologies. Women processed wild foods using grinding stones and

forced people to spread out in the Great Basin uplands, where plants and animals were more restricted. The more efficient bow and arrow replaced the atlatl, but something seems to have gone wrong. Hunters began leaving split-twig figurines of bighorn sheep in high cliff crevices where the sheep traveled, perhaps as hunting fetishes designed to attract the real thing. Game and plants may have been severely affected by drought, leading shamans to undertake long pilgrimages to sacred sites to pray for help.

Camped beneath sheer sandstone cliffs in southern Utah, they painted images in red hematite on the walls: herds of bighorn sheep,

made twined baskets for harvesting plants, which they carried on the forehead using a tumpline, the same way they carried their babies. The men made nets to catch small game, such as rabbits, and used an atlatl, or spear thrower, which allowed them greater precision in bringing down game. Excavations at Hogup Cave indicate that they enjoyed a diverse diet. Archaeologists have uncovered the remains of four species of large mammals (deer, antelope, mountain sheep and elk), 32 species of small mammals, 34 species of birds and 36 plant species.

By 2000 BC, Archaic families were found throughout Utah, and the expanding population

flowing water and oversized triangular figures with long thin bodies and huge, empty eyes. These limbless beings hover wraithlike above sandy washes in the labyrinthine canyons of the Maze District of Canyonlands National Park. They seem like the overwrought visions of a hungry, worried people calling to the gods for help.

Early farming

By AD 500, Archaic people were trying something new: cultivation of a domesticated wild grass from Mexico called maize. Agriculture made its way to the Four Corners region from Mexico via traders from the south, beginning in the early Christian era. From the Hohokam, who practiced irrigation farming in southern Arizona, the Basketmakers, as they were called, learned how to use check dams, ditches and dry farming techniques and acquired hammers, axes and exotic goods from Mexico. From the Mogollon of the southern New Mexico mountains, they learned how to make pots using the coiled clay method and to fire them at high temperatures to make strong, airtight containers for storing and transporting grains and valuables. The refined decorated pueblo pottery from the Four Corners quickly became a sought-after trade item, reflecting the potter's aesthetic.

Farming required a sedentary life and was

children, and gather seeds, nuts and fruits.

During the early Pueblo I period (AD 700– 900), families throughout the Four Corners began building hamlets of above-ground houses made of sandstone and adobe. Pithouses were used now as underground ceremonial rooms, or kivas. Here clansmen gathered to weave cotton and discuss the most advantageous times to plant and harvest. Ritual specialists tracked the daily movements of the sun, moon and planets across the sky. As the solstices approached, planting and harvesting ceremonies were announced. These priests quickly became the most important members of the village.

much more labor intensive than hunting. Nomadic families joined together to sow, water and watch over crops in irrigated gardens. They built semi-subterranean shelters, or pithouses, with roofs made of branches covered in earth and held up by central supports, that were snug in winter and cool in summer. Corn and squash, and later beans, were harvested in fall, then stored in sealed granaries for winter. While men went off hunting, the women stayed behind to keep house, grind flour, cook, weave baskets, make pottery, raise

ABOVE: Fremont culture petroglyphs adorn a canyon wall in Capitol Reef National Park.

Chaco and Mesa Verde

In a phenomenon never seen before or since, the powerful Chaco civilization, headquartered in a remote canyon in the center of the 25,000-square-mile (65,000-sq-km) San Juan Basin, rose to prominence beginning in AD 1000. Chaco seems to have served as a ceremonial center for Ancestral Pueblo groups. It may have succeeded by redistributing trade goods from as far away as the Pacific, the Mississippi River and Mexico.

By the mid-1100s, Chaco and its hundreds of satellite villages had become ghost towns and its former wealth was scattered to the winds. Its leaders may have become straw men in the face of long-running drought, leaving desperate farming families to their own devices. They fled to surrounding highlands, including the Montezuma Valley of southwestern Colorado, just west of Mesa Verde. As newcomers poured into the area and resources dwindled, Mesa Verdeans left their mesa-top villages and moved into hundreds of warm, south-facing villages cleverly concealed in the cliffs.

At its height, Mesa Verde supported 5,000 people. Some 30,000 lived in the adjoining Montezuma Valley. Villages sprang up on every mesa with a stream. Lookout towers were built, perhaps to safeguard communities from out-

doomed all these efforts. By 1300, Ancestral Puebloans had left their homes in the Four Corners and headed southeast to live along the Rio Grande and other rivers in New Mexico and Arizona, where their ancestors, the Pueblo people, remain today.

The Fremont

The people who lived in northeastern Utah and northwestern Colorado had much in common with their neighbors immediately to the south. They too made pottery, grew corn, squash and later beans along washes, and lived together in villages. But for these people the hunter-

siders. These enclosed pueblos were hastily constructed, using large stones loosely mortared with mud, and some were built in unusual shapes, such as the oval, circular, square and D-shaped buildings at Hovenweep and Canyons of the Ancients National Monuments on the Colorado–Utah border.

People continued to move north of the San Juan River into the narrow canyons of southeastern Utah, east of the Colorado River, in places such as Horse Canyon in the Needles District of Canyonlands National Park, where they built tiny homesteads big enough for just a single family and bravely continued to farm. The Great Drought of the late 13th century

gatherer lifestyle still beckoned. The Fremont (named for their strong presence along the Fremont River in Capitol Reef National Park and adjoining lands) are less obvious in the archaeological record, perhaps because of their fondness for remote places. They developed a hardy dent-style corn that suited the highlands they lived on, fashioned plain, utilitarian pottery, and made moccasins with the dew claw of deer, for traction.

Long after the Ancestral Pueblo people of the Four Corners were building large stone villages, the Fremont found comfort in their pithouses – by far the most practical shelter in the extreme temperatures of the desert. Their rock art, too, echoed that of early Archaic people, with depictions of big-shouldered anthropomorphs and game animals and enigmatic figures, such as Kokopelli the flute player. Hundreds of Fremont pictographs can be found between the Colorado River and the Great Basin and immediately west of the Green River, in the area of Nine Mile Canyon and Range Creek in central Utah. Like the Ancestral Pueblo, the Fremont culture ceased to exist in an identifiable form around AD 1300, probably due to a combination of drought and over-utilization of natural resources.

Great Basin newcomers

The arrival of Utah's modern tribes in a region already stressed by scarce resources may have tipped the balance. The Utes, Paiutes, Goshutes and Shoshones all belong to the Uto-Aztecan language family and are part of its Numic-speaking branch, which linguists say originated in southern California by way of Mexico. These hunter-gatherers seem to have entered the Great Basin area by AD 1000 and spread into Colorado about 1300.

They were joined soon after by nomadic Athabascans, or Dineh, from northwest Canada, who split into the Navajo and Apache tribes around the 12th century. The tribes jostled for dominance throughout the region which, by the 17th century, had also attracted the attention of Spanish explorers.

The most immediate and profound change wrought by Europeans was caused by the introduction of the horse. Suddenly, people who had traveled only on foot could traverse vast distances with greater speed and freedom than ever before. Borrowing technologies from the Plains tribes, Utes and Navajos used horse-drawn sleds, or travois, to transport their possessions from place to place. Mounted Utes left their homes in the mountains of northern and eastern Utah to hunt bison on the western plains. Gone for long periods, they left behind their families to gather food, tan bison and deer skins, and make highly prized clothing at encampments of hide-covered tents, or tepees. A man's wealth was measured by the number of horses he owned; his status as a warrior was determined by the number of

LEFT: ancient Pueblo granary, Zion National Park.
RIGHT: a cartoon from 1879 expresses the anti-Indian sentiment of those advocating removal of the Utes.

horses and slaves he stole from other tribes. In addition to longstanding ceremonies such as the Bear Dance, Utes adopted the Sun Dance, a test of endurance in which men pierce their flesh with hooks, abstain from food and drink, and dance to exhaustion.

Utes drove the Navajo back into southeastern Utah and the adjoining portions of Arizona and New Mexico, where they remain today. By the early 1700s, both Navajos and Utes raided Goshutes and Paiutes for slaves to trade to the Spanish in New Mexico. Within a few short years, Goshute and Paiute populations had dropped by 90 percent, creating fear of

outsiders among tribes that had lived together harmoniously for generations.

Mormon relations

The arrival of the Mormons in the Salt Lake Valley in 1847 did little to help matters. Soon after founding Salt Lake City, Mormon farmers began a rapid colonization effort in the surrounding desert lands traditionally used by some 20,000 Indians. Settlers monopolized precious water sources and grazed livestock in areas used for hunting and gathering by Indian families, who began to starve and grow dependent on handouts. Mormons referred to Goshutes and Paiutes as "Digger" Indians for their habit of digging up the edible roots of desert plants. Ironically, when crickets and floods destroyed Mormon crops, many farmers were saved from starvation by Indian knowledge of wild foods.

Mormons were "called" by the Church to create missions to convert and teach agriculture to Indians, believing they were a fallen tribe known as the Lamanites whose dark skin would be reversed by accepting Jesus Christ. Mormon Indian farms later formed the nucleus of several Indian reservations, including the Goshute reservations at Deep Creek and Skull Valley and the Southern Paiute reservation in Cedar City.

But for most settlers living frugally on ranches in remote areas, any charitable feelings toward their impoverished Indian neighbors often evaporated when they felt threatened or lost livestock to theft. Numerous clashes took place between Mormon ranchers and Navajos, Southern Utes and Paiutes in the mid- to late 1800s, which shifting alliances among Mormons, the federal government and Indian tribes only served to complicate. These clashes continued well into the 1900s, ending with an armed standoff between white ranchers and Paiute and Ute Indians over stolen livestock in Bluff, Utah, in the late 1920s, known as the Posey War.

POWWOW HIGHWAY

Tribal gatherings, known as powwows, are held throughout Utah every year. Originally *pau-wau*, an Algonquin word, meant medicine man; as a verb it meant to perform a healing ceremony. By the 1800s, however, it applied to any gathering of Indians, and today it refers to hundreds of public events in which dancers, singers and other followers of the powwow trail come to celebrate Indian culture.

Among the best known Utah powwows are the Paiute Restoration Gathering in Cedar City in June, the Northern Ute powwows in Fort Duchesne in July and at Thanksgiving, and the Northern Navajo Fair and White Mesa Ute Bear Dance which are both held in September.

Most powwows welcome spectators, but keep a few rules in mind. Before pulling out your camera, check to see if photography is allowed or a permit required. Always ask permission before snapping the shutter; sometimes a small payment is appropriate. Dress modestly and try to be unobtrusive; avoid asking questions about traditions and customs. Don't join a dance unless invited. Non-Indians may be encouraged to participate in the Round Dance, which celebrates the universality of all humankind. For more information, contact the Utah State Division of Indian Affairs at 801-538-8803.

Reservation life

After picking up farming, weaving and pottery from Pueblos and acquiring horses from Spaniards, then systematically raiding both, Navajos were forced to accept American rule in 1868, after a four-year incarceration at Fort Sumner in central New Mexico. They agreed to a reservation spanning portions of Arizona, New Mexico and Utah, which today encompasses 29,000 square miles (75,000 sq km) and has the largest tribal population in the country – some 300,000 people.

Utes were also forced onto reservations beginning in 1864, after the 1853 Walker War

Mountain Ute Reservation, also in Colorado, while some members of the band chose to move to White Mesa, Utah, where they now number 250 people. Finally, in 1880, following the massacre of missionary Nathan Meeker at White River, Colorado, the White River and Uncompahgre/Tabeguache bands were forced to move from their mountain homeland to the desolate Uintah Basin. Today, the million-acre reservation is known as the Uintah and Ouray Reservation.

The fate of Utah's Northwestern Shoshone remains up in the air. Some 250 members of the tribe encamped on the Bear River were

led by Ute leader Wakara against Mormon settlements ended with a peace treaty requiring the Indians to move to the Uintah Basin. Utes along the Wasatch Front, including the Timpanogos, Corn Creek and Spanish Fork bands, made the move, but the San Pete band, led by Black Hawk, continued to raid settlements until the early 1870s. The Moache Utes were moved to Ignacio, Colorado, where they became known as the Southern Ute Tribe. The Weeminuche settled at Towaoc on the Ute

LEFT: Navajo kids play at their Red Mesa home on the Navajo Reservation.
ABOVE: Southern Paiute tribal leader.

massacred in 1863 by the U.S. Army, and they lost all their traditional lands in Utah. In the late 1990s, the tribe launched an effort to acquire a 6,400-acre (2,600-hectare) ranch on the Utah–Idaho border.

Even more remarkable is the triumphant story of the Southern Paiutes. After having its tribal status "terminated" by the federal government, the tribe has reorganized and is making strides in health, housing, education and employment for its members. Every June, the Paiutes hold an annual Restoration Celebration in downtown Cedar City in southern Utah. For all who attend, the message is loud and clear: We are still here. ❑

TRAILBLAZERS

Explorers and soldiers were the first Europeans to penetrate the Utah hinterland,
followed over time by an assortment of others – including a pair of adventurous padres

U tah was for a long time the undiscover'd country, remote and uninviting. Inevitably, intruders began showing up, arriving from the south, the east and the west, to penetrate its forbidding terrain. Spaniards came first, up from Mexico and Nuevo Mexico, seeking material treasure and/or souls for salvation, while ever keeping a jealous eye out for other intruders – chiefly French, British, and home-grown Anglo-Americans.

In the vanguard were soldier-explorers, Franciscan friars, traders seeking to do business with the indigenous people, and then a variety of opportunists – fur trappers, gold-diggers, map-makers, farmers, land-hungry expansionists. Most of them, early on, were transients passing through and around. But their probes and ramblings succeeded in putting Utah, or what became Utah, on the map as they carved out trails later to be followed by emigrant settlers.

Most famous of Utah's settlers would of course be the Mormons, who in the 1840s found their promised land in what generally had been thought a most unpromising place. They were pioneers, too, if not exactly trailblazers. The real trailblazing had taken place up to three centuries earlier, starting with Francisco Vasquez Coronado's famous expedition into the region in search of more of the precious metal that was being unearthed elsewhere in New Spain. Coronado's expedition may have left tracks in present-day Utah when a detachment of his men, under Captain Garcia Lopez de Cardenas, crossed over into land south of the Colorado River.

Coronado returned to Mexico in 1541 with little material treasure to speak of, and little effort was expended on going that far north again. There were thrusts here and there, into the farther reaches of New Mexico and beyond to Arizona and Colorado, but not much of lasting impact. People were certainly aware of the

Ute bands that roamed western Colorado in the Utah region, from which awareness came the term "Yuta" or "Yutta." It was the Spanish spin on the indigenous self-reference for "people of the mountains." The term seems to have gained currency with the Spanish from about 1610, arising largely out of trading exchanges

between native people and the European-descended newcomers in places like Taos, New Mexico. Anglos gave the term their own linguistic twist, spelling it "Utah."

Breaking ground

It was a trading exchange in Taos that helped open a new chapter in Utah history. The exchange occurred in 1765 when an old Ute Indian known as Cuero de Lobo, or "Wolfskin," aroused curiosity in the Taos area by offering to trade an ingot of silver. To find out where more of the precious stuff might be mined, a small expedition headed by Juan Maria Antonio de Rivera was sent north. Following trails known to Spanish and Ute traders, Rivera's party got as far as the Dolores River in western Colorado before turning back.

A second expedition was immediately mounted, again under Rivera, to search for the source of such a lode of silver and also to check on the veracity of the various legends that surrounded the people and the land beyond the Colorado River. This time Rivera made it all the way north into Utah northeast of present-day Monticello. His group went by the La Sal Mountains, found a good place to cross the Colorado River, observed the lifestyle of the native people, heard intriguing reports of a far-off

The explorer priests

Even more decisive in opening up Utah's modern history was an exploration that occurred a decade after Rivera's penetration of 1765. This time the protagonists were two Spanish padres named Escalante and Dominguez. They made their move in 1776.

Francisco Atanasio Dominguez, born in Mexico, had a twofold agenda: (1) inspect the Catholic Church's far-flung outposts in New Mexico, and (2) seek a better overland route connecting the old communities centered at Santa Fe with newly established missionary outposts in Monterey and southern California.

"great lake" – which was of course the Great Salt Lake – and left a large inscribed cross claiming Spanish sovereignty before heading home.

Rivera's basic accomplishment was to forge a trade route from Santa Fe north to the Colorado River and into central Utah that was a first step along what became legendary as the Old Spanish Trail. This was a passageway arching up through southeastern Utah and then veering off westward in the direction of California. Following an ancient trail, it developed as a major trade route 1,120 miles (1,800 km) long between Santa Fe and Los Angeles, touching six states. It remained "Spanish" in formal identity until 1848 and the American takeover in the West.

For help, Dominguez called on the services of the Spanish-born priest Silvestre Velez de Escalante, who long had ministered to the needs of Christian Indians in New Mexico.

They planned to set forth on July 4, 1776, that most historic of American dates, though they didn't actually leave until July 29 owing to a delay caused by a Comanche Indian assault in the region. The two priests were accompanied by eight other Spanish colonials and, eventually, two native people recruited along the way as guides. Taking a circuitous route so as to avoid contact with the dreaded Chiruma Indians, the Escalante-Dominguez expedition proceeded north through western

Colorado, then westward into Utah. The Colorado–Utah border (as we know it today) was crossed on September 12, near the present-day Dinosaur National Monument.

Eventually the 12-member group reached Utah Valley and found a land rich with water, game, fish, timber, firewood and other resources. Also encountered were communities of Timpanogos, friendly indigenous people whom the priests deemed likely candidates for religious conversion. Escalante and Dominguez promised to return for that purpose, although they never did.

Early snowfall and signs of a harsh impending winter impelled the two priests to abort their planned trip to California, and they headed south for home. They arrived in Santa Fe on January 2, 1777, after a journey of more than 1,700 miles (2,700 km). Their search for a more secure route around hostile Indian territory as well as impossibly arid desert and rugged mountains was unfulfilled. But they had succeeded in finding a most hospitable land up north which they depicted in detailed journals and maps. Their published account served as an introduction to the land, however skewed by their imperfect sense of the actual geography involved.

Trappers and traders

Spaniards never did establish permanent settlements in Utah, although their sovereignty over the land was formally affirmed by the Adams-Onis Treaty of 1819 hammered out by diplomats in Madrid and Washington. When in 1821 Mexico broke off from Spain and declared itself a republic, control over the Utah territory shifted. In fact, however, the distance from Mexico City was too great for any meaningful control to be exerted. Still, Hispanic traders

bartered actively in Utah, offering goods such as corn, firearms and liquor in exchange for furs.

But it was the advent of fur-trapping activity in the north and west, much of it Anglo-inspired, that sowed the seeds for a major change of identity that would be fully realized in 1848 with the American military victory over Mexico.

British withdrawal after the War of 1812 had helped open the way to an increase in American private enterprise (as opposed to government-sponsored activity) in pursuit of fur-trading profit by companies operating in the American West. Large-scale trading activity began to develop along such routes as the Old Spanish Trail, and fur was destined to play a major role

LEFT: an early impression of the Great Salt Lake by artist Thomas Moran.
ABOVE: a modern mountain man rendezvous.

in Utah's development. Mexican authorities protested from time to time, to little avail.

Fur became an object of conspicuous consumption early in the 19th century. Suddenly, beaver hats were exceedingly fashionable with the urbane gentlemen of New York, London and Paris, and the profits to be won from trappers foraging along ponds and streams in the central Rocky Mountain region attracted British and American business interests.

Major players were the American Fur Company, organized by that prototype American millionaire John Jacob Astor; the Hudson's Bay Company; and the Rocky Mountain Fur Company. They employed a force of trappers, known famously as "mountain men," whose dogged pursuit of beaver fur brought them into intimate contact with the land and waterways of Utah and enlarged on such trails as had already been plied by native people, explorers, missionaries, early traders or whomever else. British tended to come from the northwest, Americans from the east and southwest.

It was a party of Astor's trappers that discovered, in October 1812, a gap in the Central Rockies in Wyoming, just above Utah, that would provide a passageway to an eventual stream of mobile Americans heading west. This

THE FUR TRAPPER

Utah's prodigious landscape was penetrated by such early voyagers as the Canadian-born fur trader Peter Skene Ogden, who spent his entire career with the Hudson's Bay Company. This scion of Loyalist forebears became a chief operative for that Anglo-oriented company, and two of the five "Snake Country" trapping expeditions he led between 1824 and 1829 brought him face to face with Utah.

In the first of the five forays, Ogden and his 131-man brigade pushed south starting in December 1824 along the Bear River and into Utah territory. They trapped the Cache and Ogden Valleys, set up camp as far south as Mountain Green, and ultimately exited after their famous confronta-

tion with dreaded American trappers. Whether Ogden himself entered the area memorialized by his name, or encountered the Great Salt Lake, is uncertain, but the expedition provided the first written account of northern Utah via his journal and that of aide William Kittson.

Four years later Ogden was back, in an 1828–29 expedition that was his last Snake Country venture. Moving along what later became tagged as the Humboldt River, Ogden and his trappers explored the region north of Great Salt Lake before returning home.

Ogden lived out his life in Oregon's Fort Vancouver, founded by the Hudson's Bay Company, and died in 1854.

strategic gap in the Rockies – that mountain range often called "Uncle Sam's backbone" – was the South Pass. The year 1824 brought another notable contingent of trappers, led by William H. Ashley of the Rocky Mountain Fur Company. These pacesetting mountain men crossed South Pass and established Fort Ashley at Lake Utah. Centered there in the late 1820s and early 1830s was the first Rocky Mountain fur-trading province.

Mountain meetings

Out of Ashley's pioneering effort came the custom of annual meetings, or rendezvous, starting

A kind of new "national road" was taking shape, with the Utah region lying in its path. The man often considered the greatest of Utah's trailblazing pioneers, Jedediah Smith, crossed Utah in 1826 en route to completing the first overland journey to California by an American. Smith, who had been one of Ashley's trappers, was also the first non-native to traverse Utah from north to south, and the first to cross the Sierra Nevada and the deserts of the Great Basin. He would fall victim to Comanche Indians in 1831 on the Santa Fe Trail.

First of these travelers to come upon the Great Salt Lake, or so many historians believe,

in 1825. At these prolonged and often raucous gatherings, trappers swapped their stored-up fur caches for supplies brought overland into the mountains from places like Ashley's adopted St. Louis. Before the rendezvous series came to an end in 1841 there were 16 such meetings, early ones being held in northern Utah. Among the mountain men involved were such famous names as Jedediah Smith, Jim Bridger, Tom Fitzpatrick, Milton and William Sublette, Etienne Provost and David Jackson.

LEFT: an inscription left by French trapper Denis Julien is scrawled on a rock wall in Desolation Canyon.
ABOVE: "prairie schooners" crowd an emigrant camp.

was another of the legendary mountain men, the young Jim Bridger. At the age of about 20, Bridger spotted the lake while searching for the source of the Bear River in 1824 as a scout for the Ashley expedition. His trek had taken him beyond the Green River valley and down into Utah. Tasting the saline waters of this unexpected natural resource, he mistook it for the deep blue sea. "Hell," he is said to have declared, "we are on the shores of the Pacific."

Utah's northwest corner was crossed in 1833 by the Tennessee-born fur trader and explorer Joseph Walker during an arduous journey that took him all the way to California. Walker reported such difficult conditions that no one else even attempted the route for the rest of the decade, but waves of emigrants would follow his trail in later years.

Meanwhile, the fur trade was hitting its peak in the early 1830s, giving rise to the establishment of frontier forts and outposts for collecting the pelts while storing up supplies to sustain the trappers. One of the earliest posts was set up by Antoine Robidoux at Uintah Basin in 1832. The annual rendezvous system went into effect whereby trappers would display the furs they had snared. They did the bulk of their trapping in fall and spring, before streams froze over. Then, in the winter, they went into hibernation along with, in many cases, their Indian wives.

The first meeting in the new rendezvous system initiated by Ashley was held at Henry's Fork on the Green River. Utah likewise was the site for some subsequent annual meetings before the venue shifted to other territories in the region. But by 1840, the year of the 16th and last rendezvous, the fur business had declined sharply. There was much less consumer demand for beaver. But the trappers had played an important role in providing the American public with a sense of the region's geography, a bare-bones knowledge of its land and resources and opportunities, and thereby facil-

THE WRONG TURN

Rightly or wrongly, the blame for the tragic Donner Party disaster of 1846-47 has usually been pinned on Lansford W. Hastings, author of *The Emigrants' Guide to Oregon and California* and propagandist for western expansion. Hastings' 1845 book was read widely, and he gave credence to a short-cut route supposedly capable of abbreviating the arduous western passage. Emigrants could bypass the normal route via Fort Hall in eastern Idaho, head south for the Great Salt Lake and then turn due west.

Alas, it proved disastrous for George Donner, age 60, of Springfield, Illinois, his wife and children and many others. Of the original group of 87, only 46 survived. They had opted in July 1846 for Hastings' Cut-off, failed to connect with Hastings himself at Fort Bridger in Wyoming, and embarked on a hellish ordeal.

The party traveled through the Wasatch Mountains and around the southern end of the Great Salt Lake before striking out across the Bonneville Flats. Mud beneath the salt crust soon bogged down the emigrants, who abandoned several wagons, livestock and equipment. They dashed across Nevada but, exhausted by their ordeal in Utah, couldn't make up for lost time. Trapped by early snow in the Sierra Nevada, the famished emigrants resorted to cannibalism for sustenance.

itated access to the golden lands, fertile valleys and nourishing waterways of the West and Far West and Pacific Northwest.

Emigrants on wheels

Now would come the wagon trains, or "prairie schooners," creaking along the rough paths and wide-open plains of Utah and adjacent regions, over homely trails that in later times would serve as super-fast highways for motorized transport. An early contingent in the emigrant wave that began rolling through the territory was that headed by John Bidwell in 1841. Organizer of the Western Emigration Society, he led the first wagon train, with 69 adults and children, through South Pass. It then divided into two groups, one heading north to Oregon Territory and the other making a grueling journey west before reaching Sacramento, California. Included were the first non-native women known to have traveled overland across the territory into Nevada and all the way to California.

There could be plenty of bumps along the way. The Bidwell emigrants skirted the edges of the Great Salt Lake and the Great Salt Lake Desert, encountering daunting and often inaccessible twists and turns. Many a wagon broke down and had to be abandoned on such passages. No journey proved as wretchedly unfortunate as that undertaken by the ill-fated Donner-Reed party of 1846.

In an ill-conceived short-cut maneuver aimed at lopping off 400 miles (640km) from the scheduled passage to California, the Donner-Reed wagons became bogged down in the mud of the Great Salt Lake Desert. Drivers had wasted three weeks hacking their way to the Salt Lake Valley, they and their families surviving only to experience the harrowing ordeal of a snowed-in winter that caused starvation and a desperate resort to cannibalism in the Sierra Nevada. Nearly four dozen emigrants would perish along the way.

The route taken in that lamentable episode had already been traversed by the soldier-adventurer John C. Frémont, who, with the famed Indian scout Kit Carson and three others, explored the northern Great Salt Lake in a rub-

ber boat in 1843. Frémont was bound for Oregon and California in the first of his five famous western expeditions. A year later, in 1844, he and another expeditionary force passed through Utah again, going north to Utah Lake and then east through the Uintah Basin and Browns Hole. And in still another trip in 1845 Frémont circled the southern shore of Great Salt Lake before heading across the Great Salt Lake Desert to California.

By the mid-1840s, thanks to the carving out of these trails and related circumstances, Utah's modern history was unfolding in a full sense. Its first permanent Anglo settlement, for exam-

ple, was built in 1845 by Miles Goodyear, a Connecticut-born trapper and trader. He called it Fort Buenaventura, out of which arose the town of Ogden. In 1848, Goodyear took a pack train from Great Salt Lake to Los Angeles, and eventually Mormons turned the western part of the Spanish Trail into a wagon route conveying pioneers to California.

The year 1848 also brought the start of one of the most transforming events in American history, the California gold rush. And a wave of emigrants and transients succeeded in transforming the public perception of Utah territory as a terra incognita. The secrets were being unlocked. ❏

LEFT: pioneer re-enactment.
RIGHT: rock piles mark pioneer graves in Skull Valley in the unforgiving desert lands of western Utah.

THE MORMON BATTALLION 1846&

PROMISED LAND

"This is the place" where a people of faith-based determination left
an indelible mark on an arid land they transformed into a bountiful Zion

If 1848 was a golden time for America, equally imposing was 1846. That latter year encapsulates the great leap forward a young nation was making toward the middle of the 19th century. Americans were on the move, by land and by sea, and usually westward. "Go west!" young men were admonished. Most fatefully, 1846 marked the start of a war by which Mexico would be supplanted as landlord over a big chunk of territory, transforming the U.S. from developing nation to continental colossus.

It was an important moment, too, for an incipient Utah, that remote territory hard by the Rockies that was long disdained as a bleak netherworld somewhere between East and West. One early visitor dismissed it as a "Great American Desert." Anybody heading that way was, likely as not, a passerby en route to some more rewarding place, like the greener pastures of Oregon and California.

Wagon trains were rolling in the 1840s, conveying emigrants over frontier routes like the Oregon Trail and into such hinterlands as the Utah region. It was a time when Americans were picking up and starting over, and why not? As the boosters of Manifest Destiny were proclaiming, this land is your land.

Out of such expansionist striving did Utah take shape, first as a Territory in 1850, finally as a State in 1896. Other states would emerge, too, but none in quite the way Utah did. In her case the driving force was what we nowadays call a faith-based initiative. It impelled a new breed of reformist Christians who called themselves Mormons – formally, the Church of Jesus Christ of Latter-day Saints, or LDS – to establish a sanctuary in the far-off western hills and desert after the most famous mass migration in American history. For the "Saints," 1846 was the central year of passage in a quest for a promised land, a new Zion, far from the madding crowds of eastern unfriendliness.

LEFT: the Mormon Battalion marches toward "Zion."
RIGHT: the angel Moroni gives Joseph Smith mystical spectacles with which to translate the Book of Mormon.

Saints and sinners

The Church had been founded in 1830 in upstate New York by a young farmer named Joseph Smith. Born in Vermont in 1805, Smith grew up poor in a period of intense religiosity and revivalism known as the "Second Great Awakening." As a boy, he was given to attempt-

ing to "divine" where precious old relics or treasure might be buried, and while still a teenager he experienced the first in a series of supernatural revelations of long-lost Christian principles.

Smith, revered by Mormons as their original "Prophet," was reputedly directed to unearthing a cache of inscribed golden plates. They provided, along with the revelations and the Holy Bible, the basis for a renewed Christian faith whose tenets he set forth in The Book of Mormon. Its millennialist message – the Second Coming was expected imminently – attracted followers from the outset. Non-believers, on the other hand, were repelled by the doctrinaire claim to religious truth and the Mormon rejection of much traditional theology. To many of them, Smith was a charlatan, while to the Mormons, non-believers were disdained as "Gentiles."

One of Smith's early revelations caused him and his followers to relocate to Kirtland, Ohio, in search of a peaceable religious haven. But the newcomers' radical Christian doctrines and "evangelical socialism" aroused resentment, and the Mormons made subsequent moves. In western Missouri, with its strong pro-slavery sentiment, the newcomers were widely detested as trouble-making "Yankee invaders." Tension there reached fever pitch by October 1838, when an attack by the Missouri Militia on a Mor-

long troubled relationship with the outside world.

The practice was at first denied outright, then kept under wraps. Joseph Smith first spoke of it publicly in 1843, as an approved doctrine, and in 1852 the practice of plural marriage received the church's official blessing.

Meanwhile, the tense situation in Illinois that was developing came to a murderous climax in June 1844. Provoked by an editorial attack on the Mormon message, Smith's fulmination incited some of his co-religionists to smash the offending newspaper's printing press. Accused of causing a riot, Joseph and his brother Hyrum were confined to a jail at Carthage while

mon settlement at Haun's Mill caused 18 deaths. Joseph Smith, his brother Hyrum and five of their co-religionists were convicted of treason. They escaped death by fleeing to Illinois.

There, at a village on the Mississippi River called Nauvoo, the Saints built a bustling community that grew to be one of the most prosperous in the state. It was dominated by a great hilltop Mormon temple – until the building was burned down by Gentiles. Hostility to the Mormons became sorely aggravated by reports that polygamy was being widely practiced. This practice of plural marriage, known in Mormon parlance as "celestial marriage" and "spiritual wifery," came to be the sorest point in the sect's

charges of treason were drawn up. An anti-Mormon mob, enraged, broke into the jail and shot both fatally.

Western sanctuary

Once again, Mormons decided to leave all behind and move on, this time to some far-off land out west for a hoped-for permanent haven. Smith as early as 1842 had envisioned such a long-distance remove, telling associates to seek "a place of refuge" for a "government of our own." But plans were sidetracked when he turned his attention to making a run for the U.S. presidency in 1844.

After his death, the planning was carried forward chicfly by Brigham Young, who survived a schism in Mormon ranks to emerge as Smith's successor. Though less charismatic than his predecessor, Young was a practical genius who would guide the Church's affairs ably over the next three decades. With military-like precision, he charted the great 1,200-mile (1,900-km) exodus of 1846–47 that brought the Mormon vanguard to Utah, followed by waves of others in the following years that numbered some 16,000.

Once there, Brigham Young supervised the settlements that overcame harsh conditions to flourish in the Great Salt Lake Basin and beyond, up into the north and down below to

and three years later was named by Smith as one of the Church's original Twelve Apostles. Young was in England from 1839 to 1841 helping to recruit some of the many European converts who would join the diaspora to Utah.

The great exodus

Brigham Young sent forth a preliminary expedition in 1845 to seek out suitable areas for settlement in places that "nobody else wanted," with special consideration given to Texas, California, Oregon and Vancouver Island. And he studied with great interest published reports in newspapers and best-selling

the south. He dealt as best he could with the vexing problem of an indigenous people whose land and resources were rudely encroached on, and with a federal government that often felt sorely tested by this idiosyncratic group of believers who seemed somehow to hold themselves above and beyond the rules of normal civic and Christian conduct.

Young had also been raised in an upstate New York region rife with revivalist fervor. He had joined the fledgling Mormon movement in 1832

LEFT: Mormon prophet Joseph Smith is shown preaching to Indians in a painting by William Armitage.
ABOVE: an attack on a Mormon settlement in Missouri.

books that were stirring wide interest in the West's vast terrain. These reports represented the findings of the soldier-adventurer John Charles Frémont, who had surveyed on behalf of the U.S. Army's Topographical Corps.

Frémont, celebrated as "the Pathfinder," undertook three major western expeditions, in 1842, 1843–44 and 1845–47. His vivid descriptions of the rich landscape were firing the imagination of readers around the country, including such literary luminaries as Longfellow, Emerson and Thoreau, who were enchanted by glimpses of the grand western vistas.

Young, too, was absorbed by the descriptions. He focused on the Great Basin, situated

1,000 miles (1,600km) from the Pacific Coast and accommodating no people beyond those native to the region. Even the Ute Indian presence was tenuous, their settlements being less permanent in nature than those of the Pueblo tribes to the south. Frémont had written approvingly of the area's soil and grazing land, sheltered by the Wasatch Range. The desert chosen for settlement by Young, part of the Great Basin, was marked by dry lake beds, but there were sufficient mountain streams from which to draw water for irrigation.

By the summer of 1845 Young was decided on the region as a likely promised land. He

marriage with 19 additional partners. Many of the marriages were pro forma, undertaken not for conjugal purposes but to assure a degree of security for women who were leaving everything behind for an uncertain future.

The great trek from Nauvoo to Utah began in February 1846. Wagon trains left at regular intervals in separate caravans, inching their way along Iowa day by day, then season by season, into Nebraska, Wyoming and finally south to the Great Salt Lake Valley. The first arrival occurred in July 1847. Some 3,000 pioneers were involved in the earliest encampments in Iowa, and the number would

envisioned as his new haven for Mormons an immense expanse of land far exceeding present-day Utah. It also included most of Nevada and Arizona plus parts of Oregon, Idaho, Wyoming, Colorado, New Mexico and, even, California. For the most part he kept the destination a secret, though he did divulge it in a letter to President James K. Polk.

Moving out

Preparations were undertaken in Nauvoo for the construction of large numbers of wagons and the amassing of necessary supplies and equipment. Some of the Mormon men took on additional wives – Young himself contracted

swell to about 16,000 assembled at a site near present-day Omaha, Nebraska, that was designated as Winter Quarters.

The routine grew familiar. A bugle would sound at five o'clock in the morning, followed by prayers and breakfast, and the wagons would start rolling again. It was slow going, with many roads resisting passage. Along the way a contingent of some 500 volunteers was signed up by U.S. Army recruiters for a Mormon Battalion to assist in the war with Mexico.

There was much hardship along the way for the Mormon pioneers. Most costly was the encampment at Winter Quarters for the 1846–47 season. The camp had nearly a thousand log cabins built by the pioneers. Some 600 deaths occurred here due to cholera, malaria, bitter cold weather and conditions of near-starvation.

On the last leg of the trek, Young in April 1847 was part of a separate "Pioneer Band" of 143 men, plus a handful of women and children, that forged a route to the Great Salt Lake Valley. This so-called Mormon Trail coincided with the Oregon Trail as far as Fort Bridger before diverging to the southwest toward Utah.

Young met up with frontier experts, including the famed scout Jim Bridger, who advised that Utah was inhospitable for farm settlement. Disregarding the counsel, Young ordered the party to press on. And on July 24, 1847, he got his first look at the Great Salt Lake Valley from the mouth of Emigration Canyon. The Mormon leader, recovering from a fever that caused him to abandon his horse for the relative comfort of a carriage, lifted his weakened frame, gazed out over the arid land and uttered his memorable approval. "It is enough. This is the right place. Drive on."

Let the desert bloom

The newcomers wasted no time in putting down roots. They developed a network of ditches for irrigation and planting crops. Water, the crucial natural resource, was commonly owned. It was diverted from mountain streams via dams and canals and efficiently delivered to serve the needs of homes and gardens, livestock and orchards.

Lots were equitably assigned. Young went forth the day after arrival to mark off streets and configure whatever traffic patterns would be necessary for the central village that became Utah's great metropolis. It was first called Great Salt Lake City, then (1868) simply Salt Lake City. Situated at its heart would be Temple Square, accommodating the great religious structure that began to arise in the 1850s and would not be dedicated until 1893.

The rate of growth was phenomenal. The original 300 pioneers who reached the valley in 1847 swelled a year later to 5,000, plus a battery of houses, shops, bridges and mills and, in 1850, the first newspaper of its kind west of the Mississippi River, the *Deseret News*. Colonization was extended beyond Salt Lake Valley, first to southern Utah, then to other areas. By 1857 there were 96 separate communities in the Territory of Utah.

A thousand acres of farmland were brought under cultivation in that brief period, but in the summer of 1848 hordes of giant crickets attacked, devouring nearly everything in sight. The settlers were in despair, expecting a total blight, when flocks of seagulls from the Great Salt Lake suddenly appeared, swooping in to rid the landscape of the pests. It was in the nature of a miracle, but there would be recurring plagues of crickets and grasshoppers for years to come, sometimes causing near-famine.

A new territory

With the Mexican surrender of 1848, the vast chunk of western territory that included the Mormons' new homeland came formally under American sovereignty. A provisional State of Deseret was established in 1849, and Brigham Young and associates asked Congress for full admission within the Union. They proposed the name "Deseret," a Mormon scriptural reference for "honey bee," suggesting industriousness.

Congress rejected the idea of putting Utah on a fast track to statehood. The land mass proposed was huge, encompassing not only present-day Utah but also most of Nevada and Arizona and parts of six other states –

LEFT: Mormon emigrants cross the Platte River, 1847.
RIGHT: Joseph Smith's successor, Brigham Young, led the Saints to Utah.

including California and its highly prized seaports! This was scaled back in size by Congress to something more like today's combined Utah and Nevada plus adjacent land in Colorado and Wyoming. (When in the 1860s land was carved out to create the Nevada, Colorado and Wyoming territories, Utah assumed her present size.)

The name "Deseret" was also rejected by the Congressmen as bleakly uninviting. They opted instead for "Utah" as more fittingly representative of the region's people – the Utes, Paiutes, Goshutes and others.

Utah Territory was crafted as part of the intense jockeying between North and South that resulted in the Compromise of 1850 – the attempt to maintain a delicate balance between the admission of free states versus slave states. Mormon leaders tried to keep their distance from the searing issue – Utah was largely a neutral place during the Civil War – but this sense of apartness stirred

CASH CROP

Skeptical mountain man Jim Bridger offered to pay "$1,000 for a bushel of corn grown in the Great Salt Basin." Ironically, by the early 1900s, northern Utah was among the most productive agricultural areas on the Union Pacific line.

SIZING UP THE PROPHET

Richard Francis Burton was big on exotica, not to mention erotica, so it was perhaps natural that this much-traveled English adventurer should find himself in Salt Lake City in 1860 to examine Mormon peculiarities, like polygamy, and take personal measure of the Prophet himself, Brigham Young.

A man for all reasons – linguist, explorer, mystic, orientalist, bon vivant – Burton spent three weeks in the Utah capital after a 19-day stagecoach trek from Missouri during which he filled his notebooks with observations on Western ways. He was much taken with Young, whom he judged to be "no common man" and whom he

described in fastidious detail in a published memoir.

"He shows no signs of dogmatism, bigotry or fanaticism," Burton wrote of his personal encounter with the Mormon leader, "and never once entered – with me at least – upon the subject of religion."

Burton, equally famous for his African explorations and his 16-volume translation of the sensual *Arabian Nights* text, capped off his American visit in San Francisco before returning home to England to marry his beloved, Isabel Arundel, publish his account of the New World in *The City of the Saints* and *Across the Rocky Mountains to California* (1861), and be awarded a knighthood.

federal suspicion about the allegiances of the LDS Church and its people.

Rumors were rife that an attitude suggesting sedition was prevalent in the territory. Worse still, in public estimation, was the practice of polygamy, affirmed in 1851 and made official Church doctrine a year later. Mormons were denounced as "a pack of outlaws" by President Zachary Taylor, who deemed them "not fit for self-government." More sympathetic was his successor, Millard Fillmore. He made Brigham Young the first governor of the Utah Territory, in 1851, and Mormon leaders reciprocated by naming the site of its first capital Fillmore (later

many from abroad – British, Dutch, Scandinavians, Germans and others. Utah's population rose from about 10,000 to 60,000 in that period. To cut costs, Young initiated a Handcart Brigade scheme whereby emigrants made the trek on foot tugging only two-wheeled carts. More than 3,000 Mormons traveled that way to the Great Basin, hundreds becoming bogged down in early snowfalls and marooned in the mountains. Many perished along the way.

A troubled relationship

Inevitably, there was conflict growing out of settlers' encroachment on native grounds. Mor-

it was returned to Salt Lake City).

The territorial legislature met for the first time in 1851, moving to establish a militia and a prison, build roads and bridges and canals, and bring towns into legal existence. And to meet the threat posed by an increasing influx of non-Mormons into the region, Young encouraged the practice of plural marriage so as to raise more children into the faith.

Mormon numbers were greatly augmented by a steady flow of immigrants in the 1850s,

LEFT: Saints reunited in the promised land.
ABOVE: *Brigham Young and His Family,* by William Warner Major.

mons liked to think they were more sympathetic than most to the Native Americans they regarded as, in a sense, fellow outcasts, and whom the Book of Mormon identified as "Lamanites" of old Israelite origins. Brigham Young famously advised that "it is better to feed them than to fight them."

In 1849, Young sought out the Ute leader known as Chief Walker to seek permission to settle the Sanpete Valley of central Utah. Permission was granted, but the chief was not always able to rein in younger Ute militants angered by the constant influx of settlers, and the Walker War of 1853–54 followed. A series of Indian raids took several Mormon lives and caused the loss of about 400 head of livestock.

Relations were seriously set back when a team of U.S. Army engineers under the command of Captain John W. Gunnison was attacked by Paiute Indians in 1853 while surveying sites for a transcontinental railroad route. The massacre of Gunnison and seven others in Utah raised suspicions that Mormons were somehow at fault, and President Franklin Pierce sent an Army force to investigate and oust Brigham Young as governor. Young remained in office.

In 1863, as the Civil War raged between North and South, a large force of federal troops commanded by Colonel Patrick E. Connor dealt a severe blow to some 300 Shoshone Indians in the Battle of Bear River in southern Idaho. It put an end to hostilities involving Native Americans in northern Utah and led to creation of the Uintah Reservation for Ute Indians in 1864.

One more major uprising occurred in 1865 with the start of the four-year Black Hawk Indian War in central Utah. It was brought on when Indian militants averse to reservation life launched a guerrilla action under the young outlaw Black Hawk that cost the lives of 70 white men, the abandonment of 25 settlements, and the loss of 2,000 horse and cattle. Mormons

DOMESTIC TANGLE

Pinning down Brigham Young's wives was never easy. There were perhaps 56 in all, from Miriam Works in 1824 to Hannah Tapfield in 1872. Many of the "sealings" were expedient in nature rather than conjugal. Nonetheless, Young was presented with 57 children by 16 of his wives.

Ten of his mates divorced him. The most notorious of the relationships was that involving Ann Eliza Webb, who was married to him in 1868 – she was 23, he 66 – only to flee her polygamous coop to pen a best-selling exposé. The public was titillated and Ann Eliza excommunicated. She charged cruelty and neglect but got little legal satisfaction – a meager $100 a month – years later.

had to rely for protection on their own Nauvoo Legion, the federal government refusing to send Army troops.

Conflict with the nation

Tension between Mormons and federal officials over the doctrines and lifestyle of a Church-dominated Utah Territory that hoped to be fully accepted into the Union erupted in the Utah War of 1857-58. It started when President James Buchanan, reacting to widespread public antipathy to Mormons and their "barbaric" practice of polygamy, moved to quell the perceived "rebellion" brewing there and replace Brigham Young with a non-Mormon governor.

Escorting the appointee was a 1,500-man force of federal troops commanded by Colonel Albert Sidney Johnston.

Young denounced the action as religious persecution. "My power will not be diminished," he declared as he imposed martial law and ordered Mormon militiamen and the Nauvoo Legion to undertake guerrilla operations. They burned Fort Bridger, then a Mormon possession, for defensive reasons, and set afire U.S. Army supply trains. Government cattle were driven off, and Salt Lake City was evacuated.

Amid this conflict occurred one of the most heinous acts of civilian slaughter in western annals. It involved the Fancher party, a wagon train bearing Arkansas emigrants through southwestern Utah en route to California. In the hysteria of the moment, when Mormons feeling beleaguered were espousing "blood atonement" as righteous retribution, the intrusion of Gentiles was seen as a dire threat. At a place called Mountain Meadows, the emigrants were ambushed by an unholy alliance of Mormon militiamen and Paiute Indians.

The emigrants were deceived, then mercilessly slaughtered, women and children by the Indians, men by the Mormon force led by Indian agent John D. Lee. About 120 deaths occurred, only a few children surviving. Twenty years later, in 1877, justice was finally meted out to one perpetrator – Lee was executed by firing squad at the site of the massacre.

The Utah War came to an end when a deal was worked out that provided pardons for alleged Mormon offenses. Young accepted it, as well as his replacement, and a force of federal troops paraded through a nearly deserted Salt Lake City. Later, Mormons returned to their abandoned homes. In 1861, the last of Johnston's troops left Utah.

A question of marriage

Polygamy as an issue continued to divide Utah from the rest of the nation, and to keep the territory from becoming a state. Utah was the target of an Anti-Bigamy act passed in 1862 that outlawed plural marriage in any U.S. territory. The measure permitted Young and others to be tried in 1871 on charges of

---

LEFT: many Mormon polygamists were sent to jail rather than renounce the doctrine of plural marriage.
RIGHT: Mormon settlers.

"lascivious cohabitation," but legal appeals blocked successful prosecution.

In 1877, two years after Young's death in Salt Lake City, anti-polygamy laws were upheld by the U.S. Supreme Court. Congress made polygamy a federal crime in 1882, and many of the Mormon leaders went into hiding. They included the church president, John Taylor, who was still a fugitive at the time of his death. Arrests and imprisonment for unlawful cohabitation were becoming frequent – in all, some 1,300 polygamists were locked up. Congress passed an even harsher law in 1887 that disincorporated the Church and seized its property.

Church sanctioning of plural marriage ended abruptly in 1890 when its new president, Wilford Woodruff, issued a manifesto urging full compliance with federal laws dealing with marriage. He attributed his action to a divine revelation. It effectively brought closure to the long-simmering "Mormon problem."

In 1893, President Benjamin Harrison granted amnesty to all who engaged in the practice of polygamy, and the following year their civil rights were restored by his successor, Grover Cleveland. Finally, on January 4, 1896, after being turned down five times between 1856 and 1887, the Territory of Utah was admitted to the Union as the nation's 45th state. ❑

SAINTS AND OTHERS

*Beyond the spiritually determined Mormon pioneers came waves of
opportunists of more mundane quality who helped reshape Utah's latter-day history*

For the Mormons, Utah was a regular utopia wherein was founded a peaceable kingdom complete with self-sufficient economy. The only trouble was, others inevitably began showing up as well. Already by 1880 the percentage of the population that was Mormon had shrunk to 85 percent. In the Ogden municipal election of 1889, non-Mormons won every seat on the city council. A year later the Church of Jesus Christ of Latter-day Saints ceased trying to defend the practice of polygamy. Little by little, Utah was becoming "Americanized."

The Ogden case was instructive. This northern outpost, destined to become Utah's second-ranking city, had been founded in 1846 as Fort Buenaventura. It was sold a year later to the Mormons, who renamed it for the early fur trapper Peter Skene Ogden. In 1869 it was transformed from an agriculture-based community to an important western rail center. This occurred because America's long-awaited transcontinental railroad, which became a reality that year, was nearby, and Ogden became a "junction city."

Work on the cross-country railroad speeded up once the Civil War was over, and its coming transformed the Utah region. A horde of job-seekers and opportunists, mostly non-Mormons, was attracted and places like Ogden prospered. There was disappointment on the part of Salt Lake City that the rail line didn't go directly through *their* locale, but plenty of Utahans prospered anyway. Some 4,000 were involved in grading and various other related projects.

"The coming of the railroad unlocked Utah," historian Charles S. Peterson observed, "changing a desert fastness to a national highway and a burgeoning economic region."

A more diverse place

For the nation at large, the historic hookup that took place on May 10, 1869, at Promontory Summit in northern Utah linking the Central

Pacific and the Union Pacific signaled the fading of the frontier as a most decisive factor. Utah, meanwhile, became a more diverse place as its isolation was lessened. One result was a widened gulf between Mormons and others, another was industrial development, mining being a case in point. Utah's poor roads had

impeded the transport of ore, and the territory suffered for that reason by comparison, for example, with next-door Colorado, where mining camps boomed. Now, with easier access to markets, Utah underwent a quick time of its own.

The railroad factor also undermined the Mormon attachment to agriculture as a more wholesome way for Saints to raise families, let the desert bloom, and make of their western sanctuary a heaven-bent commonwealth. Many LDS Church leaders, including Brigham Young, were not comfortable with the prospect of breadwinners being distracted by the chancy pursuit of trying to divine where precious metals might be buried in Utah's hills and ranges.

LEFT: steel mill worker, 1942. The steel industry boomed in Utah during World War II.

RIGHT: a locomotive crosses Markham Trestle, 1914.

Links with history

A large crowd was on hand at Promontory Summit, 56 miles (90 km) northwest of Ogden, on that memorable May day in 1869 when Leland Stanford of the Central Pacific drove home a golden spike to connect the two rail lines after years of track-laying from east and west. News of the deed was sent by telegraph to a waiting crowd in Washington, D.C. It was also in Washington, several years earlier, that another signal event involving Utah – hooking up the transcontinental telegraph system in Salt Lake City – became history when a wired dispatch was received by President Abraham Lin-

mineral deposits. And they opened marketing possibilities for farmers, sheep herders, cattle raisers and a growing merchant class.

In addition to farming, the Mormon pioneers had engaged in handicrafts, some small industry, and whatever opportunities presented themselves – such as, for example, catering to the needs of all those California-bound prospectors who were passing through in the early years of the gold rush. There were thousands of them, and they needed lots of goods and services, which Utahans were pleased to supply for the right price. (Some of the original gold dust was brought back to Utah, in fact, by former mem-

coln. (The telegraph in fact superseded yet another innovation that had a Utah link – the Pony Express.)

Salt Lake City was brought into contact with the transcontinental rail system in 1870 when the Utah Central Railroad was linked with Ogden – Brigham Young and sons, among others, profiting through construction-related contracts. Still another major connection, in 1880, made Salt Lake City a station for the Denver & Rio Grande Railway.

These railroad links were a shot in the arm for Utah's mining industry, which would go on to unearth riches in the form of copper, gold, silver, coal, tin, lead, uranium and a trove of

bers of the Mormon Battalion who had been at the scene of the original California strike, and it was utilized in minting Utah money.)

Although the early emphasis was on agriculture, Church leaders in Salt Lake City had been enticed by reports of rich deposits of iron ore in southern Utah. They called on their co-religionists to go forth and establish missions beyond the Great Basin and unearth the much needed iron. Many did, and the first smelting of Utah-produced iron occurred in 1852 in Cedar City.

But the great leap forward for Utah mining came following the arrival in 1862 of Colonel Patrick E. Connor and his California Volunteers, a military force dispatched to protect the overland mail and telegraph systems from Indian raids. Connor regarded Mormons as out-and-out "rebels" and encouraged his ex-prospector soldiers to search the hills for precious metals to attract the eventual wave of Gentile fortune-seekers that he knew would follow – and thereby undermine the Church's dominance in Utah's public affairs.

Silver-bearing ores were discovered, and the 1870s saw bustling mines along the Wasatch Front, on the Oquirrh mountain range to the west and south of Salt Lake City, in central and southern Utah and in other districts. Non-Mormons and intruders of various ethnicities were numerous in the industry as entrepreneurs and laborers. Fortunes were made by such well-known speculators as George Hearst, with holdings in the richly endowed Park City District, and banker Jay Cooke, who had mining interests in southern Utah.

There were losses, too, none more spectacular than in the case of the Emma, a mine in Little Cottonwood Canyon east of Salt Lake City. Stock manipulation and fraudulent claims made the Emma an infamous case involving fleeced investors both at home and in Europe, the resulting financial debacle aggravated by the economic Panic of 1873.

'Richest hole on earth'

Copper emerged as Utah's most lucrative mining treasure late in the 19th century. One young metallurgist, Daniel Jackling, made a fortune by figuring out a system of efficiently extracting valuable ore from daunting hunks of low-grade copper deposits. In 1903 he formed the Utah Copper Company – ultimately to be acquired by the giant Kennecott enterprise – to work a huge deposit at Bingham Canyon south of Salt Lake City. Drawing on assets of the well-heeled Guggenheim family, Jackling assembled an array of super-sized steam shovels plus dump cars, locomotives and miles of railroad track to build a humongous copper-reducing facility.

From an excavation known as "the richest hole on earth," millions of tons of copper would be retrieved. The Bingham operation alone would account for about one-third of the nation's output of copper in the 20th century.

LEFT: celebrating the completion of the first transcontinental railroad at Promontory Summit, 1869.
RIGHT: a Springville prospector, about 1900.

Inevitably, labor-management troubles emerged over pay and working conditions, intensifying in the 1890s amid economic downsizing and social unrest. Radical groups agitated for reform, and such unions as the United Mine Workers fought bitterly for bargaining power in clashes with recalcitrant owners. Making things worse were hazardous workplace conditions of often lethal severity, the worst example of which came on May 1, 1900, when an explosion in a Scofield coal mine killed 200 men and boy laborers. Many would-be rescuers succumbed to lethal gas in the poorly ventilated tunnels

A strike at Bingham Canyon in 1912 involved some 5,000 workers from among Utah's growing labor force. Most famous of the militant unions was the International Workers of the World – the "Wobblies" – and from them emerged the legendary Joe Hill, a Swede with a talent for poetry and song. Convicted of the fatal shooting of two persons at a Salt Lake City store in 1914, he was sentenced to death by firing squad. Neither a personal appeal by President Woodrow Wilson nor a barrage of international protest failed to stop the penalty from being carried out, and Joe Hill became an enduring martyr of the working class.

As for the old issue of Mormonism and

divided loyalties, it resurfaced only periodically. One notable instance was the protracted campaign to bar Reed Smoot, a Church official, from taking his seat in the U.S. Senate following his election in 1902. Smoot had to endure a protracted inquiry that was malevolently directed as much at LDS Church policy as at his own allegiance to the public order. He was finally accepted by the Senate in 1907, a colleague quipping that Smoot was adjudged "a polygamist who doesn't polyg."

In a sense, this was an acceptance of Mormons and their Church into the American community after a long history of suspicion and outright hostility. Mormons became paradoxically aligned with the establishment world-view of their old Republican antagonists – as exemplified by Smoot himself. A protectionist in trade matters, he achieved notoriety as an architect of the Smoot-Hawley Tariff Act that sought to protect American firms in competition with foreign interests – thereby, as many believe, helping to bring on the Great Depression.

Farming the land

In the realm of agricultural development, water supply was crucial in dealing with Utah's abundance of arid landscape, hence the necessity of

THE LEGEND OF JOE HILL

Born in Sweden in 1879, Joe Hill (also known as Joseph Hillstrom and Joel Hagglund) was an itinerant laborer, songwriter and sometime hobo, who organized on behalf of the Industrial Workers of the World (I.W.W.), or Wobblies. He came to Utah in 1913 and worked in the Park City mines before being executed by firing squad in Salt Lake City on November 19, 1915, after being found guilty of murdering two men – a father and son – in a grocery store. Some believe the criminal charges against him were fabricated by the "copper bosses" of Utah, an anti-union state, although nothing has ever been proven conclusively.

Since his death, Hill has become a folk hero. Among his well-known songs about the life of ordinary working men, collected in the I.W.W.'s *Little Red Song Book*, were "Casey Jones," "Rebel Girl" and "The Preacher and the Slave." He is also known for two famous statements: "Don't mourn, organize!" and "I don't want to be found dead in Utah," a sentiment poignantly expressed shortly before his execution. Several books, films, plays and songs have been written about Joe Hill, including the American folk song "I Dreamed I Saw Joe Hill Last Night," by Alfred Hayes and Earl Robinson, which captured the continuing struggle for labor rights after Hill's death.

installing irrigation systems from early on. The huge Strawberry Reservoir Project, federally funded and completed in 1913, diverted water to the Great Basin and thereby increased the extent of Utah's irrigated farmland. Irrigation projects sustained a bustling dairy industry, fruit orchards, and grain and hay production. Sheep, introduced in 1870, grazed the uplands and mountain meadows.

Sugar beets became a major product with construction of a Mormon-sponsored factory at Lehi in the early 1890s that was the first of its kind in Utah. Thousands of farms cultivated beets, and sugar came to rank as a major manufacturing enterprise.

There was a downside after World War I, however, as cutbacks in government orders reduced mining profits, and farmers were hurt as well by a drop in crop prices. Even harder times followed with the financial crash of 1929 and the Depression it engendered. By 1932, fully a third of Utah's labor force was unemployed. Residents left the state in heavy numbers, and for the first time the rural population fell behind its urban counterpart. More than 60,000 residents moved away between 1920 and 1940, and severe droughts and dust storms in the 1930s wreaked havoc on irrigation-dependent Utah.

Mormons commiserated by pulling together and establishing storehouses of goods for distribution to the needy. Out of the experience came a permanent welfare program, established in 1936, which gave rise to farms and canneries. Federal relief programs helped Utah combat the Depression and inspired conservation and reclamation projects. Work began in 1967 on an ambitious effort – the Central Utah Project – to divert water from other areas of the state to help places sorely in need of it. Today, farm income derives largely from livestock products, and commercial agriculture is the major enterprise.

A boom for defense

Utah was transformed by World War II, socially and materially. The federal government pumped millions of dollars into the local economy through new and expanded programs,

LEFT: a train wreck at the mines of Bingham Canyon.
RIGHT: an avalanche swallows Alta, a mining camp at the head of Little Cottonwood Canyon.

especially for military training and defense. Uncle Sam had already lent a hand, via relief programs, to help lift the state out of the Depression. Now the gathering storm in Europe climaxed by the devastating attack at Pearl Harbor in late 1941 intensified the recovery and changed Utah from backward hinterland into cultural mainstream.

In a state in which the federal government owns nearly two-thirds of the land, there were more than a dozen military installations operating, and they provided thousands of jobs. Hill Field near Salt Lake City was a major repair and supply depot for the Army Air Force. The

Ogden Arsenal was a storehouse for arms bound for the West Coast. The old Fort Douglas near Salt Lake City was put to use as a process center for recruits. Wendover's flatland on the Nevada border was ideal for year-round navigational and bomber training.

Utah also lent itself handily to an experimental platform for deadly warfare, as with the chemical weapons tested at remote Dugway Proving Ground in Tooele County. New impetus for testing came amid Cold War tensions, but now with heightened consciousness of the dangers of contamination. A worrisome incident occurred in 1968 when 6,400 sheep were found dead after grazing in an area near Dugway poisoned by a lethal nerve agent. The federal government paid over $1 million for compensation and related costs, and there has been a persistent public concern over the threat of contaminants in the years since.

Utah contributed about 65,000 of its own men and women for military service during the course of the war. On the negative side, the prevailing anti-Japanese hysteria following the Pearl Harbor attack resulted in the establishment of an internment camp, which began operations on September 11, 1942. This was the Topaz "Relocation Center" near Delta in Millard County, ultimately taking in 8,000 Japanese-Americans. It was phased out soon after the Japanese surrender at Tokyo Bay in September 1945, and many of the former internees opted to settle in Utah.

They and the large numbers of Hispanics, African-Americans and other "outsiders" attracted by wartime economic opportunity added a degree of cultural diversity to the state's population, resur-

TOO HOT TO HANDLE

A proposed nuclear waste dump on the Goshute Indian Reservation in Skull Valley has been a hot topic of debate for years. The facility would provide temporary storage for 40,000 tons of waste.

THE LAST GUNFIGHT

The so-called Posey War – a short-lived violent conflict pitting Utes and Paiutes against white ranchers – took place near Blanding in March 1923. It was sparked by the escape of two young Utes who had been arrested for robbing a sheep camp, killing a calf, and burning a bridge. Forty years of friction between Indians and ranchers rapidly erupted into all-out confrontation. A large posse of angry, trigger-happy men rounded up Ute men, women and children in the nearby community of Westwater and held them in a barbed-wire stockade in Blanding. They then tracked down a 60-year-old Paiute named Posey who had married into the Ute band in Allen Canyon and gained a reputation for arrogance and thievery. A gunfight between Posey and his followers and the posse ensued. The Indians killed a horse, just missed three passengers in a Model T Ford, and made headlines in national newspapers.

Unknown to the sheriff, Posey was fatally wounded in the gunfight, but his body was not recovered for a week, during which time innocent Utes remained in captivity. Upon their release, these Utes were given individual land allotments in Allen Canyon by the federal government and their children were sent to school at Towaoc, the Ute Mountain Ute Agency in Colorado. The last major gunfight in the West was over.

gent after years of stagnancy. Totaling half a million in 1940, the population doubled by 1970 and quadrupled by 2000. After the war, the military-defense buildup continued as the state became a missile center, with plants at Ogden, Salt Lake and Brigham City. By 1960 the federal government was Utah's largest employer, and the state's economic emphasis had shifted from agricultural enterprises to industry and manufacturing.

There was strong activity in food processing, petroleum refining, and manufacturing of computer software. Many steam and hydroelectric plants were built, and there was a major resurgence in uranium mining following the 1952 discovery of a rich deposit in desert land near Moab. The discovery set off a latter-day "uranium fever" that rewarded investors and prospectors handsomely.

Industrial growth was fueled in the 1960s by the construction of dams, most notably Flaming Gorge and Glen Canyon. Copper production fell off following a price decline in the 1980s. Utah nonetheless leads the world in the output of beryllium, it is a major producer of coal, and it is the only state that turns out Gilsonite, an adhesive agent used in road and asphalt paving.

Postwar affluence combined with Utah's abundance of natural resources has made tourism an important sector of the economy. Visitors are attracted by recreational opportunities in skiing, hunting, fishing, hiking, camping and snowmobiling. Skiing has become an especially important attraction, furthered by a steady upgrading of facilities. The state is blessed with a trove of national forests, parks and monuments in addition to nearly four dozen state parks.

Zion National Monument was the first of the major federal preserves, designated as of 1909 and the administration of President William Howard Taft. Nearly nine decades later, President Bill Clinton proclaimed the newest: Grand Staircase-Escalante National Monument, encompassing 1.7 million acres (688,000 hectares) centered on spectacular red-rock terrain in southeastern Utah. In remarks at Grand Canyon in 1996 directed at the designs of coal companies, Clinton said "we shouldn't have mines that threaten our national treasures." It was an allusion that reflects the debate between developers and conservationists over the issue of land use and how to keep a lid on mushrooming growth.

Olympic gold

Perhaps no institution is more identified with growth than the Church of Jesus Christ of Latter-day Saints, which has slipped the bonds of regional containment to spread its message of Christian commitment around the world through an army of missionaries. For both church and state, diversity is emphasized. Pub-

lic facilities like swimming pools long ago ceased invidious racial practices, and in 1978 the LDS Church declared the priesthood open to all worthy males. The following year brought professional basketball, via the improbably named Utah Jazz.

Sporting exposure was most pronounced in 2002 when Salt Lake City entertained the XXII Olympiad, only the second American site to be thus selected (the winter games were held at Lake Placid in both 1932 and 1980). A worldwide audience of more than 2 billion viewers watched the televised broadcast emanating from Utah over 16 days and involving 2,200 athletes from 77 nations. ❑

LEFT: protesting a proposed nuclear waste dump.
RIGHT: the 2002 Winter Olympics thrust Utah onto the world stage.

THE CULTURAL LANDSCAPE

Though 75 percent Mormon, Utah's population is unexpectedly diverse,
with Native people, Hispanic immigrants and LDS converts from around the world

In February 2002, thousands of international sports enthusiasts flocked to Salt Lake City to attend the Olympic Winter Games. Many had prepared themselves to endure what some dubbed the "Mormon Games," dominated by dour followers of the Church of Jesus Christ of Latter-day Saints who would try to convert everyone they met. With rumors of arcane alcohol licensing laws, downtown streets that were rolled up at 9pm, and locals whose idea of living life dangerously is to bring a new flavor of Jello to the annual Pioneer Day family picnic, it hardly seemed the recipe for a successful world party.

The reality was, of course, completely different. Almost overnight, it seemed (though not to the residents who had spent a decade enthusiastically laying the groundwork to host the Games), Utah had morphed into the sixth most urban state in the Union. Salt Lake City proudly unveiled spanking new freeways, one of the American West's busiest commuter airports, and attractive downtown neighborhoods filled with renovated historic homes, tree-lined boulevards, parks, malls and rapidly growing high-tech businesses.

There was everything a cosmopolitan traveler might desire: five-star hotels, historic bed-and-breakfasts, nearby ski resorts, gourmet restaurants, nightclubs, bistros, coffeehouses, independent bookstores, high-end shopping, a well-regarded university and medical research center, museums, and world-class arts and music. And for those traveling with their personal computers, there was an added bonus: Salt Lake City had recently been nominated one of the 46 most important high-tech centers by *Wired* magazine. According to a survey, 73 percent of households owned at least one computer, part of a successful statewide push by Governor Mike Leavitt to link public agencies and private business throughout the state.

PRECEDING PAGES: Wasatch Mountains camping trip.
LEFT: a member of the Southern Paiute tribe.
RIGHT: fans from around the world cheer on skiers at the World Cup races in Park City.

The Games themselves went off without a hitch. Far from being dominated by Mormons, they were deemed an all-out success for the United States as a whole – bold, commercial, technologically savvy, well run, devoid of security problems and highly photogenic, set against the picture-perfect Wasatch Mountains under

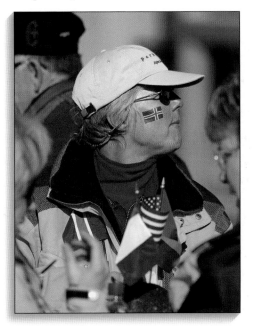

clear blue skies. Although the story was very different for those venturing into the more conservative Mormon strongholds of rural southern Utah, few visitors to Salt Lake City recalled even meeting a Mormon. This was lauded as a triumph for the Salt Lake Olympic Committee, whose avowed intention to de-Mormonize the Olympics was symbolized by a showy champagne toast a year before the games began. What most visitors remembered, instead, were the huge number of polite and welcoming Utah residents and the surprising ethnic diversity of the people they met.

It was no illusion. Ever since its founding as a Mormon sanctuary for converts from around the world, Utah has had a strong international makeup. When the Mormons arrived, the territory was under Spanish rule. For centuries it had been home to a prehistoric Indian culture dating back thousands of years, then members of the Ute, Paiute, Goshute, Shoshone and Navajo tribes who now make up nearly 30,000 of the state's residents. Mormon proselytizing in Britain and Scandinavia attracted thousands of immigrants to settle in Brigham Young's new State of Deseret. They were joined by migrant cowboys, farm workers and poor laborers from Greece, Italy, Russia, Finland, Ireland, China and elsewhere, who arrived in Utah with the railroads and mines. Today, new immigrants are increasingly Mormons from Polynesia, Latin America and Africa as well as refugees from Tibet, Somalia and other trouble spots throughout the world. By 2010, one in five of the state's projected 3 million residents will be a minority, making it the state with the fourth-highest percentage of ethnic minorities.

Ancient roots

The state's Indian tribes remain deeply attached to traditional lifeways, particularly in southern Utah, where ancient and modern Indian cultures sit side by side on the Ute, Paiute and Navajo reservations. Indian residents account

IOSEPA AND THE HAWAIIAN CONVERTS

Unknown to many, a farming community of several hundred native Hawaiian converts to the LDS faith under the leadership of I. W. Kauleinamoku was established in Tooele County's Skull Valley in 1889, close to the Mormon farm that eventually became the Skull Valley Goshute Indian Reservation. Iosepa *(yo-see-pa)*, or "Joseph" in the Hawaiian language, was named after the LDS Church's founder, Joseph Smith, and a later missionary of the same name who visited the Hawaiian Islands in 1854.

In true Hawaiian style, Iosepa's residents raised pigs and fished for carp in ponds in addition to growing crops.

When their crops failed, many residents began to work in local gold and silver mines during the late 1890s. The community was never self-sustaining and was largely supported by funds from the LDS Church, which had also paid the travel expenses of the new converts.

A combination of the harsh, dry environment and several cases of leprosy, a disease to which Hawaiians were particularly susceptible, doomed Iosepa. In 1917, Hawaiian Mormons returned to Laie on the island of Oahu, to live next to the newly constructed Hawaiian LDS Temple. The old Iosepa cemetery is now included on the National Register of Historic Places.

for more than half of San Juan County's population of 13,640. The county encompasses the Four Corners region, which was once the homeland of the Ancestral Pueblo, or Anasazi, whose descendants now reside in villages in New Mexico and Arizona.

Near the San Juan River, residents of the Navajo Nation and Southern Ute reservation live in family compounds next to empty stone pueblos left behind by departing Anasazi in AD 1300, while the people of the Uintah and Ouray Ute Reservation near Vernal and the Southern Paiutes headquartered in Cedar City still use lands once inhabited by the lesser-known Fremont Indians. In places with good hunting or plenty of water, such as the Green River canyons, images painted or incised on rock have been left behind by hundreds of generations of native people, signifying their passage.

The once nomadic Great Basin tribes share a number of material traditions, including basketry, leatherworking, drum making and beading. Mythology centers on the culture hero Wolf, who made heaven and earth, and Coyote, the creative trickster responsible for fire, arts and crafts, and the origin of many plants, animals and natural features, also celebrated in Navajo winter tales. Contact with Pueblos and Spaniards led the Navajo to develop distinctive crafts, such as silvermaking, pitch-glazed pottery, basketry and rug weaving. Paiutes and Navajos both make ceremonial baskets in the Navajo Mountain area, after centuries of living next to one another. Intermarriage and pan-Indian powwows bring all of Utah's tribes together at seasonal events like the Ute Bear Dance, a shuffling round dance held in spring to signal the rejuvenation of the natural world, symbolized by a bear awakening from hibernation.

American Indians hold special significance for Utah's Mormons. The Church teaches that Indians are descendants of the Lamanites, one of the fallen tribes of Israel documented in the Book of Mormon. According to Mormon doctrine, special efforts must be made to bring these "fallen" angels back into the Christian fold so that their skin may become white and "delightsome" again. Missionaries have worked among the Indians since the LDS Church

arrived in 1847, and the Church oversees an active adoption and mentoring program with the tribes.

A mixture of paternal concern and outright hostility has frequently characterized the relationship of Indians and Mormons in Utah's history. At the political level, these conflicting attitudes have led to tragic outcomes at times, such as the ill-fated termination policy sponsored by Utah Senator Watkins in the 1950s that ended federal recognition of the Southern Paiute Tribe until 1980. Still other Mormons, such as William Palmer, a leading citizen of Cedar City, became passionately interested in the ethnogra-

phy of the Paiutes, interviewing families and amassing an extraordinary collection of Paiute-made baskets, now on display at Southern Utah University and Iron Mission State Park.

After 150 years of contact, many of Utah's Indian people have been baptized into the Mormon faith. Many participate in the Church regularly while still keeping alive traditional Indian ceremonies – a duality that comes naturally for any minority forced to walk in more than one world. This same pragmatic pan-traditional approach can be seen throughout the Indian world today and allows tribal people to draw from a variety of influences that has strengthened tribal ties rather than weakened them.

LEFT: football practice at Monument Valley High School on the Navajo Reservation.
RIGHT: Navajo sandpainting.

The British influx

The same can be said for the many thousands of people from all over the world who have left their homelands to come to Utah, whether as converts to the Mormon faith or as immigrants seeking a better life.

The British Mormon Mission, organized in 1837, was among the most successful in drawing new converts to the Mormon city of Nauvoo, Illinois. When the word went out for a "gathering of Zion" in the Salt Lake Valley, thousands

CELEBRATING TRADITION

Salt Lake City's Living Traditions Festival is a three-day celebration of cultural diversity, featuring more than 600 artists, dancers and musicians representing 40 ethnic communities. The event is held on the third weekend in May.

Pioneer Day pageants. And Dutch oven cooking over a campfire is a tradition at thousands of family and church picnics, not just for its sentimental connections to cowboys and trail rides but for the larger connection to pioneer roots that inspires so many Utahans.

By the beginning of the 20th century, 50,000 British converts had made the journey to Utah, and a quarter of Salt Lake City's population was British-born. Brits could be found in positions of political power, busi-

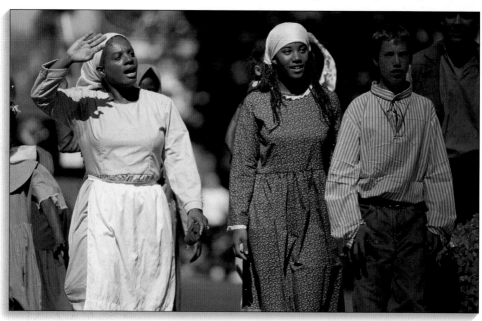

more made the sea crossing from England, Wales, Scotland, Ireland and elsewhere in Europe, paid for by the Mormon Perpetual Emigrating Fund, which between 1852 and 1887 directly assisted some 26,000 immigrants. They prayed and sang hymns on the long sea voyage, then pulled their belongings 1,000 miles (1,600 km) by handcart to Utah.

Mormon history holds a special place for these hardy "handcart pioneers," whose faith was tested by many hardships as they crossed the prairie. Handcarts, wagon wheels and other pioneer paraphernalia are proudly displayed in front yards all across Utah. Every year, young people re-enact portions of the epic voyage at

ness, the media, the arts and the trades. Leading businessmen included banker David Eccles (for whom Rice-Eccles Stadium in Salt Lake City is named) and Charles Nibley in lumber and sugar. Among the Brits who became editors of leading periodicals was George S. Godbe, founder of *Utah Magazine*, forerunner of the *Salt Lake Tribune,* who, along with Welsh immigrant Joseph Morris, founded the Godbeite Movement, dissenting from Mormonism in the late 1860s and 1870s.

Scottish-born Ebenezer Bryce, a shipbuilder, erected the state's oldest church in Pine Valley in southwestern Utah and went on to pioneer a ranch at Bryce Canyon in southern Utah, in the national park that now bears his name.

A British woman, May Anderson, founded what would become Primary Children's Hospital in Salt Lake City and also established kindergartens. British women sometimes also became polygamous wives in remote desert areas such as southern Utah's Arizona Strip, where one unsuspecting woman married a Cane Beds rancher. There is something forlorn about the accounts of such women, far from Britain's green pastures and not even allowed to indulge in a cup of tea or other simple comforts.

The thousands of quaint cottage gardens sporting hollyhocks, roses and other English country flowers, even in Utah's driest deserts, are a reminder of the state's strong British heritage. Also prevalent are numerous cultural organizations such as the Caledonia Society, founded in 1884, that organizes Scottish dancing, bagpipe bands and other highland pastimes at festivals throughout the state.

"Barn in a born"

Scandinavians, who with 30,000 immigrants by 1900 became the second most numerous group of Mormon converts, have also put their stamp on the state. Danish farmers and artisans were especially prominent in Box Elder and Cache counties north of Salt Lake City and Sanpete County to the south (which was one-third Danish by 1870), and in towns like Mantua, which was nicknamed "Little Copenhagen." One Danish immigrant, Anthony Lund, settled in Sanpete County in 1862 and later served in the territorial legislature and became a Church historian.

Today, Sanpete retains a strong Scandinavian influence. Highway 89 between Nephi and Salinas offers numerous glimpses of small pioneer towns with strong Danish roots, visible in the traditional farm buildings and workshops where musical instruments and other "Old World goods" are produced. Particularly interesting for visitors is the quaint, turned-about dialect heard throughout southern Utah – a combination of Scandinavian, British and American accents. You may hear jokes about people being "barn in a born" (born in a barn) and be asked how you enjoyed your visit to the national "porks"

(parks). Transportation is in "cores" (cars) and "courts" (carts), and folks eat "carn" (corn) for dinner. When bothered, folks are known to utter the expletive, "oh, my heck."

Mines and mayhem

A more typical western influence on Utah's cultural landscape are the many immigrant groups who came to Utah to work the mines, railroads, farms and ranches. Early Mormons were encouraged to establish agricultural enterprises, so mining fell to non-Mormon immigrants from Europe and Asia, many of whom were part of the westward migration to the California gold-

fields. Irishmen, Italians, Greeks, Slavs, Japanese, Chinese and others worked in the coal mines of Carbon and Emory counties, the hardrock mines of Summit, Salt Lake, Tooele and Juab counties, and in railroad construction.

While Mormon immigrants were assisted by the LDS Church and encouraged to integrate, non-Mormons immigrants tended to congregate in ethnic communities that sprang up near industrial areas. Many were paid lower wages than Americans and were assigned more dangerous work; discrimination of various sorts was all too common.

Nevertheless, many of these temporary workers ended up putting down roots in Utah, mar-

LEFT AND RIGHT: African-Americans and Maori dancers participate in the Pioneer Day parade in Salt Lake City, a sign of the city's growing diversity.

rying "picture brides" from back home and building strong civic institutions. Their influence can be detected throughout the state. Greek Orthodox churches, traditional Mediterranean foods and colorful celebrations have become a key part of Utah's cultural makeup.

Hispanic heritage

Today, the fastest growing immigrant group, as elsewhere in America, is Hispanics from Mexico and other Latin American countries. They now number an estimated 250,000, or 15 percent of the population, and are the largest minority group in the state.

The Spanish were absentee landowners in Utah when the Mormons arrived in 1847. In the 18th century, Spanish explorers named the Abajo and La Sal ranges and other landmarks in southern Utah, and the Old Spanish Trail was well established by the early 1800s. Spanish mining and ranching practices were important to the founding of those industries in Utah. By 1900, Hispanics from neighboring New Mexico and Colorado were working as sheepherders and cowboys, and later miners in the Monticello area. At the same time, Mexican immigrants were settling in Salt Lake City and Ogden, where they worked on the railroad and in the mines. During World War II, Hispanics were recruited to work in defense industries.

During the last 30 years, ever-increasing numbers of Hispanics have arrived from Central and South America. Hard-working people from those countries fill low-paid service jobs other Utahans refuse to do, including processing turkeys in factories in Moroni in the Sanpete Valley, cleaning office buildings in Salt Lake City, and working construction and day labor jobs. Determined to escape the poverty of their own countries and create a better life in Utah, men often take several jobs at once, live together to save money and, after gaining citizenship, send for their families. An increasing number are entrepreneurs who start their own taco stands, restaurants and other businesses, where their strong work ethic has led to numerous successes.

Hispanics have much in common with Mormons – strong families, an emphasis on home life, hard work and personal ambition, and a close connections with their church – yet the sheer exuberance of the culture and its celebrations, as well as religious differences, often collide with conservative Mormon culture. Although some Hispanics have converted to Mormonism, many congregate in their own Spanish-speaking neighborhoods, or colonias, on Salt Lake City's largely immigrant West Side, where they attend Catholic churches and are served by Spanish newspapers, television and radio stations, and businesses.

Salt Lake City's Hispanics make up about 25 percent of the population, and their political and purchasing power is growing (Hispanics in Utah spend an estimated $3.6 billion). Although Utah is far behind other states in representation, the state does have an Office of Hispanic Affairs and two Hispanic state senators who are working hard to improve race relations. In Sanpete Valley, the LDS and Catholic churches have come together to create Friendship Days to promote mutual understanding and tolerance. Fiestas and Hispanic community celebrations, such as folklorico dancing and mariachi music, are also popping up throughout the state.

"When we create a sense of celebrating, we tear down walls that divide us," commented forward-thinking Salt Lake City mayor Rocky Anderson in 2000. "Unfamiliarity is eliminated when we come together." ❑

LEFT: Mexican dancer performs *ballet folklorico*.
RIGHT: prayer at a Mormon Trail re-enactment.

EMPIRE OF SAINTS

Noted for tight-knit communities and missionary zeal, the Church of Jesus Christ of Latter-day Saints is one of the world's fastest-growing religions

It's 8.45am on a warm Sunday in August in Santa Clara, near St. George. In every neighborhood of this historic community in southwestern Utah, parents shepherding large families of scrubbed children in their Sunday best climb into equally large cars and head to church. Already the temperature is climbing into the nineties, and the bright Mojave sun is beating down on the black mesa above the town. New ranch-style houses sprawl above the sturdy brick homes and cottage gardens of the old town. Dogs bark and cicadas hum on this sleepy morning in rural America.

A stream of polished vans and cars winds along wide city streets on either side of the highway, past the irrigation ditch that brings water from Santa Clara Creek to fruit orchards and gardens. They pull into the parking lot of a large, modest building, which sports no spires, crosses or stained-glass windows. The occupants park and call out an affectionate hello to their brethren as they enter the meeting house.

Worldwide growth

It's a scene that plays out all across the Christian world every Sunday. But this particular group stands out. They are members of the Church of Jesus Christ of Latter-day Saints, commonly called Mormons. And since their church's founding, in 1830, they have proved themselves far from ordinary. The LDS Church, as it is known to its members, is the most successful religion ever founded on American soil. It now numbers 12 million members worldwide, a growth rate of 33 percent since 1994, with the rolls expanding by an astonishing 900 members a day, most of them in Latin America and Africa.

Utah, however, remains home base. It was here, in 1847, that second Church president Brigham Young led his weary followers to safety after the murder of Church founder Joseph Smith and his brother Hyrum in

LEFT: the LDS Temple in Salt Lake City.
RIGHT: devout Mormons observe Family Home Evening, dedicated to scripture study and prayer.

Carthage, Illinois, by an angry mob of "Gentiles." Inspired by Young's canny leadership and vision for a new life in an American Zion, poor converts from Great Britain, Scandinavia and all across Europe flocked to Utah by wagon, handcart and later trains and automobiles, founding small, preplanned agricultural

communities throughout the Salt Lake Valley.

Here, the genius of the LDS Church came into full flower, making the "desert bloom like a rose." No matter your station in life, if you lived a blameless life according to the tenets of LDS belief, you were assured of success. Eager and hardworking converts from the poorest neighborhoods in Europe embraced their new life in the desert, sharing in the community's wealth and ranching, farming, practicing trades, opening successful businesses and looking forward eagerly to Jesus Christ's second coming on American soil in the Latter Days, or End Times, thought to be imminent at the beginning of the 21st century.

By the early 1850s, the most successful of the first wave of converts had been "called" to colonize the remote canyon country of southern Utah. Pushing farther into the Great Basin, they built communities in northern Arizona, Nevada, Idaho, southern California and Mexico, fired up by Young's vision of a Mormon homeland, ever-after known as Deseret, where they could live away from others and practice their faith in peace.

Santa Clara was founded in 1854 by elder Jacob Hamblin, a missionary to the Paiute Indians. By 1861, he had been joined by 30 families of new Swiss converts, as the Church established the Cotton Mission in a warm, irrigated

desert area that came to be known, on the eve of the U.S. Civil War, as Utah's Dixie. Despite famine, drought, floods, crop failures due to insect infestation, malaria and Indian unrest, they endured, becoming self-supporting by raising fruit, vegetables, cotton and, for a time, silk.

Today, in common with the majority of small communities all across Utah, 75 percent of Santa Clara's 4,500 residents are active members of the LDS Church. As ever more people move into the St. George area, attracted by its warm climate, economic and recreational opportunities, and proximity to Las Vegas, Nevada, the numbers continue to climb.

Fifth-generation Santa Clara resident Lyman

Hafen, a one-time bronco-riding champion, historian, writer, businessman and former bishop of one congregation, or ward, in the Santa Clara Stake, has seen firsthand the changes in his hometown. Over the past 20 years, he says, the LDS Church in the Santa Clara Stake has grown from one to 13 neighborhood congregations, each made up of 300 to 600 residents. Three separate wards now share each meetinghouse, one reason why getting the money to construct new buildings is an ongoing affair, accounting for the numerous cake sales, charity events and other fundraisers in Mormon communities.

Social life

Meetinghouses are a hive of activity most days of the week. On Sunday, each ward offers three-hour services, beginning at 9am and continuing until 4pm. On Wednesday evening, youngsters return for Church-sponsored sports and other activities; and throughout the week, adult members of the Church hold meetings of various LDS organizations, such as the Women's Relief Society, the longest-running charity in the country, which sees to it that all Church members in need are taken care of within each ward. The one night of the week when you can expect to find LDS faithful at home is Monday evening, when devout Mormons observe Family Home Evening, a two-hour period when parents join their children to study scripture and share quality. Unlike most LDS activities, which are little changed since the Mormons arrived in Utah, Family Home Evening was introduced in the late 1960s as a way of strengthening family values during a period of social unrest.

Today, devout Mormons must commit to at least 14 hours of Church-associated activities, many more if they serve as lay clergy. This commitment to the Church is often cited as the main reason it is so difficult for Gentiles to connect with residents in LDS strongholds. For casual visitors, encounters with Mormons frequently take place in Utah's tourist businesses: souvenir shops, art galleries and bed-and-breakfasts, as well as tours of Church-run historic sites, temple visitor centers and tabernacles such as those in St. George and Salt Lake City.

During off-hours, you're most likely to meet Mormons on the 75 percent of the state set aside as public lands, including the many national parks in southern Utah. Visitors who time their visit to coincide with a community celebration, such as the weeklong Swiss Days celebration held in Santa Clara in September, get a unique opportunity to meet local residents. July 24 is Pioneer Day throughout Utah, commemorating the day Brigham Young and his followers arrived in the Salt Lake Valley in 1847. Most towns observe the day with a variety of events, from parades, floats and cookouts to family reunions and historic re-enactments. Communities like Huntington in Carbon County put on spectacular pageants that rank among the most photogenic events in Mormon Country.

specific assignments, all on a volunteer basis.

Children are indoctrinated into the Church through Primary Association lessons aimed at kindergarteners and Sunday school, which all church members attend. Only males may be ordained as priests and hold positions of power. They begin training early. Between 12 and 14 years of age boys become Deacons, from 14 to 16 they become Teachers, and between 16 and 19, Priests, responsible for collecting monthly "fast offerings" from member households, working as a Home Teacher with a senior male, and administering the sacraments during communion.

Church hierarchy

Under the patriarchal authority of the LDS Church, decisions on both religious and temporal matters are made by the Church President, or Prophet, and his two counselors, a Quorum of Twelve Apostles, and a Quorum of Seventy. Church affairs are administered locally by the bishop of an individual stake, consisting of 8 to 12 individual wards, each of which has its own bishop and counselors. In a typical ward, some 200 lay members are "called" to

LEFT: Pioneer Day honors the Mormon pioneers of 1847.
ABOVE: LDS General Authorities convene at the Church Conference Center in Salt Lake City.

Spreading the message

At 19, Mormon young men become Elders and most prepare for a two-year, self-financed Mission, where they are "called" to spread LDS doctrine worldwide and bring converts into the Church. The mission, carried out by passionate young believers, is at the heart of the success of the LDS Church. Presently, more than 55,000 missionaries serve in countries throughout the world. Foreign missionaries undergo training in 50 different languages at Church-owned Brigham Young University in Provo.

Proselytizing missions are the most visible sign of the Church in neighborhoods the world over. Carried out 12 hours a day by pairs of clean-cut young men living frugally away from home for the first time, the mission is considered excellent training for future leadership roles in business, politics and the Church. Among those who have taken advantage of this male Mormon training ground have been the hotelier J. W. Marriott, who went on to start his expansive hotel chain with funds from fellow Mormons, as well as politicians like Senator Orrin Hatch.

Women and family

Mormon women, by contrast, remain subordinate to males in the LDS hierarchy but are essential to the day-to-day running of the

sels for "preexistent" souls waiting to be saved in the LDS Church. This is no minor role. Central to the Mormon faith is a belief that the family bond is sacred and eternal, and the devout will be reunited in heaven, at the side of God and His Heavenly Wife. Over half of Utah's $5\frac{1}{2}$ million Mormons are under 24. Utah's birth rate – 31.66 births per thousand in 1977 – is more than twice as high as the national average.

Devout Mormons visit a temple whenever possible to make the appropriate preparations for the afterlife. Here, they don special clothing and receive secret "endowments" in church teachings, undergo baptism, and

Church. If men are the generals planning every move and communicating it to the faithful via sermons, conferences, letters, satellite links and the Church's vast media holdings, women are the foot soldiers carrying out the on-the-ground ward activities. Today, although more than a third of Mormon women work outside the home, the number of daily activities required of devout LDS members and an impressive family-first mentality often make it expedient for one parent to stay home.

Under LDS doctrine, women are the equals of men. In practice, their lives are circumscribed by their primary sacred task to marry and bear children who will become mortal ves-

"seal" their marriages. Of special importance are the legions of volunteers who carry out genealogical research by searching records, databases and cemeteries worldwide and creating family trees of ancestors. Once the names have been collected, these ancestors are then baptized by proxy in the temple by young people who consider it an honor to be chosen for a task that will ensure families can be reunited in heaven.

Code of conduct

Only those LDS members who are deemed "worthy" by their bishop may enter a temple. A worthy life is central to Mormon belief and requires the faithful to adhere to what is called the Word of Wisdom, formulated by first Church president Joseph Smith. Mormons, he taught, should live a busy, productive and blameless life, improve their minds, serve others, participate in their local ward, attend weekly meetings, study the Bible and accompanying Book of Mormon and Pearl of Great Price daily, tithe 10 percent of earnings to the Church, and fast one Sunday a month and donate the money that would have been spent on meals to the poor. Best known to outsiders is the requirement that a Mormon shun sexual relations outside marriage, exercise regularly, and avoid alcohol, tobacco, coffee and tea – a lifestyle that has made Mormons among the healthiest and longest-lived people in the world.

People in the LDS faith who find that they cannot follow the Word of Wisdom completely are frequently called Jack Mormons. Most families can count at least one Jack Mormon in their ranks, and Jack Mormons tend to be the most visible members of the Church in Utah, frequenting bars and cafés and other Gentile meeting places that devout Mormons shun.

Falling at the other end of the spectrum are breakaway sects of the LDS Church whose adherents attempt to restore what they consider to be the Church's original teachings. One such teaching is polygamy, which was abandoned by the Church in 1890. Polygamy has continued openly in Colorado City, a remote desert community on the Utah–Arizona border, where reports of forced marriages of young girls have sparked anger in the mainstream LDS Church as well as among Gentiles.

Family secret

One aspect of the LDS Church that sometimes disturbs Gentiles is that, despite its ubiquitous presence in every walk of life, the Church remains shrouded in secrecy. Even devout Mormons, such as former Church historian Leonard Arrington, who attempted to gain access to documents held in vaults for a multivolume history, encounter problems. Arrington, widely respected as a historian inside and beyond the LDS Church, was reprimanded by the Governing Authority and demoted from Church life. Others,

less lucky, are excommunicated completely if they speak out against the Church's positions.

From the beginning, though, Mormons have been encouraged to keep daily journals, which is one reason there exists a growing Mormon literature, much of it written by those still within the Church. Santa Clara's Lyman Hafen, a longtime journalist and former editor of *St. George* magazine, writes regularly about the people and history of southern Utah, offering a uniquely modern yet devout Mormon perspective on his corner of the state. And one Mormon writer – passionate political activist and nature writer Terry Tempest Williams – has succeeded in

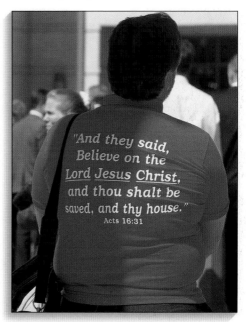

reaching an international audience with her books. Williams' thoughtful essays on people and place, sparked by a deep love for her Mormon roots and Utah's extraordinary environment, offer a window into what it means to be female and Mormon as well as a Westerner, an American, and a citizen of the world.

In fact, Mormons living in Utah have been atypical Westerners from the start. With their tight-knit communities, emphasis on family and faith, and attractively laid-out, prosperous towns, they are the antithesis of the rugged individualism that has always been part of the Western myth. For those living in Utah, the dream of Deseret is not dead. It is still unfolding. ❑

LEFT: Mormon boys prepare for the sacrament.
RIGHT: a protestor voices his opinion at an LDS conference in Salt Lake City.

THE NAKED EARTH

A labyrinth of canyons, arches and soaring cliffs
sprawls across Utah's spectacular landscape

The mile-high Colorado Plateau, a 130,000-square-mile (340,000-km) uplift that covers half of Utah as well as parts of New Mexico, Arizona and Colorado, is geology for the masses: a place where even the most casual visitor is forced, through sheer awe, to look more closely and ask why rocks behave in such incredible ways. Canyonlands. Arches. Capitol Reef. Bryce Canyon. Zion. All of Utah's national parks preserve different aspects of the geology of this colorful and spectacular region, where heat, aridity, uplift and erosion have laid bare the bones of the earth.

Although you can see ancient metamorphic gneisses and schists dating back to the Precambrian Era at Arizona's Grand Canyon and east of Moab in Westwater Canyon, these much older rocks are most visible in the northern part of the state, where recent volcanism and erosion in the Uinta and Wasatch Mountains have exposed deeply buried strata. Northern Utah's mountains are on the fringe of the Southern Rockies and have a consistently alpine look, more akin to Switzerland than the Desert Southwest. In little-known Dinosaur National Monument, which straddles the Utah–Colorado border and contains the converging Yampa and Green Rivers and an important dinosaur quarry, the geological story is even more complete than the Grand Canyon, with 19 different rock formations spanning 2½ billion years visible in the deep river canyons and Uinta Mountains.

The Wasatch Range forms the backbone of the Beehive State, giving way in southwestern Utah to a subdivision of the Colorado Plateau, known as the High Plateaus. This transition zone, pushed up by the major Hurricane and Sevier Faults, includes parks like Zion and Bryce Canyon and has the highest plateaus in North America. One of the highest and most visible is 11,000-ft (3,400-meter) Markagunt

Plateau, which drops off abruptly on the west parallel to Interstate 15, with the High Plateaus on the east and the searingly hot Basin and Range province on the west. Significantly younger than other geophysical provinces and still highly active, the north-south-trending mountains and vast basins of the Basin and

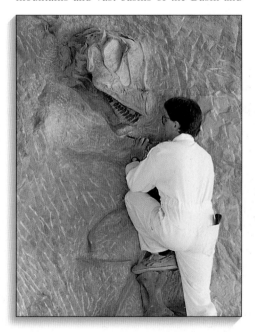

Range stretch as far as the eye can see through Nevada to California, the result of the earth's crust thinning between the Wasatch Fault on the east and the San Andreas Fault on the west.

Marine origins

The Precambrian Era encompassed about 85 percent of our planet's 4½-billion-year history. Throughout the Precambrian and subsequent Paleozoic Eras, the great laboratory of life was still in the early experimental stages, out of sight, beneath an ebbing and flowing ocean. About 3.2 billion years ago, the first life on earth evolved in the form of bacteria and blue-green algae. North America was part of a vast

---

PRECEDING PAGES: Canyonlands National Park.
LEFT: a flash flood inundates Flat Pass near the La Sal Mountains of southern Utah.
RIGHT: Wall of Bones at Dinosaur National Monument.

global supercontinent that tilted down at its western edge, allowing the sea to encroach. Lime deposits from early calcareous algae and other marine life-forms mingled with the coastal sands. As these deposits settled, they were compressed and hardened into horizontal strata cemented by calcium, manganese and iron. The Southwest's first sedimentary rocks – limestone, sandstone and shale – formed during this time. The earliest fossils, algae known as stromatolites, are found in these formations. By 750 to 700 million years ago, marine invertebrates had begun to appear.

Utah lay at the edge of the Pacific Ocean;

The ocean continued to cover western Utah into the Cambrian Period (570 to 505 million years ago) at the start of the Paleozoic Era, or Era of Ancient Life. The sea was now filled with trilobites, brachiopods and other marine invertebrates whose shells built up at the bottom of the ocean when they died. Calcium in the shells of these dead creatures precipitated into the ocean and cemented sand and other sediments into limestone embedded with marine fossils. For the next 100 million years, western Utah lay under water even as eastern Utah remained a featureless plain above sea level. New life-forms appeared, including the first ver-

Nevada and California had not yet emerged from the sea. Late in the Precambrian, western Utah subsided and sediment deposition increased. Brief episodes of mountain building and volcanic activity alternated with long periods of erosion and sedimentation. Movements in areas of weakness, known as faults, provided a conduit for heat to escape from the earth's mantle. Molten rock, or magma, was injected into sedimentary rocks, uplifting and folding them into tall mountain chains with a core of metamorphic gneiss, schist and granite. Attacked by water and wind, they eventually wore down into sediments again, which redeposited, hardened, uplifted and folded several more times.

tebrates, a kind of primitive fish, that swam in warm, tropical, shallow seas amid coral reefs, which hardened into dolomite as they died.

All of Utah was under water by 400 million years ago. The Stansbury uplift in north-central Utah developed into a prominent ridge above sea level late in the Devonian Period, and the first amphibians split their time between the sea and dry land. Throughout the Mississippian and Pennsylvanian Periods (360 to 300 million years ago), fusilinids, brachiopods and conondants were among the abundant life-forms in cyclical seas. Large quantities of limestone were laid down in the Oquirrh Basin in northwestern Utah, trapping organic matter that would yield massive quantities of oil and gas in the 20th century.

As the Pennsylvanian Era gave way to the Permian Era (290 to 245 million years ago), the basement rocks beneath Canyon Country in southeastern Utah were laid down. Uplift along the Ancestral Rockies in present-day Colorado pushed up the Uncompahgre Uplift and adjoining Paradox Basin near present-day Moab. As the sea ebbed and flowed, thousands of feet of salt, potash and organic-rich sediments from the highlands filled the shallow mountain basin, also trapping oil and gas. When the ocean withdrew and land appeared in the late Permian Period, large reptiles began to dominate the area.

Desert invasion

A drastic drying of the climate and withdrawal of the western ocean allowed enormous reptiles known as dinosaurs to dominate at the dawn of the Mesozoic (or Middle Life) Era. Wind-blown sand dunes from the north covered the shoreline of the Paradox Basin in southeastern Utah beginning in the Triassic Period (245–208 million years ago). The dunes alternated with thick layers of red silt and mud washed down from the adjoining Uncompahgre Uplift. The interfingered red-and-white rocks of the Cutler Group – consisting of the White Rim Sandstone, Organ Rock Shale, Cedar Mesa Sandstone and Elephant Canyon Formation/Halgaito Shale – have eroded beautifully into banded spires in the Needles District of Canyonlands National Park above the San Juan River. Below the river, in Monument Valley Navajo Tribal Park, Organ Rock shale forms the pedestals of enormous, highly eroded formations sculpted by the wind from swirling De Chelly Sandstone.

Volcanoes rimmed the western and northwestern margins of Utah and spewed ash across large areas of the Southwest. Silica in the ash mingled with groundwater and entered the woody core of huge conifers that had toppled from riverbanks into swamps. Over time, these silicates changed the woody core of the trees into quartz and other colorful minerals. Petrified wood is common in the multicolored layers of the Chinle Formation, and can be seen at Escalante Forest State Park and adjoining

Grand Staircase-Escalante National Monument in southeastern Utah.

The crumbly Chinle and younger Morrison Formations have also yielded large deposits of uranium. Moab boomed as the Uranium Capital of the World in the 1950s, and uranium exploration on the Colorado Plateau became widespread. Large caches of dinosaur bones in these formations have been unearthed in the Cleveland-Lloyd Quarry near Price, Utah, and in the famous Dinosaur Quarry in northeastern Utah's Dinosaur National Monument, part of a region dubbed the Dinosaur Diamond.

Aridity continued to affect the whole of Utah

throughout the Jurassic Period (208 to 144 million years ago), allowing an enormous Sahara-like desert to form dunes up to 3,000 ft high (90 meters). Swamps between the dunes were haunted by huge allosaurs, camptosaurs and other dinosaurs, who left behind footprints in mud that hardened into the Kayenta Formation, a red ledgy shale found below sheer cliffs of Navajo Sandstone.

The Navajo desert that spread across the West during the Jurassic lasted a long time, but eventually the climate changed again and became more moist. The sea returned, laying down marine and seashore sediments that lithified into Dakota Sandstone, Mancos Shale and the Mesa

LEFT: confluence of the Green and Colorado Rivers.
RIGHT: dinosaur bones, many from Utah's "Dinosaur Diamond," are stored beneath a Provo stadium.

Verde Group of the Four Corners. Below them, Wingate and Navajo sand dunes thousands of feet thick petrified so perfectly you can see which direction the wind was blowing when they formed. Calcium cemented the large quartz grains into sandstone. Hematite, derived from iron, tinted it a range of reds, pinks and oranges.

Iron in Zion's Navajo Sandstone creates rust, which changes hue as it washes down through the sandstone. Iron and manganese tinted Bryce Canyon and Cedar Breaks into rainbow hues and are also responsible in part for "desert varnish," the distinctive shiny red, brown and black streaks that spill down sandstone walls and served as blackboards for ancient Indian rock art. Desert varnish is caused by a combination of minerals, blowing clay and dust that is fixed on the dripping cliff faces by resident bacteria and microfungi.

Sea and sand

Today, sandstone is the most recognizable formation in the West. Throughout Utah, it is found in exposures of Wingate, Navajo and Entrada Sandstone. The Wingate forms the golden cliffs along the Fremont River in Capitol Reef National Park, the Circle Cliffs in the Escalante Canyons district of Grand Staircase-

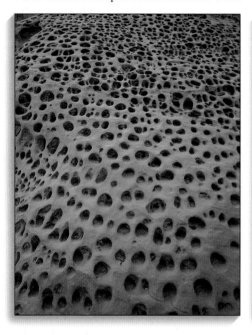

THE BIG ROCK CANDY MOUNTAIN

One of the most famous geological landmarks in Utah is a taffy-hued mountain beside the Sevier River named Big Rock Candy Mountain. It is made from Bullion Canyon volcanic rocks deposited 35 to 22 million years ago by a cluster of nearby stratovolcanoes, like the one that built Mount St. Helens. The distinctive yellow, orange and red colors derive from iron oxides mixed with creamy alunite and kaolinite, rich in potassium.

The mountain is named after a well-known folk song recorded by Burl Ives, describing a hobo's colorful fantasy of a life of ease, originally penned by a railroad brakeman named "Haywire Mac" McClintock. The song depicts a fanciful place where "the bluebird sings... to the lemonade springs."

The story has it that soon after the song was released in 1928, local boosters placed a sign at the base of the mountain christening it the "Big Rock Candy Mountain" and the nearby cold springs, the "Lemonade Springs." For thousands, the song's evocative lyrics symbolize the escapist frame of mind found throughout the American West. The late western writer Wallace Stegner, who grew up in Salt Lake City, certainly thought so. He titled his first book, a biography of his restless father, after a Utah mountain.

Escalante National Monument, and the soaring headland that makes up Island in the Sky in Canyonlands. Differential erosion of the brick-red Dewey Bridge siltstone, the lowest of three different "members" of Entrada Sandstone, is responsible for the "hoodoos" in northern Capitol Reef and nearby Goblin Valley State Park. On the other side of the Colorado River, the Entrada's younger two members – the pink Slick Rock sandstone and hard white Moab Tongue limestone, laid down in a seashore environment – offer perfect rock for arches to form.

Late in the Jurassic, shallow seaways from the north invaded Utah. In central Utah, the Ara-

pien Basin developed, trapping more than 6,000 ft (2,000 meters) of gypsum and other sediments. The first birds evolved at this time. During the Cretaceous Period (144 to 66 million years ago), lake and river systems gradually declined. In eastern Utah, the sea invaded from the east and southeast, forming an inland seaway from Mexico to the Arctic. This inland seaway was filled with strange creatures, including the plesiosaur, a fearsome marine reptile whose fossilized remains have been unearthed on the

LEFT AND ABOVE: erosion sculpts sandstone into a variety of shapes and patterns, including honeycombs, swirls and striations.

Kaiparowits Plateau near Lake Powell. Land-based dinosaurs and other reptiles wandered through major coal-forming barrier islands in swamps and marshes near the coastline, which gradually retreated east from central Utah.

In western Utah, the Sevier Mountains rose due to thrust faulting. Paleozoic rocks folded over younger rocks, and Utah rose. The highlands were attacked by the elements, and coarse sediments began to shed eastward into what is now the Great Basin.

Bulges, warps and meanders

For the dinosaurs and other living things, the end came when an asteroid collided with the earth at the end of the Cretaceous Period, 65 million years ago, paving the way for other life-forms – flowers and mammals. This was the beginning of modern Utah. Pangaea broke apart into separate continents. Hot lava from the earth's interior escaped through a trough in the Atlantic Ocean, widening the rift between the plates and forcing the North American continental plate west. Inevitably, the North American Plate collided with the eastern edge of the Pacific Oceanic Crust off present-day California. The reverberations sent seismic shock waves eastward through deep-seated Precambrian faults in the bedrock. The Rocky Mountains, the Uintas and the Colorado Plateau began to rise.

The Colorado Plateau warped and folded as it rose, creating huge swells, or monoclines, such as the Waterpocket Fold in central Utah as well as anticlines (upwarps) and synclines (downwarps), clearly visible in the Four Corners. This warping also created large basins, such as the Uinta Basin, that filled with freshwater along with organic matter including fish fossils and oil shales.

In the Oligocene and Miocene Epochs (38 million to 5 million years ago), igneous intrusions of hot molten lava along faults beneath heavy layers of sandstone pushed up and deformed much of Utah, creating mountain ranges such as the Henrys, the Abajos and the La Sals. Magma rose along zones of weakness, spread laterally between sedimentary layers, pushed them up into a dome, and the granite has now been uncovered by erosion.

A San Juan River trip, from Mexican Hat to Clay Hills Crossing, offers a rare opportunity to view these rock strata and float through the

Goosenecks of the San Juan, technically an entrenched meander, where uplift of the Colorado Plateau caused an older river to cut down several thousand feet into its sandstone course and form hairpin bends. Rivers won't meander for long without seeking a more direct route past obstacles. In this case, the grinding action of the river currents punches a hole in a meander wall, widens it, and eventually leaves behind a natural bridge like those at Rainbow Bridge and Natural Bridges National Monuments. Natural bridges are water formed; arches are formed by erosion along joints in sandstone, creating linear fins and eventually arches.

Basin and Range

Western Utah's basin-and-range country is much younger and more mobile than the Colorado Plateau and largely the result of pulling apart, not pushing up. Starting about 20 million years ago, the earth's crust beneath the Great Basin began to extend, thin, overheat, and crack along a roughly north-south trend. Stone blocks of earth started to break and tilt, forcing chunks of land to rise and others to drop. The ones that dropped formed basins and began to fill with sediments washing down in huge alluvial fans. Some basins contain 15,000 ft (4,600 meters) of fill. The Great Basin has no outlet to the sea.

The Wasatch Fault, which created the Wasatch Mountains, the dramatic backdrop of Salt Lake City, is second only to the San Andreas Fault for activity. Volcanic action along a northwest-southeast trend within sedimentary rocks, such as limestones, is thought to be the reason why the Bingham Mining District, west of Salt Lake City, has such huge copper deposits.

One theory is that the continent drifted northwest over a hot spot in the earth's mantle. Copper ores may have been the last substances to crystallize out of the magma. Associated minerals such as silver were found in sandstone in 1866 in southwestern Utah's Silver Reef Historic District. Between 1866 and 1881, Silver Reef had 2,000 residents and was southwestern Utah's biggest town. It is now a ghost town just north of St. George.

Fire and ice

Uplift along the Wasatch, Hurricane and Sevier Faults in western Utah pushed up the Wasatch Mountains and High Plateaus of southwestern Utah, starting about 15 million years ago. The Colorado, Green and Yampa Rivers and their tributaries cut into their meandering courses, creating deep sandstone canyons. In the Quaternary Period, volcanic activity continued to spew lava flows atop the high plateaus, forming the million-year-old basalts atop the Grand Staircase, a series of colorful plateaus in southwestern Utah.

During this time, the climate became colder and wetter, ushering in the last Ice Age. In Utah, glaciers carved valleys in the northern mountains and could be found as far south as Cedar Breaks National Monument, where glacial till made up of ground-up rock can be seen below Brian Head. Great Salt Lake and its smaller siblings are remnants of much larger Lake Bonneville, which covered the valleys of northern and western Utah during the Ice Age.

About 10,000 years ago, Lake Bonneville shrank. Island-dotted Great Salt Lake and two smaller lakes to the south are all that remain of Lake Bonneville. Today, Great Salt Lake is northern Utah's biggest geological attraction. It supports several major industries, including, naturally, salt production, and is important to wildlife as well as people, who use the lake for recreation. ❑

LEFT: a geologist takes core samples near Snowbasin.

There Be Monsters

Ninety million years ago, southeastern Utah was at the edge of an expansive interior seaway that split North America in half. Within this seaway lived huge crocodile-like reptiles known as plesiosaurs, which fed on sharks and fish. On the shores were the last survivors of dinosaurs that had dominated the region in Triassic and Jurassic times, 200 million years ago. The fossilized skeletons and footprints of these early predecessors now lay buried beneath deep sediments deposited in a succession of sandy deserts, beaches, streams, rivers and oceans. Small land-based mammals had begun their inexorable rise. The Age of Mammals was at hand.

Fossil remains from this Late Cretaceous Period are few and far between. That's why recent discoveries of a hadrosaur skull and two intact plesiosaurs in Grand Staircase-Escalante National Monument and neighboring Glen Canyon National Recreation Area have created so much excitement among paleontologists. "To find one intact is really rare," said Barry Albright, a Museum of Northern Arizona curator. "This is what we live for." After examining the two plesiosaurs and the ammonite-rich Tropic Shale in which they were found, Grand Staircase-Escalante National Monument paleontologist Alan Titus had further good news. These plesiosaurs – with 6-ft-long (2-meter) skulls and 25-ft-long (8-meter) bodies – apparently represent a new genus and may be older than any ever discovered in North America.

But the real story here is that of young people with a passion for paleontology, scooping the experts with finds of their own. The plesiosaurs were discovered by 15-year-old David Rankin and his friend Wryht Short of Big Water, Utah, while they were hiking in Glen Canyon National Recreation Area. After spotting a piece of bone sticking out from the hillside, they alerted their friend Merle Graffam, an amateur paleontologist, who contacted Albright and colleague David Gillette at the Museum of Northern Arizona. In 2000, a crew including Rankin, Graffam and others went to the sites and removed the remains.

The hadrosaur skull was also unearthed by young people. Since the 1930s, students from Webb School in Claremont, California, have been participating in paleontology digs under the auspices of the Raymond M. Alf Museum of Paleontology, the only nationally accredited paleontology museum on a high school campus in the world. After working for several seasons on the remote Kaiparowits Plateau, the students struck gold when they unearthed a 400-pound (180-kg) hadrosaur skull in the 75-million-year-old Kaiparowits Formation. It is the only hadrosaur skull to be found south of Montana and the first intact dinosaur skull ever excavated in southern Utah.

If all these bones get you wondering what the real-life great lizards looked like, you'll enjoy the Dinosaur Museum (754 South 200 West, Blanding, UT 84511; 435-678-3454), the brainchild of artists Sylvia and Stephen Czerkas, whose life-like recre-

ations of dinosaurs grace museums all over North America. They opened this small museum in their adopted hometown of Blanding in 1995. Galleries trace the evolution of dinosaurs around the world, and include the real skeletons of an Argentine *Herrerasaurus*, a Mongolian *Tarbosaurus*, and a clawed *Deinocheirus*, as well as the Czerkas' own sculptures, which include a huge *Allosaurus*, *Albertosaurus*, and *Carnotaurus*. Other exhibits emphasize how recent discoveries have altered scientists' understanding of the appearance of dinosaur skin and reproduction. The museum also offers a fun exhibit focusing on dinosaurs in the movies – evidence, if any were required, of the major role dinosaurs play in the popular imagination. ❑

RIGHT: dinosaur artists Sylvia and Stephen Czerkas, with their depiction of *Carnotaurus*.

LIFE IN A DRY LAND

*From the forested slopes of the Wasatch Range to the sun-blasted flats
of the Great Basin, Utah encompasses a fascinating array of plants and animals*

From Skyline Drive atop Utah's Wasatch Plateau, the surrounding country is a study in contrasts. The 11,000-ft (3,350-meter) Wasatch Plateau – one of central Utah's High Plateaus – has been uplifted by volcanism more than a mile above the desert; from the top visitors can take in all of Utah's ecosystems in a unique panorama. From up there, it's easy to imagine the sense of possibility felt by LDS Church president Brigham Young when he gathered his followers above the Salt Lake Valley on July 24, 1847, and declared it "the right place."

Atop the plateau, on either side of a dirt road that follows the mountain spine, are dense forests of hardy conifers threaded with icy mountain streams and grassy alpine basins inhabited by mule deer, elk, marmots, raptors and other denizens of the high country. At lower elevations, stands of Gambel oak, bigtooth maple and aspen form a border around the tall evergreens. These deciduous forests are the shape shifters of the mountains: bright green in the warm temperatures of spring, softening into a tapestry of magenta, russet, gold and ochre in late September, weeks before deep snow claims the highlands for the winter.

The lay of the land

Autumn colors compete with the rumpled Technicolor rocks of Canyon Country, sprawling to the southeast. Immediately east of the Wasatch Plateau, at the heart of Castle Country, is the 1,000-ft-high (300-meter) San Rafael Swell, the most dramatic of several sandstone monocline uplifts soaring above the canyons carved by the Colorado River and its tributaries on the Colorado Plateau. The rivers spilling west from the Wasatch Front couldn't be more different. Born in the highlands of the Uinta and Wasatch Mountains, water from the highlands sinks unceremoniously into the sere, monochromatic expanse of the Great Basin, a desert spanning western Utah and Nevada with no outlet to the sea.

The Bear and other rivers pouring from the highlands form lakes, swamps and other wetlands at the base of the Wasatch Mountains before disappearing into the salty, sterile waters of the Great Salt Lake. A century and a half of damming have helped make the Wasatch Front a productive area for agriculture as well as for

migratory and residential waterfowl. Birds by the thousands, including 37 species of swans, geese and ducks, descend on the surrounding wetlands seasonally.

Far to the southwest, the Great Basin Desert and Colorado Plateau are joined by a third desert – the Mojave – creating a major ecosystem where Utah, Arizona and Nevada meet along the Virgin River. Here, in a pocket-sized corner of Utah populated by Joshua trees, riparian streams and the craggy Beaver Dam Mountains, two nature preserves – the Lytle Ranch and nearby Red Cliffs Reserve – protect three desert vegetative zones and endangered species such as the Virgin River chub and desert tortoise.

LEFT: a biologist researches flammulated owl chicks.
RIGHT: mule deer, Fremont River Canyon.

Sea of diversity

With an average 13 inches (33 cm) of rainfall a year, Utah is one of the most arid states in the Union; only neighboring Nevada is drier. Happily, though, with a topography that ranges from an elevation of 2,500 ft (760 meters) in the south to 13,528 ft (4,123 meters) at Kings Peak, precipitation varies greatly, from a low of a few inches to a high of over 30, allowing a wide variety of plants and animals to find a suitable niche. Some 600 vertebrate species and thousands of plant families call Utah home. Many are endemic, meaning they exist nowhere else, such as species of milkvetch found only in

the selenium-rich soil of Zion National Park. With varied topography, soil and climate, Zion is particularly blessed with wildlife. More than 80 percent of the total wildlife found in Utah live within its boundaries, making it an important nature preserve as well as geological landmark in the High Plateaus of southern Utah.

To date, 23 animals in Utah are endangered or threatened, mostly due to habitat loss from rapid development. The list includes major predators such as the grizzly bear, gray wolf, bald eagle and California condor; smaller creatures such as the Mexican spotted owl, peregrine falcon, blackfooted ferret, burrowing owl and Utah prairie dog; and tiny natives such as

the Kanab ambersnail and Virgin River chub that hang on in a few scattered preserves but have disappeared elsewhere in their range.

The Colorado River, which transects southeastern Utah, has more than its fair share of listed species, as damming has altered the natural environment of the river and its canyons. Warm water fish species such as the Colorado squawfish (now known as the pikeminnow), razorback sucker and bonytail are unable to survive in the icy conditions created by Glen Canyon Dam. Their days seemed numbered until a recent drought along the Colorado River caused Lake Powell's northern reaches to shrink, returning the lake to a river system able to support native species again, albeit temporarily. Even as fish that evolved in the warm waters of the historic Colorado River struggle for survival, those adapted to cold water, such as trout, thrive. Trout fishing below the dam in Flaming Gorge Reservoir in northeastern Utah is some of the best in the state, while the adjoining Uinta Mountains are notable for another seasonal event: the annual return of kokanee salmon, which spawn in Sheep Creek each fall, providing eggs for hatcheries throughout Utah and Wyoming.

The southwest willow flycatcher, a neotropical migrant that historically bred in the willows along the Colorado, has also declined after its preferred willow habitat was replaced by water-guzzling tamarisk, or salt cedar, along riverbanks. Tamarisk, an attractive but lethal exotic shrub introduced for erosion control and now out of control throughout the West, has sounded the death knell for native willows and cottonwoods along disturbed waterways. It is not the only nonnative plant to wreak havoc. Introduced cheatgrass, a vigorous annual with little nutritional value, has also created problems for protein-rich native grasses such as winter fat, galleta and ricegrass that have traditionally provided year-round browse for livestock on the Colorado Plateau.

Competition from man-made activity remains the greatest danger for native plants. Twenty-four are now listed as endangered. One endemic species, the pretty little kachina daisy, is found only in "hanging gardens" created by seeps in the sandstone cliffs above Indian Creek. Three other endangered plants are now protected on The Nature Conservancy's historic Dugout Ranch adjoining the Needles District of Canyonlands National Park.

Life zones

The Canyon Country of southern Utah is a particularly interesting place to view wildlife due largely to a diversity of topographical features, ranging from the Colorado River to the La Sal Mountains, which soar to 12,000 feet (3,660 meters). Broad ecological differences are particularly obvious on the Colorado Plateau, where elevation changes allow a variety of plants and animals to thrive. Such changes piqued the interest of a young naturalist named C.

RETURN OF THE CONDOR

Biologists are trying to restore the endangered California condor to the American Southwest. Among the largest flying birds, with 9-ft (3-meter) wingspans and bald heads, the scavengers are occasionally seen in southern Utah.

On the Colorado Plateau, elevations average 4,000 to 6,000 ft (1,200–1,800 meters), placing it squarely in the high desert zone but also allowing Great Basin vegetation, such as sagebrush and grasses, to cover large tracts of land used by ranchers. In Canyonlands National Park, the 6,000-ft (1,800-meter) elevation supports both grasses and pinyon and juniper. "P-J," as it is known in these parts, is useful in a multitude of ways – for nutritious nuts, berries and firewood – and is the friendliest of the

Hart Merriam, who traveled to the Grand Canyon in 1889 to study the landscape. In just 60 miles (100 km), Merriam noted, one passed through ecosystems similar to those between Mexico and the Canadian Arctic. He named and described a series of "life zones," each corresponding to a particular elevation. Modern scientists have expanded on Merriam's ideas, now recognizing that slope angle, soil type, exposure to sun and wind, moisture and other variables all contribute to local microclimates.

LEFT: a collared lizard warms itself on a boulder; the lizard is occasionally seen running on its hind legs.
ABOVE: a naturalist examines a canyon mouse.

dwarf forests to camp under, offering views of the stars at night and shelter at noon. Cedar gnats, or "no-see-ums," are active when temperatures warm up. Watch out. They give a mean bite.

Equally entrancing is ponderosa pine forest, which forms lofty stands in Bryce Canyon National Park (elevation 7,000–8,000 ft/ 2,100–2,400 meters), west of the Colorado River. Sheltered by the vanilla-smelling, platey trunks of ponderosa pine are Gambel oak and toothy maple that flare red and bronze in autumn. Mule deer are often seen here, twitching long ears and jumping away skittishly. The forest is often noisy with disputing Steller's jays and tassel-eared squirrels.

Snow is not uncommon in June on the high plateaus and mountains of Utah, so wildflowers are late bloomers. Cedar Breaks, situated atop the 10,000-ft (3,000-meter) Wasatch Plateau, has one of the best wildflower shows in the state. Watch for explosions of bluebells, lupines, columbines, Indian paintbrush, penstemons, woolly mullein and numerous asters and sunflowers thronging disturbed roadsides in August and September. Above 8,000 ft (2,400 meters), pioneer deciduous species like quaking aspen take over subalpine meadows in silver profusion, but are eventually overshadowed by spruce, fir and, at higher elevations,

lodgepole, limber, Jeffrey and gnarled bristlecone pines, the world's oldest trees, often reaching ages of 3,000 to 4,000 years.

River corridors

Spring runoff demands a fast response from wildflowers, birds and other living things in high-altitude parks like Cedar Breaks, a veritable Monet painting of bright, splashy blooms roused from their snowbound slumber in early June, along with hibernating bears, pikas and marmots. Townsend's nutcrackers make fast work of seeds as the season rolls on. Rushing mountain streams spilling into the lowlands

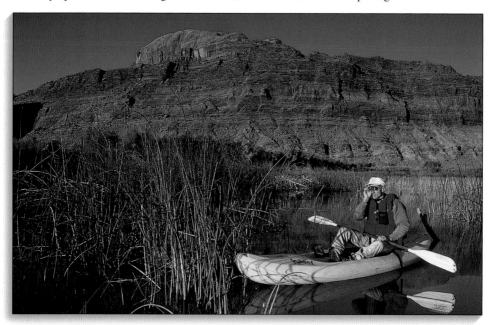

DESERT OASIS

Serious birders will want to visit Fish Springs National Wildlife Refuge (801-831-5353), an isolated wetland oasis, 78 miles (125 km) northwest of Delta in the Great Salt Lake Desert. Five major springs and several lesser seeps flow from a faultline at the base of the eastern front of the craggy Fish Springs Mountains. These mineral-laden, saline springs provide virtually all of the water for the refuge's 10,000-acre (4,000-hectare) marsh system. Since they maintain a year-round temperature of between 70°F and 80°F (21°–27°C), they provide a home for 5,000 to 6,000 wintering birds representing more than 250 resident and migratory species. The second largest population of snowy

plovers can be found here. The springs have been a vital water source not only for birds but for humans, including local Goshute Indians, early explorers like Jedediah Smith and Pony Express riders along the 1860-1861 Pony Express Trail. A well-preserved 133-mile (214-km) portion of the historic trail can be driven on an unpaved scenic backway through western Utah from Stage Coach Inn State Park, in Fairfield, one of the original Pony Express stations, to Ibapah, near the Utah–Nevada border. Brochures are available from the BLM. This is an extremely remote area, so start out with a full tank of gas, bring food, water and spare tires, and let someone know your itinerary.

slow to a trickle and ice up in places as winter arrives. Lack of rainfall and damming of major waterways mean that many smaller rivers – dry arroyos much of the year – are flooded by seasonal runoff and summer rains, a danger for hikers caught there at the wrong time.

But where mighty rivers like the Colorado, Fremont, Yampa and Green run, they form green corridors of cottonwood, box elder, willow, exotic tamarisk and other water-loving plants that provide a respite from the heat and a habitat for many creatures. Deep canyons, such as those along the Escalante River and the North Fork of the Virgin River, offer cool,

shaped by aridity. This is primarily a rain-shadow region of desert basins trapped between high peaks and plateaus, which capture what little Pacific moisture makes it over the 14,000-ft (4,300-meter) barrier of California's Sierra Nevada. It's no exaggeration to say that finding water, trying to hold onto it, and adapting to its absence are the main preoccupations of life.

At the lowest desert elevations in Utah, which include the Mojave and Great Basin, the most successful plants – cacti – take advantage of infrequent but hard rains by employing an extensive root network and conserving water in expandable, gelatinous tissues. Waxy trunks

moist microclimates in which a Douglas fir might grow across from a pricklypear cactus. Groundwater here percolates through sandstone, sustaining monkeyflower, columbine, shooting stars, maidenhair fern and other moisture-loving plants to form luxuriant hanging gardens. Also glorious is the cascading song of the canyon wren: often heard, rarely glimpsed, and truly the top of the hit parade of southwestern crooners.

Diverse as it is, all life in the Southwest is

LEFT: bird-watching at the Matheson Wetlands Preserve along the Colorado River near Moab.
ABOVE: kids search for bugs in the Wasatch Range.

and paddles protected by spines are used for photosynthesis instead of leaves. The cacti lure moth and bat pollinators with bright flowers and produce tasty autumn fruits that are eaten and disseminated by many animals. Some trees and shrubs shed their leaves and virtually shut down to conserve water; others close up or tilt fleshy, waxy leaves to keep cool.

The desert seems quiet during the day because three-quarters of the animals are nocturnal. Visit a water hole at dusk or dawn for a glimpse of coyotes, kit foxes, bobcats, badgers, perhaps even rare bighorn sheep, which have been reintroduced in Canyonlands and Arches National Parks. During the day, look skyward to see red-tailed hawks, golden eagles, lightning fast peregrine falcons and enormous desert ravens. These birds patrol the skies from cliff aeries in search of unsuspecting cottontail rabbits or Uintah ground squirrels, which keep themselves cool by holding their feathery tails over their backs as they rush from rock to rock. Smaller birds, such as tits, finches, vireos, tanagers and hummingbirds, flocks in huge numbers to riparian zones in sheltered canyons.

Reptiles keep cool hiding under bushes and rocks, becoming active at twilight and leaving strange slither marks and tracks in sandy soil. Collared lizards and whiptails are often seen in

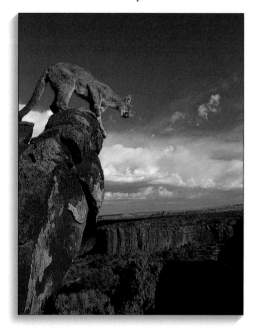

low-elevation regions; if you're lucky, you may even glimpse the huge and colorful Gila monster, North America's only venomous lizard, in the Mojave Desert west of St. George. Venomous creatures are plentiful in the desert, using poison to immobilize prey, aid in digestion, or defend themselves. The giant desert hairy scorpion, more than 5 inches (13 cm) long, is less poisonous than the pale, inch-long scorpion, whose sting can be deadly. In addition to rattlesnakes and coral snakes, poisonous desert dwellers include an 8-inch-long (20 cm) centipede, black widow and brown recluse spiders, cone nose bugs and tarantulas.

On the Colorado Plateau, spadefoot toads sim-

ply bide their time throughout the year, waiting in the bottom of dried-up potholes for the drumbeat of rainfall, which signals the time to spawn. Spadefoot toads are only one of many species that inhabit desert potholes. Perhaps the most fascinating are tadpole shrimp, which can withstand dessication (like packaged "sea monkeys") and come back to life again when it rains. Some animals, such as kangaroo rats, have lost the need to drink water at all, recycling it from seeds.

Not a drop to drink

The Great Salt Lake, as Utah naturalist Terry Tempest Williams writes in her memoir *Refuge: An Unnatural History of Family and Place,* is a "liquid lie" in the desert, a mirage, water that does not support life. This relic of Ice Age Lake Bonneville – now northern Utah's most popular natural attraction – is rendered almost lifeless by extreme salinity, but its seasonal fluctuations have a profound effect on adjoining wetlands, such as Bear River Migratory Bird Refuge, which was set aside in 1928 as the nation's first waterfowl preserve.

Two species manage to live in the lake's salty environment. Green algae thrive in briny water and multiply so rapidly the lake shallows often take on a green hue. In late summer, green algae form the main diet of brine shrimp, which consume so much of the green algae the water begins to clear. The algae also attract swarms of brine flies. The flies, along with algae, reptiles and small mammals, are the major attraction for hundreds of species of birds that visit the wetlands surrounding the lake. They include avocets, phalaropes, eared grebes, pintail ducks, white pelicans and thousands of tundra, or whistling, swans, which migrate through in fall.

Utah Mormons have a special place in their hearts for the 80,000 or so gulls that nest and feed around Great Salt Lake. In 1847, shortly after the Mormons had planted their first crops, an infestation of crickets threatened to destroy what little food the people had managed to grow to get them through the winter. At the last moment, when all seemed lost, a flock of gulls came to their rescue, killing and eating the crickets, and saving the crops. The grateful Mormons never forgot this reprieve. Today, the gull is Utah's state bird. ❏

LEFT: mountain lions prey on deer and small mammals.

Sea Monkey Business

You won't find any fish to catch in the Great Salt Lake. What's there, actually, is the peculiar creature known as brine shrimp. That's the common name for this member of the crustacean class. Brine shrimp have also become known popularly as "sea monkeys," and therein lies a tale.

Although they're of the class that includes the lobster and the crab, brine shrimp are absent from oceans while being prevalent in inland saltwaters or wherever salt water evaporates. The species involved here is *Artemia*, and the most familiar example in the United States is *Artemia franciscana*, the name deriving from the San Francisco Bay area in California. Another chief location is the Great Salt Lake of Utah.

Brine shrimp lack bones. They come equipped with exoskeletons – outer shell-like skeletons that cover their bodies. Starting out as tiny larva, the shrimp reach their adult size of about one centimeter in four to six weeks. The eggs can dry out and remain viable for years, and then, under the right conditions, begin to hatch.

Beginning in the 1950s, a big business developed whereby adult shrimp were harvested on the Great Salt Lake for use as fish food for America's aquarium trade. By the 1970s there was a build-up of commercial demand for brine shrimp eggs, or cysts, in connection with the feeding of shrimp, prawns and some fish in the seafood industry.

Hatched in late February and early March, the cysts float on the surface before being hauled in by a horde of commercial fishermen, who descend each October on the Great Salt Lake. The eggs are so tiny that fifty could easily fit on the head of a pin. As seen from planes employed in the harvesting, the cysts take on the appearance of rosy swirls or reddish-brown streaks on the water.

The trade has become highly lucrative, with *Artemia* cysts selling for upwards of $35 a pound. In the mid-1990s the harvest was totaling some 15 million pounds, although only about half the amount reeled in can actually be marketed.

There has been much environmental concern lately centering on the intense commercial harvesting, and wildlife agencies have been monitoring the population of brine shrimp. A major worry is the effect which a diminished population could

have for the millions of shorebirds and waterfowl that depend on the shrimp for sustenance in the course of their migratory journeys. Limits on cyst harvesting have been tried, to the dismay of the commercial shrimp harvesters.

The term "sea monkeys" arose when a variety of the brine shrimp began to be marketed as pets in the 1960s with great success. A few years earlier, in 1957, an eccentric New Yorker named Harold von Braunhut chanced upon the phenomenon of brine shrimp and their ability to spring to life after a long shelf life. As cysts, they appeared to exist in a state of suspended animation, only to revive when introduced to water.

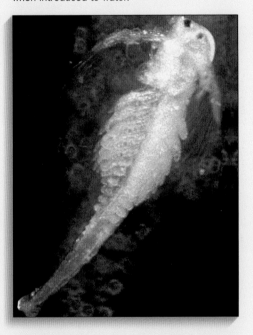

Braunhut decided to offer the shrimp as pets for children which could be sold through the mail. In 1960 he advertised the packaged shrimp as "Instant Life" in ads he placed in the back of comic books. Legions of youngsters would respond over years to come. Dubbing the shrimp "sea monkeys" after their tail-like appendage once they morphed into life, Braunhut touted their ability to cavort in water settings – racing and performing acrobatic maneuvers – to the delight of youngsters the world over.

Braunhut's success in selling billions of the Sea Monkeys was offset by controversy stemming from his political extremism. He was identified in a 1996 Anti-Defamation Report as belonging to the Ku Klux Klan and the Aryan Nations. He died in 2003. ❏

RIGHT: brine shrimp are harvested in the Great Salt Lake and sold as "sea monkeys."

OUTDOOR ADVENTURE

Slot canyons, whitewater rapids, mountain heights and slickrock trails
beckon travelers with an itch to experience the wild side of the Beehive State

The National Sporting Goods Association regularly conducts state-by-state surveys of how many people participate in each of 34 sports and fitness activities, ranging from backpacking, mountain biking and downhill skiing to bowling, darts and working out at fitness clubs. According to recent NSGA surveys, Utah ranks among the top five states in every activity except saltwater fishing. In fact, compared to the national average, Utahans are more than twice as likely to participate in sports and fitness activities.

One reason for the high ranking is the Mormon emphasis on physical fitness, a corollary of the belief that the body is a temple. Even in the 19th century, when many churches associated play with idleness and most "outdoor adventures" were a matter of survival, Mormons strongly advocated recreation as part of a wholesome lifestyle. According to historian Rex A. Skidmore, Brigham Young "not only enjoyed recreational pursuits himself, but some of his august religious speeches were on this subject."

There's another reason that outdoor sports are so popular: Utah is built for adventure. This is a land of slickrock canyons, whitewater rapids, sandstone cliffs, alpine meadows, crystalline lakes and wilderness so rugged that some areas have only been surveyed from the air. Viewing it through a windshield can't come close to truly experiencing it. And that's where the adventure begins.

Wet and wild

If you explore the great outdoors in Utah long enough, you're sure to cross paths with the ghost of John Wesley Powell. A geology professor and Civil War veteran, Powell became the spiritual father of adventure travel in 1869, when he ran the rapids of the Colorado River in a wooden boat. Poised with his 10 men and four boats at the upper end of

Cataract Canyon, the start of nearly 1,000 miles (1,600 km) of whitewater wilderness, Powell declared, "We are now ready to start on our way down the Great Unknown. We have an unknown distance yet to run, an unknown river to explore. What falls there are, we know not; what rocks beset the channel,

we know not; what walls ride over the river, we know not. Ah, well!"

Every year some 2,000 people raft through Cataract Canyon in the heart of Canyonlands National Park. Unlike Powell, today's whitewater enthusiasts know what lies ahead: 25 rapids, several of them rated Class IV (the second-highest level) in just 37 miles (60 km). At the end of the four-day trip, a small plane or van returns them to their starting point. Their spiritual bond with Powell is clear. Each of them has undertaken a journey fraught with danger for the promise of a remarkable, once-in-a-lifetime experience.

Rafting, like other outdoor adventures, comes

LEFT: Sulphur Creek, Capitol Reef National Park.
RIGHT: a backpacker cools off in a desert stream.

in all degrees of difficulty and risk. If Cataract Canyon sounds too intimidating, rafting companies in the Moab area offer trips on smooth-as-glass stretches of the Green and Colorado Rivers. Farther afield, the Green River flows through Dinosaur National Monument on a trip that is placid one minute and thrilling the next, but always magnificently scenic. Place names like the Gates of Lodore and Rainbow Park lend a Tolkienesque mystique to the multi-day, Class-III journey.

NATURE CALLING

When nature calls, answer with a trowel. Dig a hole at least 6 inches (15 cm) deep for human waste and bury or carry out toilet paper. Pick a site at least 200 ft (60 meters) from water sources.

see are a few sailboats. Since kayaking is best when there's no wind, kayakers often find that they have the water all to themselves.

In contrast, Lake Powell – on the Colorado River between Canyonlands and the Arizona state line – is one of the most celebrated boating lakes in the West. More than 100 miles (160 km) long and fringed with countless side canyons, the lake is best known for houseboating vacations. Often lasting for a week or longer, the journey unfolds at a leisurely pace, with

While virtually all rafting in Utah is done on the Colorado and Green Rivers, kayaking is different. A kayak opens up more possibilities than any other watercraft. You can rent a kayak at any marina on Lake Powell and spend a weekend or longer paddling and camping along the lake's remote tributaries. Or you can test your mettle against one of the fast, cold rivers that pour down canyons along the Wasatch front. Ogden even has a kayak practice park within its city limits.

You can also kayak on the Great Salt Lake. The lake's extreme salinity corrodes the metal parts of motorized boats, so aside from kayaks and canoes, the only watercraft you're likely to

plenty of time to investigate remote areas by kayak or canoe and fish for dinner in waters that haven't seen an angler all season. Reservations must be made far in advance; the cost per week is about the same as a posh resort.

Elsewhere in the state, boaters and anglers can explore the waters of alpine reservoirs such as Pineview, Deer Creek, Jordanelle and Strawberry. There are a number of natural lakes, too, including broad, shallow Utah Lake near Provo and aquamarine Bear Lake, which spills into Idaho. Sailboats, bass boats, windsurfers and sunbathers share all these waters. So do scuba divers, though by far the top dive areas in the state are the submerged slot canyons of Lake Powell and, even more popular, an underground warm spring called Homestead Crater near Heber City.

On the trail

For some, hiking is adventure enough. They owe no apologies. A slow, steady walk in the wilderness seems relatively harmless, but hiking can be risky for several reasons. First, it is the activity people are most likely to undertake without an experienced guide. Second, it is tempting and far too easy to set out on a hike without equipment that may prove essential. And third, it is more likely than any other activity to leave you at the mercy of the elements without an easy way back to safety.

What gets most people into trouble isn't snakebite, flash floods or falling off cliffs but the far more mundane risk of dehydration – a critical loss of moisture due to extreme heat and aridity. The condition is particularly insidious because in the desert even mild exertion, like hiking, can cause the body to loose moisture faster than the brain can generate an urge to drink. In other words, you become dehydrated before you feel thirsty.

Prevention is simple enough. Carry plenty of water and drink it at regular intervals, whether or not you feel thirsty. The rule of thumb is one gallon (4 liters) per person per day, but it's best to take more than you think you'll need just in case you want to extend your trip or you lose your way. Getting lost is notoriously easy to do in the desert, where the absence of trees and other landmarks leaves you with few reference points and the bare ground makes it easy to stray from even a well-marked trail. Coupled with the symptoms of mild dehydration – fatigue, lightheadedness, disorientation – losing your way can quickly spiral into a life-threatening situation. Carry a map and compass (or GPS unit) and know how to use them, and leave a travel plan with someone at home, so they know when and where to start looking if you don't turn up.

Other basics you'll need to take with you are a hat, sunglasses and sunscreen with a high SPF. The Utah sun is unrelenting, and shade is scarce. Left unprotected, your skin and eyes will be fried in no time.

LEFT: rafters on the Colorado River plunge through Cataract Canyon in Canyonlands National Park.
RIGHT: Fisher Towers Trail outside Moab.

Foot notes

As a hiker, you will rely almost entirely on your feet, so keep them in good shape with the best hiking boots you can afford. Gone are the days of heavy leather clunkers that took forever to break in. Modern boots are lightweight but sturdy enough to protect your feet from cactus and thorny underbrush and need little or no breaking in, which helps avoid painful blisters. Wearing polypropylene liner socks under a thick pair of poly-wool outer socks will wick moisture away from your feet and prevent blisters. Avoid cotton socks, which soak up moisture and tend to be rough. If a hot spot develops,

cover the area with moleskin (available at most camping supply shops) or white athletic tape and allow yourself extra time to rest.

Overnight trips are naturally more complicated to plan and require a rather daunting list of additional equipment, including a backpack, sleeping bag, tent, water-purifying kit and camping stove. The design and quality of camping gear has never been better, though choices (and prices) can quickly become overwhelming. Unless you have an experienced friend to show you the ropes, the best advice is to start by doing a little research in books and magazines and on the Web, then go to a reputable camping-supply retailer and work with a salesperson who's willing to take the time you need to make the right decisions. Remember: comfort is key. Roughing it in the outdoors shouldn't be rough at all. The idea is to simplify your life, unload stress, and enjoy the place, people and moment, not aggravate yourself with ill-fitting or poor-quality equipment that leaves you cold, hungry, achy and generally miserable.

Hoofing it

In the 19th century, Utahans like mountain man Jim Bridger and outlaw Butch Cassidy roamed the mountains and canyons on horseback with a freedom that modern travelers dependent on maintained roads can only envy or, if they wish, emulate. Unless you're the kind of serious equestrian who travels with a horse trailer in tow, the first step in booking a backcountry riding trip is to find a reputable stable or outfitter. Among the best areas for horseback riding are Bryce Canyon and Capitol Reef national parks, the Escalante Canyons, the San Rafael Swell and the Uintah Plateaus. For trips of more than one day, most stables require that you arrange a trip through an outfitter who will make sure you and the horses return safely. Outfitters who guide pack trips in the national parks or forests must be certified by the managing agency.

SKY HIGH

Topping the list of skyscraping thrills is hot-air ballooning, which lets you experience the freedom of drifting high on the wind to the dragon-like roar of a propane burner, lifting you a world away from the terrain far below – whether it be the wilds of Canyonlands National Park, the rugged Wasatch Mountains or the Great Salt Lake. Balloon trips usually take off early in the morning, when the cool air provides the best lift. Balloon companies operate out of Moab, Park City, Provo and Ogden.

Other sky-high adventures include paragliding and hang gliding at Point of the Mountain Flight Park, about 13 miles (21 km) south of Salt Lake City. Tandem flights, which team a "passenger" with a seasoned flier, allow even rank beginners to get airborne on their first outing. An airport near the flight park was Utah's main skydiving zone for more than 30 years until the area became too developed for safe landings. Now skydiving has moved to the Tooele Valley Airport in Erda, a desert location 20 minutes west of Salt Lake City.

Travelers who dream of soaring can do so in a fixed-wing glider at Heber Valley Airport. If you prefer a vehicle with a motor, several companies offer helicopter and airplane tours over some of the most spectacular terrain in all of the West.

Horses are an especially appealing alternative in wilderness areas where wheeled vehicles are prohibited. Llamas are becoming a popular alternative, too. Though you can't ride them, llamas can carry as much weight as a human, turning a back-breaking schlep into a comfortable stroll. Llamas make amiable trail companions and getting to know one can be the most memorable part of the trip.

Thrills on wheels

Nothing since the advent of downhill skiing has transformed outdoor recreation in Utah as much as mountain bikes. Invented around 1980 in the ski towns of central Colorado and popularized in the redwood forests of northern California, this new breed of bicycle with extra-strong frames and heavy-duty tires had been around for a while before cyclists realized that Moab's slickrock country was a mountain biker's paradise. It started when off-road cyclists pioneered the Kokopelli Trail, an ambitious 142-mile (229-km) cross-country trek from Loma, Colorado (near Grand Junction), to Moab.

Once there, mountain bikers soon discovered Moab's Slickrock Trail, a technically challenging 12-mile (19-km) route across sloping sandstone surfaces that was first developed by motorcyclists in 1969. Today Slickrock is said to be the world's most popular mountain bike trail, used by more than 100,000 cyclists each year. The White Rim Trail, a 100-mile (160-km) four-wheel-drive road around the base of the Island in the Sky district of Canyonlands National Park, makes for a spectacular two- to three-day trip that has enhanced Moab's reputation as a mountain biking mecca. Today, Moab's main street has more bike rental shops than restaurants.

Mountain bike rentals and tours can be arranged in towns near all national parks. Unless otherwise posted, cycling in the parks is limited to roads open to motorized vehicles. A notable exception is Zion National Park, where a 3-mile (5-km) bikes-only trail offers a shortcut between two scenic drives. Biking is an ideal way to bypass the traffic congestion that often plagues Bryce Canyon National Park, as well as to experience the unpaved scenic routes in and around Capitol Reef National Park.

LEFT: a paraglider floats over Monument Valley.
RIGHT: a mountain biker splashes through a stream in the Wasatch Mountains near Park City.

Visit any bike shop for information on nearby trails, many of which traverse land managed by the National Forest Service or BLM. Some of the biking adventures awaiting discovery are epic in scope, such as a 50-mile (80-km) cycling route along the historic Pony Express Trail across the Great Salt Lake Desert. If you haven't brought your own bike, you'll find rentals in sizable towns throughout the state, from Price in the northeast, where the 19-mile (30-km) Castle Valley Ridge Trail challenges even the most advanced riders, to St. George in the southwest, where Snow Canyon State Park, Gooseberry Mesa and the Green Valley

Loop are popular biking destinations.

The most ambitious effort to create a trail network for mountain bikers has taken place around Park City, a popular ski town in the Wasatch Mountains. Here, many ski shops have discovered that bike rentals are an ideal off-season business. With their support, cycling organizations have established more than 300 miles (480 km) of trails designated for mountain bikes. Chairlifts equipped with bike racks operate in summer at ski resorts, allowing cyclists to ride to the top of the mountain and spend hours coasting down ski trails. Other relatively effortless trails in the Park City area include the 28-mile (45-km) Historic Union

Pacific Rail Trail, an old railroad grade stripped of its tracks and ties. The Park City trail system also includes short, technical routes like the Round Valley Trail that challenges bikers of all skill levels.

Elsewhere in Utah, cyclists enjoy excellent opportunities for road touring. Bike routes separated from traffic lanes have been established along a number of scenic drives in the Wasatch Mountains, such as Ogden and Provo Canyons. Perhaps the most memorable spot is Antelope Island State Park, set on an island in the Great Salt Lake. A 7-mile (11-km) causeway connects the island to Syracuse, near Ogden, and an 8-

mile loop road leads through the park, home of a free-ranging bison herd.

Climbing and canyoneering

For a uniquely Utahan experience, consider "canyoneering," a hybrid sport that involves hiking, boating and rock climbing techniques such as rappelling and "chimneying" as well as navigation and survival skills. The sport is ideal for guide services, which offer a wide range of adventures depending on the participants' skill.

Rock climbing can be the focus of advanced canyoneering, or it can be a passion all its own. From the tortured rock faces of Zion National Park to the granite cliffs of the Wasatch Range,

those in search of a vertical vacation will find an inviting menu of possibilities. Though technically demanding, rock climbing has become much easier for novices to try. Guides in popular rock-climbing areas like Moab tailor their services to the needs of beginners, offering supervised ascents on short, clearly blazed climbing routes and rappels down cliff faces that are more thrilling than hazardous. Advanced climbers, on the other hand, can take advantage of year-round opportunities, tackling the cool canyons of the Wasatch Range in summer and shifting to desert areas in spring and fall. On those rare days when the weather is miserable, there are indoor climbing walls where residents and visitors alike hone their skills. Perhaps the most spectacular of these manmade walls is at the Cliff Lodge at Snowbird Resort, where a 120-ft (36-meter) International Climbing Competition Wall spans the west face of the 10-story hotel.

For information on guides and climbing routes, contact the Salt Lake Climbers Alliance (www.saltlakeclimbers.org). Also helpful is the American Canyoneering Association (ACA), based in Cedar City (www.canyoneering.net). The 450-member group trains canyoneering guides, search and rescue teams, backcountry rangers and law enforcement officials. When undertaking any canyoneering adventure, it's prudent to select an ACA-certified guide.

At least as important as the guide's qualifications are your own. Each traveler bound for Utah's backcountry should evaluate honestly his or her tolerance for adventure. This is especially true in the realm of climbing and canyoneering, where the array of trips can range from mild to death-defying. Guides will usually interview you to ascertain your experience so they can help you select the most suitable trip. Avoid hubris or exaggeration; your objective is not to impress your guide.

With that word of caution in mind, seize the opportunity to go boldly into the Utah backcountry. Whether by water or land, you'll discover landscapes so wild and strange they might as well be on a distant planet. You may discover something about yourself, too – hidden reserves of strength, courage and wonder that will change forever the way you relate to the natural environment. ❏

LEFT: a rock climber in Arches National Park.
RIGHT: a quiet moment in Capitol Reef National Park.

SNOW SPORTS

Huge vertical drops and tons of light, dry powder lure skiers and snowboarders to this Olympic-quality kingdom of snow

In winter, a chill wind out of the west howls across the salt flats most of the time. As it reaches the Great Salt Lake, churning up choppy waves on the surface of water too saline to freeze, evaporation occurs rapidly, saturating the desert air with humidity. Reaching the other side of the lake, the wind slams into the near-vertical rock faces of the Wasatch Front, creating an updraft that hurls the moisture-laden air upward a mile or more into the sky, where the temperature drops by as much as 50°F (10°C). The water content in the air flash-freezes into tiny crystals that drop in the form of fluffy white powder on the mountain slopes below. The result of this unique phenomenon is an astonishing average of 500 inches (1,270 cm) of snowfall each winter. That's more than 40 ft (12 meters) of snow – enough to bury a five-story building.

By way of comparison, the most famous ski resorts in neighboring Colorado – Aspen, Vail and Breckenridge – average only about 300 inches (760 cm) of snow a year. From 1985 to 1997, Utah license plates bore the slogan, "Ski Utah! The Greatest Snow on Earth." And yet, Utah's snow remained a local secret. In the 1990s Vail alone attracted more skiers than all the ski areas in Utah combined. But that was before the Winter Olympics came to town.

Best kept secret

Of the dozen downhill ski areas in Utah, 11 are in the Wasatch Mountains within an hour's drive of Salt Lake City, Provo, Ogden or Logan. Four areas – Solitude (801-534-1400) and Brighton (801-532-4731) in Big Cottonwood Canyon and Alta (801-359-1078) and Snowbird (801-742-2222) in parallel Little Cottonwood Canyon – are less than 30 miles (48 km) from Salt Lake City International Airport and less than half that distance from Interstate 215, the beltway along the east edge of the city, making them the most accessible major ski

areas in the United States. These areas have always been popular with local skiers but, until recently, all but ignored by out-of-towners.

Most of the others, farther from Salt Lake City, were little family-run resorts with one lodge and two or three chairlifts. They include places like historic Beaver Mountain (435-753-0921) in Logan Canyon, Utah's first ski resort, built in 1939, and Sundance (801-225-4107) in Provo Canyon, owned by actor Robert Redford and better known for its namesake film festival than for its easygoing elegance, uncrowded slopes and the last tow rope in the West.

Before the Olympic Games came to Utah in 2002, the state's only slopes adjacent to a real ski town was Park City Mountain Resort (435-649-8111), which got its start in 1963 as a small day-use area. In those days, Park City Mountain used a train and elevator to carry skiers through an old mine shaft – a far cry from the present-day megaresort, with its 3,300 skiable acres (1,335 hectares), 100 runs and 14 lifts.

LEFT: Olympic medalist Picabo Street chats with fans.
RIGHT: a skier flies down an Alta slope.

The Games change everything

When Salt Lake City was nominated to host the 2002 Winter Olympic Games, the skiing world immediately took notice. Articles about Utah's little-known ski resorts flooded the ski magazines. Soon, allegations began to emerge about bribery, fraud and corruption on the part of the original organizers of the Salt Lake City Games. Although some officials were forced to resign, the scandal created an avalanche of publicity for Utah skiing. Before ground was broken for the Olympic facilities, Utah's snow became an instant legend among skiers. One question remained: Could Salt Lake City

its main chairlifts with a detachable quad that offers summit-to-base skiing with a single lift. It established a lift-served connection with nearby Snowbird for a combined 4,700 skiable acres (1,900 hectares) – the second-largest ski area in Utah – for the price of a premium lift ticket. Alta also offers Nordic ski trails and Snow Cat ski trips to nearby Grizzly Gulch.

Big and small

The largest ski area in Utah, Powder Mountain Winter Resort (801-745-3772) near Ogden, has expanded to 5,500 skiable acres (2,225 hectares), including 700 acres (280 hectares)

deliver on the massive preparations required of an Olympic host?

The results astonished just about everyone. Within less than two years, the city and state not only built an array of special-use facilities including ski jumps, bobsled runs, Nordic ski courses, snowboard pipes, a skating rink and a ceremonial stadium, but also widened highways in several canyons and met stringent demands for security. The Salt Lake City Games are widely regarded as one of the best organized in Olympic history.

The legacy of the 2002 Olympics has been an expansion of Utah's ski industry beyond all expectations. Alta, for instance, has replaced

SPEED DEMONS

The Olympics are long gone, but the Winter Sports Park in Park City is busier than ever. Not only do U.S. Olympic contenders train there, but the facilities are open to teams from other countries during international training weeks to practice bobsledding, luge and skeleton. If watching isn't thrilling enough, you can ride a bobsled yourself. The Park provides the pilot and brakeman; two passengers ride in between. It costs about $200 per person, and the ride is over quickly (the course record is 48 seconds), though it may seem to last forever. You can also take a half-day introductory course in ski jumping or ride a luge or skeleton with a protective shell.

of powder and tree skiing accessible by Snow Cat, 1,200 acres (485 hectares) of backcountry skiing, and 800 acres (325 hectares) set aside for guided powder skiing tours. The sprawling slopes also offer night skiing until 10pm. On the opposite side of Pineview Reservoir, Snowbasin (801-620-1000) is smaller but features spectacular slopes and trails, including race courses and two terrain parks. It has recently been upgraded with two gondolas and a tram in addition to six lifts.

Park City has become Utah's premier resort town. Not only has Park City Mountain Resort expanded, but two other prestigious

just north of Cedar Breaks National Monument. With just over 500 skiable acres (200 hectares) and eight lifts, it's tiny compared to the behemoths of the Wasatch Front, but it holds a reliable snow base despite its southerly location due to a 11,307-ft (3,446-meter) elevation. In fact, its base elevation is higher than the summits of most Salt Lake City ski resorts.

Halfpipes and terrain parks

The 2002 Winter Games also gave a new air of respectability to snowboarding, a sport that most serious skiers had previously viewed as a type of juvenile delinquency. Snowboarding's

resorts – Deer Valley (435-649-1000) and The Canyons (435-649-5400) – have added more downhill skiing options for a total of 8,550 skiable acres (3,460 hectares) served by 45 chairlifts and three gondolas, all within easy shuttle distance of the cafés and boutiques that line the town's historic main street.

Finally, no survey of Utah ski areas would be complete without the only ski resort outside the Salt Lake City vicinity. Brian Head (435-677-2035) is situated in Dixie National Forest

LEFT: passengers hurtle down the bobsled course at the Utah Winter Sports Park in Park City.
ABOVE: keeping warm in Snowbird's cold climate.

Olympic debut, four years earlier at the Winter Games in Nagano, Japan, had been marred by scandal when Canadian Ross Rebagliati, the first-ever gold medalist in snowboarding, was stripped of his title after testing positive for marijuana. (The Court of Arbitration in Sport restored his medal after ruling that cannabis was not a prohibited "performance-enhancing drug.") Equally embarrassing, the snowboarding team from the United States, where snowboards had been invented and international snowboarding races had been held for almost 20 years, took no gold or silver medals.

Once again, Utah's ski resorts capitalized on the Games, this time by developing world-class "terrain parks" – special areas with halfpipes, jumps and other features designed to provide maximum thrills. Park City Mountain Resort, home of the world's first competition superpipe, added three new snowboard areas with a total of 61 rails, jumps and "funboxes." They have been named the world's top terrain parks by both *Snowboarder Magazine* and *Transworld Snowboarding Magazine*. Neighboring Deer Valley added a unique Skier Cross course, a specially modified alpine slalom with banked turns, jumps and rolls that is set up to be timed; boarders compete only against their own records, not other competitors. Park City's third ski resort,

The Canyons, premiered a high-altitude terrain park to provide more reliable powder. The Canyons also features seven halfpipes throughout its ski area, including one a full mile long.

Other ski areas that emphasize snowboarding include Snowbird, with three terrain parks for boarders of varying skill. Due to their popularity, Snowbird's advanced Baby Thunder Terrain Park and its intermediate Big Thunder Terrain Park are being expanded every season. Brighton has three interconnected terrain parks that let boarders ride hips, tabletops and jumps from the top of the highest chairlift to the base of the mountain.

Powder Mountain, Snowbasin and Solitude have also added terrain parks, as has Brian Head

in southwestern Utah, leaving Alta as the only ski resort in Utah that does not allow snowboarding. Alta, too, has created its own terrain park, allowing extreme skiers to put their hotdogging techniques to the test without the inconvenience of snowboarders getting in the way.

Without a lift

Of course, you don't need a ski slope to ski. Utahans have been doing it ever since the 1870s, when snowbound miners in the Wasatch Range got around by strapping on 12-ft (4-meter) skis made from lumber. By 1912, the Wasatch Mountain Club was taking recreational cross-country ski treks into the wilderness. Before the Olympic Games came to town, skiers were flocking to trails groomed by resorts and Nordic ski clubs, while others skied into the national forests of the Wasatch and High Uintas Mountains.

The 2002 Winter Olympics included 12 cross-country ski competitions ranging from sprints to 30-kilometer endurance races. The site chosen for the Nordic ski course was Soldier's Hollow, an area of Wasatch Mountain State Park in the Heber Valley south of Park City. Unlike most other Olympic facilities, cross-country ski courses need not be permanent; the groomed trails melt away in the spring. Soldier Hollow, however, has proved so popular with local skiers that the Olympic course is regroomed annually and set aside for cross-country skiing in winter. It's the second-largest groomed Nordic ski park in Utah. Only Ruby's Inn near the entrance of Bryce Canyon National Park is larger, with 30 miles (50 km) of trails; all trails within the national park are open for cross-country skiing in winter.

Other resorts in the Salt Lake City area with groomed cross-country ski areas are Homestead Resort with 7½ miles (12 km) of trails, Solitude Ski Area with 12 miles (20 km), and Sundance Resort with 9 miles (15 km). Brian Head in southwestern Utah also has a cross-country ski course, and tour operators in Moab guide tours into the nearby mountains during the winter months. And what could be more convenient than Park City, which has groomed cross-country trails right in town – on the golf course? ❑

Left: covered in snow, a skier happily recovers from a tumble in the powder.
Right: a skier rockets over a ledge at The Canyons.

PLACES

*A detailed guide to the entire state, with principal sites
clearly cross-referenced by number to the maps*

On a weekend morning, a steady stream of locals is driving or bicycling up Emigration Canyon to a favorite breakfast restaurant in Salt Lake City: Ruth's Diner. The second-oldest restaurant in Utah, Ruth's has been in business for 75 years, 56 of them in the old trolley car it now occupies in the foothills of the Wasatch Mountains. Its former owner, an independent-spirited cabaret entertainer named Ruth with a penchant for cigarettes, chihuahuas and cussing, died in 1989. She wasn't your average Utah resident, but she was much loved, nevertheless. "In a perfect world, every town would have a diner like Ruth's," *Salt Lake Weekly* food critic Ted Scheffler once wrote.

Ruth's continued popularity is surely not because the food or the building are anything fancy. "The cooking," said another critic, is "like grandma's – with a few sassy additions." No, it's simply that, in a state founded by large numbers of immigrants, nothing is more important than keeping alive tradition. The diner's spectacular setting – at the mouth of the canyon from which Brigham Young pronounced Salt Lake Valley "the right place" – doesn't hurt. On the way up, you can take in some of the best scenery, historic sites and outdoor recreation in Salt Lake City.

This can't-fail combination of setting, history and culture is not just limited to the Wasatch Front – home of three-quarters of Utah's population and world headquarters of the LDS Church – but a feature of the whole state. Go just about anywhere in Utah, and you'll find an array of travel options and often striking contrasts.

For example, in central Utah, in a lightly traveled region known as Castle Country, you'll discover a former mining town transformed into an artist haven, the hideout of outlaw Butch Cassidy, and a dinosaur museum across from 6,000-year-old Indian rock art. Just a quick drive from hip Moab, the "mountain bike capital of the world" and a mecca for all stripes of outdoor adventurers, are the gravity-defying spans of Arches and Canyonlands National Parks as well as the forested ramparts of the La Sal Mountains. Within sight of rapidly growing St. George in the southwestern corner of the state is Zion National Park, the state's third-most visited attraction, as well as pioneer homes, a unique wildlife refuge on a former ranch, and a historic Mormon outpost.

Around Salt Lake City, travelers can visit the headquarters of the LDS Church, take in first-class theater, stroll through a bustling farmers market, and treat yourself to a gourmet feast. There is Scandinavian culture in the Sanpete Valley, Navajo culture around Monument Valley, cowboys and ranchers on vast expanses of rangeland, and, of course, tight-knit Mormon communities throughout the state.

All this and more can be found in the pages that follow, the very best of what Utah has to offer.   ❑

PRECEDING PAGES: a sandstone wall towers over a lone hiker in the desert near Arches National Park; Archangel Cascades, Zion National Park; Zebra Canyon, Grand Staircase-Escalante National Monument.
LEFT: "mule ears" bloom at the base of Courthouse Towers in Arches National Park.

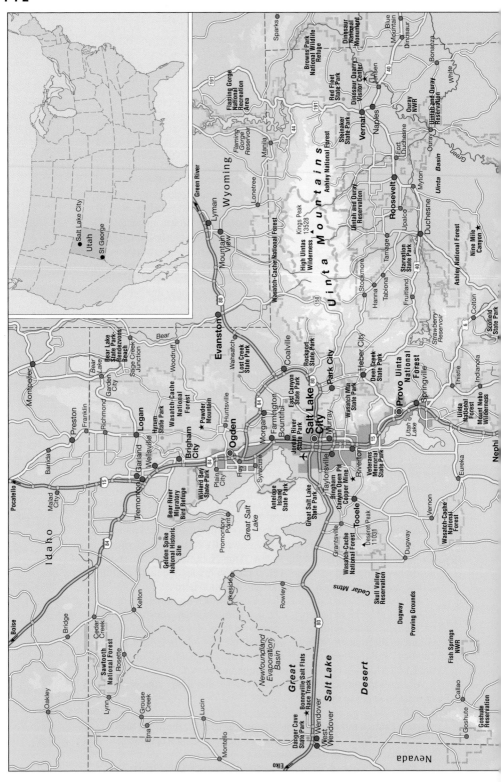

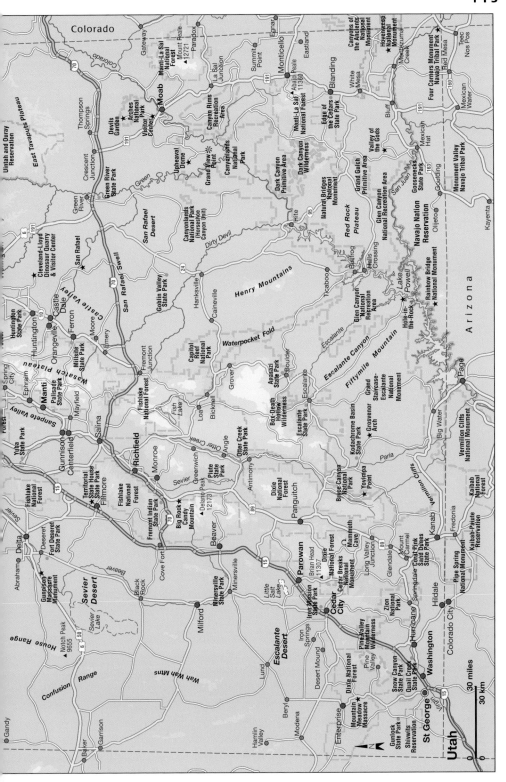

NORTHERN UTAH

Utah's largest metropolitan area is snugged between the Great Salt Lake Desert and Wasatch Mountains

From the summit of Mount Olympus, you can see northern Utah laid out before you in all its dramatic contrasts. On the hazy western horizon lies the Great Salt Lake Desert, the saline remains of Lake Bonneville, the vast inland sea that covered much of Utah 15,000 years ago. Today it is one of the most desolate places in North America, utterly devoid of the essentials to sustain life.

Closer, the Great Salt Lake – a part of ancient Lake Bonneville that never evaporated away – is nearly as lifeless, sustaining only tiny brine shrimp, brine flies and, in its depths, a newly discovered microscopic life-form unknown elsewhere on the planet. In the middle of the lake, mountainous Antelope Island hosts an abundance of improbable creatures, from sea gulls and pelicans to free-roaming herds of bison, but no human inhabitants.

Along the lakeshore, ragged with marshes and salt evaporation ponds, the urban corridor encompassing Ogden, Salt Lake City, Provo and their many suburbs stretch unbroken for 100 miles (160 km) north to south, yet only 10 miles (16 km) across at its widest point. In this hazy strand of skyscrapers, sprawling neighborhoods and strip malls live 1.75 million people – about 80 percent of the entire population of Utah.

To the north, east and south, Mount Olympus is surrounded by other granite and limestone crags of the Wasatch Front – Twin Peaks, Gobbler's Knob, Grandeur Peak, Mount Timpanogos and many others – along with equally dramatic gorges such as Big and Little Cottonwood Canyons and American Fork Canyon.

What is most striking about these mountains is the abruptness with which they rise out of the urban sprawl. The climb up Mount Olympus begins within the town limits of Salt Lake City and rises more than 4,200 ft (1,280 meters) in elevation in less than 4 miles (6.5 km) of climbing, so that from the summit you feel like you're looking straight down into suburban backyards. Strenuous though it is, this is a popular trail, and on weekends you may find yourself sharing the view from the top with 50 other hikers.

As impressive as the bird's-eye view of northern Utah is, there's more to be discovered by exploring at ground level. Within this one-of-a-kind region you'll find such marvels as the center of the Mormon faith at Temple Square. You'll find farms that still operate just as they did at the end of the 19th century, and bobsled runs and ski jumps where future Olympic contenders train. You'll find parks where life-size dinosaur sculptures lurk in the woods and kayakers practice whitewater paddling within blocks of downtown.

This is northern Utah, and there's no other place on earth quite like it. See for yourself. ❏

PRECEDING PAGES: Stewart Cascade, Mount Timpanogos Wilderness, near Sundance. **LEFT:** skiers pause in a high-country basin at Snowbird Ski Area in the Wasatch Range southwest of Salt Lake City.

OGDEN AND ENVIRONS

*Utah's second-largest urban cluster is home
to the state's oldest settlement and a gateway
to its remote northern corner*

Map on page 122

Most travelers are drawn to Utah's northernmost tier by the **Great Salt Lake**. For a close-up view, drive the 7-mile (11-km) causeway from **Syracuse**, a small bedroom community just southeast of Ogden, to **Antelope Island ❶**. Encompassing more than 25,000 acres (10,000 hectares), it is the lake's largest island and Utah's largest state park.

Hikers who reach the summit of **Frary Peak**, the island's high point half a mile above water level, can see the entire Great Salt Lake spread out before them. Sunbathers bob like corks in the salt-saturated water of two bays near the island's north end (where there are also campgrounds), and mountain bikers cycle among hundreds of free-ranging bison. The island also lures birders, who spot species as diverse as bald eagles, pelicans and burrowing owls.

Named for the pronghorns explorers found grazing there, Antelope Island served for much of the 19th century as a private hunting preserve for Mormon elders, who quickly exterminated the native antelope but introduced other game species, including bison and elk. After a causeway was built, the island became a park, although an unexpected rise in water level destroyed the road and left the island isolated for more than a decade. Completion of the present causeway allowed the island to be reopened to the public. By that time, the original herd of 10 bison had multiplied to more than 600, which graze on the golden grass and drink from freshwater springs along the east shore. Near the south end of the island, the **Garr Ranch** was recently acquired by the Utah Division of Parks and Recreation. The ranch house, which now serves as a museum, is the oldest building in Utah in its original location.

Despite its recreational opportunities, Antelope Island is most striking for its emptiness. Even on busy weekends, the number of visitors on the island is only in the dozens – a dramatic contrast to the mainland, where more than 100,000 people reside in Ogden and the smaller towns that comprise Utah's second-largest urban area, filling the delta of the Ogden and Weber Rivers, which flow from the mountains and meander all over town before spilling into the Great Salt Lake.

PRECEDING PAGES:
Golden Spike National Historic Site.
LEFT: Antelope Island rock formation.
BELOW: Snowbasin skier.

Shady past

Ogden ❷ claims to be the oldest settlement in Utah because mountain man Miles Goodyear built a trading post there in 1845, then sold out to the Mormons two years later. A reconstruction of Goodyear's stockade and cabin can be seen today at **Fort Buenaventura State Park** (Apr–Sept daily 8am–8pm, 8am–5pm in Mar, Oct and Nov; 2450 A Ave, 801-621-4808), a wooded site on the Weber River. Brigham Young renamed the burgeoning community after Peter Skene Ogden, a fur trapper who led the first Hudson's Bay

Company expedition into the Wasatch Range, in 1825. Many of Ogden's men deserted him and joined another fur expedition led by John Weber, for whom the county is named, taking Ogden's beaver pelts with them. Ogden left empty-handed and never returned to Utah or saw the town named after him.

The completion of the transcontinental railroad in 1869 transformed the quiet farming community almost overnight. Ogden became the largest railroad hub between Denver and Sacramento, with up to 120 trains coming and going every day. The commercial center of town shifted several blocks south of the Mormon Temple to 25th Street, where the passenger terminal was situated. Today, no passenger train services Ogden, and the refurbished **Ogden Union Station** (Mon–Sat 10am–5pm, Sun hours in summer; 2501 Wall Ave, 801-629-8535; admission) houses a museum complex. Featured here are the **Utah State Railroad Museum**, **Natural History Museum** and **Browning Firearms Museum**, which chronicles the accomplishments of Ogden native John M. Browning, who designed weapons for Colt, Remington and Winchester.

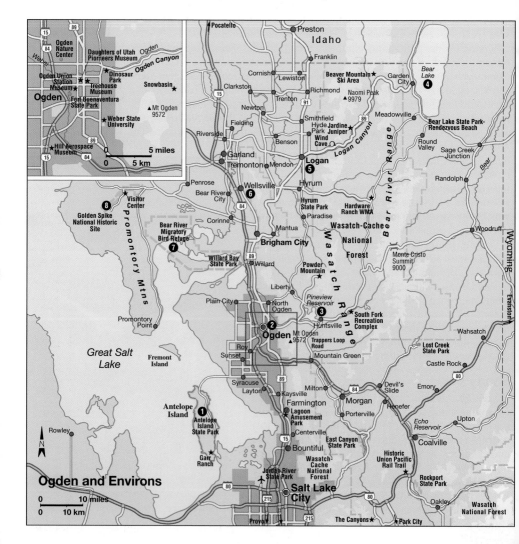

Map on page 122

During the railroad era, 25th Street became notorious for its opium dens and houses of ill repute – an oasis of vice amid Utah's clean-living Mormon settlements. With the decline of passenger trains, 25th Street was in danger of being razed. A citizen movement succeeded in gaining recognition for the **25th Street Historic District**, opening the way to gentrification in the form of galleries, boutiques, restaurants and "private clubs" (that is, bars). Anchoring the east end of the district, **Peery's Egyptian Theater** (2415 Washington Ave) is one of the last survivors among the grand old movie palaces of the 1920s. Its lavish decor features towering columns covered with hieroglyphs, as well as mummies and a golden "sun" that moves across the lofty ceiling. It now serves as an overflow venue for the Sundance Film Festival and presents community theater.

Living down its seamy past, Ogden became the wholesome, economically balanced community one sees today. It is home to the 15,000-student **Weber State University** (3750 Harrison Blvd, 801-626-8750), a former agriculture school that is shifting its emphasis to science and engineering in an effort to attract technology companies to the city's new high-tech center. You can learn about military history and see retired jet fighters at the **Hill Aerospace Museum** (daily 9am–4pm; Hill AFB, I-15, 801-777-6818).

Children's attractions

The Ogden of a century ago may have been a den of iniquity, but today it's a scrubbed and wholesome community with an abundance of attractions designed for kids. The **Treehouse Museum** (Mon–Sat 10am–5pm, to 6pm in summer; 455 23rd St, 801-394-9663; admission) is packed with play exhibits that encourage literacy, artistic expression and an interest in history – like a replica of the president's desk in the White House. The museum isn't really in a treehouse, but it does have two-story playhouses shaped like castles and mountains.

More than 27,000 kids a year visit the **Ogden Nature Center** (Mon–Fri 9am–4pm, Sat 10am–4pm; 966 W. 12th Ave, 801-621-7595; admission), a 150-acre (60-hectare) park where you can spot birds and deer, plus gardens and mews (homes for hawks and other birds of prey). The center cares for hundreds of rescued wild birds, and visitors can meet many of them up close.

Most kids agree that the coolest place in town is **Dinosaur Park** (Mon–Sat 10am–6pm, Sun noon–5pm; 1544 E. Park Blvd, 801-393-3466; admission), near the mouth of Ogden Canyon. Full-size replicas of more than 100 dinosaurs lurk behind trees and underbrush waiting for you to find them. In a new museum at the park, visitors can watch scientists carefully preserve real dinosaur bones.

Lovers of old-fashioned amusement parks will be thrilled at **Lagoon** (summer Sun–Fri from 11am, Sat from 10am; weekends only in spring and fall; Farmington, 801-451-8000; admission), set near the lakeshore 5 miles (8km) southeast of Ogden. Opened in 1886, Lagoon retains a nostalgic cotton-candy flavor with a vintage roller coaster and Wild Mouse ride and a huge Ferris wheel with spectacular views of the Great Salt Lake. There are also newer gravity-defying thrill rides and **Pioneer Village**, a restoration of an

BELOW: neon reflections in downtown Ogden.

A U.S. ski team racer at Snowbasin, site of alpine events during the 2002 Winter Olympics.

early Utah town with carriage and gun collections. Musical events are presented at Lagoon throughout the season. In the past, it has hosted performers such as Louis Armstrong, the Beach Boys, Jimi Hendrix and the Rolling Stones.

The great outdoors

A unique attraction for whitewater enthusiasts right in metropolitan Ogden, the **Kayak Rodeo Park** (24th Street at Exchange Road) was born when the city asked for ideas to beautify city parks. One artist, who was also a kayaking fanatic, proposed moving boulders to strategic locations in the Weber River to create a series of holes and eddies. When the mayor cut the ribbon across the river in 2002, the course of perfect rapids – and eager hordes of college students – made Ogden the kayaking capital of Utah overnight.

Ask Ogden residents about the key to the quality of life, and most will tell you it's outdoor recreation. The mouth of **Ogden Canyon**, which provides access for hiking, skiing, camping, boating and fishing in the Wasatch Mountains, is a five-minute drive from downtown via East 12th Street or a gentle walk or bike ride along the paved, 3-mile (5-km) **Ogden River Parkway**. Within the canyon, UT 39 – officially designated the **Ogden Canyon National Scenic Byway** – winds between sheer limestone and shale cliffs. Along the way are parking areas for anglers hoping to catch brown trout or wild cutthroat trout, as well as trailheads for several hiking and mountain biking trails. Among the most popular are the edgy, hikers-only **Indian Trail**, which runs up the canyon 4 miles (6.5 km) high above the river, and the challenging **Beus Canyon Trail**, which takes hikers, bikers and equestrians to the 9,572-ft (2,917-meter) summit of Mount Ogden, a 6-mile (10-km) trip with more than 4,000 ft (1,200 meters) of altitude gain.

BELOW:
historic Union
Station houses a
museum complex.

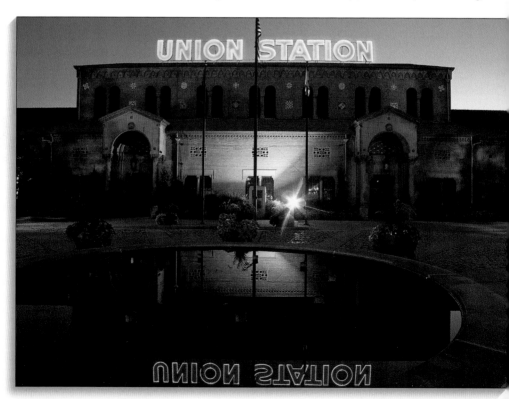

Map on page 122

Long and winding road

Ogden Canyon is the starting point for a spectacular 200-mile (320-km) road trip through the heart of the Wasatch Range. About 12 miles (19 km) up the road, the canyon fans out into a broad, green valley surrounded by mountain peaks. In the center of the valley is **Pineview Reservoir ❸**, a favorite of bass fishers, waterskiers and sailing enthusiasts. Surrounding the lake, a hodgepodge of new palatial homes stands side-by-side with farms, some dating to the 19th century.

From Pineview Reservoir, sightseers can follow a paved road that switchbacks up to **Snowbasin** (3925 E. Snowbasin Rd, Huntsville, 801-620-1000; www.snow-basin.com), a ski resort built in the 1930s by the same developers who built Sun Valley in Idaho. Snowbasin remained a local secret until it was selected as the site for several alpine events in the 2002 Olympics. Four hundred inches (1,000 cm) of natural snowfall a year plus one of the world's largest computer-controlled snowmaking systems assure ideal skiing conditions. Lodges and restaurants at the foot of the slopes have transformed it into a year-round resort.

The road to Bear Lake

At **Huntsville**, the little town at the lake's southeast tip, motorists can abbreviate their scenic drive by turning onto UT 167, known locally as **Trappers Loop Road** because it runs between rivers named after the area's most famous old-time mountain men, Peter Ogden and John Weber. The paved road traverses the back side of Mount Ogden for 9 miles (15 km), climbing steep grades as it makes its way among hills covered with oak and aspen before joining I-84, which runs through **Weber Canyon**, at the village of **Mountain Green**. From there, motorists can be back in the Ogden metro area in 10 minutes or detour

BELOW: skiing fans young and old cheer on contestants at a Snowbasin event.

A broom maker demonstrates his skills at a modern mountain man rendezvous.

BELOW: "mule ears" blossom at the base of Mount Ogden.

about 18 miles (29 km) east on the interstate to see **Devil's Slide**, a unique geological landmark where two 40-ft-tall (12-meter) reefs of white limestone run down the mountainside a mere 20 ft (6 meters) apart.

For a longer scenic drive, continue east from Pineview Reservoir on UT 39. Re-entering the **Wasatch-Cache National Forest** a few miles east of Huntsville, the two-lane blacktop highway takes you along the South Fork of the Ogden River to the **South Fork Recreation Complex**, where seven small campgrounds offer a total of 139 tent and RV sites designed with trout fishermen in mind. As the road veers north into the **Monte Cristo Range**, highway traffic fades away, leaving you alone on the open road. When you reach Monte Cristo Summit, you can see why few people come out here: mountain forests drop away as you make an abrupt descent into the barren foothills that lie in the rain shadow of the Wasatch Range. By the time you turn north on UT 16 in the don't-blink-or-you'll-miss-it town of **Woodruff** near the Wyoming state line, you may find yourself wondering what inspired you to come way out here, almost 90 miles (145 km) from Ogden.

Soon, after you turn left onto UT 30, the most dramatic sight in this remote corner of the state comes into view. Surrounded by desert, the startlingly turquoise water of **Bear Lake** ❹ fills a natural basin 8 miles (12 km) wide and 20 miles (32 km) long, extending across the Idaho state line. The unique color is produced by the sun reflecting from countless tiny limestone particles suspended in the water. Geologists believe the lake is a relict of ancient Lake Bonneville, which filled most of northern Utah 28,000 years ago. As evidence, they point to four unique species of fish – the Bonneville Cisco, Bonneville whitefish, Bear Lake whitefish and Bear Lake sculpin – that live nowhere else

on earth but Bear Lake. Fur trappers exploring the Wasatch Range used Bear Lake as a rendezvous as early as 1819, and **Rendezvous Beach** is still the site of one of America's largest "mountain man" gatherings each April.

Continue your loop drive by turning west on US 89 at **Garden City**. The road climbs by switchbacks up the arid hillsides, each view of the lake more spectacular than the last. Cresting the mountains, you'll pass the entrance to **Beaver Mountain Ski Area**, a family-run operation that began in 1939.

Map on page 122

A world apart

At the mouth of the canyon, the town of **Logan** ❺ seems a world apart from Ogden and the I-15 corridor, just a few miles away on the far side of a roadless wall of granite, the **Wellsville Mountains**. Walking Logan's timeless Main Street is like strolling through a Norman Rockwell painting. Main Street highlights are the **Logan Tabernacle** (50 N. Main St, 435-755-5594; tours daily in summer) and nearby **Latter-day Saints Temple**, two of the finest examples of 19th-century Mormon architecture. Construction of the tabernacle was begun in 1865 but was left half-finished while workmen turned their efforts to building the Temple; it was completed in 1891. The Temple, built to the exact proportions of King Solomon's Temple in Jerusalem as set out in the Bible, is the third-oldest Mormon temple in Utah. The tabernacle is used for religious meetings, lectures and concerts, and contains a large genealogical library in the basement.

Another Main Street sight that's a must for history buffs is the **Daughters of Utah Pioneers Cache Museum** (Tues–Fri June–Sept; 160 N. Main St, 435-752-5139; donation) in the former Hall of Justice. Exhibits include old-time musical instruments, weaving equipment and such curiosities as a hair

BELOW: a kayaker muscles through whitewater in Logan Canyon.

THE BEAR, WITCH AND TREE

Despite its steep walls, Logan Canyon offers a variety of great hiking and biking trails. Three of the most popular lead to curiosities that can't be reached by car. Near the upper end of the canyon, for example, is a 4½-mile (7-km) trail that leads to the Jardine Juniper. Believed to be the oldest living thing in the region, the gnarled tree was a seedling some 3,400 years ago, around the time of Moses. Today only the tip of its lightning-split trunk still bears needles.

At the lower end of the canyon, a short but steep trail leads to Witch's Castle, also known as Wind Caves. The "castle" is a small cave and three delicate arches; the site offers spectacular views of Logan Canyon.

The 5½-mile (9-km) trail to Old Ephraim's Grave is a moderate all-day hike or bike trip. A grizzly bear standing 11 ft tall (3.5 meters), Ephraim gained notoriety for his voracious appetite for livestock and an uncanny ability to evade hunters. The bear was buried here by the man who killed him, in 1923. A Boy Scout troop later dug up his remains and sent the skull to the Smithsonian Institution, which sent it back. The skull now resides at the Utah State University library in Logan. Old Ephraim was the last wild grizzly in Utah.

Birders flock to the Bear River Migratory Bird Refuge (tel: 435-723-5887) in late spring for an annual birdwatching festival, featuring special tours, photography seminars and bird identification workshops.

BELOW: drought has caused Robert Smithson's monumental "earthwork" *Spiral Jetty* to emerge from the Great Salt Lake.

wreath, which women made from the hair of their relatives and wore like a hat.

Logan also has a long tradition of theatrical arts. While exploring the historic district, visit the grand **Ellen Eccles Theater** (43 S. Main St, 435-752-0026). Built in 1923 and restored in 1993, it is host to ballet, symphonic music, opera and musical theater. An even older venue, the 1913 Victorian-style **Caine Lyric Theater** (28 W. Center St, 435-797-1500), has also been restored and now houses a repertory company. The Art Deco **Utah Theater** (18 W. Center St, 435-752-3072), a reconstruction inspired by the movie palaces of the 1930s, shows first-run films nightly.

College town

Much of Logan's unique character comes from the student population of **Utah State University**, an agricultural school. With a student body of 22,000 in a community of only 43,000 year-round residents, it's no wonder that the whole town seems to radiate youthful exuberance. The campus sprawls across the northeast of Logan; 500 North Street takes you directly to the school's hallmark edifice, the **Old Main Building**. The **Nora Eccles Treadwell Harrison Museum of Art** (Tues–Fri 10.30am–4.30pm; 650 North 1100 East St, 435-797-0163; free) features a collection of 20th-century paintings, photographs and ceramics.

The small **Willow Park Zoo** (daily 7am to dusk; 419 West 700 South St, 435-750-9893; donation) has no lions, giraffes or elephants. The largest animals are elk, pronghorn antelope and bobcats. Water is diverted from the Logan River for a series of ponds, streams and water holes that occupy more than half of the zoo's total area, providing habitat for a wide assortment of North American, European, Asian and Australian waterfowl.

Six miles (10km) southwest of Logan, just off the highway to Brigham City, the

EARTH AND ART

Artists in the late 1960s began shifting their attention from gallery walls to the great outdoors, employing nature to create a new genre called, variously, "earthworks," "land art," "public art." Down with salon artifice, up with primordial reality.

An exemplar was Robert Smithson. Born in 1938 and trained at New York's Art Students League and the Brooklyn Museum, he never got over his childhood fascination for the objects on display at the American Museum of Natural History, and in 1970 he put his budding sculptural inclination to work in Utah on a monumental scale.

Using a bulldozer, Smithson piled up basalt rocks and mud from around the Great Salt Lake in a symmetrical design, creating a coil at Rozel Point stretching counterclockwise 1,500 ft (460 meters) into the water. It is called *Spiral Jetty* and ranks as an earthwork classic.

Owing to the whims of Mother Nature, *Spiral Jetty* has mostly been submerged, although a protracted Western drought has caused it to re-emerge in recent years. The Jetty is situated on the northern lakeshore about 15½ miles (25 km) miles over unpaved roads from the visitor center at Golden Spike National Historic Site.

little mountain town of **Wellsville** ❻ is home to the **American West Heritage Center** (Mon–Sat 10am–5pm, summer only; 4025 US 89/91, 435-245-6050; admission). The Center is a living-history museum designed to simulate the experience of the American frontier. Costumed interpreters demonstrate such skills as dancing, gunfighting and woodworking. Shoshone Indian and Mountain Man encampments share the 160-acre (65-hectare) park with a pioneer settlement. Visitors can make advance arrangements to stay overnight in one of the Indian tepees. Adjoining the heritage center, the **Jensen Historical Farm** (435-245-4064) re-creates a working 1917 Mormon farm. Staffers show how to cultivate fruits and vegetables with nothing more sophisticated than a horse-drawn tractor.

About 21 miles (34 km) east of Wellsville is the **Hardware Ranch** (Utah 101, 435-753-6168; winter weekends only), a wildlife preserve where more than 600 elk graze during the winter months and bear calves in early spring. Horse-drawn sleighs take visitors over the meadows for better views of the herd. Hardware Ranch is also the hub of a snowmobile trail system that extends to Logan Canyon; rentals are available.

Birds, boats and trains

Return to I-15 at **Brigham City**. Fruit stands along the way are filled in summer with locally grown cherries, apricots and peaches. On a steel archway over Main Street is a neon sign that reads, "Welcome to Brigham – Gateway – World's Greatest Bird Sanctuary." The sanctuary is **Bear River Migratory Bird Refuge** ❼ (off Utah 83, 435-723-5887; dawn to dusk). Whether it is the "greatest" may be debatable, but it's certainly the oldest, created by a special act of Congress in 1928. The 74,000-acre (30,000-hectare) refuge is enclosed by a 12-mile (19-km) manmade dike that separates the lake's briny water from the fresh water carried down from the mountains by the Bear River. Visitors drive a loop along the top of the dikes and watch for birds. More than 200 species frequent the wetlands. Depending on the time of year, they may include whistling swans, Canada geese, white ibis and snowy egrets. Even rare and exotic "accidentals" are occasionally spotted here, such as American flamingos and roseate spoonbills. Just to the south, another dike encloses the waters of **Willard Bay State Park** (435-734-9494; Mar–Nov), a popular spot for swimming, sunbathing, boating and fishing.

About 32 miles (52 km) west of Brigham City is **Golden Spike National Historic Site** ❽ (435-471-22; June–Sept daily, Oct–May Wed–Sun 9am–5.30pm; admission), where the final spike was driven into the country's first transcontinental railroad. The job fell to Leland Stanford, a grocer-turned-railroad-mogul who traveled from California for the event. Stanford swung a silver hammer… and missed. But a telegraph operator sent out a triumphant message anyway. *Dot. dot. dot. Done.* A Central Pacific locomotive crept forward from the west, a Union Pacific engine from the east. Their cowcatchers kissed. Recently sundered by the Civil War, the United States was now united by rail. Visitors may also wish to follow a partially paved scenic road that runs down to **Promontory Point**, a remote peninsula jutting into the Great Salt Lake. ❑

Map on page 122

BELOW: a replica of locomotive No. 119 steams down the tracks at Golden Spike National Historic Site, where the country's first transcontinental railroad was completed.

SALT LAKE CITY

Thrust into the spotlight by the 2002 Winter Olympics, Utah's capital – the headquarters of the Church of Jesus Christ of Latter-day Saints – has matured into a world-class urban center

Map on page 134

Salt Lake City

Years ago, **Salt Lake City** had the reputation of a straitlaced provincial town. Back then, travelers could rightfully wonder: "Is there life in Salt Lake City after the local Woolworth's closes?" Today, all that has changed. Salt Lake City is now one of the New West's fastest-growing and most vibrant metropolitan areas. An influx of high-tech and energy-related industries and other corporate interests, as well as the robust growth of the Wasatch ski resorts (a short drive from downtown), have helped transform the city into a cultured, contemporary urban center that was propelled onto the world stage by the 2002 Winter Olympics.

Capping the city's cultural life are a number of hot new restaurants and nightclubs. It is still illegal to buy liquor by the drink except in private bottle clubs (where visitor memberships can be purchased), but nightlife in Salt Lake is no longer limited to an evening of bingo, as popular nightspots compete to meet the demands of "Gentile" immigrants and local "jack" (inactive) Mormons.

What makes Salt Lake truly unique, however, is that it is the capital – the Vatican City, if you will – of the LDS Church. Set on the southeastern edge of the Great Salt Lake between the jagged peaks of the Wasatch Range and the sere, copper-rich Oquirrh Mountains, this was the site chosen by Brigham Young to begin building the Mormons' new Zion. It is impossible to understand Salt Lake City, and much of Utah, without first understanding the centrality of the LDS Church and the legacy of the Mormon pioneers.

Temple Square

By day, the heart and hub of Salt Lake City is the sandstone and adobe walled grounds of **Temple Square** (801-240-4446; tours 9am–8.30pm, free), naturally the place to begin a visit. Shortly after reaching the Salt Lake Valley in 1847, Brigham Young, with cane in hand, consecrated the site between two forks of City Creek for the construction of the **LDS Temple Ⓐ**. For over 40 years, oxen teams hauled granite blocks from nearby quarries in the Wasatch Mountains until the majestic, six-spired, neo-Gothic structure was complete.

Perched atop the temple is a gold statue of Moroni, the angel who, in Mormon doctrine, appeared to Joseph Smith. The temple itself is used for the holy ordinances of the LDS Church, such as baptisms, weddings and family "sealing" ceremonies. As with all Mormon temples, only Church members in good standing may enter. The general public may wander about the manicured grounds of Temple Square (a delight at Christmastime, when it is aglitter with thousands of lights) where two visitor centers feature exhibits on Mormon history and beliefs. Young, neatly attired missionaries are stationed throughout the

PRECEDING PAGES: Christmas lights illuminate the LDS Temple.
LEFT: Utah State Capitol.
BELOW: a fan of the University of Utah Utes puts on a game face.

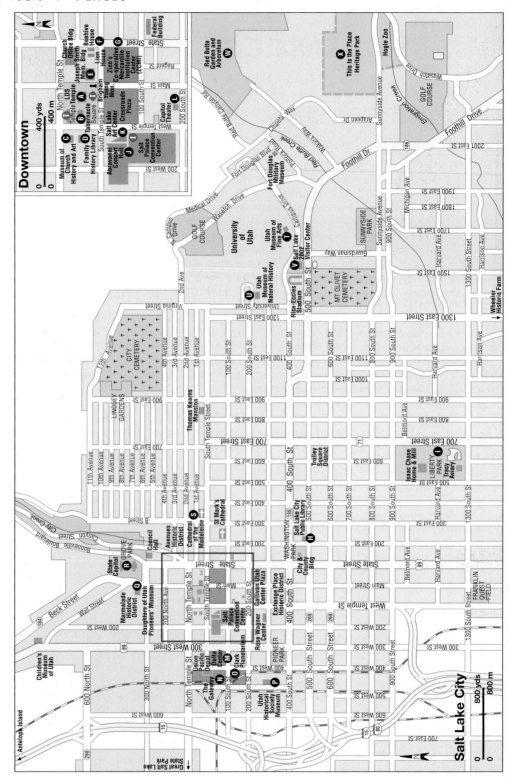

Downtown

A. Museum of Church History and Art
B. Temple
C. LDS Temple
D. Family History Library
E. Joseph Smith Mem. Bldg
F. Beehive House
G. Zion's Co-operative Mercantile Institution (ZCMI)
H. Brigham Young Mon.
I. Salt Lake Art Center
J. Abravanel Concert Hall
K. Salt Palace Convention Center
L. Capitol Theatre

400 yds
400 m

Salt Lake City

A. Children's Museum of Utah
B. Marmalade Historic District
C. State Capitol
D. Daughters of Utah Pioneers' Museum
E. Council Hall
F. Avenues Historic District
G. Cathedral of the Madeleine
H. St Mark's Cathedral
I. Salt Lake City Public Library
J. City & County Bldg
K. Exchange Place Historic District
L. Gallivan Utah Center Plaza
M. Delta Center
N. The Gateway
O. Clark Planetarium
P. Utah Historical Society Museum
Q. Rose Wagner Center
R. Salt Palace Convention Center
S. Thomas Kearns Mansion
T. Utah Museum of Fine Arts
U. Utah Museum of Natural History
V. Salt Lake 2002 Visitor Center
W. Red Butte Garden and Arboretum
X. This Is the Place Heritage Park

800 yds
800 m

Antelope Island
Great Salt Lake State Park
Isaac Chase Home & Mill
Tracy Aviary
Liberty Park
Trolley Square District
Wheeler Historic Farm
Hogle Zoo
Fort Douglas Military Museum
University of Utah
Rice-Eccles Stadium
Mt Olivet Cemetery
City Cemetery
Lindsey Gardens
Grove Park
Sunnyside Park
Golf Course
Franklin Quest Field
Pioneer Park
Washington Park
Union Pacific Depot

Square and often chat up visitors. They are a good source of information if you have questions about the grounds, but if you would rather not talk, a polite "No thanks, I'm not interested" is sufficient.

Notable sights are **Assembly Hall**, completed in 1882, and the **Seagull Monument** commemorating the "miracle of the gulls" that saved the first Mormon pioneers from a swarm of crickets. Don't pass up an opportunity to visit the **Tabernacle B** (tours 9am–8.30pm, organ concerts daily at noon and 2pm; 801-240-3221), home of the Mormon Tabernacle Choir. The choir offers free admission to its rehearsal on Thursday evening and its broadcast on Sunday morning, the oldest continuous broadcast in the world.

Walk about

From Temple Square it is only a short walk in several directions to other noteworthy Church sites. Exiting the west gate, you can't miss the **Museum of Church History and Art C** (Mon–Fri 9am–9pm, Sat–Sun 10am–7pm; 45 N. West Temple St, 801-240-3310; free), where exhibits on Church leaders, the Mormon migration and other topics chronicle the evolution of the faith.

Next to the Museum, the **Family History Library D** (Mon 8am–5pm, Tue–Sat 8am–9pm; 35 N. West Temple St, 801-240-2331; free) houses the Mormon genealogical library, the largest institution of its kind in the world. Millions of birth, baptism and death certificates from around the world are stored in its archival collection, and a staff of librarians speaking some 40 languages is on hand to help you dig up the roots of your family tree.

Directly east of Temple Square is a full block of Church-related buildings. Exit through the south gate of Temple Square, near the **Brigham Young Monument**, and walk east toward the historic **Hotel Utah**, which now houses the **Joseph Smith Memorial Building E** (Mon–Sat 9am–9pm; 15 E. South Temple St, 801-240-1266; free) and a giant-screen film about the Mormon migration. Directly north and east, the hotel is flanked by magnificent fountains, flower gardens and lawns around a complex of noteworthy Church buildings. The massive modern building to the north is the **Church Office Building**; an observation deck on the 26th floor has glorious views of the city.

Aross the plaza are the former residences of Brigham Young and many of his 27 wives. Built in 1854, the **Beehive House F** (Mon–Sat 9.30am–6.30pm, Sun 10am–1pm in summer, abbreviated hours off-season; 67 E. South Temple St, 801-240-2671; free) was the official residence of Brigham Young who, as Church president and territorial governor, received President Ulysses S. Grant, Samuel Clemens, General William T. Sherman and other prominent visitors in the Long Room. Now a historic landmark, the Federal-style residence is named for the carved beehive, a symbol of Mormon industry, atop the cupola.

Next door is the **Lion House** (1855), a "supplementary" domestic residence used by some of Young's wives and 56 children. An impressive stone lion stands guard at the entrance. The women were lodged on the main floor while the children stayed in the upstairs rooms with their 20 gabled dormer windows.

Map on page 134

BELOW: a street artist at work in Salt Lake City attracts a cluster of onlookers.

Brigham Young statue on Temple Square, headquarters of the LDS Church.

BELOW: exploring a "luminarium" at the Utah Arts Festival.

Commercial rather than spiritual values are the stock in trade across South Temple Street at the **ZCMI Center** , an enclosed shopping mall operated by the LDS Church, with some 70 stores and restaurants. The building's facade is from the original Zion's Co-operative Mercantile Institution, which was established by Brigham Young to distribute goods to Church members. There's more shopping next door at the four-story **Crossroads Plaza**, which encompasses more than 100 stores, three movie theaters, 22 restaurants and a rooftop sports facility.

Drifting a couple of blocks south on State Street, you come to the **Gallivan Center**, an outdoor plaza with an intriguing design, featuring an ice skating rink, a giant chess board and space for concerts, a farmers market and other events. Farther down State Street, on the edge of **Washington Park**, is the new **Salt Lake City Public Library** (Mon–Thur 9am–9pm, Fri–Sat 9am–6pm, Sun 1pm–5pm; 210 E. 400 South, 801-524-8200), which features an eye-catching six-story, crescent-shaped glass wall and rooftop garden. Fireplaces on each floor create a cozy ambience for winter book browsing. A few small shops and a café, as well as an art gallery and indoor and outdoor performance spaces elevate the complex far beyond the traditional concept of a library. The handsome Romanesque Revival building across Washington Park is the **City and County Building**, completed in 1894 and the seat of municipal government.

Five long blocks to the west, the **Trolley Square District** encompasses a series of renovated 1908 trolley barns that have been converted into a bustling, brick-paved shopping, dining and theater complex. A few blocks south on Seventh East is **Liberty Park** , a popular spot for roller blading, riding paddle boats, catching a concert and strolling the landscaped grounds. Visit the historic adobe **Isaac Chase Home and Mill**, then take a leisurely walk and listen to the

trumpeter swans, rare Andean condors and hundreds of other bird species at the **Tracy Aviary** (daily 9am–4.30pm, extended summer hours; 589 E. 1300 South, 801-596-0900; admission), one of the world's oldest public aviaries.

Map on page 134

Room for the arts

Large civic structures dominate the western edge of the downtown area, including the sprawling **Salt Palace Convention Center** (90 S. West Temple St, 801-521-2822), which has a visitor information area, and **Abravanel Hall ❶** (123 W. South Temple, 801-355-2787), an architectural gem and home of the Utah Symphony. Next door, the **Salt Lake Art Center ❸** (20 S. West Temple, 801-328-4201) mounts about a dozen exhibitions a year, with an emphasis on the work of Utah artists. The Utah Opera Company and Ballet West perform several blocks away at the historic **Capitol Theater ❶** (50 W. 200 South, 801-355-2787), which also stages Broadway road shows and concerts.

Devereaux Plaza at Triad Center, about three blocks west of Temple Square, has fine shops, restaurants, private social clubs, an ice-skating rink, and the restored Devereaux Mansion.

The largest venue in the downtown area is the **Delta Center ❿** (300 W. South Temple St, 801-325-7328), a 20,000-seat arena where basketball fans cheer on the NBA Utah Jazz. It is also used for rodeos, concerts and other large-scale events.

Just beyond the Delta Center is the imposing **Union Pacific Depot** (400 W. 100 South St), built in 1909 as the city's main railway terminal. Western scenes are depicted on murals and stained glass in the interior. The building now serves as a portal to the **Gateway ❶** (801-456-0000; Mon–Sat 10am–9pm, Sun noon–6pm), a 30-acre (12-hectare), two-level, outdoor complex of shops, restaurants, movie theaters and offices built around numerous plazas and performance spaces. Kids love to splash around in the Olympic Snowflake Fountain at **Olympic Plaza**. Anchoring the south end of the complex is the **Clark**

BELOW: the Beehive House is the former residence of Brigham Young.

Planetarium  (110 S. 400 West St, 801-456-7827; daily from 11am; admission), which features state-of-the-art star shows and an IMAX theater.

Another railroad-related landmark, the **Rio Grande Depot**, just south of the Gateway, houses the **Utah Historical Society Museum** (Mon–Fri 8am–5pm, Sat 10am–3pm; 300 S. Rio Grande St, 801-533-3500; free), which interprets the state's rich and varied past. Nearby **Pioneer Park** is the scene of a lively farmers market on Saturday morning, July through October.

Capitol Hill

Return to Temple Square and head north on Main Street past the elegant **McCune Mansion** (home of mining mogul Alfred McCune) to the **Daughters of Utah Pioneers' Museum** (Mon–Sat 9am–5pm; 300 N. Main St, 801-538-1050; admission). Here there's a warren of chambers and glass-enclosed exhibits stuffed with thousands of artifacts, from period furniture to military paraphernalia.

Across the street from the museum, the copper-domed, Renaissance Revival **State Capitol** (Mon–Fri 10am–4pm; 350 N. Main St, 801-538-3000; free), the temporal seat of power in Utah, overlooks Temple Square from **Capitol Hill**. On a clear day or night, from the steps beneath its Corinthian marble columns, there is a panoramic view of the Wasatch Mountains and the platted streets below.

Inside the capitol a 165-ft (50-meter) rotunda rises above the building's main features: the 23-karat gold-leaf reception room, an exhibition hall with displays on Utah history, and marble staircases. Outside there is a 40-acre (16-hectare) park with strolling gardens and other sites to visit, such as the Gothic Revival **White Memorial Chapel** and **Council Hall**, which was constructed in 1866, moved to this spot in 1963, and now houses a visitor center and bookstore.

The skull of a toothy Carnotosaurus is on display at the Utah Museum of Natural History.

BELOW:
kids cool off in a Gateway fountain.
RIGHT:
McCune Mansion on Capitol Hill.

Adjacent to Capitol Hill are two historic neighborhoods. West of the Capitol is the **Marmalade Historic District** – its streets are named after fruits – where many early English and Scandinavian immigrants resided. East of City Creek Canyon is the **Avenues Historic District**, where one finds a wide variety of architectural styles, including many restored Victorian houses.

A number of buildings in the neighborhood are noteworthy. They include the **Cathedral of the Madeleine ⓢ** (Mon–Fri 8am–5.30pm; 331 E. South Temple St, 801-328-8941; free), a handsome Romanesque-style church. Also notable are the mansions of two silver magnates: the **Keith-Brown Mansion** and the **Thomas Kearns Mansion**, now the official residence of Utah's governor.

Pioneer past

East of downtown Salt Lake City is the **Emigration Visitors District**, a scenic triangle of parks and museums situated near the mouth of **Emigration Canyon**. The dominant presence here is the **University of Utah** (801-581-7200), the state's largest institution of higher learning and the home of two fine museums.

The **Utah Museum of Fine Arts ⓣ** (Tues–Fri 10am–5pm, Sat–Sun 11am–5pm, Wed to 8pm; 410 Campus Center Dr, 801-581-7332; admission) presents traveling exhibitions as well as selections from its collection of American and European paintings, classical artifacts, American Indian art, Chinese ceramics and other Asian works. The **Utah Museum of Natural History ⓤ** (Mon–Sat 9.30am–8pm, Tues–Sat 9.30am–5.30pm; 1390 E. President Circle, 801-581-6927; admission) cares for more than a million objects that trace the biological and cultural diversity of Utah and the intermountain region. Exhibits cover natural history and Utah's native people. Most impressive is the dinosaur collection, much of it

Map on page 134

BELOW: the Hispanic float at the Pioneer Day parade.

Map on page 134

retrieved from the Cleveland-Lloyd quarry. Tens of thousands of specimens are housed in the sprawling basement paleontology department, including mounted skeletons of such Jurassic-era monsters as Allosaurus, Ceratosaurus and Stegosaurus, as well as an extensive collection of Triassic plant fossils.

Also on campus, **Rice-Eccles Stadium** (500 South St at Guardsman Way, 801-581-8314) is the home of the university's football and soccer teams and the site of concerts by big-name performers like the Rolling Stones and U2. The stadium won international recognition (and a $50 million face-lift) when it was selected as the venue for the 2002 Winter Olympics opening and closing ceremonies.

Established after World War II to promote world peace, the International Peace Gardens (1060 South 900 West) has botanical displays representing more than 20 countries .

Adjacent to the stadium, **Olympic Cauldron Park** enjoys a hillside vantage overlooking the city. In the park, the **Salt Lake 2002 Visitor Center** (Mon–Fri 10am–6pm) displays Olympic images taken by leading sports photographers, as well as a theater dedicated to a breathtaking multimedia presentation about the Winter Games. The **Hoberman Arch** originally stood over the plaza where Olympic award ceremonies were held; today the 36-ft-high (11-meter) moving spiral of sandblasted aluminum stands near the Olympic Cauldron, the towering beacon lit by the Olympic Flame. Each winter on the anniversary of the Games, the cauldron burns for 17 nights, sending flames 24 ft (7 meters) into the sky.

From the stadium it's a short hop to **Fort Douglas** (Tue–Sat noon–4pm; 32 Potter St, 801-581-1251; free), built in 1862 to protect stage routes into the city. Just beyond, the **Red Butte Garden and Arboretum** (summer Mon–Sat 9am–9pm, Sun 9am–5pm, limited hours in other seasons; 300 Wakara Way, 801-581-4747; admission) has 150 acres (60 hectares) of thematic gardens, waterfalls, nature trails and an outdoor performance space as well as a 1,500-acre (600-hectare) arboretum with trees from around the world.

BELOW: This is the Place Monument.

Both kids and adults will enjoy the modest but appealing **Hogle Zoo** (2600 E. Sunnyside Ave, 801-582-1631; daily 9am–4.30pm, extended summer hours; admission), which has more than 1,100 exotic animals in naturalistic "habitats."

Living history

Utah's pioneer past comes to life across from the zoo at **This Is the Place Heritage Park** . The site includes **Old Deseret Village** (2601 E. Sunnyside Ave, 801-582-1847; summer Mon–Sat 10am–5pm; admission), a re-creation of a 19th-century Mormon settlement, including Brigham Young's Forest Farmhouse, built by Young in the 1850s. Costumed interpreters demonstrate period crafts and skills such as blacksmithing, weaving and carepentry. Nearby, a statue of Young and his councilors, known as the **This is the Place Monument**, stands at the spot where, on July 24, 1847, Young stopped and gazed over the Salt Lake Valley. "It is enough," he declared. "This is the right place."

For another living-history experience, check out the **Wheeler Historic Farm** (Mon–Sat 9.30am–5pm; 801-264-2241; free) on the outskirts of the city at South 900 East Street. The site re-creates a family dairy farm from the early 20th century. Only manual and animal labor are used. Children are welcome to join the farmers at 11am or 5pm to help milk the cows and gather eggs. Tours of the 1898 farmhouse are offered hourly. ❑

Urban Wilderness

S alt Lake City is only a hop, skip and hike away from some of the most rugged mountain terrain in Utah. Find out for yourself by walking or jogging the much-loved 6-mile (10-km) City Creek Canyon Trail, which starts right behind the state capitol. After a half-mile stroll through grassy Memory Grove, the trail steepens, a dramatic gateway leading from downtown into the forests of the Wasatch Range. The creekside trail shaded with cottonwoods is closed to cyclists, who ride on a paved road winding past picnic areas in oak glens.

City Creek also provides access to the remarkable Bonneville Shoreline Trail, which contours along a terrace notched into the flanks of the mountains by prehistoric Lake Bonneville. A 13-mile (21-km) section between City Creek and This is the Place Heritage Park is usually busy with hikers, joggers and mountain bikers in warm weather and snowshoers and skiers in winter. Perched above The Avenues neighborhood and University of Utah, and running right through Red Butte Gardens, the Shoreline Trail provides lovely views over the Salt Lake Valley and the Great Salt Lake. Spur trails lead to rugged mountain bike routes and to the crest of the Wasatch Range.

For more challenging hikes, head south on Interstate 215 to 3900 South, for Mill Creek Canyon, and to 6200 South, for Big Cottonwood and Little Cottonwood canyons. In all three canyons, steep trails follow drainages into the adjacent Twin Peaks and Mount Olympus Wilderness Areas. At the south end of the valley, Lone Peak Wilderness Area surrounds its namesake – the first Congressionally designated "urban wilderness," centerpiece of the 1978 Endangered American Wilderness Act.

Though the Cottonwood canyons are best known for winter resorts at Alta, Snowbird, Brighton and Solitude, their steep granite and limestone walls also attract rock climbers, ice climbers and geologists. Backcountry skiers take advantage of 500 inches (1,270 cm) of Wasatch powder each winter.

All these canyons start within the city limits and pass into Wasatch-Cache National Forest, connecting more than a million people with roadless wilderness that covers half the range along the Wasatch Front. These mountains also serve as the city's watershed, so dogs are not welcome. Mill Creek Canyon is the dog-friendly exception; a small fee is required to drive up to Mill Creek's trailheads.

Fall color in the Wasatch goes beyond the usual yellows and golds of aspen trees to include crimson canyon maple and orange and rust accents from Gambel oak. Mill Creek and Big and Little Cottonwood Canyons are good choices for autumn leaf-peeping. A favorite dirt road from Brighton to Deer Valley leads over Guardsman's Pass and through glorious aspen groves.

This rich wilderness experience immediately adjacent to a major city is one of the defining characteristics of Salt Lake City. The city lies between the Wasatch Range and the wild public lands of the Great Basin. This is indeed "the place," for there is no other place quite like it.   ❑

RIGHT: Bonneville Shoreline Trail.

PROVO, PARK CITY AND THE WASATCH RANGE

Travelers here will find an absorbing palette of mountains, canyons and rivers as well as an international film festival and some of the finest skiing in the West

Map on page 146

ocation, location, location. If you were looking for a new place to start a business, you could do worse than the city of **Provo ❶**. After all, this community of 105,000 has been identified variously as "America's number one entrepreneurial city," one of the "Top Ten Places for Business and Careers" and "the least stressful midsize city in the nation." The city's university offers one of the most prestigious MBA programs in the country (though you have to be a Mormon to go there). Yet if you ask a typical Provo resident what he or she likes most about Provo, the reply will probably be "the mountains."

The mountains are a constant presence in Provo, where 11,068-ft (3,375-meter) **Provo Peak** rises in the east so steeply that its summit is only 4 miles (96 km) as the crow flies from downtown. **Park City**, the winter sports capital of Utah, is a picturesque one-hour drive away.

Much of this chapter describes a 116-mile (187-km) road trip, with many potential detours and diversions, that motorists can take from Provo. It takes in spectacular Provo Canyon, the lakes and golf links of the Heber Valley and sporty Park City, home of the Sundance Film Festival and the 2002 Winter Olympic Games. Before setting out, though, why not visit nearby Utah Lake or take your pick among Provo's many museums?

In search of history

Unlike many Utah towns, Provo does not wear its history on its sleeve. Redevelopment has long since eliminated most of the old buildings. Nothing remains of the trading post started in 1825 by Québécois fur trapper Etienne Provot, who gave his name to the river and the settlement on its banks. (The *t* was dropped to encourage correct pronunciation.)

Later, in 1849, Brigham Young directed a group of 30 families to establish a fort and farming community there. The Ute Indians of the area, who depended on fish in nearby Utah Lake, allowed the Mormons to stay on condition that they never force the Indians off their land. But if any trace of the Utes or settlers remains today, it is most likely to be found in the **Daughters of Utah Pioneer Museum** (Feb–Nov Wed, Fri–Sat noon–4pm; 500 North 500 West St, 801-852-6609; donation) and **Sons of Utah Pioneer Village** (1pm–4pm Mon–Wed, Fri–Sat, summer only).

One of several dozen settlements along the Wasatch Front, Provo did not become noteworthy until 1875, when it was chosen as the site of **Brigham Young University**. The university got its start as the Brigham Young Academy, housed in a stately three-story sandstone building with a mansard roof and bell tower

PRECEDING PAGES: historic Main Street, Park City. **LEFT:** Park City's Egyptian Theatre, site of the Sundance Film Festival. **BELOW:** skiing at The Canyons.

All smiles at a Park City balloon festival.

situated in what is now downtown Provo. After the school was relocated to its present campus, the academy building became a high school and then a library. Abandoned when the library moved to more spacious quarters, the structure's date with the wrecking ball was approaching fast when the people of Provo passed a $17 million bond issue, and the Brigham Young Academy kicked in another $6 million, to restore the building. It is now once again part of the **Provo City Library** (Mon–Fri 9am–9pm, Sat 9am–6pm; 550 N. University Ave, 801-852-6650).

Mormons and museums

LDS-owned Brigham Young University has a student body of more than 30,000. About 98 percent of the students are members of the Church of Jesus Christ of Latter-day Saints, including 12 percent "multicultural" students who come from Mormon missions in other parts of the world. To apply, students must submit ecclesiastical recommendations and agree to a strict honor code. The BYU campus has magnificent views of the mountains and 97-ft-tall (30-meter) **Centennial Carillon Tower**, which fills the air with the music of 52 bells played by keyboard. You can see the campus on one of the riding tours offered by the BYU Hosting Center, located in the former president's residence (801-422-4678).

The main attractions on the BYU campus are four free museums. The **Museum of People and Cultures** (Mon–Fri 9am–5pm; 700 North 100 East St, 801-378-6112) features artifacts from the Great Basin, American Southwest, Mesoamerica, South America and Polynesia. Among the most striking are the casts of the Stele V "Tree of Life" and the "Tablet of the Cross," both pre-Columbian crosses found in Mexico that were offered in earlier times as proof that Jesus Christ visited ancient America as described in the Book of Mormon.

BELOW:
historic Miner's Hospital, Park City.

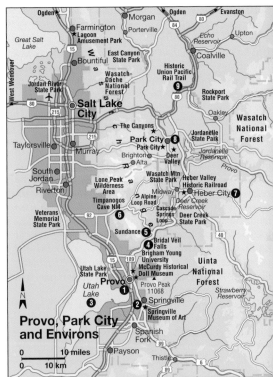

Provo, Park City and Environs

The **BYU Museum of Art** (Mon–Fri 10am–9pm, Sat noon–5pm; N. Campus Dr, 801-378-2787) has extensive painting, photography and sculpture collections. The focus is on works by 19th- and 20th-century American artists, though there are also exhibits of Asian, Egyptian, Greek and Roman art. The Sacred Subjects collection features traditional biblical themes, scenes from the Book of Mormon and images of the Mormon migration to Utah.

Exhibits at the **Monte L. Bean Life Science Museum** (Mon–Fri 9am–5pm; Sat 10am–5pm; Bean Building, 801-378-5051) include dioramas depicting the wildlife of Utah and Africa. The **Earth Science Museum** (Mon–Fri 9am–5pm, Sat noon–4pm; 1683 N. Canyon Rd, 801-378-3680) is noted for its collection of dinosaur and prehistoric mammal fossils. Particularly striking is the skeleton of a Utahraptor, a dinosaur found near Moab in 1991. Fast, intelligent and much larger than the velociraptors depicted in the film *Jurassic Park,* paleontologists believe it may have been the deadliest dinosaur to have roamed the earth.

Of all the museums in Provo, the most remarkable is the **McCurdy Historical Doll Museum** (Tues–Sat noon–6pm, limited winter hours; 246 North 100 East St, 801-377-9935; admission). Kids and adults enjoy this extensive collection of dolls, started by a turn-of-the-century teacher. The museum has more than 4,000 dolls displayed in rotating exhibits on themes such as international folk clothing, U.S. presidents and women in the Bible.

About 7 miles (11 km) south of Provo in the suburb of **Springville ②** is the **Springville Museum of Art** (126 East 400 South St, 801-489-2727; Tues–Sat 10am–5pm, Sun 3pm–6pm; free). Utah's oldest art museum, it was founded in 1903 with paintings donated to the local high school. Today it presents works by Utah artists of the late 19th and 20th centuries, along with traveling exhibits.

Canyon loop

Utah Lake ③, 24 miles (37 km) long and 11 miles (18 km) wide but only 9 ft (2.7 meters) deep, is the state's largest body of fresh water. **Utah Lake State Park** (4400 W. Center St, 801-375-0731) has campsites, picnic areas, a marina and boat rentals. The park is packed on summer weekends with anglers out to catch channel catfish, bass, walleye and seven native species of panfish. In winter, part of the lake is roped off for ice skating; the rest is used by ice fishermen.

Of all the canyons along the Wasatch Front, perhaps the most dramatic is **Provo Canyon**, northeast of Provo on US 189 (University Avenue). Sadly, the canyon lost much of its seclusion when the formerly narrow, winding road was widened for the 2002 Winter Games in Park City. Still, the towering rock walls have lost none of their majesty. Parking areas along the route give motorists a chance to get out of their vehicles for a close-up look and provide parking space for anglers along one of Utah's most popular trout streams. Cyclists can pedal the 32-mile (52-km) climb from Provo to Heber City on a paved bike path partly separated by barriers from highway traffic: some cyclists arrange shuttles to the upper end for the thrill of coasting back down.

A must-see, **Bridal Veil Falls ④** is just 4 miles (6.5 km) up Provo Canyon. A short trail from the riverside

Map on page 146

BELOW: the dinosaur collection at the Earth Science Museum in Provo.

picnic area leads you to the foot of the 607-ft-high (185-meter), two-tiered cataracts, which spill hypnotically down sheer rock faces, filling the air with mist. In winter, the falls attract ice climbers from all over the West.

The steep canyon walls don't allow much in the way of hiking or off-road biking. For that kind of adventure, turn north onto SR 92, clearly marked for "Sundance" and "Alpine Loop." It's the only paved road that turns off the main highway within the canyon.

The road first takes you past **Sundance ❺**, Robert Redford's resort and film institute, which some critics credit with a renaissance in American independent filmmaking. In 1980, when the actor bought a small family-run ski resort, his idea was to establish a filmmaking colony outside the influence of the Hollywood mainstream. The Sundance Film Institute, which occupies part of the resort grounds, selects 13 projects a year out of more than 1,000 submissions. Among the projects the institute has developed are *Boys Don't Cry, Slums of Beverly Hills, Smoke Signals* and *Hedwig and the Angry Inch.* The institute also sponsors the **Sundance Film Festival** (www.sundance.org), where independent filmmakers often gain recognition and financial backing for their work. The week-long festival is held in Park City, with additional venues in Salt Lake City and Ogden.

The event brings in more than $40 million in tourism money and attracts a battalion of Hollywood heavyweights, leading some critics to wonder if the festival has become a victim of its own success. Meanwhile, the Sundance Institute carries on quietly in this secluded valley, each year adding new programs such as the Sundance Documentary Fund and the Film Music Program.

Continue past Sundance to **Uinta National Forest** and the entrance station to the **Alpine Loop Road** (closed in winter), a narrow, paved route that winds

A park ranger leads a tour through Timpanogos Cave National Monument.

BELOW:
Bridal Veil Falls cascades down the sheer walls of Provo Canyon.

through a forest of aspen and Douglas fir. This is one of the most beautiful drives in the Wasatch Mountains. Trailheads along the road lead to the **Mount Timpanogos** and **Lone Peak Wilderness Areas** as well as mountain bike trails like the 21-mile (34-km) **Cascade Springs Loop**. Cascade Springs can also be reached by car, following an unpaved road that forks off to the east. Interpretive nature trails lead visitors around the springs, which pour 7 million gallons (26 million liters) of water a day down a series of pools before vanishing underground.

Farther along the Alpine Loop is **Timpanogos Cave National Monument** ❻ (801-756-5239; daily 7am–5.30pm, last tour one hour before closing; admission), actually a series of three limestone caverns discovered at different times and linked together by manmade tunnels. The caverns have the stalactites, stalagmites and stone curtains typical of limestone caves but are especially notable for their rare helectites – hollow, gravity-defying calcite formations that grow in unpredictable directions. What many people remember most, however, is the trail to the cave entrance, climbing nearly 1,100 ft (335 meters) in 1½ miles (2.4 km).

Valley of lakes

Rocky cliffs yield to water views at the upper end of Provo Canyon as you pass **Deer Creek Reservoir** at the south end of the agricultural **Heber Valley**. To the north is the even larger **Jordanelle Reservoir**. The lakeshores are developed for recreational use at **Deer Creek State Park** and **Jordanelle State Park**. Both offer fishing, boating, swimming and other water sports as well as camping. Deer Creek has a marina with a restaurant and boat rentals and is a favorite of windsurfers and sailors.

Also in the Heber Valley is **Wasatch Mountain State Park**, Utah's largest,

Map on page 146

BELOW: performing at the Sundance Outdoor Theater.

with a manicured 36-hole golf course, hiking and horseback riding trails, and a Nordic skiing facility called **Soldier Hollow**, which saw Olympic action during the 2002 Winter Games. Nearly 20 miles (32 km) of groomed trails are available for cross-country skiing and snowshoeing in winter and mountain biking in summer.

Between the two lakes is **Heber City ❼**, an unpretentious farm and ranch center, and its rustic "suburb," **Midway**. Heber City's top attraction is the **Heber Valley Historic Railroad** (450 South 600 Street West, 801-654-5601; June–Oct 11am and 3pm Tues–Sun; admission), an early 20th-century steam train that chugs past Deer Creek Reservoir and into Provo Canyon.

Scuba diving in the mountains? You'll find it at **Homestead Crater** (Homestead Resort, 700 N. Homestead Dr, 435-654-1102; daily 10am–8pm; admission), just outside Midway in a natural hot spring set inside a 55-ft-high (17-meter) rock dome. The amazingly clear water is 65 ft (20 meters) deep and 96°F (37°C). The crater is on the property of the Homestead Resort, which operates a small rental shop with scuba and snorkeling gear. Swimmers are welcome; the dive shop offers "scuba experiences" for visitors who don't have their certifications.

An engineer takes a break on the Heber Valley Historic Railroad.

After the gold rush

About 20 miles (32 km) north of Heber City is **Park City ❽**, a gold rush-era mining town that's been refurbished beyond recognition. Some folks liken it to Aspen, a comparison that many Park City residents detest. But some similarities are hard to ignore – the multimillion-dollar houses, ski resorts and frequent sightings of movie stars.

Connect with the town's sometimes seamy past at the **Park City Museum** (Mon–Sat 10am–7pm, Sun noon–6pm; 528 Main St, 435-649-6104; free), which features vintage photographs and the original town jail. Park City got its start in 1870, when prospectors discovered silver, lead, zinc and a little gold in the surrounding mountains. Within two years, the town grew to 5,000 people – nearly its present-day population. Most of the mines shut down after the 1893 silver crash, though the population doubled in the next several years as laborers from Colorado came looking for work in the few mines that remained open.

Part of the secret of Park City's survival was illegal liquor. The rough-and-ready boomtown had long held itself apart from the clean-living Mormons who lived on the other side of the mountain. Its 26 saloons thrived thanks to the city folk who occasionally slipped off to the mountains to tie one on. Business was especially good after the enactment of Prohibition in 1921, thanks largely to police officers who looked the other way. But the high times didn't last. The town's alcohol-fueled economy foundered after Prohibition was repealed in 1933. By the 1950s, it was regarded as one of Utah's best-preserved ghost towns.

Then in 1963, with the opening of a small ski area, Park City was reborn. At first skiers were carried to the top of the mountain by mine cars that went up the shaft of the old Silver King Mine. When a gondola, chair lift and two J-bars were installed, Park City quickly became one of the state's most popular winter sports destinations.

History buffs can still find vestiges of the gold-rush days in the four-block-long **Main Street Historic District**, listed on the National Register of Historic Places. A walking-tour brochure is available at the Park City Museum. Don't miss the fully restored **Egyptian Theatre** (328 Main St, 435-649-9731),

Map
on page
146

BELOW:
inflating a hot-air
balloon, Park City.

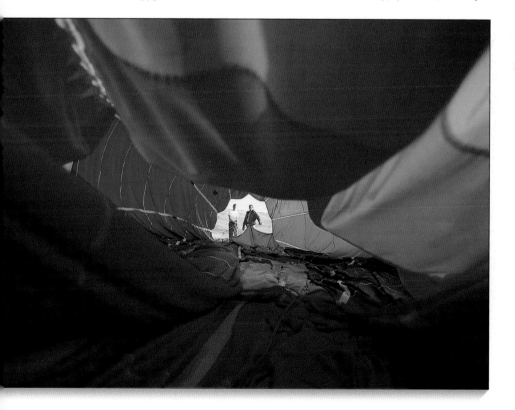

Map on page 146

centerpiece of the Sundance Film Festival. Built as an opera house around 1898, it was redesigned in faux-Egyptian style in 1920s.

Slip sliding away

Winter is peak season in Park City, which is blessed annually with 300 to 350 inches (750–900 cm) of some of the world's best snow. **Park City Mountain Resort** (1310 Lowell Ave, 435-649-8111 or 800-687-9915), the town's original ski area, has been improved and expanded. It now encompasses three new terrain parks and has the greatest lift capacity in town. Another standout feature is the Eagle Superpipe, built for Olympic snowboarding competitions and much larger than regulation halfpipes at other ski areas. **Deer Valley Resort** (2250 Deer Valley Dr, 435-649-1000 or 800-558-3337), the smallest (or as the marketing people put it, "most intimate") of the three ski areas, has dramatic ridgeline runs and a 3,000-ft (900-meter) vertical drop. Elegant lodges and four gourmet restaurants make Deer Valley the high-end choice. The latest entry is **The Canyons** (4000 The Canyons Resort Dr, 435-615-3465 or 866-604-4169), which has the largest ski and snowboard area in Utah.

Adrenaline junkies might want to forgo the ski slopes for a once-in-a-lifetime ride on a bobsled at the **Utah Olympic Park** (3000 Bear Hollow Dr, 435-658-4200; daily 9am–5pm). The four-man sleds, under the control of certified drivers, reach 80 miles per hour (130 kmh) and 4Gs of force. The price is as steep as the bobsled run – around $200 per person. Slightly less costly are the half-day introductory classes offered in Nordic jumping, slopestyle skiing, luge racing and skeleton racing. The less adventurous can tour the park and see where U.S. Olympic contenders practice on ski jumps up to 360 ft high (110 meters), then visit the **Alf Engen Ski Museum**. You'll find an exhibit on the 2002 Winter Games at the park's **Joe Quinney Winter Sports Center**.

Summer fun

In summer, the sports scene is dominated by mountain biking. More than 300 miles (480 km) of trails have been set aside for non-motorized use (biking, hiking and horseback riding) in the Park City area. Bikers can ride chairlifts at Park City Mountain Resort and Deer Valley Resort and spend the day coasting downhill or explore some 35 miles (55 km) of municipal bike trails. For a moderate ride, the **Historic Union Pacific Rail Trail ❾**, an old railroad bed, runs 28 mostly level miles (45 km) from Park City to Echo Reservoir. Or you can put your technical skills to the test on **Sweeney Switchbacks**, a tough 2-mile (3-km) trail that climbs to the Park City Mountain Resort trail system.

With so many bikes whizzing around, hikers may want to seek the relative calm of the **Swaner Nature Preserve** (Kimball Junction, 435-649-1867), a 1,160-acre (470-hectare) island of rolling alpine meadow. Also available in summer is the **Alpine Slide** (Park City Mountain Resort, 435-649-8111; Mon–Thur noon–9pm, Fri–Sat 10am–10pm), a sled-like contraption that zips down a winding track. Or you can wander over to watch the young and daring at the largest concrete skateboard park in Utah. ❑

BELOW: a mountain biker splashes through a stream in the Wasatch Mountains outside Park City.

Hollywood in Utah

Utah has been the backdrop for hundreds of movies, from *Stagecoach* (1939) and *Brigham Young* (1940) to *2001: A Space Odyssey* (1968), *Butch Cassidy and the Sundance Kid* (1969) and many others. So it seems fitting that the state has come to play host to one of the major North American attractions for film lovers and movie moguls: the Sundance Film Festival.

Spawned by the Utah Film Commission, the festival began its run in Salt Lake City on a September week in 1978, then shifted in 1981 to Park City about 30 miles (48 km) down the road. Its original name was the Utah/US Film Festival, and movies by independent filmmakers – "indies" – were encouraged.

By the mid-1980s the festival, now staged during January in a bid to cash in on the ski season, was catching the eye of the media and the imagination of the public at large. The big breakthrough came after 1984, the year that saw the festival fall under the wing of Robert Redford's Sundance Institute. Redford ultimately became board chairman of the Sundance Film Festival, as the annual event was retitled – after his role in *Butch Cassidy and the Sundance Kid.*

Thanks to Redford and the Institute, the festival enjoyed wider contacts and increased prestige, furthered the independent cause in moviemaking, and cast a spotlight on innovative talent. Two early examples from the 1985 festival were the Coen brothers, with *Blood Simple*, and Jim Jarmusch, creator of the offbeat *Stranger Than Paradise*.

The festival has become more ambitious since that opening program in 1978, when three theaters provided showings of classic American films and patrons listened to panel discussions focusing on theory and technique. Also shown were eight feature films made by novice moviemakers.

In the years ahead, competition was opened up to include documentaries, short films, videos and other forms, and as Sundance's prestige as a "happening" has swelled, there has been increased criticism centering on festival hype and commercialization. As the common complaint has it, the streets of Park City are now ubiquitous each January with a gaggle of power brokers and talent scouts manipulating cell phones for, hopefully, lucrative payoffs.

Some notable films were given showings at Sundance. They include Woody Allen's 1986 entry *Hannah and Her Sisters* and Quentin Tarantino's 1992 entry *Reservoir Dogs.* Among others: *The Usual Suspects* (1995), *Shine* (1996), *Memento* (2000) and *In The Bedroom* (2002).

But most significant, by general agreement, was the 1989 showing of a decidedly offbeat film by an erstwhile Sundance volunteer worker, Steven Soderbergh. The movie was entitled *sex, lies and videotape,* and its success at box offices far and wide, to the tune of over $25 million, is widely thought to have turned the corner for Sundance. This Utah event, now showing well over 100 feature films, ranks on a global scale with such distinguished festival venues as Cannes, Venice, Toronto and Berlin. ❏

RIGHT: movie critic Roger Ebert takes a coffee break during the Sundance Film Festival.

DINOSAUR, FLAMING GORGE AND THE HIGH UINTAS

Dinosaur quarries, a beautiful lake, scenic drives and a vast mountain wilderness lure travelers to a region once traversed by mountain men and outlaws

Map on page 158

"Wildlife Through the Ages." That's what the tourism board calls the 59-mile (95-km) Flaming Gorge–Uintas Scenic Byway between Vernal and Manila near the Utah–Wyoming border. Nature is indeed the focus of this beautiful scenic mountain drive up US 191 and UT 44 in Utah's down-to-earth, rural northeastern corner. Fifteen interpretive wayside pullouts, four nature trails, and four scenic backways highlight animals that live in eight different life zones over an elevation change of 7,000 ft (2,100 meters). You may see everything from raptors and kokanee salmon to moose, black bear, elk and bighorn sheep, depending on where and when you visit.

Even more amazing, you'll have the chance to go back in time, geologically speaking, as you climb in elevation. The highway passes through increasingly older rocks exposed by uplift along the adjoining Uinta Fault. One billion years of earth's history – a more complete record than even the Grand Canyon – is on display, containing within 23 different strata a remarkable look at the evolution of life on earth. This ancient wildlife includes an abundance of dinosaurs, which turn up so regularly in the fossil record here that they have led to the region's nickname: Dinosaurland.

Stop west of the highway to enter the Uinta Mountains and Ashley National Forest. Travel in farther on foot or pack animal and you'll reach the **High Uintas Wilderness** surrounding Utah's highest mountain, 13,528-ft (4,123-meter) **Kings Peak**, a backcountry region beloved by generations of Utah backpackers. East of the highway, the more accessible Flaming Gorge National Recreation Area offers scenic drives, birdwatching, camping, hiking, boating, hunting, rustic cabins and lodges, and the distinct possibility of reeling in the largest fish in the state at Flaming Gorge Reservoir, one of the prettiest man-made lakes in the country.

River paradise

The 502-ft-high (153-meter) **Flaming Gorge Dam** backs up the Green River where the Uinta Mountains meet the Red Desert of Wyoming. In Flaming Gorge, named by explorer John Wesley Powell in 1869 for its fiery sandstone, river trips on the Green begin beneath the dam. Rafts and kayaks meander gently through canyons and a series of broad openings, or "holes," so named by mountain men who trapped beaver and traded with Indians in Browns Park in the 1830s.

River runners of all ages will enjoy floating the flat water and gentle rapids here. A pleasant trip of one to three days takes you through the authentic Wild West – 1,000-year-old Fremont Indian sites, a national

Salt Lake City

PRECEDING PAGES: Green River, Desolation Canyon. **LEFT:** the "bone wall" at Dinosaur National Monument. **BELOW:** a collared lizard warms itself in the morning sun.

wildlife refuge, historic ranches, outlaw hideouts, and high desert scenery of quiet, mesmerizing beauty.

Takeout is just before you reach **Dinosaur National Monument** ❶ (4545 E. US 40, Dinosaur, CO, tel: 970-374-3000, www.nps.gov/dino; daily; admission), where the river turns to whitewater at the Gates of Lodore. Dinosaur National Monument, the highlight of any visit to Utah's northeastern corner, sprawls across the Utah–Colorado border. Within its boundaries, the Green River joins the wilder Yampa River in 800-ft-deep (240-meter) **Echo Canyon**, the heart of the monument.

Echo Canyon is reached via a rugged 13-mile-long (21-km) dirt road in the lightly visited Canyons section of the monument, just north of the town of **Dinosaur** in Colorado. The labyrinthine canyons and quiet high-country grasslands can be seen from the 23-mile (37-km) **Journey Through Time Scenic Drive**. It's easy to see what drew the Chews, the Mantles, the Ruples and other early ranchers: a sense of space, abundant grass, reliable water and plenty of game.

The attraction for which the monument was named – dinosaurs – can only be

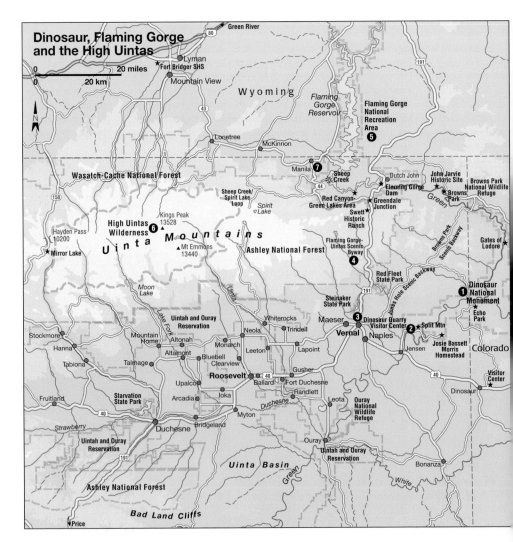

seen on the Utah side at the **Dinosaur Quarry Visitor Center ❷**, 7 miles (11 km) north of **Jensen**. The "Wall of Bones," as it is known, contains 10 different Jurassic-era dinosaur species, including Camarasaurus, Stegosaurus, Diplodocus and Dryosaurus, first discovered here in 1909 by Carnegie Museum paleontologist Earl Douglass. Since then, excavations have uncovered more than 2,000 dinosaur bones. This is just a fraction of the dinosaurs that were entombed here when a catastrophic river flood wiped them out 150 million years ago.

Douglass's discovery triggered a stampede to uncover fossils that threatened to strip the area of dinosaur bones. The quarry was protected as a national monument in 1915. The Green and Yampa river canyons of eastern Dinosaur National Monument were added in 1938. Environmentalists successfully prevented dams from being built at Echo Park and Split Mountain in 1956. Briefly, little-known Dinosaur basked in the national spotlight, only to return to obscurity when more high-profile environmental battles, such as the building of a dam at Glen Canyon, took over the headlines.

Map on page 158

Dino-land

Protected by an attractive glass-and-steel structure, the Wall of Bones is open year-round and will appeal to the whole family. In summer, visitors park at the bottom of the hill and – shades of Disney here – hop aboard a tram, where a taped introduction to the quarry keeps everyone happy for the few minutes it takes to get to the top. Trams leave regularly all day, so you can spend as much time as you wish in the quarry building, listening to ranger talks, viewing exhibits, and visiting the gift shop. This part of the monument sits below Split Mountain, a huge, tilted formation with a plated profile that looks oddly like a Stegosaurus.

BELOW: hikers take in the view near the confluence of the Green and Yampa Rivers in Dinosaur National Monument.

A butterfly alights on a Rocky Mountain beeplant in Dinosaur National Monument.

BELOW: T. rex lurks in the "dinosaur garden" at the Utah Field House of Natural History.

The 22-mile (35-km) **Tilted Rocks Scenic Drive** offers a closer look at Split Mountain and the Green River, both of which have campgrounds heavily used by hikers and river runners. A prehistoric rock shelter that was used by Paleo-Indians as long ago as 7000 BC can be viewed at the start of the scenic drive; it also has many examples of Fremont Indian art. At the end of the road, in Cub Creek, you'll find the fascinating **Josie Bassett Morris Homestead**. This pioneer woman spent her early years in Browns Park, just north of the park, and knew Butch Cassidy. When she died in 1964, her homestead became part of the park.

If you're driving from Colorado on US 40, you'll want to stop at the Dinosaur Quarry first. Tour information is available at the **Jensen Welcome Center** and **Dinosaur Quarry Visitor Center**. Otherwise, begin this tour of northeastern Utah in friendly little **Vernal ❸**, gateway to Flaming Gorge and the eastern Uintas.

Ancient creatures and fiery rocks

Everything you ever wanted to know about dinosaurs can be found at Vernal's **Utah Field House of Natural History** (daily 8am–9pm, to 5pm after Labor Day; 235 E. Main St, tel: 435-789-3799; admission), which, in 2004, reopened with new displays, including reconstructed dinosaur skeletons, a regional map chronicling a billion years of geologic history, and exhibits on Indian cultures.

Perhaps because the physical landscape lacks a certain drama, northeastern Utah really works the dinosaur theme – a surefire winner with young children. Dinosaur-themed buildings scale new heights of kitsch in quiet Mormon communities gradually awakening to the possibilities of tourism. A giant replica of a dinosaur welcomes visitors in neighboring **Roosevelt** while, at the Utah Field House, 18 life-sized sculptures lurk in their own Dinosaur Garden.

WILD HORSES ROAM FREE

Horses were brought to North America by Spaniards in the mid-1400s and quickly became an important means of transportation for Europeans and Indians alike. In the West, horses that escaped from farms, ranches or the U.S. Cavalry headed for the open range and formed large herds. Wild mustangs were rounded up by early pioneers to replenish their stock. By the turn of the 20th century, though, demand had declined, and unscrupulous mustangers rounded up wild horses and sold them for meat and pet food from the 1920s to the 1950s.

Nevada's Velma Johnson, also known as Wild Horse Annie, and thousands of schoolchildren were instrumental in getting the Wild Free Roaming Horses and Burros Act of 1971 passed, providing for the protection and control of wild horses on public lands. In Utah, approximately 2,500 wild horses and 100 burros roam freely within 22 herd management areas overseen by the Bureau of Land Management. Regular Adopt-a-Horse auctions allow the public to purchase excess animals, learn how to train them at clinics, and show them in the annual Wild Horse Festival.

Look for wild horses in Hill and Range Creeks and Bonanza in the Uinta Basin. For more information, contact the BLM in Vernal at 435-781-4400.

Map on page 158

Leave the kids to play among the fake dinosaurs and pick up tour information at the **Vernal Orientation Center** (435-789-7894), which shares the building. Vernal and neighboring Roosevelt serve as the main shopping centers on the northern periphery of the massive Uinta Basin, a vast expanse of monochromatic Cretaceous-era rocks dotted with oil pumps, farms, ranches, Ute tribal lands and wetland preserves that attract huge numbers of waterfowl.

The **Flaming Gorge–Uintas Scenic Byway ❹** leads north from Vernal to **Flaming Gorge National Recreation Area ❺** (tel: 435-784-3445, www.fs.fed.us). Two state parks on either side of the highway a few miles north of Vernal feature small reservoirs surrounded by a Jurassic landscape of bright, upended rocks. **Steinaker State Park** has a nature trail that offers a good introduction to the geology and wildlife of the area. **Red Fleet State Park**, named for its red sandstone formations, which do indeed look like ships on the water, has boating and camping.

Red rocks are also spectacularly carved at **Red Canyon**, off UT 44, a few miles past the turnoff for Flaming Gorge Dam. A short drive leads to **Red Canyon Visitor Center** (summer only) and views of the blue waters of Flaming Gorge Reservoir that contrast strikingly with the red rocks. Red Canyon Lodge has cabins and a restaurant on a small lake, where you can boat or watch for wildlife in the forest.

Before you get to Red Canyon, stop at Red Cloud Pullout (mile marker 14) to view interpretive panels about animals that "live on the edge" in meadows that serve as a transition zone between summer and winter ranges for deer and other animals. The 45-mile (72-km) **Red Cloud Loop Drive** leads to **McConkie Ranch**, a good place to view Fremont Indian rock art in Dry Fork Canyon.

Slow down as you approach forested **Greendale Junction**. The meadows to the west are a great place to glimpse elk, moose and deer in early morning and

BELOW: Steamboat Rock towers over rafters on the Green River in Dinosaur National Monument.

evening. US 191 continues northeast toward Flaming Gorge Dam at the junction, passing **Swett Historic Ranch**, open for tours in summer, and several Forest Service campgrounds. Campers will find excellent facilities at Firefighters' Memorial Campground, which commemorates "smokejumpers" who gave their lives in this fire-altered landscape. Across the road is Flaming Gorge Lodge, which has reasonably priced rooms, a coffee shop, a gas station and raft rentals to float or fish the Green River.

Flaming Gorge Dam was dedicated in 1964 and is 502 ft (153 meters) tall, 1,285 ft (393 meters) long and 131 ft (40 meters) wide at the base. Tours are offered daily. Stop at one of the overlooks off US 191 on the east side of the dam for breathtaking sunset views. You'll find some of Utah's best fishing here. Trout, bass, catfish and other stocked species grow to huge size in the reservoir.

Anglers cast for trophy-sized bass, trout and other fish at Flaming Gorge Reservoir.

BELOW:
llama packing in the High Uintas Wilderness Area.

Wildlife events

If it's native fish you're interested in – rare enough in the cold waters of desert reservoirs – continue on US 44 to the bridge at Sheep Creek Overlook where, during August and September, bright-red kokanee salmon return to Sheep Creek to spawn in huge numbers. Ten-mile (16-km) **Sheep Creek National Geologic Area Scenic Backway Loop**, a must-see for any visitor to Flaming Gorge, offers numerous delights: glimpses of kokanee salmon; the chance to see reintroduced bighorn sheep on the steep cliffs; and a close look at the Uinta Fault, which has tilted billion-year-old Precambrian rocks into vertical strata.

Spirit Lake Scenic Backway begins at the southern end of the Sheep Creek loop and is your best bet for reaching the **High Uintas Wilderness Area ❻** from Flaming Gorge. The 17-mile (27-km) dirt road passes Ute Fire Lookout Tower,

built by the Civilian Conservation Corps in the 1930s and open for tours in summer, and dead-ends at Spirit Lake, which features a rustic lodge and campground, a restaurant, horseback riding and trails leading into the High Uintas Wilderness.

The northern end of the Sheep Creek loop is about 4½ miles (7 km) south of **Manila ⑦**, where UT 44 joins WY 530/UT 43 on the north side of the Uintas. Manila is the headquarters of the Flaming Gorge Area Chamber of Commerce (435-784-3154, www.flaminggorgecountry.com) and Ashley National Forest Flaming Gorge Ranger District (435-784-3445, www.fs.fed.us). Both have centers at the junction of UT 44 and UT 43, where you can pick up info on traveling into the recreation area, which sprawls northward into Wyoming.

Continue north toward the Wyoming side of Flaming Gorge via WY 530 or head northwest on WY 414 to historic Fort Bridger on US 80. If you're interested in seeing the west side of the Uintas, drive west on US 80 and drop south on UT 150, also known as **Mirror Lake Scenic Byway**. This paved route is a complete contrast with the east side of the mountains, which attracts a largely urban crowd from Salt Lake City to its many trails, campgrounds and mountain vistas.

Outlaw Trail

Once you reach Manila, you're in the historic stronghold of mountain men and outlaws. The area was a favorite haunt of Butch Cassidy and the Wild Bunch, whose dubious achievements are commemorated during Vernal's annual **Outlaw Ride**, a four-day event featuring trail rides, cookouts, camping and live entertainment. For a real backcountry adventure, consider a visit to **Browns Park**, an isolated valley on the Green River where a number of mountain man rendezvous took place in the early 1800s. The best way to reach the site is the **Jones Hole Scenic Backway**, a 40-mile (65-km) four-wheel-drive-only trip that begins just north of Vernal.

Allow lots of time for this drive: The road (impassable in winter) climbs 2,600 ft (800 meters) to Diamond Mountain Plateau, then picks up **Browns Park Scenic Backway**. A short side trip takes you to the **John Jarvie Historic Site**, a ranch and store owned in the late 1800s by a well-liked Scotsman who was murdered in Browns Park. Contact the BLM in Vernal (170 S. 500 East, tel: 435-789-1362) for more information.

By far the easiest way to see Browns Park is on a river trip between Flaming Gorge and Dinosaur National Monument. South of Dinosaur, the Green River passes through the largely inaccessible Desolation and Gray Canyons. A 12-mile (19-km) stretch of the Green is protected as **Ouray National Wildlife Refuge**, home to 209 resident and migratory bird species.

East of the river is the undeveloped Hill Creek Extension of the **Uintah and Ouray Indian Reservation**. The Uintah and Ouray Tribe have had an uneasy history with whites in the Uinta Basin and now maintain a low profile in the area. They are most visible at their annual **Northern Ute Indian Powwow** during the July 4th weekend and **Thanksgiving Powwow** in November, both held at **Fort Duchesne**. You may also encounter them taking part in the **Dinosaur Roundup Rodeo** held in Vernal in November, which commemorates the region's Wild West heritage. ❑

Map on page 158

BELOW:
horseback riders cross an alpine meadow in Ashley National Forest.

CENTRAL UTAH

Desert canyons, ghost towns and villages with a Scandinavian flavor await travelers in the state's varied heartland

Deseret, as Utah was once known to faithful Mormons, is a word from the Book of Mormon for the honey bee, symbolizing the industry the Saints brought to the task of building towns, growing food, creating successful businesses, and making the desert "bloom like a rose." The best place to understand this industriousness is central Utah, where farmers, ranchers and miners have successfully harnessed the natural resources of the mountains and deserts since the mid-1800s.

Tintic Mining District, which grew up around Eureka in the Great Basin in 1869, was one of the top three producers of precious metals in the state, with a total production of about 16,654,377 tons valued at $570 million during its century of operation. Equally wealthy was Carbon County, on the far side of the Wasatch Plateau in Castle Country. It has been called "Eastern Utah's Industrialized Island" by historian Philip Notarianni whose Italian forebears were among the thousands of immigrants who came to Utah to work in the coal mines in Helper and Price, and stayed. Nowhere else in rural Utah is more cosmopolitan in character than Castle Country, nor as rich in natural and cultural history, from the thousands of dinosaurs bones that have been unearthed at Cleveland-Lloyd Quarry to desert canyons throughout the extraordinarily scenic San Rafael Swell that once sheltered Desert Archaic, Fremont and Ute Indians and outlaws like Butch Cassidy.

Immigrant "towns" contrasted dramatically with the larger Mormon culture, which, although drawn from around the world, emphasized assimilation rather than segregation. Yet few immigrants leave their culture behind, as is abundantly clear for visitors driving through the rural heartland of Sanpete Valley along Scenic Byway 89. In the 1850s and 1860s, Mormon converts from Norway, Sweden and Denmark founded neatly laid-out small towns in this agricultural valley between the Wasatch Plateau and the Sanpitch Mountains, all named for important places and people in the Book of Mormon.

Isolated from the rest of Utah, Sanpete's hardy old-world pioneers cobbled together a way of life that has sustained them for nearly 150 years. Even today, pioneer activities, such as rug weaving, tatting, crochet, quilting, soap making, pottery, furniture making and handmade musical instruments thrive in studios all along US 89 in towns such as Moroni, Ephraim and Manti. Here you'll find some of the most unique historic districts in the state and a love of storytelling and old-world humor, celebrated in town festivals, books and Scandinavian families whose roots are as deep as the rich soils of the valley.   ❏

PRECEDING PAGES: a young hiker in the Wasatch Range finds a shady spot to write entries in her journal.
LEFT: rafters survey the landscape from a bluff above the Green River.

CASTLE COUNTRY

*Ancient rock art, old-time mining towns and the stark beauty
of the San Rafael Desert attract visitors to a land
where dinosaurs – and outlaws – once roamed*

Map
on page
172

I t was early April, 1897. Outlaw Butch Cassidy had been hanging around the mining town of Castle Gate, near Price, Utah, for nearly a week. With his blond hair and clean-cut good looks, the affable young cowboy stood out from the town's residents, many of them non-English-speaking, dark-skinned miners of European birth. Every day, Butch visited a saloon, chatted with the patrons, then rode his lively gray mare to meet the train. Rumor had it that Butch, a skilled horseman, and his companion, Elza Lay, were using the steep trails to train their mounts for an upcoming race. The story held water. Horses in Indian Canyon were an anomaly; it was so narrow the train could hardly make it through. Most of the population simply walked.

Townspeople had heard of Butch Cassidy and the Wild Bunch, of course. Word of their daring robberies in Wyoming and Colorado had spread throughout the West, but no one knew what the thieves looked like and they had never yet struck in Utah. Just in case, the Pleasant Valley Coal Company, owners of the Castle Gate Mine, had taken the precaution of varying the delivery schedule for payrolls. A holdup seemed highly unlikely under the circumstances.

PRECEDING PAGES:
San Rafael Swell.
LEFT: Little Wild
Horse Canyon.
BELOW: playing in
Muddy Creek, San
Rafael Swell.

Butch's cover held, and on April 21 his patience paid off. While meeting the train, he noticed that the bags being unloaded were heavier than usual and, pulling a six-gun, successfully held up the paymaster and his two assistants. Among the witnesses were several hundred men waiting for their paychecks, but no one made much of a move to stop the thieves, and with the town's telegraph wires cut by Butch, word of the robbery took a while to get out.

Butch and Elza dodged a posse from Castle Dale and Huntington. Along the way, the outlaws were helped by other gang members and ranchers who gave them fresh horses (including the head of one posse, who had secretly loaned his horse to Butch for the robbery). South of Price, they rode through 70 miles (110 km) of the San Rafael Desert, passing the geological landmark known as the San Rafael Swell, until they reached Robber's Roost, their canyon lair near Hanksville, in what is now the Maze district of Canyonlands National Park.

Today, there are few signs of the Wild Bunch and other self-styled "businessmen" who dominated the rugged San Rafael Swell country in the late 1800s. Time and the vast wilderness of the Tavaputs Plateau have swallowed up these Wild West characters, making them seem larger than life.

Beneath the surface

Nearly 100 million years before this landscape was pushed up by the same geologic episode that built the Rocky Mountains, the bone-dry San Rafael Desert was a sticky tropical swamp filled with supersized

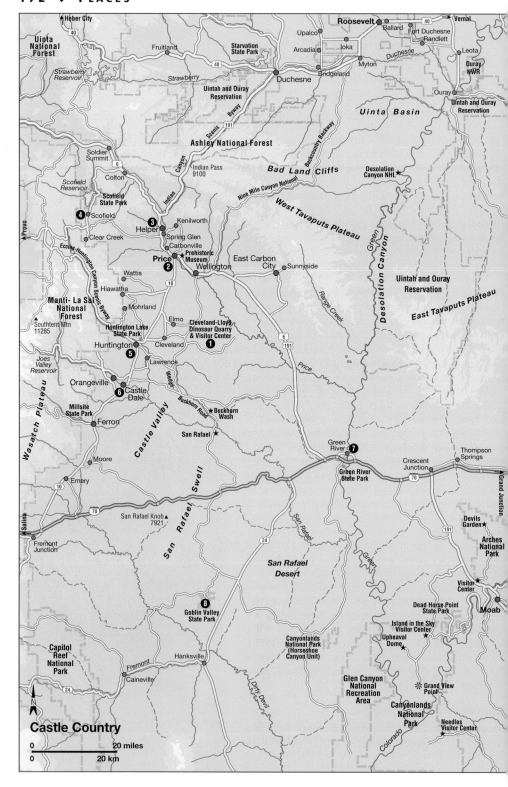

Heber City

Uinta
National
Forest

40

Fruitland

Strawberry
Reservoir

Strawberry

Roosevelt

Upalco   Ballard   Fort Duchesne
                           Randlett

Arcadia   Ioka

40

Vernal

Leota

Duchesne

Starvation
State Park

Scenic 191

Uintah and Ouray
Reservation

Bridgeland   Myton

Duchesne

Ouray
NWR

Ouray   Uintah and Ouray
         Reservation

Ashley National Forest

Soldier
Summit

6

Colton

Scofield
Reservoir

Scofield
State Park

4 Scofield

Clear Creek

Indian Pass
9100

Indian Canyon

Nine Mile Canyon National

Uinta   Basin

Bad Land Cliffs

Backcountry Backway

West Tavaputs Plateau

Desolation
Canyon NHL

Green

Ecclas Huntington Canyon Scenic Byway

3 Helper

Kenilworth

Spring Glen
Carbonville

2 Price

Prehistoric
Museum

Wellington

East Carbon
City   Sunnyside

Desolation Canyon

Uintah and Ouray
Reservation

East Tavaputs Plateau

Wattis

Manti-La Sal
National
Forest

Southtent Mtn
11285

Hiawatha

Mohrland

Huntington Lake
State Park

5 Huntington

Cleveland

Lawrence

Elmo

Cleveland-Lloyd
Dinosaur Quarry
& Visitor Center

1

6

191

Range Creek

Price

Joes
Valley
Reservoir

Orangeville

6 Castle
    Dale

Wasatch Plateau

Millsite
State Park

Ferron

Moore

Emery

10

Castle Valley

Wedge

Buckhorn Road

★ Buckhorn
  Wash

San Rafael ★

Green
River   **7**

Green River
State Park

70

Crescent
Junction

Thompson
Springs

Grand Junction

Salina

70

Fremont
Junction

San Rafael Knob ▲
7921

San Rafael Swell

San Rafael

24

San Rafael
Desert

San Rafael

Green

191

Devils
Garden ★

Arches
National
Park

Visitor ★
Center

Moab

Capitol
Reef
National
Park

8

Goblin Valley
State Park

Fremont

Caineville

24

Hanksville

Dirty Devil

Canyonlands
National Park
(Horseshoe
Canyon Unit)

Glen Canyon
National
Recreation
Area

Dead Horse Point
State Park

Island in the Sky
Visitor Center

Upheaval
Dome ★

☀ Grand View
  Point

Canyonlands
National
Park

Needles
Visitor Center ★

Colorado

N

Castle Country

0   20 miles
0   20 km

Map on page 172

conifers, ferns and dinosaurs. Millions of years later, those same swamps would harbor so much coal and uranium that Castle Country would become Utah's most important center of coal mining and energy production.

Castle Country would also yield other important secrets, including huge caches of dinosaur bones at **Cleveland-Lloyd Dinosaur Quarry ❶**, just south of Price; an intact skeleton of a mammoth hunted by spear-wielding Paleo-Indians; and an extraordinary array of ancient Indian rock art, spanning 6,000 years, in the San Rafael Swell and remote Nine Mile Canyon just east of Price.

If you plan to drive the popular **Nine Mile Canyon National Backcountry Backway** (www.ninemilecanyoncoalition.org) – a rough, almost completely unpopulated 70-mile (113-km) dirt road between Wellington and Myton – here's some important advice: Don't begin the drive without stocking up on water, food and a free Nine Mile Canyon map showing the main sites. Most of the land in the canyon is privately owned and road signs are few and far between and sometimes confusing. The only food and lodging in the canyon are at historic Nine Mile Canyon Ranch, a western experience dubbed "bunk 'n' breakfast."

Most people opt to stay in **Price ❷**, the seat of Carbon County off US 191/6, just west of Nine Mile Canyon. Founded as a coal mining camp in the 1870s, Price is still a coal town but, after violent clashes between foreigners and Americans earlier in its history, it now proudly embraces its international roots. Mexican, Italian and Greek influences are particularly strong, reflected in Price's many inexpensive ethnic restaurants. The popular Greek Festival, held the second weekend in July, features food, music, dancing and tours of the 1916 Hellenic Orthodox Church of the Assumption (61 S. 200 East, tel: 435-637-0704), Utah's oldest Greek Orthodox church.

BELOW:
Castle Country encompasses some of the richest deposits of dinosaur bones in the western states.

DINOSAUR GRAVEYARD

A lumbering Camarasaurus wades into a pond to slake its thirst. As the dinosaur drinks, its stout, elephantine legs sink into the viscous clay. Struggling to escape, it only sinks deeper. The beast bellows an alarm, which lures three hungry allosaurs. The carnivores rush in to chomp the flanks of their prey, but before they can reach the helpless camarasaur, they too become mired in the swamp.

This scenario, or one much like it, played out some 147 million years ago at Cleveland-Lloyd Dinosaur Quarry, 30 miles (48 km) southeast of Price, the highlight of the western Dinosaur Diamond, a series of major dinosaur sites stretching from Moab, Utah, to Grand Junction, Colorado. More than 12,000 bones representing 70 individuals, including 44 allosaurs, the top predator of the Jurassic period, were uncovered at the quarry between 1939 and 1990. Stained jet black from manganese oxide in the groundwater, they constitute one of the most intriguing dinosaur die-off sites.

Visitors can see in-situ fossils and casts of other bones beneath two metal sheds over the quarry site. More bones, a mounted allosaur skeleton and an allosaur egg are displayed in a small visitor center. For more information, contact the BLM office in Price; 435-636-3600.

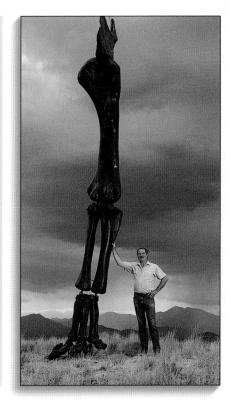

A ghostly pictograph adorns the wall of Black Dragon Wash.

BELOW:
a spring rain coaxes beeplant and phacelia from the cracked earth of the San Rafael Swell.

Dinosaurs and Indians

In Price, stop at **Castle Country Regional Information Center** (800-817-9949) inside the **College of Eastern Utah Prehistoric Museum** (Apr–Sept daily 9am–6pm, Oct–Mar Mon–Sat 9am–5pm; 155 E. Main, tel: 435-37-2514; donation) for maps and information. The adjoining bookstore sells an excellent mile-by-mile guide to Nine Mile Canyon, a good investment for those interested in the Fremont culture. The museum's eastern wing and an upstairs gallery have exhibits tracing the Indian presence in the area, including blow-up photographs of regional rock art and a full-size reproduction of the Barrier Canyon pictographs in the Horseshoe Canyon unit of Canyonlands National Park. Don't miss the "Pilling Figurines," 10 unbaked clay objects possibly used as fertility fetishes by the Fremont Indians, discovered by Clarence Pilling on his ranch in Range Creek.

The museum is also famous for its dinosaurs. The West Wing is filled with enormous Allosaurus, Camptosaurus, Camarasaurus and Stegosaurus skeletons uncovered at **Cleveland-Lloyd Dinosaur Quarry** (daily in summer 10am–5pm; tel: 435-636-3600; admission), a major dinosaur die-off site off UT 10, where more than 12,000 dinosaur bones have been uncovered. Unique to this museum are Early Cretaceous dinosaurs, found in the Cedar Mountain Formation, dating to about 120 to 110 million years ago.

Museum staff and volunteers have recovered more than 2,600 bones belonging to at least 10 new species of dinosaurs, ranging from 3 ft to 70 ft (1–21 meters) in length, including Utahraptor, Gastonia, Animantarx, Nedcolbertia and Eolambia. These highly specialized creatures occupied a unique ecological niche at the end of the dinosaur era. Much smaller than the better-known great lizards, Animantarx and Gastonia look almost like pony-size armadillos.

Miners and artists

Northwest of Price, sandwiched between railroad tracks and the highway, is historic **Helper ❸**. Like so many mining towns in the West, Helper is being revived by a community of artists. Every August, the historic district is shut down for the popular **Helper Arts Festival**, which includes a plein air painting competition.

Helper's main visitor attraction is the **Western Mining and Railroad Museum** (May–Sept Mon–Sat 9am–5pm, Oct–Apr Tues–Sat 11am–4pm; 296 S. Main, tel: 435-472-3009, www.mrrm.org; donation), which occupies an old railroad hotel. Displays in the three-story building and adjoining outdoor park feature early 1900s dentist offices, a beauty salon and outlaw history. Model trains and old mining gear highlight Helper's rich mining and railroading past, which saw the development of ethnic towns, fights over miners' unions led by legendary activist Joe Hill, and three horrific mining disasters in 1900, 1924 and 1984.

US 191 continues north from Helper to **Duchesne** via 45-mile-long (72-km) **Indian Canyon Scenic Byway**, a lovely highway that offers a glimpse of the area's coal-mining past and amazing fall colors. US 191 passes the Castle Gate Power Plant and the old Castle Gate cemetery, where victims of the 1924 coal mine explosion are buried, then continues into **Ashley National Forest** via 9,100-ft (2,770-meter) Indian Pass.

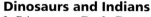

Map on page 172

Northwest of Helper, near the little town of **Colton** on US 6, is an entrance to **Manti-La Sal National Forest**. Here UT 96 leads to **Scofield Reservoir**, a state park offering boating, swimming and fishing. Nearby is the historic mining town of **Scofield ❹**, where more than 100 miners were killed in an explosion in 1900. UT 96 joins UT 264 and then connects with UT 31, also known as **Eccles-Huntington Canyon Scenic Byway**. This is also the intersection for the north-south **Skyline Drive**, a scenic route across the 10,000-ft (3,000-meter) plateau with numerous forested campsites and hiking trails.

UT 31 intersects with UT 10 at **Huntington ❺**, a mining town with a power plant producing electricity from coal mined on the plateau. **Huntington Lake State Park**, next to the highway, is a good place for camping and birdwatching. **Millsite State Park** near **Castle Dale ❻** is also popular with travelers on UT 10. Expect to be self-sufficient in this traditional Mormon area; there are few services.

Given the dearth of visitor services, the modern **Museum of the San Rafael** (Mon–Fri 10am–4pm, Sat 1pm–4pm; 64 N. 100 East, tel: 435-381-5252; donation) in Castle Dale is quite a surprise. It has its own glassed-in paleontology room, featuring mammoth and dinosaur skeletons, and a nautilus-shaped exhibit hall displaying local wildlife as well as arrowheads, spear points and the Sitterud Bundle, a collection of artifacts dating from AD 1250–1450.

East of Castle Dale is the best-marked road into the **San Rafael Desert**, following the route of the Old Spanish Trail, used in the 1800s by Spanish traders and explorers John Gunnison and John C. Frémont. At Buckhorn Flat, turn south to view some of the area's best Archaic pictographs in **Buckhorn Wash**. The badly vandalized paintings, made about 6,000 years ago, were completely restored in 1995 and are an area highlight today.

BELOW: a party of camel trekkers ventures into Eagle Canyon in the San Rafael Swell.

Buckhorn Wash emerges at San Rafael River Campground, an unshaded but well-maintained BLM campground on the San Rafael River, the only one in this part of the San Rafael Swell. The road brings you out to I-70, just west of Black Dragon Wash, one of several pictograph panels you can reach from the highway.

Down by the river

The nearest visitor facilities on this scenic stretch of I-70 are at **Green River ❼**, which is set on the waterway of the same name and has become a mecca for river runners, who descend on the town in droves year-round. Like other towns in these parts, Green River grew up around mining and the railroad and boomed briefly following World War II, when uranium was discovered. Today, it has reinvented itself as a tourist stop with plentiful gas stations, lodgings and eateries. If you're passing through Green River in the late summer and fall, be sure to stop and buy one of the delicious sweet melons grown in the area.

The big attraction in Green River is the carefully thought-out **John Wesley Powell River History Museum** (daily 8am–5pm, to 8pm in summer; 885 E. Main, tel: 435-564-3427; admission). Named for the man who first explored the Green and Colorado Rivers, in 1869 and 1871, this airy museum is a homage to river aficionados and their watercraft, from historic figures like Powell to guides like Bert Loper. Inside the lobby doors, you'll find **Emery County Visitor Information Center**, where you can get maps and help with trip planning.

South of the bridge is Green River State Park, which sits on the river and has numerous campsites amid the tamarisks. A variety of river companies in Green River and nearby Moab offer float trips on the Green as far as the Maze district of Canyonlands National Park, before it turns into the whitewater of

An abandoned truck gradually disintegrates in Muddy Creek.

BELOW: a dusting of snow lays upon the sandstone "hoodoos" of Goblin Valley.

Cataract Canyon. Some also offer more unusual upriver outings. Holiday Expeditions (800-624-6323, www.holidayexpeditions.com), for example, arranges week-long fly/float trips to Butch and Jeanie Jensen's Tavaputs Ranch (435-637-1236) high on the Tavaputs Plateau above Desolation Canyon. From Green River, you can fly to Tavaputs Ranch, relax on the ranch for several days, then float back on the Green, viewing Fremont artifacts near Range Creek, one of the premier archaeological sites in the region.

Map on page 172

The heart of the Swell

The **Maze**, the wild western section of **Canyonlands National Park**, may be reached overland from US 24, just west of Green River. Drive south through what's known as Sinbad Country, the extraordinary, uptilted landscape of the San Rafael Swell, until you reach Temple Junction, named for the highest point on the Reef, 6,773-ft (2,064-meter) Temple Mountain. East of the junction, a 30-mile (48-km) dirt road takes you to **Horseshoe Canyon**, where you can view remarkable pictographs. A series of old ranch and mining tracks take you overland past Hans Flat Ranger Station and into the Maze country that once sheltered the Wild Bunch. A four-wheel-drive is essential for deeper explorations of this rough country. Bring food, water, extra gas and spare tires. This is a very remote area.

West of Temple Junction is the paved road that leads directly into the heart of the San Rafael Swell, passing Archaic and Fremont rock art panels, old mines, wilderness study areas, wild horse herds and Swasey's Cabin, a backcountry ranch built by the highly "entrepreneurial" Joe Swasey in the early 1900s. You're welcome to camp in dispersed sites throughout the majestic San Rafael Swell, which is fast becoming one of south-central Utah's most popular pristine backcountry experiences.

BELOW: ancient rock paintings, some as much as 6,000 years old, are found throughout the San Rafael Desert.

If that seems too intimidating (and never underestimate this country; its remoteness, heat and aridity can make it very dicey in summer), base yourself in delightful **Goblin Valley State Park** ❽, which offers numerous comforts for the self-sufficient traveler in an awe-inspiring setting at the edge of the San Rafael Swell. The park is set about 20 miles (32 km) from UT 24 via paved roads and has everything even a neophyte backcountry explorer might desire: plenty of well-conceived, clean campsites with attractive metal gazebos, showers, toilets, trails and knock-your-socks-off scenery that has starred in numerous movies.

The "goblins" are actually eroded red Entrada sandstone, the same formation found in Cathedral Valley in nearby Capitol Reef National Park. The campground is sheltered right below them, in the far valley, and is much more intimate than you would expect. Friendly on-site rangers are passionate about this place and love to share information with visitors. Despite its remote setting, the park is quite popular with campers (the whole campground is occasionally reserved by movie crews); reserving a site ahead of time is advisable. Bring your mountain bike, hiking shoes and a camera, and plan on spending a couple of nights. Castle Country doesn't get much better than this. ❏

SANPETE AND SEVIER VALLEYS

*Scandinavian immigrants have left their stamp on this
region of farms and ranches settled by Mormon
pioneers in the mid-19th century*

Map on page 182

Most travelers heading south through Utah drive Interstate 15, a fast, modern freeway running parallel to the yawning Great Basin and the high mountain ranges and plateaus that together make up what tourism officials call Panoramaland. The Salt Lake City metropolitan area peters out at Spanish Fork, east of Utah Lake, giving way to long stretches of desert freeway punctuated by small towns in the shadow of mountain highlands.

The sights along I-15 are few and far between. **Nephi ❶** is home to July's **Ute Stampede** (435-623-7102), one of Utah's most popular rodeos. In quiet, staid **Fillmore ❷**, you'll find the 1855 territorial state capitol, the oldest government building in Utah, protected now as **Territorial State House State Park and Museum** (Mon–Sat 9am–6pm; 50 W. Capitol Ave, tel: 435-743-4723; admission). At the junction of I-15 and I-70, blink and you'll miss **Cove Fort ❸** (8am–sunset, tel: 435-438-5547, www.placestovisit.lds.org; free), an 1866 stone fortification built by pioneers and now operated by the LDS Church.

Even farther south is **Beaver ❹**, with over 200 historic buildings from its heyday as a gold and silver mining town adjacent to the Tushar Mountains, the third-highest range in Utah.

PRECEDING PAGES:
wildflowers at the
base of Mount Nebo.
LEFT: pioneer
heritage comes
alive at a historic
re-enactment.
BELOW: rabbitbrush
and maples, Uinta
National Forest.

Slow and easy

East of I-15, life settles into the slow lane. Visitor services aren't immediately obvious along Highway 89, Utah's award-winning "Mormon pioneer cultural corridor," which passes through the isolated Sanpete Valley, then drops into the scenic Sevier River valley, south of I-70, the gateway to southern Utah. That's because agricultural Sanpete County may well be Utah's most traditional Mormon stronghold, and there's not a lot of occasions for farm folks to eat out, drink coffee or strong liquor, and engage in other activities that go against the strict Word of Wisdom.

Sanpete County attracted so many Scandinavian immigrant Mormon pioneers in the 1850s and 1860s that it was dubbed "Little Denmark." Today, the Scandinavian stamp is everywhere – in historic buildings now housing bed-and-breakfasts, mom-and-pop cafes, museums, art studios and shops, as well as in the folklore and deadpan, self-deprecating humor for which the region's Scandinavian communities are known.

The story is different south of I-70 and the scenery even more dramatic. Next to the north-flowing rapids of the Sevier River is the historic cold-springs resort of Big Rock Candy Mountain, where, according to Burl Ives' famous song of the same name, "the bluebird sings to the lemonade springs." In nearby **Circleville** are the remains of the log cabin that served as the boyhood home of famed outlaw Robert Leroy Parker,

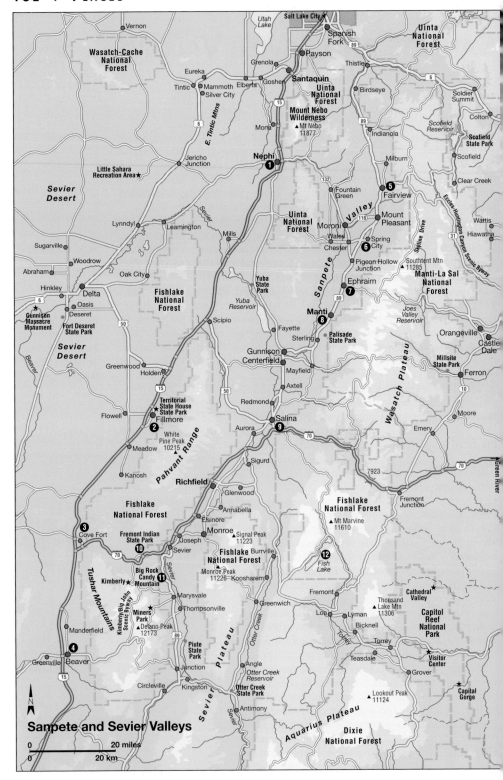

Salt Lake City
Utah Lake
Spanish Fork
Uinta National Forest
Vernon
Wasatch-Cache National Forest
Payson
Thistle
Eureka
Grenola
Soldier Summit
Tintic
Mammoth
Elberta
Goshen
Santaquin
Birdseye
Silver City
Uinta National Forest
Colton
Scofield Reservoir
Scofield State Park
Mount Nebo Wilderness
Indianola
Scofield
Mona
▲ Mt Nebo 11877
89
Clear Creek
Sevier Desert
Jericho Junction
Nephi ①
Little Sahara Recreation Area ★
132
Fountain Green
5 Fairview
Wattis
Lynndyl
Leamington
Uinta National Forest
Moroni
116
Mount Pleasant
Hiawatha
Mills
Wales
Spring City
31
Sugarville
Woodrow
Chester
6 ⑥
Skyline Drive
Abraham
Oak City
Pigeon Hollow Junction
Southtent Mtn ▲ 11285
Manti-La Sal National Forest
Hinkley
Delta
Fishlake National Forest
Yuba State Park
Ephraim ⑦
89
Joes Valley Reservoir
6
Oasis
Deseret
Yuba Reservoir
Manti ⑧
Orangeville
Gunnison Massacre Monument
Fort Deseret State Park
Scipio
Fayette
Sterling
Palisade State Park
Castle Dale
Sevier Desert
Greenwood
Holden
Gunnison Centerfield
Mayfield
Millsite State Park
Ferron
Beaver
50
Axtell
10
Territorial State House State Park
Fillmore ②
50
Redmond
Moore
Flowell
White Pine Peak 10215
Aurora
Salina ⑨
Emery
Meadow
70
70
Kanosh
Sigurd
7923
Fremont Junction
Richfield
Glenwood
Fishlake National Forest
Fishlake National Forest
Annabella
▲ Mt Marvine 11610
Pahvant Range
Elsinore
Cove Fort ③
Fremont Indian State Park
Monroe
Signal Peak 11223
Joseph
Sevier
Burrville
12 ⑫ Fish Lake
70
Fishlake National Forest
Kimberly ★
Big Rock Candy Mountain ⑪
Monroe Peak 11226
Koosharem
Fremont
Cathedral Valley ★
Tushar Mountains
Marysvale
Greenwich
Thousand Lake Mtn ▲ 11306
Capitol Reef National Park
Miners Park ★
Thompsonville
Loa
Lyman
Manderfield
▲ Delano Peak 12173
Otter Creek
Bicknell
Beaver ④
89
Piute State Park
Torrey
Teasdale
Visitor Center
Greenville
15
Junction
Angle
Grover
Capital Gorge
Circleville
Kingston
Otter Creek Reservoir
Otter Creek State Park
Lookout Peak ▲ 11124
Aquarius Plateau
Antimony
Dixie National Forest

Sanpete and Sevier Valleys

N

0 ————— 20 miles
0 ————— 20 km

Map
on page
182

alias Butch Cassidy. It was here the young Mormon planned his escape from a life of grinding poverty by changing his name to that of mentor Mike Cassidy, a ranch hand and sometime rustler who taught Butch the tricks of the trade.

Violent past

Start your tour in **Payson**, at the northern end of **Mount Nebo National Scenic Byway**, which travels for 38 miles (61 km) behind 11,877-ft (3,620-meter) **Mount Nebo**, the highest peak in the Wasatch range. The winding road passes through oaks and aspens in **Uinta National Forest** for fabulous views of Mount Nebo Wilderness, Utah Valley and the Wasatch Mountains. Most people drive the byway in late October, when fall colors really pop.

At UT 132, turn east into the Sanpete Valley, passing through **Fountain Green**, a camping site for Mormon pioneers immigrating to Sanpete Valley in the 1850s. A few miles farther is **Moroni**, originally named Mego and Sanpitch, after local Ute leaders, and later renamed for the angel who led LDS Church founder Joseph Smith to the golden plates on which the Book of Mormon was recorded.

From Moroni, take a detour north on UT 116 to pick up US 89 near **Fairview ❺**, where a historic school now houses the homegrown **Fairview Museum of History and Art** (Mon–Sat 10am–6pm, Sun 2–6pm, 85 N. 100 East, tel: 435-427-9216). Exhibits tell the sad but all-too-familiar 19th-century tale of conflicts between Utes and whites in settling the valley, while highlighting the unique world view the newcomers brought with them. In the 1860s, Brigham Young advised the residents of Fairview to "fort up" to protect themselves during the Blackhawk War, named for the fierce young Ute leader who, together with other starving Indians, raided cattle herds and killed whites in an attempt to drive the interlopers from the valley. The long-running war was eventually settled by federal troops. Several Ute bands were then banished from their homeland to a reservation in the desolate Uintah Basin, a far cry from the lush valley in which they once roamed.

Sanpete Valley

Although the towns in Sanpete Valley are just a few miles apart, each has developed separately, giving every community an individual look. A wealth of 19th- and early 20th-century buildings made from local limestone and often adorned with traditional Scandinavian carved wood and stained glass are slowly being restored. South of Fairview, the attractive Main Street of **Mount Pleasant**, which prospered with the arrival of the railroad, is still intact, with many buildings dating from 1880 to 1905.

At nearby **Spring City ❻**, the second oldest community in Sanpete County, the whole town is on the National Register of Historic Places and has become an artist haven. A little off the highway, it has several attractive bed-and-breakfasts and artist studios. The town hosts **Heritage Days** each spring, with tours of historic homes and studios, wagon rides and a barbecue.

Another Biblical-sounding town – **Ephraim ❼** – is home to **Snow College**, which was founded in the 1880s in a two-story stone building on Main Street that has also served as a mercantile and community

BELOW: flying the colors at a small-town parade.

Hungry travelers dig into rib-sticking home-cooked meals at Mom's Cafe in Salina.

BELOW:

Cove Fort was built in the 1860s as a way station for Mormon settlers.

center. The two-year college now has 2,500 students and is well regarded in the state. Ephraim was founded in 1854 and, at one time, 90 percent of the town's population hailed from Denmark. The meticulously restored former ZCMI store now houses the **Sanpete Sampler** (96 Main St, 435-283-6654), showcasing the work of 80 local artisans. If you're interested in Scandinavian art, check out the **Central Utah Art Center** (86 Main, 435-283-5110), set in a classic limestone building. Other artists can be visited in working studios in town. The **Scandinavian Heritage Day Festival** is held in Ephraim every Memorial Day weekend.

Manti ❽, founded in 1849 at the invitation of Ute chief Wakara (also known as Walker), is the oldest town in Sanpete County and the county seat. It is best known for its imposing **Mormon Temple**, built at a cost of $1 million between 1877 and 1888. The temple's mix of Victorian architectural styles echoes those found in other early Mormon towns in the Midwest, and it is certainly one of the most photogenic buildings in the area. Only "worthy" Mormons may enter the building; gentiles can learn more at the adjoining **Mormon Temple Heritage Center**.

The temple serves as the backdrop for the spectacular springtime **Mormon Miracle Pageant** (435-835-3000), a retelling of an epic tale in the Book of Mormon using a cast of hundreds. Learn more about Manti at **Patton House** (300 North 100 West), an 1854 pioneer rock house that serves as the town museum.

Chief Wakara's welcome rapidly chilled when he clashed with antislavery Mormons over the Ute practice of selling Paiute children to Spanish traders. When the Walker War erupted in the 1850s, settlers across the region took shelter in three forts built from logs and stone. The war began when Spanish traders were intercepted by a posse from Manti and a trial ensued, pitting Utes, who had long traded with Spaniards, against Brigham Young's fledgling State of Deseret.

Map on page 182

Fatal encounters with angry Indians didn't affect only Mormons. In 1853, Captain John Gunnison, an American surveying the newly acquired US territory, was killed by Indians nearby. The town of **Gunnison** is named for him.

Sevier Valley

The Scandinavian-influenced Sanpete Valley gives way to the Sevier River valley at **Salina** ❾, where US 89 meets Interstate 70. If time permits, stop at **Miss Mary's Museum** (435-529-3968), which tells the story of Mary McCallum, a missionary and teacher who ministered to the needs of Japanese-American internees at the remote Topaz Relocation Center during World War II.

Salina was named for the salt beds formed at the bottom of an ancient sea and later pushed to the surface by intense volcanism. Just north of town, in **Redmond**, you can tour the **Red-Mound Salt Mine** (tours Apr–Oct, 435-529-7402), which produces a pinkish, mineralized salt found in gift shops throughout the area.

One museum in the Sevier Valley that you should not miss is the **Fremont Indian State Park** ❿ (daily, 435-527-4631, admission), southwest of **Richfield** in the foothills of the Pahvant Mountains. During construction of the interstate highway in 1985, archaeologists discovered a thousand-year-old Fremont Indian village and hundreds of rock art panels on the walls of Clear Creek Canyon. Inside the visitor center are exhibits of reconstructed pithouses, pottery and other artifacts. Three trails lead to pictograph panels. The park sponsors popular events, including a Mountain Man Rendezvous, atlatl (spearthrower) competitions and pottery workshops.

US 89 continues south opposite the park and follows the Sevier River into dramatic red-rock country. Even amid southern Utah's canyon scenery, **Big Rock Candy Mountain** ⓫ (435-326-4321) stands out for its whimsical colors and huge profile, rising sharply above the river. Stop at the rustic resort for refreshments. Raft trips on the river begin here.

BELOW: a family of fishermen try their luck in the headwaters of the Fremont River in Fishlake National Forest.

There are numerous hiking, biking and ATV trails in the area. West of **Marysvale**, the 2½-mile-long (4-km) Canyon of Gold scenic drive takes you from Bullion Canyon to Miners Park in the Tushar Mountains. Pick up a brochure at the start of this drive interpreting old mines and mill sites. Miners Park has mining exhibits and makes a good picnic spot. Another scenic drive into mining country begins at Junction, a few miles north of Circleville. The 40-mile (64-km) **Kimberly/Big John Scenic Byway** winds into the Tushar Mountains to the old mining camp of Kimberly, which, in the late 1800s and early 1900s, employed 300 miners. It closed in 1907 and is now a ghost town.

UT 153 continues east through dramatic Kingston Canyon (UT 62) and passes through a rugged volcanic gorge to the fishing and boating haven of **Otter Creek State Park** (435-642-3265). UT 62 connects with scenic UT 24, the main highway between pretty Sigurd and Loa, at the far end of the Torrey River valley. A left turn onto **Fishlake Scenic Byway** (UT 25) will take you to Thousand Lake Mountain, which has not a thousand but certainly many lakes. The largest, **Fish Lake** ⓬ (435-896-9233), is one of the state's premier hunting and fishing spots. It has plentiful mackinaw and rainbow trout in summer and ice fishing in winter. Game hunting for elk and deer takes place seasonally. ❑

THE GREAT BASIN

Detours here and there will lead the serendipitous traveler to ghost towns, intriguing museums and other unexpected sights in the harsh desert lands southwest of the Great Salt Lake

Map on page 190

I n the heat of the day, mirages shimmer on the salt flats like the ghosts of an ancient sea. Mountain ranges rise from the silvery illusions like the islands of Atlantis, their summits crowned with dark, distant forests that look less real than the mirages themselves. City skylines, too, occasionally appear, reflected from beyond the horizon and magnified by heat waves, then vanish like phantoms. In a landscape lacking the bare essentials to sustain life, the air itself dances.

The only part of west-central Utah that travelers routinely see is the I-80 corridor, one of the longest, hottest and emptiest freeways in America. Most motorists are en route to California or West Wendover, the tiny "Sin City" on the Nevada state line just 90 minutes from Salt Lake City. In most cases, the main objective is to get across this mind-numbing expanse as quickly as possible. But if time and temperament allow, there are several detours off the main drag that lead to intriguing museums, ghost towns, stark deserts and island-like mountains.

PRECEDING PAGES: Saltair Resort. **LEFT:** salt formations emerge from the drought-depleted Great Salt Lake. **BELOW:** lakeshore sunset.

Oolite and Copper

About 15 miles (24 km) west of Salt Lake City, for example, is the exit for **Great Salt Lake State Park ❶** (801-250-1898). The park consists of a 300-slip sailboat marina and miles of wide, grayish-white beaches along the lake's south shore. On summer weekends, city folks by the thousands pack the beach to bob like apples in the dense salt water and walk barefoot in the strange, squeaky sand, called oolite, which is made of the waste of billions of tiny brine shrimp coated in salt.

A hundred years ago, the lakeshore was the site of several elaborate beach resorts. One offered steamboat rides. Another had an elegant restaurant, a nightclub and a covered boardwalk. The most spectacular was Saltair, built in 1893 in a whimsical architectural style, with broad staircases, towers topped by bulbous Russian-style domes, and a ballroom under a five-story neo-Moorish atrium. Amusement park rides provided family entertainment, and dining options ranged from a fancy restaurant to picnic tables along the water. But with gradually declining water levels, the widening beach revealed a disadvantage of oolite sand: under the constant trampling of bathers' feet, it turned into foul-smelling mud. The resorts were gradually abandoned and, by the 1940s, demolished. Saltair, the last one left standing, was destroyed by fire in the 1960s.

Today, a smaller reproduction of **Saltair** stands on the site, the resort's trademark copper-clad Russian domes glinting in the sun. Conceived as a bed-and-breakfast, the new incarnation of Saltair has turned out to be something of a white elephant, though it is occasionally used as a pop music concert venue.

An easy side trip south of the park leads to the

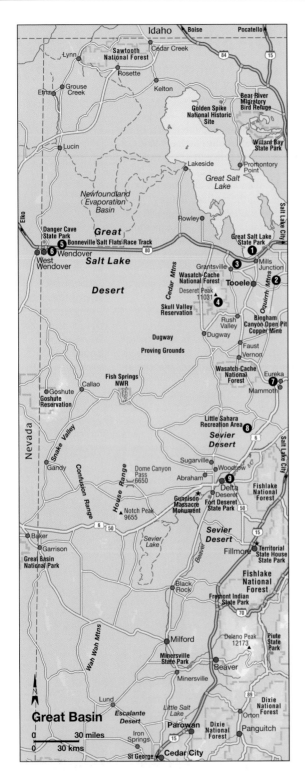

Bingham Canyon Open Pit Copper Mine ②, the largest excavated site on the planet. More than three-quarters of a mile deep (1.2 km) and 2½ miles wide (4 km), the copper pit has produced in excess of 16 million tons of copper in the past century, along with a fortune in gold, silver and molybdenum. In total, the pit has produced more tonnage of commercial metals than the California, Comstock Lode and Klondike gold rushes combined. View the pit from a visitor center perched on the rim (daily Apr–Oct 8am–8pm; UT 48, 801-252-3234).

Back on I-80, exit 99 leads to **Mills Junction**, site of **Benson Historic Grist Mill** (May–Oct Mon–Sat 10am–4pm; UT 138 and 36; 435-882-7678; free), built in 1854 by Brigham Young to grind grain for Tooele County farmers. Cabins, an old-fashioned blacksmith shop and a museum can be found at the site.

Continue south on UT 36 along the western slope of the **Oquirrh Mountains** to **Tooele**, where the principal employer is the Tooele Army Depot, a vast munitions repository. Vine Street in Tooele becomes scenic **Middle Canyon Road** and runs east for 15 miles (24 km) to 7,780-ft (2,370-meter) **Butterfield Pass** (where the pavement ends) for a panoramic view of the Salt Lake Valley. (Only high-clearance four-wheel-drive vehicles should continue over the pass.)

Salt, speed and Skull Valley

Back on I-80, exit 88 leads 10 miles (16 km) south to **Grantsville ③**, where you can visit the morbidly fascinating **Donner-Reed Museum** (Cooley and Clark Sts, 435-884-3411; appointment only). Most people familiar with Western history know the grizzly tale of the Donner party, the ill-fated pioneers who were trapped by snow in the Sierra Nevada, eventually resorting to cannibalism to survive. At the suggestion of an incompetent guide, the Donners had attempted a "short cut" across the desert, only to have their wagons bog

Map on page 190

down in the salt-encrusted earth. By the time they reached the mountains, winter was upon them. The museum preserves the possessions that the party threw away on their hellish trek across Utah, which follows roughly the same route that I-80 takes today.

Six miles (10 km) south of Grantsville, South Willow Road turns off from UT 138, providing access to an isolated section of **Wasatch-Cache National Forest** around 11,031-ft (3,362-meter) **Deseret Peak ❹**, the high point of the **Stansbury Mountains** and one of the tallest summits in the Great Basin. The peak is set within a designated wilderness area and can be climbed only on foot or horseback along a 3½-mile (5.5-km) trail that gains 3,650 ft (1,110 meters) in elevation as it ascends into cool aspen and fir forests and alpine meadows spangled with wildflowers. The summit offers what may well be the most spectacular view from any Utah mountaintop, a 360-degree panorama that takes in the Wasatch Front, the Great Salt Lake, the full expanse of the salt flat desert and the vast wastelands of the military munitions testing ranges.

Farther west on I-80, at exit 77, UT 196 runs south along the formidable western slope of the Stansbury Mountains. The road leads to the east gate of **Dugway Proving Grounds**, where the U.S. military tests chemical and biological weapons. The site is off-limits to the public. En route to Dugway is the **Skull Valley Indian Reservation**, home to about 125 Goshute Indians, the traditional inhabitants of the Great Salt Lake Desert. Surrounded by military and industrial facilities (including a weapons storage facility with the world's largest nerve-gas incinerator, a coal-fired power plant and a radioactive waste disposal site), the tiny tribe has considered using reservation land for storage of spent nuclear rods and using the income to move to another location.

BELOW: setting up camp in the Stansbury Mountains.

Signs marks the route of the Pony Express Trail across the western desert.

BELOW:
a gravestone in Skull Valley marks the final resting place of a Hawaiian convert to the Mormon faith.

To the west, I-80 runs straight as an arrow for some 75 miles (120 km) across the Great Salt Lake Desert. The barren, sugar-white salt flats are a remnant of **Lake Bonneville**, an inland sea the size of Lake Michigan that partly evaporated 15,000 years ago. This is the setting for the **Bonneville Salt Flats Race Track** ❺ (I-80 exit 4, 801-977-4300), where automobiles have been setting land speed records since 1914. The first unofficial record, set by celebrity daredevil Teddy Tezlaff, was 141.73 mph (228.1 km/h); in 1970, Gary Gabolich's rocket car reached 622.4 mph (1,001.7 km/h), which is still the record for Bonneville Salt Flats, though a speed of 763 mph (1,227.9 km/h) was set in 1997 at Black Rock Desert in Nevada.

Pressed up against the state line is the little town of **Wendover** ❻, most of whose 1,600 residents work at adjacent Wendover Air Force Base or the nearby potash mines. The town's main street is lined with modest mom-and-pop motels, now prospering thanks to the cluster of casino resorts that loom just inches from the state line in West Wendover, Nevada. For those interested in exploring the backcountry, the unpaved 54-mile (87-km) **Silver Island Mountain Loop** heads north along the edge of the Great Salt Lake Desert. The byway passes Danger Cave State Park, where archaeologists have discovered evidence of human habitation from 11,000 years ago, the oldest such site in Utah. The park is undeveloped; the cave entrance is blocked with an iron gate to prevent vandalism.

Lonely road

Another route across Utah's Great Basin is US 6, dubbed "the loneliest highway in America." Running roughly southwest from I-15 to the Nevada border, it's a passage into the stark beauty of the western desert.

GREAT BASIN NATIONAL PARK

Situated in Nevada, just over the Utah border, Great Basin National Park encompasses a fascinating array of ecosystems, ranging from low-lying, sun-blasted desert to the stony crags of 13,063-ft (3,982-meter) Wheeler Peak. The park's best-known feature, Lehman Caves, is a limestone cave complex filled with stalactites, stalagmites and other bizarre rock formations. Ranger-guided tours are available.

On the surface, the Wheeler Peak Scenic Drive winds up the mountain to an overlook with sweeping views of the surrounding landscape. From here, a demanding 5-mile (8-km) trail leads intrepid visitors to the summit. One of the highlights of driving the mountain road is getting a close-up view of Great Basin bristlecone pines, some more than 4,000 years old. Slow growth rates and unremitting winds account for the trees' gnarled appearance.

Another highlight is Lexington Arch. Quite different from the sandstone arches of southern Utah, the existence of this 75-ft-high (23-meter) limestone span baffles geologists. Some theorize that it is the remnant of a cavern eroded from entrances at both ends.

The park is about 100 miles (160 km) west of Delta via US 6/50. It has a visitor center and primitive campgrounds.

Eureka ❼, 35 miles (56 km) southwest of Spanish Fork, was the center of the silver-rich Tintic Mining District. Today, this village of weather-beaten shacks and boarded-up storefronts has a single tourist attraction: the **Tintic Mining Museum** (daily 10am–4pm; 241 W. Main St, 435-433-6842 or 435-433-6869), which occupies the old brick city hall and nearby train station. Among the exhibits are the interior of a typical miner's home, a replica of an old saloon, and a scale model of a silver mine.

About 3 miles (5 km) south of Eureka is the ghost town of **Mammoth**. Though not completely abandoned (there are still about 60 residents), it's a mere shadow of the bustling mining camp that stood here in the 1890s.

Just off US 6, about 35 miles (56 km) southwest of Eureka, is the **Little Sahara Recreation Area ❽** (435-743-6811), the largest expanse of sand dunes in Utah, some standing 700 ft high (215 meters). The dunes owe their existence to windborne sand scoured from the Sevier Desert to the southwest and deposited at the foot of the **Tintic Mountains**. The recreation area, a favorite of off-road vehicle enthusiasts, also has a 9,000-acre (3,600-hectare) nature preserve where only hikers are allowed. There are four campgrounds as well as picnic areas.

Farther along US 6, in the little town of **Delta ❾**, is the **Great Basin Museum** (Mon–Sat 10am–4pm; 328 West 100 North, 435-864-5013; donation). In addition to Indian and pioneer artifacts and a collection of historic photographs, the museum has an excellent exhibit on the Topaz Relocation Camp, where more than 8,000 Japanese-Americans from California were confined during World War II. Topaz was situated about 17 miles (27 km) northwest of town.

South of Delta, near the tiny town of **Deseret**, is **Fort Deseret State Park**. The undeveloped site encompasses the ruins of an adobe fort built as a defense against Paiute Indians during the Black Hawk War of 1865–68. The fort was never attacked, though local settlers huddled within its walls for about a month. After the war, the structure was occupied by Indians, who used it for shelter and storage.

The **Gunnison Massacre Monument**, about 6 miles (10 km) farther south, memorializes the killing of a U.S. government survey party by Indians during an earlier conflict, the Walker War of 1853. Historians still debate whether the local Mormons, who resented federal incursions into Utah, warned the surveyors of hostile Indians or simply sent them to their deaths.

From Delta, US 6 runs about 100 miles (160 km) across the barren expanse of the **Sevier Desert**, where the usually dry bed of Sevier Lake extends southward for nearly 40 miles (65 km). Travelers with an adventurous spirit and a rugged vehicle can follow the unpaved 50-mile (80-km) **Notch Peak Loop** into the **House Range**. The route crosses the mountains at 6,430-ft (1,960-meter) **Dome Creek Pass** and then follows the western slope back to US 6. The highway passes through the picturesque **Confusion Mountains** before descending into the **Snake Valley** near the state line. **Great Basin National Park** is 18 miles (29 km) across the border in Nevada. ❑

BELOW: kids play in Davenport Creek in the Stansbury Mountains, a precious source of water in the parched Great Basin.

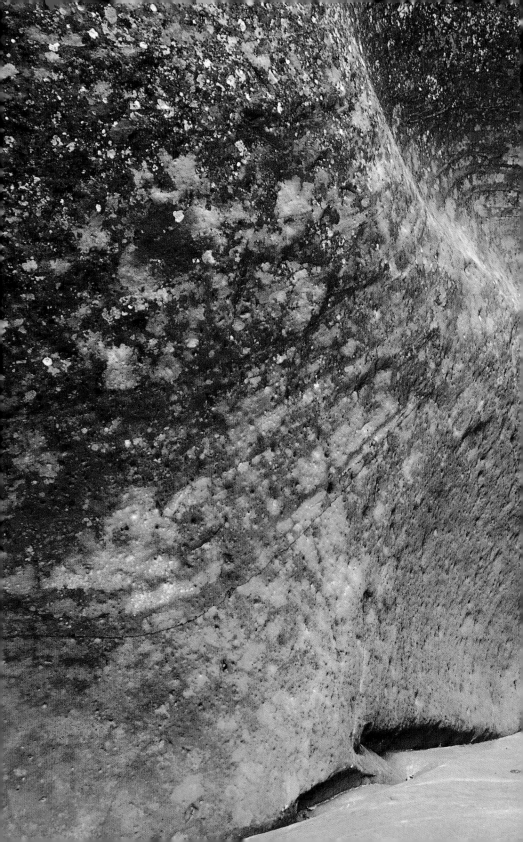

SOUTHERN UTAH

Rock is the leitmotiv of this otherworldly landscape – layers
and layers of it, rearranged by time and the elements

In 1869, after a two-month journey down the Green River from Wyoming, an expedition led by explorer John Wesley Powell reached the confluence of the Green and Colorado Rivers, one of the most remote spots on the North American continent. Here, in the heart of what Powell called "the Great Unknown," both rivers lay deep within the earth, imprisoned by sheer cliffs of their own making, part of a mile-high, 130,000-square-mile (330,000-sq-km) elevated geophysical province known as the Colorado Plateau.

Today, travelers can drive across southern Utah in a matter of hours on paved roads, but there remains no fast route to appreciating the beauty and scope of the geography that so captivated Powell: you simply need time, and plenty of it – anywhere from a week to a year to a lifetime. Nature, pure and simple, rules here, in a continually meta-morphosing landscape whose predominant feature is bare sedimentary rock rearranged by volcanism along deep faults and eroded by water, weather and time.

Within a 250-mile (400-km) radius lie 12 national parks, 14 national monuments, seven tribal parks, 17 wilderness areas, seven state parks and six national forests – such a wealth of extraordinary destinations, it has been dubbed the Grand Circle. Southern Utah is the meeting place of three deserts and a series of progressively higher plateaus on its west side known as the Grand Staircase, elevated by recent volcan-ism and carved into breathtaking river canyons by tributaries of the Colorado. East of the Colorado River and above the San Juan River, southeastern Utah is even more remote. This is the heart of Canyon Country, preserved in Canyonlands and Arches National Parks, Glen Canyon National Recreation Area and Monument Valley, centerpiece of the Navajo Nation.

Interstates 15 and 70 and scenic byways 89, 12, 24, 95 and 191 wrap around this broken country of arches and natural bridges; standing fins of rock; monoclines, anticlines, synclines and laccoliths; collapsed salt valleys; and cool forested volcanic peaks and drifting mesa tablelands. The population is sparse, the few towns of any consequence – St. George, Kanab, Escalante, Torrey, Hanksville, Green River, Moab, Monticello, Blanding and Mexican Hat – many miles apart and deter-minedly Mormon. It is country difficult to travel through and easy to get lost in, as human travelers, from prehistoric desert nomads and mounted Utes and Navajos to pueblo-building Indians, Spanish and American explorers, Mormon settlers, and an increasing number of outdoor lovers, can attest. That, for most, is its greatest attraction. ❑

PRECEDING PAGES: a hiker takes a break while exploring Heath Wash in Cottonwood Canyon near St. George.
LEFT: a backpacker crosses Uranium Arch in the red-rock wilderness near Moab.

ZION NATIONAL PARK AND THE ST. GEORGE AREA

*Soaring cliffs, sandstone monoliths and narrow canyons
are a few of the attractions that lure travelers to this
spellbinding red-rock wilderness*

Maps:
Area 211
Park 202

Set in the rocky heart of southern Utah's convoluted canyon country, **Zion National Park ❶** is nature at its most eloquent, a dramatic juxtaposition of towering sandstone monoliths, narrow slot canyons, fast-flowing water, dense greenery and myriad wildlife. From afar, the park's enormous buttes and domes rise like temples beckoning the faithful. Up close, its sheltering walls offer a protected sanctuary. For the Mormon settlers who came here in the mid-1800s, this seemed to be Zion, "the Heavenly City of God." A national park since 1919, Zion annually draws 2½ million "worshippers" who marvel at the extraordinary geology and natural beauty found in these precipitous canyons.

Dramatically eroded sedimentary rocks are what give Zion its character and have led to its fame. Eight different rock strata may be found in the vicinity, all of which were deposited over a period of 260 million years, as geologic instability and changing climates and topography brought a succession of inland seas, lakes, rivers, streams, volcanic debris and even a dune-filled desert into the region. It is the latter that was responsible for the park's dominant rocks, the sheer, creamy-pink Navajo Sandstone cliffs, which reach a height of 2,200 ft (671 meters).

PRECEDING PAGES:
San Juan River.
LEFT: the Watchman
rises over a field of
daisies in Springdale.
BELOW: a badger
emerges from its
burrow near Zion
National Park.

Reading the rocks

The best way to "read the rocks" is to drive into Zion from the west, via Hurricane, along UT 9, following the course of the pretty Virgin River through spick-and-span villages into the park's South Entrance. From Hurricane, 25 miles (40 km) away, you drive over the dramatic Hurricane Fault in the Kaibab Limestone cliffs, whose marine sediments make up the rim-rock of Grand Canyon, and into the Virgin River Canyon, encountering progressively younger rocks on the journey east.

Near the community of **Virgin**, the banded Moenkopi Formation is visible. A little farther along, above the colorful gardens of postcard-pretty Rockville, the mul-tihued Chinle Formation forms crumbling hills scattered with dinosaur-era petrified wood. At **Springdale**, the red mud shales of the Moenave are visible beneath vermilion-colored Kayenta rocks that sometimes display dinosaur tracks. The sheer cliffs of Navajo Sandstone are now everywhere in sight, topped occasionally by the rounded bald domes of the Great White Throne and other landmarks. In the farther reaches of the park, younger Carmel Limestone and Dakota Formation appear on only the highest mountains.

The corrosive power of flash-flooding rivers, ephemeral waterfalls and seeping water is primarily responsible for the deep canyons, etched rock faces,

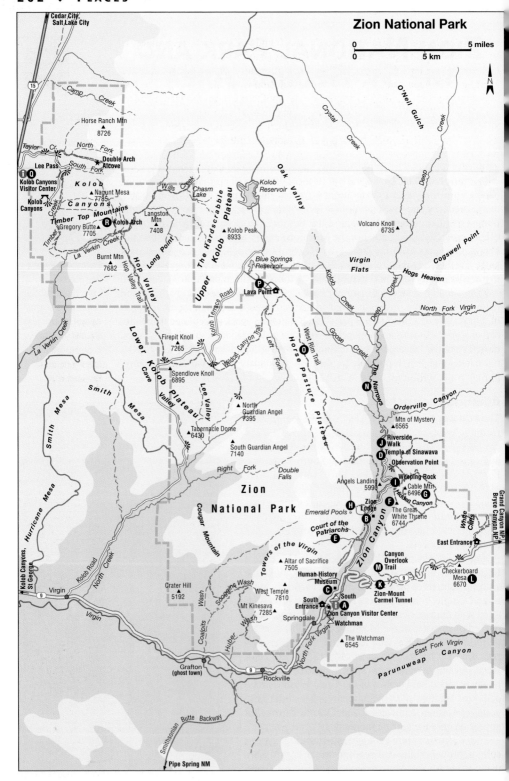

Zion National Park

0   5 miles
0   5 km

Cedar City,
Salt Lake City

O'Neil Gulch

Camp Creek

Crystal Creek

Horse Ranch Mtn
8726

North Fork

Taylor Cr.

South Fork

Double Arch
Alcove

Lee Pass

Kolob Canyons
Visitor Center

Kolob
Canyons

Kolob Canyons

Nagunt Mesa
7785

Kolob
Canyons

Wills Creek

Chasm
Lake

Kolob
Reservoir

Oak Valley

Deep Creek

Cogswell Point

Volcano Knoll
6735

Timber Top Mountains

Gregory Butte
7705

Kolob Arch

Langston
Mtn
7408

Kolob Peak
8933

The Hardscrabble

Upper Kolob Plateau

Blue Springs
Reservoir

Lava Point

Virgin
Flats

Hogs Heaven

North Fork Virgin

Burnt Mtn
7682

Hop Valley

Long Point

La Verkin Creek

Hop Valley Trail

Kolob Terrace Road

Wildcat Canyon Trail

West Rim Trail

Horse Pasture Plateau

Kolob Creek

Goose Creek

Deep Creek

Firepit Knoll
7265

Lower Kolob Plateau

Cave Valley

Spendlove Knoll
6895

Lee Valley

Left Fork

The Narrows

Orderville Canyon

La Verkin Creek

Smith Mesa

Smith

Mesa

North
Guardian Angel
7395

Tabernacle Dome
6430

South Guardian Angel
7140

Mtn of Mystery
6565

Riverside
Walk

Temple of Sinawava

Observation Point

Right Fork

Double
Falls

Angels Landing
5990

Weeping Rock

Cable Mtn
6496

Hidden Canyon

Zion

National Park

Cougar Mountain

Emerald Pools

Court of the
Patriarchs

Zion
Lodge

The Great
White Throne
6744

White Cliffs

Zion Canyon

East Entrance

Grand Canyon NP/
Bryce Canyon NP

Kolob Canyons,
Hurricane Mesa

Kolob Road

North Creek

Crater Hill
5192

Altar of Sacrifice
7505

Towers of the Virgin

West Temple
7810

Human History
Museum

Canyon
Overlook
Trail

Checkerboard
Mesa
6670

Kolob Canyons,
St George

Virgin

Virgin

Scoggins Wash

Coalpits Wash

Huber Wash

Mt Kinesava
7285

South
Entrance

Springdale

South
Entrance

Zion Canyon Visitor Center

Watchman

Zion-Mount
Carmel Tunnel

The Watchman
6545

Grafton
(ghost town)

Rockville

East Fork Virgin

Canyon

Parunuweap

North Fork Virgin

Smithsonian Butte Backway

Pipe Spring NM

smooth domes and colorfully streaked rocks found at Zion. Hard though it is to believe, the North Fork of the Virgin River (a modest-sized tributary of the Colorado River), which rises at 9,000 ft (2,750 meters) on the tableland of the Markagunt Plateau just north of Zion, carved Zion Canyon.

Map: opposite page

Beginning some 15 million years ago, the southern Colorado Plateau underwent a period of violent geologic activity that caused it to break and weather along faults into distinctive plateaus. The Hurricane Fault, a southern spur of the Wasatch Fault, rivals California's San Andreas Fault for activity. In 1992, a powerful earthquake centered in St. George caused a large rock slide in Springdale, still visible along UT 9. Zion is riddled with fractures in the soft rocks, which, combined with water erosion, account for the unusual U shape of its canyons and the great spalling arches (locally called "bridges") in its sheer walls.

The Virgin River cut into its course as the land rose around it, scouring soft rock and bearing away sediments, which end up in Lake Mead far to the south. The Colorado and its tributaries remove strata from this portion of the uplifted Colorado Plateau at differing rates, giving the canyon country a colorful, stepped look, referred to as the Grand Staircase. This can best be seen looking north over the Arizona Strip from a viewpoint on the Kaibab Plateau, south of Zion.

The reds and pinks (and, occasionally, yellows and browns) found in the rocks at Zion generally result from iron within the rock, which has been washed through by percolating groundwater. Dark streaking, as on the Altar of Sacrifice, occurs when water falling over sheer precipices leaches minerals from vegetation or caprock. Weathering of organic material on rock faces also causes shiny "desert varnish," fixed by bacteria on the face of the rock, perhaps the most dramatic of all rock coatings in the Southwest.

BELOW:
a dinosaur footprint is preserved in sandstone outside St. George.

All aboard

Most visitors arrive in Zion via the South Entrance, which adjoins the gateway community of Springdale. In 2000, the community of Springdale and Zion National Park unveiled an integrated transportation and visitor services plan that has won awards as a model for how public-private partnerships can work elsewhere in the park system. The linchpin of this plan is a two-loop, free shuttle system, operating from April 1 to October 31, which run about 3 miles (5 km) from Springdale, then about 9 miles (14 km) from the visitor center to the top of Zion Canyon. The 60-seat buses run from 5.30am to 11pm and arrive every 6 to 10 minutes during the peak summer season.

You can now park at one of several lots next to hotels and restaurants in Springdale, hop aboard the Springdale shuttle and go directly to the visitor center to pick up the Zion Canyon shuttle, without ever dealing with overcrowded parking lots. The virtue of this for busy sightseers is that you can effectively enjoy a pleasant, two-hour narrated bus tour of one of the most popular national parks (free with park entrance) and still easily get on and off at major attractions in the canyon to hike popular trails and visit historic Zion Lodge. Best of all, narrow Zion Canyon has been positively transformed from a clogged, noisy thoroughfare deserted by all but the boldest wildlife into a quiet, idyllic Southwest river

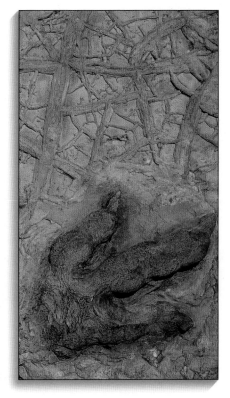

A shaft of light illuminates the Virgin River Narrows.

BELOW: cairns mark the route of the Emerald Pools Trail.

canyon, where the emphasis is back on appreciating nature, scenery and walking.

Zion Canyon Visitor Center (9am–5pm, to 7pm in summer; 435-772-3256), just inside the park boundary in the shadow of the **Watchman**, **West Temple** and **Towers of the Virgin**, has been relocated, rethought, and improved. Now sited on the south bank of the East Fork of the Virgin River, the handsome building has been constructed in a harmonious neo-rustic architectural style using native sandstone and heavy timbers, echoing the architecture of the 1930s, much of it carried out by the Civilian Conservation Corps, which built lodges and other infrastructure in Zion and Springdale. Modern touches include passive solar and twin state-of-the-art evaporative cooling towers that make the building a pleasant haven when summer temperatures soar into the triple digits.

New and improved

The role of water in shaping Zion is now obvious. From the riverside patio, you can listen to the river burbling over rocks and trickling through irrigation ditches while you plan your visit to the park using outdoor interpretive panels or listen to a ranger talk. Inside the building, three short films give an overview of the park, and the large bookstore run by the Zion Natural History Association sells maps, books and other interpretive materials. Staffed kiosks offer registration for Zion Lodge and backcountry permits, required for overnight backpacking trips in the park and backcountry hikes in such places as Zion Narrows, the Subway and Mystery Canyon. Canyoneering, a sport that involves rappelling into narrow slot canyons, is wildly popular in Zion, and you may have difficulty getting a permit for the best-known hikes if you don't reserve ahead of time. Contact the Backcountry Office for more information. Frequent back-

country hikers in Zion can now reserve and pay for permits on the park website (www.nps.gov/zion) but only after visiting the park in person to sign up and view a video on safe travel in the backcountry.

There are two developed campgrounds in Zion Canyon itself. The 160-site **Watchman Campground** and 161-site **South Campground**, just beyond the visitor center. Sites in Watchman Campground can be reserved by calling 800-365-CAMP or logging on to www.reservations.nps.gov; South Campground is first-come, first-served. The primitive 6-site **Lava Point Campground** next to the West Rim Trail on Kolob Terrace is open only in summer, has no water, and is also first-come, first-served. The log-framed **Zion Lodge ❸** (303-297-2757; www.amfac.com) in Zion Canyon was built in the 1920s by the now-defunct Utah Parks Company to accommodate well-heeled park visitors and is now on the National Register of Historic Places. With its ice-cream fountain, pleasant gift shop, manicured lawns, shady trees and woodsy cabins, it's a good spot to take a breather or get something to eat or drink. Just don't expect to stay here without reservations; bookings must usually be secured a year in advance. Most people spend the night in one of the many inns, motels and bed-and-breakfasts in pretty little Springdale, which also has an excellent assortment of restaurants, from juice bars and espresso joints to steak houses and nouvelle cuisine.

Map on page 202

Seeing the park

The first shuttle stop after the visitor center is the new **Human History Museum ❻** (9am–5pm, to 7pm in summer), housed in the old park visitor center. The museum tells the human story of Zion from the Virgin Anasazi Indians and Kaibab Paiutes who used the park seasonally to Mormon pioneers like the Behunin, Heaps and Rolfe families who first home-steaded the canyon, across from Zion Lodge, in 1862. The 6-mile (10-km) scenic drive begins at the stone bridge where the North and East Forks of the Virgin River join, then heads north, paralleling the tree-lined banks of the Virgin River all the way to the amphi-theater of the **Temple of Sinawava ❶** and the popular **Riverside Walk**. Within this short drive are the **Court of the Patriarchs ❸**, the **Great White Throne ❺** and **Cable Mountain ❻**, as well as shady hiking trails surrounded by dripping rocks and colorful hang-ing plants. From here, you can set out on longer hikes into the high country, or simply dream away the day deep in the canyon paddling in the river shallows.

BELOW: a hiker takes in the view of Zion Canyon from Angels Landing.

Three short hiking trails – to **Emerald Pools ❶** (2 miles/3 km), **Weeping Rock ❶** (1½ miles/2 km) and **Riverside Walk ❶** (2 miles/3 km) – meander through side canyons populated by singleleaf ash, manzanita, cliff rose and Gambel oak. Here, contact between the porous Navajo Sandstone and impervious Kayenta river sandstones and shales below it has created seeping rocks, known as springlines, which are home to delight-ful "hanging gardens" of mosses, ferns, monkeyflowers and columbines, as well as the park's unique Zion snail. Another leitmotiv of the park is sacred datura or jim-sonweed, known locally as Zion lily, a poisonous, white-trumpeted flower that opens at night along waysides.

Other trails, most of them found close to Zion

Lodge, lead to famous landmarks, such as the **Court of the Patriarchs** (300 ft/ 90 meters), **Angels Landing** (5 miles/8 km) and **Hidden Canyon** (2 miles/3 km, between Cable Mountain and the Great White Throne). Eight-mile (13-km) **Observation Point Trail** skirts the base of Cable Mountain before climbing through woodlands, offering stunning views of the Great White Throne, Cable Mountain, the West Rim, Angels Landing and Zion Canyon.

Zion is the most popular national park in Utah, with more than 2.4 million visitors a year.

The East Rim

Many people choose to drive or bicycle 10 miles (16km) to the East Rim of Zion via the **Zion-Mount Carmel Highway** (UT 9), which follows a tributary of the Virgin River. The road climbs in dramatic zigzag fashion through the canyon until it enters the 1-mile-long (1.6-km) **Zion-Mount Carmel Tunnel 🅚**, built in 1930 to shorten the route between Zion and Bryce Canyon and Grand Canyon National Parks. (Note: There are strictly enforced size restrictions on vehicles using the tunnel. Check with the park in advance.) Just before you reach the tunnel, the road passes beneath a huge blind alcove known as the Great Arch of Zion.

On the other side of the tunnel, you climb to an elevation of 7,000 ft (2,000 meters), where the highway passes through a landscape of marvelously eroded formations, which are exactly what they look like: "petrified" sand dunes. The most distinctive is spectacular **Checkerboard Mesa 🅛**, a huge, creamy giant with crosshatched surfaces caused by horizontal cross-bedding in the dunes and later deepening of vertical fractures by water erosion. If you have time, hike the **Canyon Overlook Trail 🅜** next to the East Portal of the Zion-Mount Carmel Tunnel. It sits directly above the Great Arch of Zion and offers an unusual view of Zion Canyon and a superb introduction to some of Zion's key natural features.

BELOW: snow-covered trees frame a view of the Towers of the Virgin and the Beehives.

Map on page 202

Wildlife and white water

Four different life zones are to be found in the 3,650–8,725-ft (1,100–2,650-meter) elevations at Zion, encompassing desert, riparian, woodland and coniferous forest. In the low, dry areas of the canyons, heavy-fruited pricklypear cactus is found alongside desert residents, such as whip-tailed and desert spiny lizards, slow-moving chuckwallas and, occasionally, western rattlesnakes.

The river is a perfect refuge when temperatures reach 100°F (38°C) or higher in summer. Throngs of Fremont cottonwoods, box elders, willows and velvet ash crowd its banks, sharing the location with bank beavers, gnatcatchers and insects, as well as footsore hikers. The high country supports ponderosa pine, Rocky Mountain juniper and sagebrush, as well as oak, Douglas fir, quaking aspen and numerous wildflowers.

At twilight, you may glimpse a coyote, mule deer or bighorn sheep, the latter a recent return resident at Zion. Mountain lions, bobcats, badgers, foxes and weasels lead very private lives here and are rarely encountered. Your companions throughout much of the park will be sociable little ground squirrels, camp-robbing ringtails and noisy ravens and pinyon jays, whose chatter usually drowns out the melodic descant sonata of canyon wrens and other songbirds. During the summer rainy season, the full impact of water on rock is evident. Torrents pour off vertical rock faces in magnificent waterfalls, and the swollen Virgin River speeds noisily over and around boulders.

In spring, when snowmelt is greatest, or during summer rainstorms, don't even think of wading the 16-mile (26-km) **Narrows Trail Ⓝ**, which follows the Virgin River through Orderville Canyon, a slot canyon that is 2,000 ft (600 meters) high and in places only 20 ft (6 meters) wide. During heavy rainstorms,

BELOW: a party of hikers crosses the Virgin River on the popular Narrows Trail.

ZION'S PARKITECTURE

Almost as memorable as Zion's naturally sculpted cliffs and canyons are the many examples of the rustic architecture preserved in the park. This building style dominated park architecture in the 1920s and 1930s and required buildings and other man-made structures to match their surroundings in scale, materials and color. The 1930 Pine Creek Bridge, for example, is an acknowledged work of art made entirely of Navajo Sandstone with a cemented rubblestone core and hand-hewn sandstone slabs reflecting all the colors of Zion – tan, brown, pink, red, purple, even green.

Much of this attractive "parkitecture" was built by young recruits in the Civilian Conservation Corps, organized during the Depression as a government-sponsored labor force. This was more than a make-work program designed to assist unemployed youth. The young men of "Roosevelt's Tree Army" embodied a resurgence of America's pioneer ethic and native optimism. In Zion, the Corps constructed trails, houses and park buildings and cut and shaped stone at a quarry a mile west of Springdale. They also built and maintained irrigation ditches, providing a visible link between the pioneers and the young men who sought to emulate them years later.

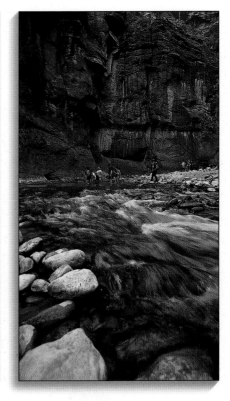

flash floods may funnel through the canyon at the speed of a runaway train, destroying everything in their path. Plan to make the trip in dry summer months, and even if you are just wading the southern section from the end of Riverside Walk, get a weather forecast before starting out. The Narrows Trail is in the riverbed, so be prepared to stay wet for hours in a chilly, sunless environment. Don't try to do the whole hike in one day – wading through water for 12 hours is grueling. Reserve a campsite inside the canyon and enjoy the hike.

Equally strenuous is the one-way 13-mile (21-km) **West Rim Trail O**, which links Zion Canyon with **Lava Point P** through breathtaking mountainous country in the central Kolob Terrace area of the park. Extend the trip by taking Wildcat Canyon Trail into the beautifully carved Finger Canyons of the Kolob district. You can also drive to **Kolob Canyons**, proceeding west on UT 9, then north to Exit 40 on Interstate 15.

Check in at **Kolob Canyons Visitor Center Q** (8am–4.30pm, extended summer hours; 435-772-3256) before taking the 5-mile (8-km) scenic drive through the folded and eroded vermilion-colored cliffs. A lot of people miss visiting Kolob Canyons because of its distance from the main park, but there are some fascinating hikes in this section, including a strenuous, 14-mile (23-km) round-trip to 310-ft (94-meter) **Kolob Arch R**, the world's longest natural arch.

Beyond the park

BELOW:
a bigtooth maple is aflame with autumn color at Emerald Pools Falls.

Base yourself in Springdale for a few days and explore southwestern Utah's scenic byways and backways. The unpaved **Smithsonian Butte Backway** links Rockville with UT 59 on the Arizona Strip, passing **Grafton** on the south side of the river, a ghost town that was abandoned after the Great Flood of 1861–62.

For years, Rockville residents, descendants of the original settlers, looked after the town and farmed adjoining fields. The whole town is now preserved as a historic site. Roadside interpretive signs can be found opposite the townsite, on UT 9, just before you get to Rockville.

The scenic backway offers an excellent shortcut to the Arizona Strip, which gets its name from the narrow swath of Arizona that borders Utah between the Grand Canyon and the Vermilion Cliffs. Drive east on UT 59 into Arizona, where the highway changes number to AZ 389. After 30 minutes, you'll reach **Pipe Spring National Monument ❷** (visitor center daily 7am–5pm in summer, 9am–5pm in winter, tours every 30 minutes in summer; 928-643-7105; admission), one of those small but fascinating units that abound in the park system but often get overlooked. Prehistoric Virgin Anasazi people, Kaibab Paiutes (whose reservation surrounds Pipe Spring), and early western settlers were all attracted to this spot because of the natural springs that come bubbling up the Sevier Fault in the Vermilion Cliffs. Pipe Spring is a fortified ranch built by the Mormons in 1870 to accommodate the Church's burgeoning cattle herds. During the 1880s, it served as a hideout for the wives of polygamous elders in nearby communities like Fredonia and Kanab, which were under surveillance by the federal government.

The fort and its outlying cabins, corrals, pens and ponds have been preserved very much as they were in their heyday, when Anson Winsor and his wife constructed the two modest stone houses that were dubbed Winsor Castle (a punning reference to Winsor's British roots). Pipe Spring served as a base for John Wesley Powell, the Colorado River explorer, during his survey of the region in 1871-72.

Descendants of the original Kaibab Paiute and Anglo settlers still live in the area and maintain a strong attachment to Pipe Spring. The administrative offices

> **Maps:**
> **Area 211**
> **Park 202**

BELOW: Mount Kinesava looms over Grafton ghost town on the banks of the Virgin River.

Coyote tracks mark the rippled surface of Coral Pink Sand Dunes State Park.

BELOW: the St. George temple was the first Mormon temple dedicated in Utah.

of the Kaibab Band of Paiutes is across the road, and the tribe operates a small campground next to the park, holds a powwow in October, and offers guided hiking tours of rock art sites. The tribe and the National Park Service are also involved in a joint partnership: a new museum in the park visitor center containing 12 exhibits interpreting the Ancestral Pueblo, Kaibab Paiute and Mormon cultures.

Hollywood favorite

Directly ahead is the AZ 389/US 89 junction in the tiny Mormon hamlet of **Fredonia**, which has a smattering of homestyle restaurants and motels. From here, you can either drive south to the Kaibab Plateau to visit the North Rim of the Grand Canyon or head north on US 89 to Kanab, just over the border back in Utah.

Kanab ❸, at the crossroads of US 89 and 89A, is a fine place to spend the night, have a meal, and explore the surrounding canyons, which, for decades, have been used as backdrops in the movies. The Bureau of Land Management, which manages adjoining Grand Staircase-Escalante National Monument and the little-known Grand Canyon-Parashant National Monument, south of the highway, has an office in downtown Kanab (435-644-2672), where you can get information on visiting their lands. Return to Zion by heading north on US 89, turning left onto UT 9 at Mount Carmel and driving into the park through the East Entrance. Just south of Mount Carmel is a turnoff for **Coral Pink Sand Dunes State Park** (UT 43, 435-648-2800), a 3,730-acre (1,510-hectare) expanse of rust-colored dunes deposited by winds funneled at great speed through a notch in the mountains. The park is a favorite with drivers of motorcycles and ATVs. A section is reserved for hikers, though in summer the dunes are sizzling hot.

Blink-and-you'll-miss-it **Mount Carmel ❹** was a favorite of famed western artist Maynard Dixon, who, in the 1940s, spent his summers here, painting the Grand Staircase and other colorful formations that are now called Maynard Dixon Country. Between May and October each year, volunteers offer guided tours of the rustic **Maynard Dixon Home and Studio** (435-648-2653, www.maynarddixon.com). The foundation also sponsors an annual three-day gala featuring 15 to 20 artists and an art sale at Dixon's former home.

Map below

Around St. George

Kanab is an excellent base for day trips to sites on the east side of the Markagunt Plateau, such as Zion, Pipe Spring, Cedar Breaks, Bryce Canyon and Grand Staircase-Escalante National Monument. More convenient to the I-15 corridor, though, is **St. George ❺**, southwestern Utah's largest town and, at two hours from Las Vegas and four hours from Salt Lake City, the area's fastest growing community.

Founded in 1861 by members of the Cotton Mission and known as Utah's Dixie because of its moderate winters, St. George was chosen by Brigham Young as the site of his **Winter Home**. Here, Young oversaw construction of the dazzlingly white **St. George Temple** and the sandstone **Tabernacle**, both completed in the 1870s by workers who, incidentally, were fed by meat and cheese from Pipe Spring's dairy herds. Only Mormons in good standing may enter the Temple, but the adjoining visitor center is open to all and is a good place to find out more about the LDS faith (daily 9am–9pm; 435-673-5181; free). You can also take a guided tour of the Tabernacle (daily 9am–6pm; 435-628-4072). Docents at these sites are friendly, older Mormons, volunteering to fulfil their "second mission" – designed to bring converts into the Church. If you already have a religious affiliation, be sure to say so, to avoid any efforts at proselytizing.

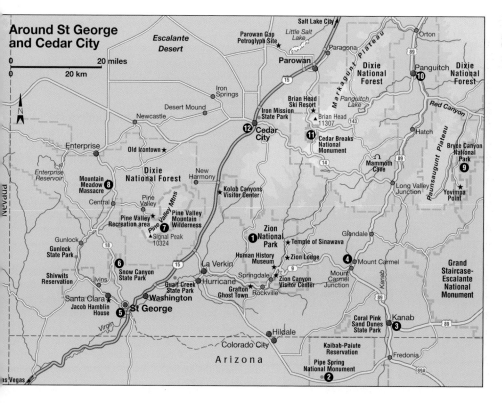

Around St George and Cedar City

Map on page 211

Artifacts from the town's pioneer days are exhibited at the **Daughters of the Utah Pioneers Museum** (Mon–Sat 10am–5pm; 435-628-7274; free). The museum, Winter Home, Temple, Tabernacle and other historic buildings are within walking distance of **Ancestor Square** in the town center. Ancestor Square includes several historic buildings that have been converted to restaurants, stores and businesses. You may also enjoy strolling around the Dixie College campus, south of Main. Like Southern Utah University in Cedar City, it is a four-year college and hosts cultural events, including a popular arts festival. Located on the northern edge of the Mojave Desert (with its characteristic Joshua trees), St. George gets pretty hot in summer, but with 10 golf courses, a premium store outlet and other attractions, it's a good base for visitors.

If you have time, take the drive west of St. George to several important natural and cultural attractions. In the pastoral, fruit-growing town of **Santa Clara**, you can visit the **Jacob Hamblin House** (June–Sept, 9am–9pm; 435-673-2161; free), built by the famous Mormon missionary and friend of John Wesley Powell, in 1862. A 24-mile (37-km) loop from St. George takes you to **Snow Canyon State Park ❻** (daily 6am–10pm; 435-628-2255; admission), which combines red Navajo Sandstone and lava formations in a unique setting. The surreal landscape around Snow Canyon has been a favorite with filmmakers for years. John Wayne made several movies here. Camping, picnicking and horseback riding are available; several backcountry hikes offer an excellent opportunity to observe specially adapted desert plants and animals, such as desert tortoises, a rarely seen endangered species found in the hot, dry country around St. George.

The lava formations in Snow Canyon came from the volcano that built adjoining 10,324-ft (3,147-meter) **Pine Valley Mountain ❼**, the imposing peak that looms over St. George. **Pine Valley Recreation Area** in Dixie National Forest is a good place to escape the sizzling summer temperatures at lower elevations and has excellent cross-country skiing in winter. You can take longer hikes and backpack in the adjoining 50,000-acre (20,000-hectare) **Pine Valley Mountain Wilderness**.

BELOW: Brigham Young's Winter Home. **RIGHT:** a footbridge arches over the Virgin River in Zion National Park.

A bloody episode

UT 18 continues all the way to **Gunlock Reservoir**, a popular fishing spot. Before you get there, the highway passes through a large, quiet grassy valley where the wind always seems to be moaning. This is **Mountain Meadow ❽**, where the worst (and least talked about) atrocity in Mormon history took place in 1857, at a time when tensions between Mormons and the federal government were causing widespread anxiety. Fear turned to tragedy when a party of emigrants bound for California passed through southern Utah and harassed Mormon farmers and Indians. In anger, a group of Paiutes and Mormons led by John D. Lee cornered the emigrants in Mountain Meadows, lured them out with a promise of safe passage, and then massacred 120 people, sparing only the youngest children.

After evading capture for 20 years, Lee was forced by the LDS Church to surrender to authorities, and was tried, found guilty, and executed atop his own coffin at the site of the massacre. A somber granite marker records the names of the emigrants who perished. ❏

BRYCE CANYON AND THE CEDAR CITY AREA

Maps:
Area 211
Park 218

Erosion has sculpted a landscape of knobs, "hoodoos" and desert scenery in a corner of Utah where visitors also find such unexpected attractions as a ski resort and Shakespearean festival

Some landscapes are so remarkable that many people are never the same again after seeing them. **Bryce Canyon National Park ❾** in southern Utah is one such place. A geologic fantasyland of Kodacolor dreaming spires, natural bridges, gravity-defying arches, precariously balanced rocks and sky-filled windows carved deeply into the soft, pastel-hued cliffs of the Paunsaugunt Plateau, this is one national park you'll long remember.

To the Paiute people who have lived in the region for centuries, the remarkable formations of Bryce Canyon came into being in legendary times, when the animal people so displeased powerful Coyote that he turned them to stone. Ebenezer Bryce, a Scottish Mormon who homesteaded the Paria Valley below the cliffs in 1875–76, is said to have been more prosaic about the series of carved amphitheaters towering above him, complaining that it was "a hell of a place to lose a cow!" In fact, Bryce Canyon can be explained by the weathering action of water and repeated freezing and thawing on the east-facing edge of a lofty plateau. The ending of Bryce's story is always changing, as gravity and erosion sculpt this natural masterpiece.

PRECEDING PAGES: Cedar Breaks National Monument. **LEFT:** sunrise at Agua Canyon. **BELOW:** Navajo Loop Trail, Bryce Canyon.

Thrust upwards, torn down

The Pink Cliffs of Bryce Canyon form the sixth and uppermost "step" of the Grand Staircase, which ascends in color-coded formations – oldest to youngest – from the Grand Canyon to the Paunsaugunt Plateau, a distance of more than 100 miles (160 km) and an ascent of 5,000 ft (1,500 meters). The rocks, which were pushed up, cracked and broken into plateaus by faults 15 million years ago, originated as sediments laid down over millions of years, when a succession of inland seas, lakes, rivers, streams and even a dune-filled desert covered the Southwest. Over time, the sediments hardened into rock, colored by manganese and iron. Today, weathering has oxidized these minerals into the blues, reds, purples and yellows that bathe the rocks in a wash of pastel hues.

Bryce's Pink Cliffs are the youngest sedimentary rocks in the area, the result of silt, sand and the limey skeletons of creatures that lived in the ephemeral freshwater lakes that formed here 55 million years ago, just before geologic activity began pushing up the Colorado Plateau. Forty million years later, when southern Utah began to split into its characteristic plateaus, these rocks, known as the Claron Formation, were exposed to the action of water speeding down the eastern edge of the Paunsaugunt Plateau. In what is today a semiarid

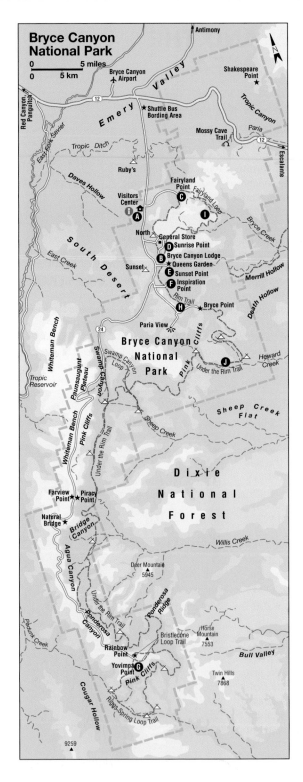

Bryce Canyon National Park

0 ___ 5 miles
0 ___ 5 km

country, there is an irony in the role water has played in creating the eerie "hoodoos" and other "rock-candy" formations that crowd the park's amphitheaters.

Exploring the park

Plan to spend at least a day here. Between May and September, large shuttle buses make it easy to get around what is usually a pretty crowded park, where spaces in small parking lots are often at a premium during peak hours. The heavily visited northern section is served by regular Red Line buses, which stop at all the main viewpoints in the main canyon. The fast Green Line buses allow you to reach the southern part of the scenic drive and do special tours.

Bryce's shuttles are voluntary but offer numerous benefits. For example, driving into Bryce has become expensive ($20 per car load). If you are alone, you can halve that cost and see the park more efficiently by taking the shuttle from the Park and Ride facility at the junction of UT 12 and 63 or from Ruby's Inn on UT 63 near the park boundary. The shuttles are free with your entrance fee or park pass.

Visitor fees have helped pay for the new stone-and-timber **Bryce Canyon Visitor Center A** (8am–8pm in summer, restricted hours in winter; 435-834-5322, www.nps.gov/brca), an airy space that evokes the rustic park architecture of the 1920s. The park museum has exhibits on the natural and cultural history of Bryce, and there is a large bookstore. Rangers at the information desk will help you get the most out of your trip. Bryce has two campgrounds. The largest and busiest, **North Campground**, is entirely on a reservation system in summer. Its 107 RV and tent sites can be reserved through the ReserveUSA program (877-444-6777 or www.ReserveUSA.com) up to six months ahead. If you're in a tent, the 101-site **Sunset Campground**, east of the viewpoint of the same name, is much quieter because noisy RV generators are restricted (neither campground has hookups). Sunset is on a first-come, first-served basis, so try to arrive early to snag a site. If you plan on hiking, this campground offers easy access to the Sunset Viewpoint trailheads, across the road.

Bryce Canyon Lodge Ⓑ (mid-May–Nov, tel: 435-297-2757), built in the 1920s by the Utah Parks Company, offers a step back into the past that may be worth the splurge. The dark, woodsy lodge with the wavy-shingled roof was designed by railroad architect Gilbert Stanley Underwood, who was responsible for rustic "parkitecture" lodges in what were then the new parks of Zion, Cedar Breaks and Bryce Canyon. Of these only 114-room Bryce Canyon Lodge survives. It is on the Register of Historic Places and was completely restored in 1988. Book at least six months ahead; this lodge is very popular. Even if you're not staying here, take a look inside the lobby. You'll get a feel for what traveling used to be like in the golden age of tourism. The restaurant is a good stop for lunch if you're here for only a day.

The 18-mile (29-km) scenic drive follows the edge of the 8,000-ft (2,438-meter) plateau through forests of ponderosa pine and summer wildflowers, such as Indian paintbrush, skyrocket gilia and penstemon. The drive takes in 15 overlooks whose names exude romance. Among them are **Fairyland Point** Ⓒ, **Sunrise Point** Ⓓ, **Sunset Point** Ⓔ and **Inspiration Point** Ⓕ. The highest spot in the park is **Yovimpa Point** Ⓖ (9,115 ft/2,778 meters). Here, the ponderosa pine gives way to subalpine conifers such as white fir and blue spruce. Rare bristlecone pines – some more than 1,000 years old – grow in exposed areas. A pleasant 1-mile (1.6-km) trail meanders through the trees to an overlook at Rainbow Point.

In the evenings, you will encounter mule deer grazing by the roadside; during the day, rodents such as ground squirrels and prairie dogs are commonly

Map on page 218

BELOW: Thor's Hammer looms over a photographer setting up a shot below Sunset Point.

sighted. Utah prairie dogs, an endangered species, are protected here but rarely seen. Out of sight but not out of mind are the shy mountain lions that prey on deer – their numbers diminished by destruction of habitat, but their presence still felt on the plateau. The skies are patrolled by red-tailed hawks and ravens, whose languid, circuitous flight is in sharp contrast to the quick, darting forays of cliff swallows. In the forests, jays jabber loquaciously from the pines, their iridescent blue feathers flashing among green needles.

The wildlife on the canyon bottom varies considerably from that on the moister, cooler rim. Pinyon and juniper trees grow alongside sagebrush, clinging tenaciously to pockets of soil in bare rock ledges. Runoff comes and goes swiftly here; there is little to hold it as it courses down steep precipices toward the Paria River, and thence to the Colorado River.

A closer look

Hikers follow Queen's Garden Trail through Bryce Canyon National Park.

Even if you have only a short time, get out of your car and hike down into the amphitheaters along one of the superb intersecting trails, which start from the overlooks. The easy 11-mile (18-km) **Rim Trail** links the scenic overlooks in the Bryce Canyon Amphitheater. The 8-mile (13-km) **Fairyland Loop** ❶ has views into Fairyland and Campbell Canyons near the park entrance. From Sunrise Point, you can descend the cliffs 320 ft (98 meters) on the easy 1.4-mile (2-km) round-trip **Queen's Garden Trail** and, if you wish, join up with the moderately strenuous **Navajo Loop Trail** (1.3 miles/2-km round-trip), which descends steeply from Sunset Point 520 ft (160 meters) and proceeds through the clustered formations of Silent City.

Hiking through these strange carved rocks is one of life's great novelties.

You won't soon forget the sight of an out-of-place Douglas fir yearning toward the sunlight from a narrow corridor on Navajo Loop Trail, nor should you miss taking a guided moonlit hike among these phantasmagoric rocks, if you visit at the right time of year. If you want a longer hike, the strenuous, 5½-mile (8-km) **Peekaboo Loop** starts at Bryce Point and meanders through the amphitheater's otherworldly formations. For overnight trips, the **Under-the-Rim Trail ❿** runs 23 miles (37 km) from Bryce Point to Yovimpa Point through some of the most remote and wildlife-rich country in the park. Be sure to consult the park rangers before attempting long backcountry hikes. Permits are required for overnight backpacking.

Maps:
Area 211
Park 218

Cedar Breaks

Leaving Bryce, head west on UT 12 through **Red Canyon**, Bryce's pretty little sister. Dixie National Forest runs a visitor center and campground on the other side of the creek, and this makes a decent alternative for overnight campers if Bryce Canyon is full. There are many other hiking and camping options in the 2-million-acre (800,000-hectare) Dixie National Forest surrounding Bryce. For more information, contact the U.S. Forest Service in **Panguitch ❿**, a few miles north of the US 89/UT 12 junction. Panguitch, meaning "big fish" in Paiute, has gas, food, lodging and other visitor services in its pleasant downtown. Continue west on UT 143 to reach several campgrounds and lakeside resorts in the high country.

If you're headed for Interstate 15, an even better idea is to drive south on UT 89, then west on UT 14, a beautiful drive at any time of year, across the 11,000-ft-high (3,350-meter) Markagunt Plateau. The Markagunt Plateau is

BELOW:
snowfall dusts the "hoodoos" of Bryce Amphitheater.

where southern Utahans come to escape the heat, and you'll find many attractions, including resorts, campgrounds, lodges, lakes, trails and viewpoints.

The undisputed highlight is **Cedar Breaks National Monument** (visitor center open daily June–late Sept; 2390 Hwy 56, Cedar City, tel: 435-586-9451; admission). This tiny gem, just off UT 14 on UT 148, preserves another highly eroded amphitheater of Claron Formation rock, but because the amphitheater is deeper, the coloration somewhat different, and descent into it discouraged, it complements a trip to Bryce rather than takes the place of it.

TIP

Cedar Breaks National Monument is open year-round. Cross-country skiers and snowshoers can follow two marked trails through the park in winter and backcountry areas above the rim are open as well.

A profusion of life

Cedar Breaks is best known for its extravagant wildflower displays, including lupine sneezeweed, yarrow and sunflowers, which begin adorning the meadows in July, shortly after the park reopens. Summer brings a rush of wildlife, which ranges from scurrying pikas, chipmunks, squirrels and marmots to stealthy mountain lions and coyotes. Mule deer browse on lush high-country meadows. Ravens and violet-green swallows swoop past colorful cliffs, and chattery Clark's nutcrackers and Steller's jays feast on the seasonal bounty of pine nuts.

A 5-mile (8-km) scenic drive follows the rim of the amphitheater and has numerous overlooks. **Alpine Pond Trail** (1 mile/1.5 km long) takes you through a cool, moist forest of spruce and fir. A completely different hike skirts the rim of the amphitheater past a large stand of thousand-year-old bristlecone pines clinging precariously to bare rock at **Spectra Point**, and out along the **Wasatch Ramparts**. The park's clean, quiet, 30-site campground is a real find. Nicely screened sites in the conifers open onto high-country meadows heavily used by wildlife. A truly idyllic spot.

BELOW: a Douglas fir reaches for the sun in narrow Wall Street Canyon at Bryce Canyon National Park.

PAROWAN GAP PETROGLYPHS

Evidence of prehistoric occupation is found throughout the Cedar City area. At least two of the area's pioneer settlements, Paragonah and Summit, were built on late Fremont sites dating to between AD 1000 and 1300, and there is evidence of human use dating back to the Late Archaic period, several thousand years ago.

Both Archaic and Fremont cultural remains can be viewed at the 2-mile-long (3-km) Parowan Gap Petroglyph Site, 15 miles (24 km) northwest of Cedar City. Parowan Gap separates Cedar Valley to the west and Parowan Valley to the east and lies along a route used by Indians and wildlife crossing Red Hills. The rock art at Parowan Gap is some of the best in Utah and is on the National Register of Historic Places. The images of mountain sheep, bear claws, snakes, lizards and other animals indicate it may have been connected to hunting rituals.

To reach the site from Parowan, head west at 400 North under Interstate 15 and continue for 10½ miles (17 km) to Parowan Gap. From Cedar City, go north on Main Street or take Interstate 15 Exit 62, then follow signs for UT 130 north for 13½ miles (22 km), and turn right 2½ miles (4 km) on a gravel road near milepost 19. Parking is available at the western end of the Gap.

In summer, you can continue north on UT 148 to UT 143, which leads to **Brian Head**. At 11,307 ft (3,446 meters), this is the highest point on the plateau. In winter, **Brian Head Ski Resort** (435-677-2035, www.brianhead.com) makes an excellent, little-known alternative to Sundance and other ski resorts in the Wasatch Mountains east of Salt Lake City. Brian Head is the highest ski resort in Utah and has 53 runs, six ski lifts and a snowboard park. It offers a wide array of condos, hotel rooms and restaurants and is open year-round.

UT 143 continues 14 miles (23 km) to the sleepy Mormon community of **Parowan**, the oldest town in southern Utah. From here, take I-15 south 18 miles (29 km) to Cedar City.

Map on page 218

Cedar City and environs

Three and a half hours south of Salt Lake City, **Cedar City** ⑫ is home to the award-winning **Utah Shakespearean Festival** (351 W. Center St, tel: 800-752-9849, www.bard.org), held over a nine-week period each summer in a specially built Elizabethan theater on the campus of Southern Utah University. The Shakespearean Festival is only one of the many events that are transforming this clean-cut Mormon town into a popular tourist destination. The self-described Festival City USA is also host to the Mid-Summer Renaissance Faire, Canyon Country Western Arts Festival, Utah Neil Simon Festival and Thunderbird International Film Festival.

Cedar City has come a long way from its pioneer roots. To find out more about the town's history, stop at **Iron Mission State Park** (daily 9am–7pm in summer, to 5pm in winter; 635 N. Main, tel: 435-586-9290), which commemorates the men of the Deseret Iron Company (many of them miners from Liverpool, England), who were "called" to help establish Cedar City in 1851. Low-tech but charming, the museum tells the story of the Iron Mission, which failed in 1860 and was supplanted by farming, ranching and other typical Mormon pursuits. Among the exhibits are numerous old wagons and carriages from 1850 to 1920, as well as the William H. Palmer Collection of Southern Paiute basketry, clothing, tools and other items collected by a prominent Cedar City Mormon in the 1940s.

Other samples of Palmer's Paiute basketry – nearly a lost art among surviving Paiutes – are on display in the Gerald Sherratt Library on the attractive campus of **Southern Utah University** (351 S. Main, tel: 435-586-7700), founded in 1897. A sizeable population of Southern Paiutes lives locally and on reservations in southern Utah and Nevada. The headquarters of the Paiute Indian Tribe of Southern Utah is in downtown Cedar City. The tribe holds an annual Paiute Restoration Gathering in June to celebrate its 1980 reinstatement as an "official" American Indian tribe.

Cedar City's most recent addition is the **Heritage Performing Arts Center** (105 North 100 East; 435-865-2882), which is situated in the historic downtown on the site of the former Escalante Hotel. The hotel was built in the 1920s by the Utah Parks Company, a division of the Union Pacific Railroad, to serve arriving railroad visitors who wished to visit area parks in grand style. ❑

BELOW: an actor mingles with the crowd at Cedar City's Utah Shakespearean Festival.

GRAND STAIRCASE-ESCALANTE NATIONAL MONUMENT

Map on page 228

Follow a river corridor or rugged backcountry road through extraordinary red-rock canyons rich with desert life and adorned with ancient pictographs

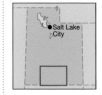

Yup! You Gotta Get Wet." The sign on the north bank of the Escalante River elicits big grins. Get wet? No problem. On any desert pilgrimage to southern Utah's famed Escalante Canyons, a river baptism is the price of admission to heaven. There'll be additional toll-takers later on - bush-whacking through willow thickets, scrambling over boulders, squeezing through water-carved narrows, creeping over the slippery sandstone known as slickrock, slogging through deep sand.

No one here would want it any other way. **Grand Staircase–Escalante National Monument ❶** (Mon–Fri 8.15am–4.30pm; 190 E. Center St, Kanab, tel: 435-644-4300, www.gsenm.ut.blm.gov) is remote and wild country. In other words, it's just the place to have an adventure.

Open space

This was one of the last regions in the continental United States to be mapped, when members of John Wesley Powell's second expedition to the West traveled overland from Kanab in 1871–72 to survey the area. They named the Escalante River after Father Silvestre Velez de Escalante, a Spanish padre who traversed the area in 1776, though he never saw the river. Even today, with a sprinkling of small Mormon ranching and farming communities on the periphery, the area remains essentially pristine, adjoined by Capitol Reef National Park to the north-east, Glen Canyon to the southeast and Bryce Canyon to the west.

The scientific implications of such a vast, intact ecosystem have become increasingly clear in recent decades. In September 1996, President Bill Clinton set aside Grand Staircase-Escalante as the country's first national monument overseen by the Bureau of Land Management. Encompassed within its 1.9 million acres (770,000 hectares) are an almost intact fossil record in exposed geological formations; flora and fauna adapted to five life zones and numerous microenvironments; and thousands of pristine archaeological sites spanning 10,000 years.

You'll barely have to leave one of the monument's surrounding paved highways or graded interior back-roads to find yourself deep within the most rugged terrain imaginable. There's only one designated trail: a 6-mile (10-km) round-trip hike to spectacular 126-ft-high (38-meter) **Lower Calf Creek Falls** between Escalante and Boulder. Other "trails" are unmarked routes through often narrow desert canyons carved by rivers, streams and washes. There are three small

PRECEDING PAGES: Escalante Canyon. **LEFT:** Buckskin Canyon, Paria Canyon–Vermilion Cliffs Wilderness. **BELOW:** Cannonville horses.

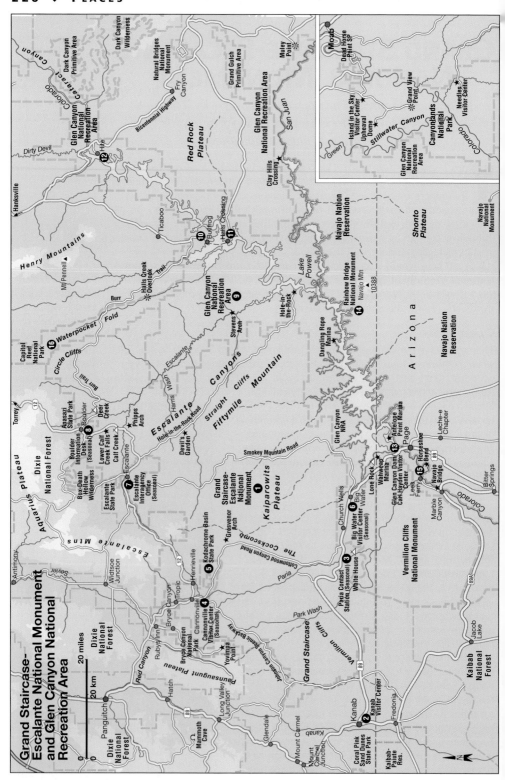

Grand Staircase-Escalante National Monument and Glen Canyon National Recreation Area

Map on page 228

primitive campgrounds next to the main highways – **Calf Creek** (off UT 12), **Deer Creek** (off the Burr Trail) and **White House** (off US 89) – as well as several developed campgrounds in adjoining state parks and national forests. Primitive camping is allowed throughout the monument (with an overnight permit) within 50 ft (15 meters) of roads and at designated areas in the backcountry.

If you're heading off-road, a compass, GPS unit, topographical map and route-finding skills are essential. Be advised that cell phones do not work in many places in the monument. Spring and fall offer cooler hiking temperatures and are blessedly free of biting flies, mosquitoes and tiny insects known as no-see-ums. Too much or too little water is the norm here, and what water one finds is notoriously unreliable or contaminated by chemicals. On the other hand, watch out for flash floods year-round, especially in summer when daily thunderstorms send surges through slot canyons with vertical walls hundreds of feet high.

Plan carefully

Be sure to stop at one of the monument's visitor centers or ranger stations for information about backcountry road conditions, which change quickly after storms, and to pick up overnight backcountry permits, get help planning your trip, and attend lectures by experts on park topics in summer. The visitor centers and ranger stations are in or near the outlying towns of Kanab, Orderville, Bryce Canyon, Big Water, Cannonville, Tropic, Escalante and Boulder. Glendale, north of Kanab, will have a visitor contact station in the next few years. All have a modest selection of gas, food and lodging. An expanding number of approved outfitters offers low-impact backpacking, mountain biking, horseback riding, llama trekking, fishing, hunting, four-wheel-drive tours and backcountry survival courses.

Bear in mind that distances between towns are great and even paved highways are lightly traveled. Make sure your car is in good working condition, keep your gas tank topped up, and bring spare tires. Carry a gallon of water per person per day (and drink it) and extra food. And don't forget a first-aid kit. Prepare to be self-sufficient; no services are available inside the monument. Last but most important: Be sure to let someone know where you're going, when you expect to return, and whom to call if you don't.

Where to go

Grand Staircase-Escalante National Monument is divided into three large, contiguous geographical provinces. The easy-to-reach **Grand Staircase** province protects a 3,500-ft-high (1,000-meter) geological "staircase" of rock strata, rising from the North Rim of the Grand Canyon to Cedar Breaks National Monument in southwestern Utah. In these massive color-coded cliffs and terraces, the Paria River and other Colorado River tributaries have carved a landscape of isolated mesas, valleys, buttes and narrow canyons homesteaded by settlers in the 19th century. **Kanab BLM Field Office** (Mon–Fri 8.30am–4.15pm; 318 N. First East, Kanab, tel: 435-644-4600) and **Kanab Visitor Center ②** (Mon–Fri 8am–4.30pm, weekend hours in summer; 75 US 89, Kanab, tel: 435-644-

BELOW: a filling station near Cannonville is a strictly self-serve operation.

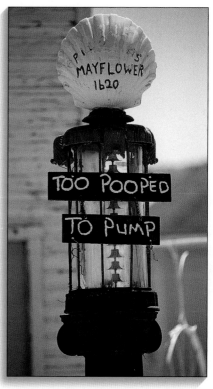

Metate Arch rises above hikers in the Devil's Garden section of Grand Staircase–Escalante National Monument.

4680) are both located in Kanab in the Grand Staircase section, a good place to start your visit if you're coming from the west.

Forty-four miles (71 km) east of Kanab, on US 89, is **Paria Contact Station ❸** (Mar–Oct daily 8.30am–4.15pm) adjoining the Paria Wilderness, a premier slot canyon that exits at the Colorado River in the northwest section of Glen Canyon National Recreation Area.

The middle province, the 800,000-acre (320,000-hectare) **Kaiparowits Plateau**, adjoins the Grand Staircase to the east and is the most remote and inaccessible area of the monument. The Kaiparowits' rugged isolation has preserved an extraordinary fossil and archaeological record in the younger rocks of the Cretaceous period. It is situated between the Straight Cliffs and a distinctive tilted formation known locally as the Cockscomb, which run 42 miles (68 km) east to Glen Canyon National Recreation Area. **Cottonwood Canyon Road Scenic Backway**, the 46-mile (74-km) route separating the Grand Staircase and Kaiparowits provinces, links US 89 with UT 12, the two paved highways encircling the monument.

At the north end of Cottonwood Road, you'll find the folksy **Cannonville Visitor Center ❹** (Apr–Oct daily 8am–4.30pm; 10 Center St, Cannonville, tel: 435-679-8981), which interprets the rich human history of the monument, from Fremont and Paiute Indians to Mormon homesteaders.

BELOW: a hiker squeezes through Coyote Canyon.

Nine miles (15 km) south of Cannonville, where the dirt Cottonwood Road rejoins pavement, is **Kodachrome Basin State Park ❺** (tel: 435-697-8562 or 800-284-2267 for reservations), named by writer Jack Breed in a 1949 *National Geographic* article extolling the beauties of the area. The park protects unique stovepipe-shaped formations known as "sand pipes" and several natural arches;

8 miles (13 km) south of the park is **Grosvenor Arch**, a rare double rock span. The nicely developed campground has showers and lots of tent and RV sites and makes a good base for touring the central section of the monument.

US 89 provides a scenic 77-mile (124-km) link between **Kanab**, Utah, and **Page**, Arizona. A few miles before you get to Page, look for the turnoff for the **Big Water Visitor Center** ❻ (Apr–Oct daily 9am–5.30pm; 100 Upper Revolution Way, Big Water; tel: 435-675-5868), which is located at the base of the rough and often impassable **Smoky Mountain Road** across the Kaiparowits Plateau. Built in the shape of a nautilus shell, this exquisite small facility has a native plant garden, sculptures, interpretive panels and dioramas interpreting the marine reptiles, dinosaurs and early mammals of the late Cretaceous Period excavated from atop the Kaiparowits in the 1990s.

Map on page 228

The wild east

The easternmost province of the monument is **Escalante Canyons**, which protects the maze of canyons cut by the Escalante River from the Aquarius Plateau to Lake Powell. The Escalante Canyons have long been the main attraction on the monument, offering riverside hikes, slot canyons, bizarre rock formations, breathtaking vistas and historic roads. The busy **Escalante Interagency Office** ❼ (Apr–Oct daily 7.30am–5pm, Nov–Mar Mon–Fri 7.30am–5pm; 75 W. Main, Escalante, tel: 435-826-5499) anchors the monument on the east side and offers in-depth information and trip planning for the Escalante Canyons and Glen Canyon National Recreation Area.

If you're arriving from the north, you'll find information in the little ranching community of Boulder at the start of the historic Burr Trail. The monu-

BELOW: a modern-day cowboy drives a herd through Escalante.

ment's **Boulder Information Desk** ❽ (435-335-7382, closed Nov–Mar) is on the north end of town in the visitor center at **Anasazi State Park** (460 N. UT 12, tel: 435-355-7308). This park preserves a huge, 13th-century pueblo known as the Coombs Site, one of the most important archaeological sites in the area. On the south side of town is the beginning of **Hell's Backbone**, the precipitous backroad that used to be the main link between Boulder and Escalante.

"I have seen almost more beauty than I can bear."

– EVERETT RUESS

Climbing a steep graveled road, this route (used by mule trains carrying mail until the 1940s) crosses **Box-Death Hollow Wilderness** and has spectacular views. Two gorgeous forest service campgrounds – **Posey Lake** and **Blue Spruce** – offer the coolest camping in the area. Don't attempt this road in bad weather. Ask about conditions before setting out.

Labyrinth of stone

The Grand Staircase section of the monument has two lightly traveled day hikes that make a pleasant introduction to the area. To reach the trailheads, drive north 16 miles (28 km) on the paved **Johnson Canyon Scenic Backway**, east of Kanab, and turn on the 34-mile (58-km) dirt **Skutumpah Road Scenic Backway** heading east. You can also get there by driving north on US 89 from downtown Kanab to **Glendale**, an old coal-mining town, then heading west on **Glendale Bench Road**. Lick Wash and Willis Creek are halfway between Cannonville and Kanab. Both offer moderate hiking in deep, narrow canyons filled with stands of Douglas fir. Ask at the Kanab or Cannonville Visitor Centers for more information.

BELOW:
juniper snags cast a silhouette against the walls of Long Canyon on the Burr Trail.

For most people, though, the main destinations in the monument are the spectacular Escalante Canyons above Lake Powell. If you've never been there before,

EVERETT RUESS

Born in California in 1914, adventurer, artist and writer Everett Ruess took to the road as a teenager along with thousands of other men seeking work during the Depression. Unlike them, though, Ruess came from a family of means: he simply traveled for the joy of it, sending home regular missives about his passion for the Arizona and Utah wilderness, the people he met and his faithful pack mule, Nemo.

On trips home, he befriended photographers Ansel Adams and Dorothea Lange and painter Maynard Dixon. Although the Bohemian life attracted him, his brooding temperament and love of wilderness drew him deeper into Utah's backcountry. In a final letter to his brother Waldo, he wrote: "I have not tired of the wilderness; rather I enjoy its beauty and the vagrant life I lead more keenly all the time. I prefer the saddle to the streetcar and star-sprinkled sky to a roof, the obscure and difficult trail leading into the unknown to any paved highway, and the deep peace of the wild to the discontent bred by cities ."

In November 1934, at the age of 20, he made his last journey, vanishing into Davis Canyon in what is today Grand Staircase-Escalante National Monument. His love of Canyon Country continues to inspire modern-day adventurers.

you'll learn more about this vast maze of stone and stay safest if you hire a local outfitter to introduce you to the area and help pack your gear. You can go the traditional route with horses, but a more unusual option is to use llamas, which need far less water than horses and can carry up to 120 pounds (55 kg) of gear. With their cushiony, two-toed feet, they have about as much impact on fragile desert soils as deer and are possessed of remarkably docile temperaments.

The Escalante Basin begins east of **Escalante**, between the 1,100-ft (335-meter) Straight Cliffs of the Kaiparowits Plateau and the great dropoff of the Waterpocket Fold. On either side of UT 12, the torqued and twisted knobs of Navajo Sandstone roiling to the horizon are almost enough to bring on seasickness. Near its confluence with Calf Creek, the Escalante River appears in a blaze of preternaturally green vegetation at the foot of ruddy sandstone. The water is only about 10 ft (3 meters) wide and usually only knee-deep, but don't laugh – this qualifies as a river in Canyon Country. Its headwaters are on the 11,000-ft (3,350-meter) Aquarius Plateau, from whence the Escalante drops toward its conjunction with Lake Powell. If the water gods had their way, this would be a straight shot, but Mother Earth has shrugged her shoulders at such plans and wrinkled the area in a series of uplifts, or monoclines, that have forced the river and its tributaries to cut deep, labyrinthine canyons.

If you stick close to the Escalante River, you won't have to sprinkle bread crumbs to find your way back. Cattle have pounded out a trail along the riverbank that's easy to follow. You'll ford the silty river numerous times, so wear good river sandals or light boots and bring spare footwear and dry socks. A number of side canyons lead to the river. On the north side, Deer Creek and The Gulch are popular access points. They join the **Burr Trail Scenic Back-**

Map on page 228

BELOW: Lower Calf Creek Falls tumbles through a cleft in a canyon wall.

way, the old rancher's road that starts in Boulder as a 31-mile (50-km) paved road below the Circle Cliffs, then turns to dirt as it crosses the Waterpocket Fold in Capitol Reef and continues into Glen Canyon National Recreation Area. On the south side, you can reach Harris Wash from the 57-mile (92-km) **Hole-in-the-Rock Scenic Backway**, which was blasted by Mormon pioneers in the winter of 1879 on their epic mission to colonize southeastern Utah.

River's path

An easy, 15-mile (24-km) overnight trip can be made along the Escalante River between Escalante and Calf Creek for great views of an arch, a natural bridge and Indian granaries and rock art. Continue down the canyon for longer trips; five days is usually enough time to reach Glen Canyon National Recreation Area and explore side canyons.

Water and other erosional forces have sculpted myriad cliffs, alcoves, arches, bridges, slots and hoodoos. Cross-bedded Navajo Sandstone, the remnant of a 190-million-year-old desert, reaches precipitously to the rim and catches fire at sunrise and sunset. Beneath the rosy Navajo, the maroon Kayenta siltstone erodes into ledges, forcing the canyon to step back in terraces and benches. Even more dramatic than the Navajo (if that's possible) is the fiery orange Wingate Sandstone, which appears deeper in the canyon and reaches its most stunning expression in the fractured Circle Cliffs to the northeast. Lengthening shadows bring out the tapestry effect on sandstone. Pour-offs have washed out manganese and iron in the rock, creating "desert varnish" fixed to cliff faces by bacteria.

The eye is constantly drawn up to the cliffs, then back down to the feet, where your passage may send crickets jumping or a dozing lizard scurrying from the

BELOW: water erosion has carved the undulating walls of a Hackberry Canyon tributary.

Map on page 228

undergrowth. Watch out for "cryptobiotic crusts" in sandy areas. These dark soils are made up of strands of cyanobacteria, lichen and algae that hold moisture and nitrogen and prevent erosion. This is where life begins in the desert, but it's easily destroyed by careless feet. To avoid "crypto," walk in washes or on slickrock.

The bank of the Escalante River is a grabby tangle of tamarisk, willow, box elder and thorny Russian olive. Scouring rushes and horsetails poke up from the shallows. Growing along the trail are woody sagebrush, rabbitbrush, greasewood and four-wing saltbush interspersed with orange-red globemallow, vermilion Indian paintbrush, scarlet gilia, skyrocket and purple-headed woolly vetch. On higher ledges, dwarf pinyon and juniper, gambel oak, old man sage and roundleaf buffaloberry find purchase in soil pockets.

Canyon song

Over the burbling of the river, listen for the descending serenade of the canyon wren accompanied by the fluting notes of robins. Egrets and herons visit at times, along with dainty water ouzels that dip for insects in the shallows. Graceful white-throated swifts swoop down to the river from cliff nests in acrobatic dives. The cliffs are also home to more than 20 raptor species, which use tree snags and ledges as staging areas for skyline sorties. Perhaps you'll be lucky enough to see a golden eagle soaring into the morning sun and follow its shadow on a cliff as it spirals. Though formidable predators, these majestic birds are no match for peregrine falcons, which, along with condors released along the Vermilion Cliffs, are the great comeback story here. It's not unknown for lightning-fast peregrines to attack and kill eagles. More than three-quarters of the monument's plants and animals use riparian corridors like this one.

BELOW: Grosvenor Arch, Grand Staircase–Escalante National Monument.

Map on page 228

In side canyons, giant Fremont cottonwoods wrap rubbery limbs around boulders and stretch toe roots into warm pools skittering with water striders and polliwogs. When you least expect it, you'll happen upon miniature hanging gardens of moss, ferns and eye-dazzling columbines, monkeyflowers and shooting stars crowding around dripping springs in the canyon walls. The water percolates down through porous sandstone. The constant dripping undermines the overlying sandstone cliffs, which crack along joints, then peel away like an onion, leaving behind huge alcoves that will one day become arches. Various creatures find refuge here: elusive bighorn sheep, timid mountain lions scanning for deer, coyotes sniffing around for cottontails and jackrabbits, and rodents like the desert-adapted kangaroo rat, which recycles all its water from seeds.

About 2 miles (3 km) down the canyon from the UT 12 bridge, a side canyon to the south follows Phipps Wash. Head east in a box canyon to view 40-ft-high (12-meter) Phipps Arch, a magnificent natural span. You'll need to scramble up several hundred feet of crumbly ledges and slickrock to reach the arch, but it's worth the effort. This is a great place for a picnic or for close encounters with turkey vultures and red-tailed hawks, which soar upon thermals through the canyon.

BELOW:
Peekaboo Gulch.
RIGHT: UT 12 winds through the Escalante Canyons section of the national monument, the Henry Mountains in the distance.

Vanishing treasures

Some of the most memorable sights in the canyons are the dwellings, granaries, stone-working sites and rock art panels left behind by the Fremont and Kayenta Anasazi people who lived here between AD 100 and 1300. The Fremont dug snug pithouses with warm southern exposures on deer and elk migration routes, gathered plants seasonally, raised corn, and appear to have subsisted on water

from *tinajas*, or potholes. The Kayenta Anasazi were pueblo builders who erected the large Coombs Site now preserved in Anasazi State Park in nearby Boulder. It's estimated that more than 20,000 archaeological sites are situated within the monument, many protected by their remote locations.

Pecked and painted rock art panels display strong Fremont characteristics – wide-shouldered human-like figures with round shields, headdresses and ear bobs, accompanied by bighorn sheep, animal tracks, handprints, joined-hand figures and concentric circles. It's hard not to admire the resourcefulness and artistry of these hardy people, though not everyone shares the sentiment, as is heartbreakingly apparent when you come upon sites desecrated by vandalism.

A greater sense of connection is what visiting wilderness is all about. "Music has been in my heart all the time, and poetry in my thoughts," wrote adventurer Everett Ruess of his experiences in the Escalante Canyons before he disappeared here in 1934. "Alone on the open desert, I have made up songs of wild, poignant rejoicing and transcendent melancholy. The world has seemed more beautiful to me than ever before... I have rejoiced to set out, to be going somewhere, and I have felt a still sublimity... I have really lived." Lying under a star-studded sky in an alcove with just the breath of a wind wafting through the canyons, you know exactly what he meant. ❏

GLEN CANYON
NATIONAL RECREATION AREA

*Boaters ply a watery labyrinth in this sprawling park
centered on a man-made lake in the heart of
southern Utah's slickrock wilderness*

Salt Lake City

I t's a sizzling June afternoon under cloudless skies on the north shore of Lake Powell. The mirror-smooth, tepid waters of the lake and surrounding mesas of pale sandstone wobble in a heat haze above Bullfrog Marina, a self-contained lakeside community in Glen Canyon National Recreation Area, south of Hanksville on UT 276, between the spectacular Waterpocket Fold and Henry Mountains. Weekenders siesta under the shady awnings of their boats or hole up in air-conditioned RVs in the campground, waiting out the heat. Some visitors, clad in long-sleeved shirts and broad-brimmed hats, stand around in the shallows, cold drinks in hand. Still others head over to the Bullfrog gas station and grocery, where a walk-in freezer containing bagged ice offers cheap thrills for an overheated body.

Sensible desert creatures are resting, too, amid the man-made sounds of car and watercraft engines and the horn blast of the departing Bullfrog-Halls Crossing Ferry. The only exception is a group of enormous desert ravens excitedly attacking an unattended picnic bag. Their harsh cawing, bouncing off the rocky walls of the marina, momentarily attracts attention. Soon enough, though, people return to enjoying the lake – for most, the high point of a week spent toiling at jobs in Phoenix, Salt Lake City and other desert cities in Arizona and Utah.

PRECEDING PAGES: a houseboat on Lake Powell cruises past Three Roof Ruin. **LEFT:** kayaking in Clear Creek Canyon. **BELOW:** a young explorer finds a canyon tree frog.

Managed by the National Park Service since 1972, **Glen Canyon National Recreation Area** ❾ (tel: 520-608-6404, www.nps.gov/glca; fee) preserves 1,961 square miles (5,079 sq km) in and around the Colorado River and its major tributaries – the San Juan, Paria, Dirty Devil and Escalante Rivers – which, since 1963, have been backed up behind Glen Canyon Dam at Page, Arizona.

Although it sees most of the visitation, 229-square-mile (593-sq-km) Lake Powell actually represents only 13 percent of the park. Glen Canyon also includes many square miles of mesas, mountains and desert canyons cut by the rivers prior to inundation beneath the reservoir. Below Glen Canyon Dam, the Colorado River continues to flow for 15 miles (24 km) to Lees Ferry, offering whitewater rafting in the lower reaches of the park.

What lies below

Since 2000, recreation in Glen Canyon National Recreation Area has been an unfolding work-in-progress. Lake levels have plummeted 118 ft (36 meters) below capacity due to an extended drought. As the lake drops, hiking and primitive camping on new beaches and side canyons are once again becoming popular. Some of the best are in the spectacular Escalante Canyons in the northern reaches of the lake, where places like Cathedral in the Desert, named by geologist John Wesley Powell on his river expedition down the Colorado in 1869, are worthy destinations in themselves.

History and archaeology buffs will be thrilled to discover the cultural remains of Archaic and ancient Pueblo people, 19th-century pioneers and contemporary Indian tribes reappearing from the receding waters like the mythical lost city of Atlantis. Glen Canyon, once mourned as "The Place No One Knew" by activists opposed to the construction of Glen Canyon Dam, is beginning to reemerge of its own volition even as the dam faces an uncertain future.

Despite its depleted state, Lake Powell – the second-largest man-made lake in the Western Hemisphere – remains the big attraction at Glen Canyon for the more than 2½ million visitors who come here annually. The dam that created this vast reservoir was authorized by the Colorado River Storage Project Act in 1956, a water-sharing arrangement between the western states of California, Nevada, Wyoming, Utah, Colorado, Arizona and New Mexico. Although it is overextended, the dam project has provided water storage, flood control, irrigation, river regulation and hydroelectric power, which, in the years since, have paid for the cost of construction.

Lake Powell extends 186 miles (299 km) upstream from the dam and has 1,960 miles (3,154 km) of shoreline – longer even than the West Coast of the United States. Water activities, such as boating, water skiing, wind surfing, swimming and fishing, predominate and are served by five marinas: **Bullfrog**, **Wahweap**, **Dangling Rope**, **Hall's Crossing** and the new **Antelope**

A sailboat on Lake Powell finds a placid mooring for the night.

Point Marina (602-952-0114), a joint project with the Navajo Nation, whose vast reservation adjoins Lake Powell to the south.

Bullfrog

If you're arriving at Lake Powell from Utah in summer, **Bullfrog Resort and Marina ⑩** (435-684-3000) is your best bet. Less than five hours from Salt Lake City, it offers both full services and the perfect introduction to the quiet beauty of the San Juan River country in the northern sector of the park. You'll find almost everything you will need at Bullfrog and nearby Ticaboo – accommodations, a campground, a large marina, a swimming beach, restaurants, gift shops, boat tours, a gas station, a fuel dock, convenience stores and a medical clinic. Bullfrog is currently the only marina renting houseboats, a popular option with vacationers. You can also rent sea kayaks and other small watercraft as well as fishing gear. Largemouth and striped bass, black crappie, catfish, bluegill and walleye predominate in Lake Powell; trophy-sized rainbow trout thrive in the cold waters below the dam.

Your first stop at Bullfrog should be **Bullfrog Visitor Center** (daily in summer 10am–7pm, limited hours in spring and fall, closed Oct–Mar; tel: 435-684-7423), a pleasant haven adjoining the medical clinic. The visitor center interprets the natural and cultural history of the region with state-of-the-art displays, video programs and a helpful staff who can give you tips on exploring the surrounding area. It has exhibits on desert animals and the alcove villages left behind by ancient Pueblo people.

Among the most interesting exhibits is a full-sized diorama of a slot canyon, a common geological feature in Canyon Country, where floodwater cuts straight

Map on page 228

BELOW: a view from Muley Point encompasses a serpentine canyon carved by the San Juan River.

The Glen Canyon Dam near the Utah border at Page, Arizona, blocks the flow of the Colorado River.

BELOW: the San Juan River follows the course of an entrenched meander or "gooseneck."

down through sandstone, leaving behind narrow, winding subterranean passageways with cool, sandy bottoms. The best-known slot canyon in the area is photogenic Antelope Canyon, on the south side of the lake near Page. There are several good slot canyon hikes near Bullfrog, too. You'll find them off the Burr Trail; inquire at the visitor center for directions

Early pioneers

The **Bullfrog-Halls Crossing Ferry** (six crossings daily in summer, four in winter; 435-684-3000; fee) makes the half-hour crossing between Bullfrog and Halls Crossing and offers non-boaters the opportunity to get out on the water, albeit briefly. **Halls Crossing ⓫** has a marina, boat launch, ferry landing, campground and store. **Hall's Crossing Boater Contact Station** (open 8am–6pm intermittently in summer) has exhibits on boater information and safety, geology and the history of the village. This remote spot was named for one of the Hole-in-the-Rock pioneers, Charles Hall, who operated a ferry across the Colorado River in the late 19th century. Business was slow, and Hall stopped running the ferry after three years, just before a gold rush in Glen Canyon would have kept him busy.

Beginning in 1945, another historic ferry was operated by Arthur Chaffin at **Hite ⓬**, the northernmost community in Glen Canyon. Situated at the junction of the Dirty Devil and Colorado Rivers, Hite was named for 19th-century prospector Cass Hite, who first came here in 1883 with Navajo headman Hoskaninni, after asking the Monument Valley leader to show him where the Navajo found silver for their jewelry. Two earlier prospectors with a similar interest had been killed in Monument Valley three years earlier, but fortunately

for Hite, Hoskaninni was willing to show him the place on the south side of the Colorado River where he had found gold dust in the riverbank.

Dandy Crossing, as Hite called the spot, was quickly mobbed by prospectors but, sadly, there was never sufficient gold to make up for the difficulty of extracting it in such remote country. Two corporations – one run by mining engineer Robert Stanton at Bullfrog Creek and one by Charles Spencer at Lees Ferry – made a major attempt. All eventually gave up, leaving their equipment to rust along the river and eventually be drowned by Lake Powell.

Modern travelers now cross the river via a suspension bridge along US 95. Lake levels have been so low that Hite – once a waterfront village – has turned into a ghost town. The boat launch is closed, but anyone with even a passing interest in desert rivers will want to drive this way to see how quickly the river is reclaiming the mudflats from the lake. **Hite Ranger Station** (435-684-2457) is open intermittently but has outdoor interpretive displays about the historic village.

Map on page 228

Glen Canyon Dam and Page

For visitors arriving at Lake Powell from Arizona, the former company town of Page is the main entrance point for Glen Canyon. **Carl Hayden Visitor Center ⓭** (daily 7am–7pm in summer; 8am–5pm rest of year; tel: 928-608-6404), next to the dam, has exhibits, interpretive presentations, a bookstore and information on hiking side canyons and arranging river trips. Glen Canyon Natural History Association offers guided tours of the 710-ft-high (216-meter) dam and power plant, which is operated by the U.S. Bureau of Reclamation. Note: security here is extremely tight. Visitors are required to pass through an electronic screening bay and no bags of any type are allowed in the visitor center.

BELOW: runoff from a summer storm swells a desert stream.

When it was begun in 1956, Glen Canyon Dam had the blessing of almost everyone concerned. By the time it was finished in 1963, conservationists such as Sierra Club's David Brower and writer Wallace Stegner had belatedly recognized that Glen Canyon was comparable in grandeur to anything – including the nearby Grand Canyon – on the Colorado Plateau. Today, many people believe that the drowning of Glen Canyon and its rich natural and cultural history was an unspeakable ecological tragedy and are advocating dismantling the dam. But while both biologists and politicians investigate ways to mitigate the effects of the dam on the downstream environment, nature has intervened, rapidly drying up the lake during a period of drought that, as of this writing, shows no signs of abating.

That said, Glen Canyon Dam is an extraordinary structure. It was built over seven years at a cost of $187 million and is the second-largest dam in the United States (after Hoover Dam, downstream at Lake Mead, Nevada). The canyon it occupies was shaped to fit the dam, not the other way around, and hundreds of rock bolts were installed by high scalers to reinforce the canyon walls and prevent rock slabs from falling. The dam designers thought of almost every eventuality. Groundwater, seeping through fractures in the sandstone, enters tunnels in the dam at 2,600 gallons (9,800 liters) a minute and is diverted through weirs and troughs and discharged to the river below. Massive diversion tunnels on either side of the dam regulate water releases during times of seasonal flood.

The dam can generate 1.3 million kilowatts of electricity through hydroelectric power, most of which is used to power the megalopolis of Phoenix and other Southwest cities. In 2002, the low levels of the lake cut this output to one-third of former capacity, forcing the Western Area Power Administration (WAPA) to

TIP

Tours of Glen Canyon Dam are not available when the terror threat is Orange or higher.

BELOW: a hiker takes in a view of Fifty Mile Canyon.

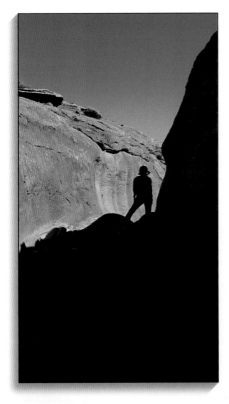

RAINBOW BRIDGE

Rainbow Bridge National Monument ⓮, set deep in the heart of Glen Canyon, is a 100-mile (160-km) round-trip by boat from Wahweap Marina near Page. Although it is possible to hike overland from Navajo Mountain, using a Navajo guide, the 14-mile (23-km) trail is unmarked, rugged and shadeless and not recommended for those who aren't in good shape or accustomed to hot desert hiking. You must obtain a permit from Navajo Parks and Recreation in Window Rock (520-871-6647) before starting out.

Most people visit Rainbow Bridge by boat. Concessionaires run popular, all-day boat trips from Wahweap for about $100 per person. With low lake levels, visitors must hike 3 miles (5 km) round-trip to view Rainbow Bridge, so wear sturdy shoes, a hat and sunscreen, and bring plenty of water. Rainbow Bridge is sacred to local tribes. The National Park Service urges visitors to approach the bridge with respect and refrain from walking beneath it.

Arrange your boat trip through the Page-Lake Powell Chamber of Commerce (tel: 888-261-7243 or 928-645-2741). For independent boaters, the closest marina to Rainbow Bridge is Dangling Rope (928-645-2969), about 40 miles (64 km) upstream of Page.

buy $135 million of power from other sources to honor existing contracts. Hydrologists estimate that if the drought continues, hydropower at Glen Canyon Dam could be eliminated within five years, affecting 10 million households.

On a daily basis, icy waters from deep below Lake Powell are released from behind the dam to coincide with peak usage times in western cities. This type of operation, known as "peaking," means that the river level below the dam rises and falls by as much as 14 ft (4 meters) a day, depending on the season. This has heavily impacted the downstream environment of the Colorado River, whose ecology was adapted to the free-flowing river. No longer can spring floods scour the riverbank and rebuild beaches. The warm, silty-red waters (for which the Colorado was named) are a thing of the past. Warm-water native fish species, such as the razorback sucker and humpback chub, are now federally listed endangered species, along with the southwest willow flycatcher, a small, drab, gray bird that nests in native willows that have been largely replaced by exotic tamarisk, or salt cedar, along the riverbank.

Map on page 228

Lessons of the past

Civil War veteran and geologist John Wesley Powell, for whom Lake Powell was named, was the first to travel down the free-flowing Colorado River in 1869. Using the Mormon community of Kanab, Utah, as a base, he returned for a second, shorter trip in 1872, photographing many features in the canyons as well as Navajos, Paiutes and other native people whom he used as guides. In his subsequent report, Powell was the first to write about the need for a realistic federal water policy for the West.

Powell's legacy is celebrated at the charming **John Wesley Powell Memorial**

BELOW: Rainbow Bridge, considered sacred by the Navajo, can be reached by tour boat.

Map on page 228

Museum in Page (Mon–Sat 8am–6pm; 928-645-9496; admission), a Grandma's-attic type of place in downtown Page, which displays old drawings and photos from Powell's life and voyages, geological displays and Indian artifacts. Among the many items of interest is Powell's old bedstead, a wooden dory rowboat used by Mexican Hat river runner Norm Nevills, the largest collection of phosphorescent rocks in the world and the complete skeleton of a giant predatory marine reptile called a plesiosaur, which lived about 90 million years ago, when this region was inundated by a huge interior seaway.

Page has grown from a makeshift shantytown for dam workers into far northern Arizona's largest community, with a variety of lodgings and restaurants. From here, you can arrange trips on Lake Powell, boat tours to Rainbow Bridge, tours of Antelope Canyon and Monument Valley, and the nearby Grand Canyon. **Wahweap Resort and Marina** (928-645-2433), just west of the dam, is the main access for the lake and has full facilities. Primitive beach camping is available at nearby **Lone Rock Beach**.

Cliffs and canyons

Busy Wahweap is a popular venue for partying boaters and vacationers. For a more back-to-nature experience, head south on US 89, then north on US 89A to Marble Canyon. When it opened in 1929, the narrow, 467-ft-high (142-meter) Navajo Bridge over the Colorado was the highest steel structure in the world. A wider bridge was opened in 1997 for automobiles, and you can walk across the old structure. The small **Navajo Bridge Visitor Center** (Apr–Oct 9am–5pm; tel: 928-355-2319) is an impressive piece of desert architecture, with pueblo-style sandstone walls and a fine little bookstore.

BELOW: pleasure boats crowd Wahweap Marina.

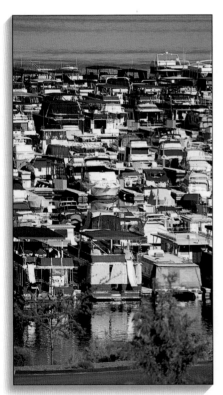

Behind the dramatic Vermilion Cliffs is **Lees Ferry** ⑮, once a ferry crossing operated by John D. Lee, a prominent Mormon elder. Lee was sent here personally by LDS Church President Brigham Young after being implicated in the 1857 Mountain Meadows Massacre of an emigrant wagon train bound for California. At the mouth of the Paria River is Lee's old homestead, **Lonely Dell Ranch**, a pretty spot with a log cabin, a blacksmith shop, ranch house and shady orchards. This is a good place to while away an hour or two, watching the river runners on the Colorado River. There is a campground at Lees Ferry and several quaint lodgings and restaurants a little farther west in the Arizona Strip. The historic **Spencer Trail**, which was built as a shortcut over the Vermilion Cliffs in 1910 by a miner and trader named Charles Spencer, makes an interesting day hike while you're in the area. You can reach the rim of these steep cliffs in one to two hours, depending on your physical condition.

By now, you'll probably be champing at the bit to get on the river itself. Wilderness River Adventures (800-528-6154) offers single-day and multiday river trips from below Glen Canyon Dam to Lees Ferry and beyond. From the dam, you'll pass through **Horseshoe Bend**, an entrenched meander, or gooseneck, cut by the river into the sedimentary rocks. From Lees Ferry, you can continue through Grand Canyon National Park, whose boundary adjoins Glen Canyon to the west. ❏

Hidden Life

The biological soil crust known as cryptobiotic soil (Greek for "hidden life") is one of the quiet miracles of Canyon Country. "Crypto," as it's known, is a living community of mutually beneficial organisms, working together to reduce erosion, retain water, and encourage soil fertility. An astonishing 75 percent of the Colorado Plateau is covered in this ancient building block of life.

Cryptobiotic communities are dominated by cyanobacteria (blue-green algae), one of the oldest life-forms on earth, as well as lichens, mosses, microfungi, bacteria and green algae. Cyanobacteria and microfungi protect themselves from sharp sand grains by secreting a sticky mucilage around their cells that helps glue soil particles in place. Mosses and lichens put down small roots that anchor the soil and keep it from blowing away.

When it rains, these organisms absorb up to 10 times their volume in water and then release it slowly into the soil. Frost-heaving roughens the surface of cryptobiotic soil, further slowing rainwater runoff. Mature cryptobiotic crusts are easy to recognize: the soil is dark, mounded, crumbly and filled with plants. Less easy to see are young soils, which look like a sandy crust.

Cryptobiosis also allows living things to shut down metabolic activity and lie dormant until conditions are favorable – a survival tactic widespread among microscopic life-forms found in potholes, the depressions atop sandstone cliffs. Potholes are carved by desert downpours that collect in depressions and dissolve the cementing minerals between grains of sand, allowing them to be removed by wind and rain.

Thousands of tiny plants and animals live in these temporary aquatic habitats. Only single-celled organisms survive in small, shallow pools. Slightly larger potholes may contain water bears, rotifers, nematodes and water mites. The largest pools contain the most diversity: fairy shrimp, water fleas and other small crustaceans; snails; mosquito larvae; diving beetles; and water boatmen.

Because rainfall is sporadic on the Colorado Plateau, many pothole dwellers have evolved survival tactics that allow them to lie dormant indefinitely, then quickly revive and reproduce before rainwater evaporates. Some fairy shrimp complete their entire life cycle in as little as four days. Once laid, fairy shrimp eggs withstand dehydration. Rotifers, tardigrades and nematodes can dry up and survive at any time in their life cycle.

Hiking, camping, bicycling, and off-road driving are destroying cryptobiotic crusts and pothole life in Canyon Country. Crushed cryptobiotic crusts contribute less nitrogen and organic matter to the ecosystem, dry out, and blow away, forming sand dunes that bury other healthy soils. Recovery can take up to 250 years. Bicycle and tire tracks are particularly damaging because they form a continuous strip and channelize water flow that quickly washes away soil. Pothole life is also fragile and easily disturbed. Never wade in a pothole, use it for washing or drinking, or even walk, ride, or drive through a dry pothole, if you can avoid it. ❑

RIGHT: primrose finds a tenuous foothold in cracked sandstone.

CAPITOL REEF NATIONAL PARK

Maps:
Area 228
Park 254

A wrinkle in the earth's crust runs through this intensely colorful park where 'sleeping rainbows,' 'golden thrones' and other formations appear to be illuminated from within

For many people, the desert Southwest seems like a vast dry ocean that stretches endlessly in every direction, its rocky floor occasionally interrupted by broad troughs, tablelands, snowcapped mountains and maze-like canyons. But in Utah, the paradox of ocean imagery amid intensely arid land goes one step farther, for here, rolling in long, colorful, petrified breakers across a desert basin, is one of the most dramatic geologic features on the American continent: the Waterpocket Fold, a 100-mile-long (160-km) warp on the earth's surface that neatly bisects southeastern Utah, from volcanic Thousand Lake Mountain in the north to man-made Lake Powell in the south. In between, 378-square-mile (979-sq-km) **Capitol Reef National Park ⑯** preserves 75 miles (120 km) of the Waterpocket Fold, its native plants and animals, and the artifacts of Fremont Indians and Mormon pioneers who made the area their home.

PRECEDING PAGES: a view of Fruita from the rim overlook. **LEFT:** the Burr Trail. **BELOW:** cowboy poet Marion Manwell at a festival in Capitol Reef National Park.

Capitol Reef is one of the lesser-known parks in the Southwest – a plus for outdoor enthusiasts who are put off by the crowds at Grand Canyon and Zion. It adjoins Grand Staircase–Escalante National Monument and Glen Canyon National Recreation Area to the south and is halfway between Bryce Canyon and Canyonlands National Parks. It is easily reached from UT Scenic Byway 12 to the south or from Interstate 70 to the north. UT 24 cuts across the park, following the winding Fremont River beneath sheer sandstone cliffs. On the east, these cliffs open into a series of humpbacks, known to the Paiutes as "the sleeping rainbow." Roads on either side of the Waterpocket Fold swing south from UT 24, providing numerous possibilities for exploring the park by car, bicycle or on foot.

Rainbow rocks

Most visitors are intrigued by the Waterpocket Fold. How did it come to be here? Geologists believe that it was created about 65 million years ago, when a period of geologic activity deep below the earth's surface began wrenching the low-lying landscape of western America into its present contorted form. It is generally thought that massive movements along the junction of the Pacific and North American Plates around that time forced up the Sierra Nevada in California and continued to reverberate eastward, squeezing the miles of sedimentary rocks that had accumulated across the Southwest.

The monolithic Colorado Plateau rose slowly under this pressure, and a series of steep, north-south monoclines, or folds, began to form across its surface, of

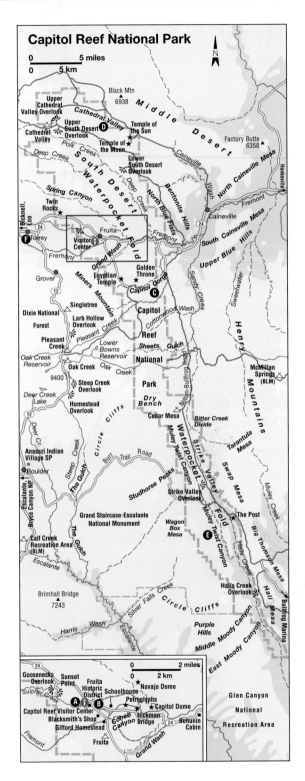

Capitol Reef National Park

which the Waterpocket Fold is one of the most spectacular examples. The exposed rock surfaces soon became vulnerable to weathering. Wind and water carved the rainbow-colored cliffs, spires, natural bridges, arches and hogbacks that characterize Capitol Reef today.

Because it follows the Waterpocket Fold, the park is much longer than it is wide and can be divided roughly into three sections: the rugged, remote northern section of Cathedral Valley paralleling the northeastern exposure of the Fold; the accessible Escarpment section, encompassing park headquarters at Fruita, the Fremont River and a particularly scenic portion of the Fold; and the southernmost section of the park, above Bullfrog Basin in Glen Canyon, where the great rock waves of the Waterpocket Fold reach 1,500 ft (460 meters) in height and are cut by a labyrinth of deep canyons.

Mormon settlers

If you haven't been to Capitol Reef before, start your visit in the Escarpment section of the park off UT 24. Park headquarters is in the pretty little former Mormon community of **Fruita**, which sits next to an emerald belt of cottonwoods, tamarisks and willows along the Fremont River. Views here are incredible, especially after a summer rainstorm. You'll be surrounded on all sides by cliffs of Navajo Sandstone atop the sheer Wingate Sandstone, which have been molded by erosion into domes, buttes, pillows and knobs that contrast with a startling blue sky.

Stop first at the **Capitol Reef Visitor Center Ⓐ** (8am–4.30pm, extended hours in summer; 435-425-3791, www. nps.gov/care) to pick up self-guided tour leaflets and hiking information, view exhibits, and buy books and maps. If you plan to do any backcountry driving on the Bullfrog-Notom Road to Lake Powell, the Burr Trail in the southern part of the park, or in Cathedral Valley, be sure to ask about road conditions before setting out. These high-clearance roads wash out after bad weather and are not recommended at such times.

Geologist and Civil War veteran Major John Wesley Powell was the first American to systematically explore the area, in 1872. He noted the way depressions in the "slickrock" filled with life-giving rainwater and dubbed the formation the Waterpocket Fold. Fruita was founded by settler Niels Johnson in the 1880s and eventually comprised 10 families, some of whom were polygamists wishing to live quiet, self-supporting lives away from the glare of government disapproval. Names like Cohab Canyon linger, commemorating these early settlers. The Mormons' preoccupation with land and government is also reflected in the name they gave the area of the Waterpocket Fold in which they had settled – Capitol Reef. In their eyes, the central section of the Fold welled up like an ocean reef, while one of its larger domes was a dead ringer for the US Capitol. Other unusually eroded rocks sparked equally descriptive names – Chimney Rock, Golden Throne, Egyptian Temple and the Castle.

With a reliable water source at hand, the residents were able to harvest plentiful supplies of apricots, peaches, cherries and apples, which they used for their own consumption or sold to neighboring towns, transient miners, cowboys and even outlaws. Butch Cassidy and the Wild Bunch, who hid out in nearby Loa and east of the park in a remote area known as Robber's Roost, were customers. Cassidy carved his signature on the wall of a side canyon, along with many other early miners, surveyors, explorers and homesteaders. A number of inscriptions are preserved at **Pioneer Register**, visible on the popular hike through Capitol Gorge. The earliest historic signatures are those of two prospectors who passed through in 1871.

Fruita residents prospered even as downriver communities like **Caineville**, snugged into the low-lying badlands, struggled with flooding. In 1884, they built a notorious wagon road known as the "Blue Dugway" through Capitol Gorge, crossing the nearly impassable ridges and smooth domes of the Waterpocket Fold to link Torrey on the west with settlements on the east. Every year, enterprising farmers hauled their produce to markets in Price and Ritchfield. It was an extraordinary undertaking, considering that in 1910 the 10-mile (16-km) wagon trip to Torrey, the closest settlement, took no less than 90 minutes – in good weather.

Growing all their own food, residents weathered the Great Depression far more successfully than the rest of the United States. Still, the community remained isolated and, in the 1930s, boosters proposed that part of the present national park be set aside as Wayne Wonderland State Park in an effort to bring visitors to the area. Instead, the area was designated a national monument in 1937 and later incorporated into the larger Capitol Reef National Park in 1971. Fruita's last few residents departed in the 1960s.

The 200-acre (80-hectare) **Fruita Historic District ❸** includes the 1896 one-room **Schoolhouse**, the 1908 **Gifford Homestead**, the **Blacksmith's Shop**, barns and the historic **Fruit Orchards**, containing roughly 3,000 trees, the most extensive in the National Park System. If you spend the night in the park's grassy campground (highly recom-

Map: opposite page

BELOW: apricot picking in Fruita's pioneer orchard.

mended), you can stroll the trails linking these historic structures and pick fruit in the orchards as it comes into season. The peaches are especially tasty.

Desert and river

This is a park that inspires strong emotions. It is remote, overscaled and desperately hot and dry in summer (unless you find yourself caught in a summer downpour, when most of the park's scant 7 inches/18 cm of precipitation falls). To keep cool, either view the park from your car or stick to one of the day hikes off the scenic drive and UT 24, such as those at **Grand Wash**, **Capitol Gorge**, the **Goosenecks Overlook**, **Sunset Point** and **Hickman Bridge**.

A dragonfly alights on a blade of grass along Halls Creek.

The tree-lined banks of the Fremont River also provide shade on days when temperatures approach 100°F (37°C). If you hope to explore the park on foot, bring adequate weather protection, water, food and backpacking equipment; supplies are not available in the park. There are numerous places where you can hike and camp off-trail. Plan your trip carefully before venturing out by obtaining a free backcountry map from rangers at the visitor center.

The river and the shallow pools at the base of seeping sandstone walls are an oasis where trees and water-loving plants, such as columbines, monkeyflowers and ferns grow. They are also popular haunts for mule deer, warblers, ringtail cats, frogs and other desert denizens who come to drink and splash during cool desert evenings and mornings. In winter, you can sometimes surprise a mountain lion or bobcat emboldened by the lack of visitors.

BELOW:
Cohab Canyon.

It is a mistake to imagine that the desert is devoid of life. In reality, the many creatures, large and small, that live here have adapted to a life beneath rocks, in underground burrows, or hidden in narrow canyons, where sunlight and human

THE MAN BEHIND THE PARK

Ephraim Portman Pectol was the owner of a store in Torrey and served as a Mormon bishop there from 1911 to 1928. He enjoyed exploring Capitol Reef and collecting Fremont Indian artifacts, which he displayed in a small private museum inside his store.

In 1921, Pectol organized a boosters club in Torrey, with the sole aim of promoting the scenic attractions of Wayne County. The club mounted a major media campaign, using articles and photographs of the area to drum up nationwide interest for a park. Wayne Wonderland Club paid Salt Lake City photographer J. E. Broaddus to take a series of promotional photographs and travel around lecturing on Wayne Wonderland.

Pectol's long campaign to establish Wayne Wonderland National Monument succeeded soon after he was elected to the legislature in 1933. Four years later, Capitol Reef National Monument was set aside by President Franklin D. Roosevelt. It was expanded and upgraded to a national park in 1971. Sleeping Rainbow Ranch, a former dude ranch along Pleasant Creek belonging to Lerton Knee, was recently added to the park. It will be operated as a scientific research center collecting data on the large number of endemic plant species found in the area.

Map
on page
254

visitors rarely interrupt their privacy. On the slippery cliffs towering above the river, pinyon and juniper trees struggle with the elements, sending roots into pockets of soil. These dune-deposited rocks were laid down in a vast desert roughly 190 million years ago and, over time, compressed into mineralized rocks several miles thick.

The scenic drive south of Fruita takes you through the dramatic western exposure of the Waterpocket Fold into Grand Wash and Capitol Gorge, two water-carved, sheer-walled canyons. Along the drive, older rocks of the Shinarump Conglomerate, Chinle and Moenkopi formations reveal their ancient origins in sluggish streams and rivers during the time of the dinosaurs.

In **Capitol Gorge** ⒸÊ (and along a roadside trail off UT 24) is 1,000-year-old rock art left behind by prehistoric Fremont people between AD 700 and 1250. These first residents of Capitol Reef cultivated fields of hardy corn along the fertile floodplain and stored crops in granaries in side canyons. They hunted bighorn sheep and deer and made unique moccasins from the hide, using a deer's dewclaw for traction on the heel. Their early pottery was unpainted gray or black, with raised or tooled surfaces. Later, they began to decorate this gray-ware with black paint – similar to Mesa Verde ceramics – possibly as a result of contact with Ancestral Pueblo neighbors to the south.

Abundant evidence of geologic activity is on view in the northern section of the park. East of the Waterpocket Fold, the enormous drainage area of **Cathedral Valley** ⒹÊ fans southeast from the base of Thousand Lake Mountain in the South Desert, where more recent volcanism and glaciation have built and sculpted the high country beyond Capitol Reef. In this extremely arid section of the park, accessible only on foot or by four-wheel-drive, thick layers of red

BELOW:
wheelwrights
demonstrate
traditional skills
during the national
park's Harvest
Homecoming Days.

Entrada sandstone have been whittled by erosion into 500-ft (150-meter) spires that seem to guard the rugged landscape. The exposed location is home to only the hardiest desert plants. Burrowing creatures such as kangaroo rats, jackrabbits and cottontails have found a way to survive here – even though these same animals form the diet of gray foxes, coyotes, mountain lions, golden eagles, ravens and other peripatetic desert dwellers.

In this remote spot, there is a single primitive five-site campground close to Upper Cathedral Valley Overlook, and another at Elkhorn in Fishlake National Forest, outside the park limits.

South to Lake Powell

For "desert rats" used to the rigors of hiking over naked slickrock, the southernmost tip of the Fold is the most alluring. It can be reached via the dirt **Notom-Bullfrog Road**, which runs down the east side of the Fold all the way to Bullfrog Marina at Lake Powell, or by turning off at Boulder along UT 12 and crossing the famous **Burr Trail Road**, the 34-mile (58-km) route across the Waterpocket Fold built by rancher John Atlantic Burr in the late 1800s. On this southern exposure of the Waterpocket Fold, Capitol Reef adjoins the wilderness that surrounds the Escalante River and its canyons in Grand Staircase–Escalante National Monument, and here the true meaning of canyon country becomes apparent.

BELOW: orchards planted by Mormon settlers "let the desert bloom."

The best way to explore the region is to hike south from the intersection of Burr Trail and Notom-Bullfrog Road through 16-mile (26-km) **Muley Twist Canyon E**. This route takes you through steep canyon narrows to an exceptionally wild area of the park around Lower Halls Creek where, for a few years

in the early 1880s, Hole-in-the-Rock pioneer Charles Hall ferried passengers across the Colorado River.

The Escalante area also harbors beautiful rock art created by prehistoric Ancestral Pueblo and Fremont Indians. Deep in the canyons are panels depicting, among other things, tall, bejeweled shaman-like anthropomorphs carrying shields and surrounded by bighorn sheep and other game. Look but don't touch. These beautiful images are one of the highlights of this unusual park and protecting them is everyone's responsibility.

Around Torrey

If, like many visitors, you're traveling east on UT 24 through Capitol Reef to Moab – all in one long day – it's easy to miss much of what makes the park and surrounding area so special. That takes a bit more time. Instead, plan to spend the night in the park's campground or in nearby Torrey and explore Wayne County – an area that is 97 percent public land.

Tiny **Torrey** Ⓕ, a mile west of the UT 12/24 junction, is a quintessential Mormon ranching and farming community, complete with irrigation ditch and a historic LDS church. But that doesn't mean culture has passed it by. It has a modest but worthwhile art gallery, a surprisingly comprehensive bookstore/ coffeehouse in a unique historic building, an enterprising visitors bureau, an organization that offers seasonal public lectures on topics of local interest, the area's only four-star bed-and-breakfast, and several high-end restaurants whose chefs serve farm-raised trout from nearby Loa and organic produce from Mesa Farm in Caineville.

The Technicolor country surrounding Capitol Reef has long attracted writers

Map on page 254

BELOW: a deer browses near the historic Gifford barn in Fruita.

Map on page 254

BELOW: a schoolhouse in the Fruita historic district has been restored to its 19th-century appearance.
RIGHT: a hiker pauses below a formation called Fern's Nipple, reputedly named after a girlfriend of one of Butch Cassidy's gang members.

and artists. Zane Grey and Wallace Stegner found inspiration in the red-rocks, as did artists Maynard Dixon and comic-book illustrator Dick Sprang, who drew his most famous character, Batman, while living here.

In the 1970s, Salt Lake City travel writer Ward Roylance fell in love with the Capitol Reef area and moved here with his wife. Until his death in 1993, Roylance fought tirelessly to preserve the area. His book, *Enchanted Wilderness,* is a little-known classic and led to the founding of the nonprofit Entrada Institute, dedicated to preserving the red-rock country and its heritage through arts and education. The Institute is a Torrey fixture, offering public workshops, readings, demonstrations and lectures every weekend in July and August on topics such as rock art, astronomy, the environment and historical characters. Entrada occupies part of Roylance's hand-built, pyramid-shaped home.

The building also houses the low-key Robbers Roost Books and Beverages (185 W. Main St/UT 24, tel: 435-425-3265; www.xmission.com/entrada), a good stop for anyone interested in the history of the area. You can buy regional books, maps and pioneer-inspired handicrafts, and relax with a latte next to the creek or fireplace. The nearby Torrey Gallery (80 E. Main, tel: 435-425-3909) displays Navajo rugs and works by Bonnie Posselli, Doug Snow and other Utah artists.

Small wonders

Continue west on UT 24 through **Bicknell**, where you can view an old grist mill from a roadside interpretive pullout. Bicknell has a few art galleries, but the town has seen better days. In late July, it hosts the smallest international film festival in the world in its restored 1945 **Wayne Theater** (11 E. Main, tel: 435-425-3123) – a popular event that attracts more people in a few days than you'll see here in a year.

Fifteen miles (24 km) from Torrey is the tiny hamlet of **Loa**, where you'll find the Road Creek Inn (98 S. Main, tel: 800-388-7688, www.roadcreekranch.com), a 21-room lodge in a converted 1912 Mormon mercantile building, on a working ranch owned by former Utah governor Mike Leavitt's family. Road Creek Ranch operates a trout hatchery, which sells tasty fresh and smoked fish to restaurants throughout the region. The inn has a popular and casual restaurant, specializing in – you guessed it – trout.

Guests at Road Creek Ranch can arrange horseback tours and chuckwagon cookouts on **Thousand Lake Mountain** and **Boulder Mountain**, which fill the horizon around this pastoral green valley. Vehicle, horseback and hiking trips as well as shuttles are available in Torrey through Hondo Tours (90 E. Main, tel: 800-332-2696). The cool, forested mountains, reaching 12,000 ft (3,660 meters) in elevation, are reason enough to stick around Torrey when the temperatures at lower elevations soar. There are numerous hiking and camping opportunities in Dixie National Forest on Boulder Mountain (off UT 12 between Boulder and Torrey) and Fishlake National Forest on Thousand Lake Mountain, reachable from Loa. For more information, contact the US Forest Service Teasdale Ranger Station in **Teasdale** (138 East Main, tel: 435-425-9500), south of UT 24, or Fishlake National Forest headquarters (115 E 900 N. Richfield, tel: 435-896-9233). ❑

CANYONLANDS NATIONAL PARK

Maps:
Area 288
Park 266

The Green and Colorado Rivers converge in the heart of Canyon Country, where ancient pueblo ruins vie for the traveler's attention with enthralling landscapes and lots of recreational opportunities

Canyonlands sprawls at the physical and emotional center of the province known as the Colorado Plateau. Here, across a tilted, tiered and carved rock stage, one of nature's longest-running dramas plays every day – an epic in which rock, river, weather and finely adapted living things all have equal roles.

Stewart Udall, who as U.S. Secretary of the Interior was midwife to the congressional bill that created **Canyonlands National Park ❶** in 1964, described the region as "a vast area of scenic wonders and recreational opportunities unduplicated elsewhere on the American continent or in the world." You will certainly need to plan your trip to this 527-sq-mile (1,365-sq km) park carefully, as it is divided into four distinct units – Island in the Sky, the Needles, the Maze, and the converging Green and Colorado Rivers – all of which deserve equal consideration.

The big picture

If you have only a day, the 6,000-ft (1,830-meter) plateau of **Island in the Sky**, situated in the northern part of Canyonlands atop the Y created by the conjoining rivers, offers sweeping views of the park, a visitor center, interpretive talks, a primitive campground, and short, rugged hikes to salt domes, arches and other geologic features. No water is available; be sure to bring plenty with you. The road to this unit begins 7 miles (10 km) north of Moab, then southwest from UT 313 for another 25 miles (40 km). Float trips above the confluence of the Green and Colorado Rivers – one of the most pleasurable ways to experience the park – are popular, as are mountain biking and four-wheel-driving.

You can arrange trips into Canyonlands with park concessionaires, located primarily in Moab or Green River. Working under contract with the National Park Service, these companies offer a variety of services, including lodging, restaurants, gift shops and backcountry tours. For a list of approved concessionaires, call or stop in at the **Southeast Utah Group, National Park Service** (2282 SW Resource Blvd, Moab, tel: 435-719-2313) or the multi-agency **Moab Information Center** at Center and Main Sts (summer 8am–9pm, winter 9am–5pm; tel: 435-259-1370).

The best way to see canyon country up close is to drive south 40 miles (64 km) on US 191, then another 36 miles (56 km) on UT 211 into the **Needles District**, where a dizzying array of sandstone arches, fins, buttes, spires and canyons rival Ancestral Pueblo ruins and rock art for beauty and abundance. The Needles has an attractive, air-conditioned visitor center with exhibits and a bookstore; the 26-site Squaw Flat Camp-

PRECEDING PAGES: crossing Mesa Arch. **LEFT:** bighorn skull. **BELOW:** camping in the Island in the Sky district.

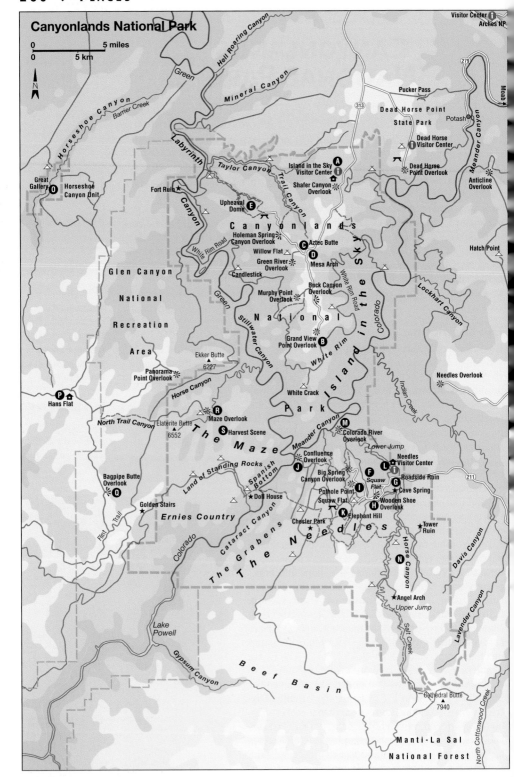

Canyonlands National Park

Map on page 288

ground; primitive backcountry campsites; and a number of unpaved roads and undeveloped hiking trails.

The remote **Maze District**, once described as "a 30-sq-mile puzzle in sandstone," can only be reached by foot or four-wheel-drive vehicle from west of the park (or from the river). If you're equipped with water, food, backpacking supplies, spare tires and winches and are willing to spend extra time in the park's remote reaches, the Maze contains a rich variety of desert landscapes and rock art.

For "river rats," there's no better way to go into the heart of this convoluted canyon country than to follow in the wake of explorer Major John Wesley Powell, who made daring runs down the Green and Colorado Rivers in 1869 and 1871–72. Below the river confluence, the swollen Colorado erupts into roaring white water for the 14 miles (23 km) that link sheer-walled Cataract Canyon with Lake Powell. River running here is challenging and carefully monitored by the National Park Service; only experienced river runners should attempt the trip.

Be aware that all day and overnight backcountry users must purchase a permit for their trip (valid for 14 days and including reserved campsites in the backcountry). Since Canyonlands is cold in winter and exceedingly hot and dry in summer, spring and fall are the most popular times. Reservations are suggested but not required and may be made two weeks in advance; cancelled permits are sold on a first-come, first-served basis. Rangers are available to answer questions and help with trip planning at the Backcountry Reservations office at park headquarters (Mon–Fri 8am–12.30pm; tel: 435-259-4351). Reservations must be made by mail or fax.

Island in the Sky

Rock is the leitmotiv of Canyonlands. In order to understand its scope, drive south from **Island in the Sky Visitor Center Ⓐ** (daily 8am–4.30pm) to **Grand View Point Overlook Ⓑ**, which is the best place to survey the 360-degree panorama that unfolds before you. Hidden in the northeast are the soaring red-rock landmarks of Arches National Park. To the east rise the tall, volcanic crags of the La Sal Mountains, imposing yet inviting. Closer to the park, beneath Dead Horse Point State Park, loop the famous "goosenecks" of the **Colorado River**, marking the park's eastern border.

To the west, the equally contorted **Green River** winds through **Labyrinth Canyon**, its narrow meanders forming the boundary with Glen Canyon National Recreation Area. To the southwest, the Henry Mountains obstruct the view of Capitol Reef National Park, their great bulk looming beyond the Maze. The view south encompasses more than 100 miles (160 km) of drifting tablelands and swirling canyons, including the junction of the Colorado and Green Rivers, bound on either side by the eroded sandstone of The Needles and the tortuous passages of The Maze. Just below this sky island is the **White Rim Road**, a circuitous, 100-mile (160-km) dirt trail that was used by prospectors mining uranium in the colorful Chinle Formation in the 1950s. This popular mountain bike and four-wheel-drive route follows a bench of White Rim Sandstone through prime bighorn sheep territory.

BELOW: mountain bikers take a break on the White Rim Road.

The scenic drive offers several places for stopping and hiking. Short trails to **Aztec Butte**  and **Mesa Arch** ❶ are clearly marked by piles of rock, or cairns, on the slickrock. Plants struggle to survive in this arid environment – in cracks in the rock and in fragile, "brown sugar" patches of cryptobiotic soil. Although it doesn't look like much, cryptobiotic soil is a primary building block of all living things in canyon country. It is actually a community of mutually beneficial living organisms – lichens, mosses, microfungii and blue-green algae – that work together to reduce erosion, increase water retention, and encourage soil fertility. These hummocks protect young pinyons, junipers, blackbrush, grasses and wildflowers and allow them to root, stabilize the desert soil, and prosper. As they say in these parts: "Don't Bust the Crust." Keep to the trail, or bypass these sensitive soils by walking in sandy washes and on the rocks. Adaptable reptiles, such as whip-tailed lizards, and ground squirrels, canyon mice and other gnawing creatures are found on the plateau. They make fine fare for peripatetic coyotes and gray foxes and alert sky patrollers, such as eagles, ravens and red-tailed hawks.

The rocks in this park contain a color-coded record of sediment deposited over the past 300 million years, in a succession of seas, beaches, deserts, rivers and streams. But the accounting is not complete; more than a vertical mile of recent strata has already been borne away by the youthful enthusiasm of the Colorado and Green Rivers, which began scouring the land as the massive Colorado Plateau was forced up. The topography is forever changing. As the sediment-laden rivers cut their paths, and ground water, ice, snow and wind break down the rocks, the eroded beauty of Canyonlands will one day be merely a memory.

One of the best ways to confront the geologic processes that brought Canyonlands into being is to hike the trail to **Upheaval Dome** ❺, a short way from the

Colorado River mudflats crack in the intense heat of the desert sun.

BELOW: a river guide takes a snooze on the banks of the Green River.

DEAD HORSE POINT STATE PARK

Situated next to the Island in the Sky district of Canyonlands, this 5,250-acre (2,120-hectare) park has breathtaking views of the La Sal Mountains, eroded cliffs, mesas, buttes and river canyons. At the base of the mesa is an enormous horseshoe bend, or entrenched meander, carved by the Colorado River.

Before the turn of the century, mustang herds ran wild on the mesas near Dead Horse Point. The promontory provided a natural corral used by cowboys for rounding up horses. The only escape was through a narrow, 30-meter "neck" of land controlled by fencing. Mustangs were then roped and broken, with the better ones being kept for personal use or sold to eastern markets.

According to one legend, a band of broomtails was left corralled on the Point. The gate was supposedly left open so the horses could return to the open range. For some unknown reason, the mustangs remained on the Point and died of thirst.

Dead Horse Point is a popular movie location; in 1991 it served as the backdrop for the final scenes of *Thelma and Louise*. The park has 10 miles (16 km) of rim trails and a 21-site campground with developed facilities, and makes a useful base for exploring the surrounding lands.

Map on page 266

main road in Island in the Sky. Just below you is a 1,500-ft (460-meter) crater filled with a jumble of rocks. Some geologists believe this is a collapsed salt dome; others, the site of a meteor impact; still others a combination of the two.

The 11 layers of sedimentary rocks on display in Canyonlands sit uneasily on a layer of salt thousands of feet thick – the remnant of evaporated seas that lay trapped here 300 million years ago. As overlying sediments pressed down on this salt – the Paradox Formation – it became soft and mobile and began to move away from the weight. Highlands blocked it on the east, so it flowed west until it encountered ancient fault blocks that forced the salt to bulge upward, forming the cracked salt domes you see throughout the large Paradox Basin. Groundwater began to seep into the fractures, dissolving the salt and deepening the joints through many layers of sedimentary rocks. This weathering of sandstone has created memorable features throughout the park – some of the most spectacular are found in the carved, banded spires of Cedar Mesa Sandstone in The Needles.

The Needles

The turnoff for The Needles district lies 14 miles (23 km) north of **Monticello**, on US 191, where paved UT 211 follows Indian Creek to **Squaw Flat F**. This is one of those rare places in Canyonlands blessed with deeper soils that allow Indian ricegrass, galleta and other useful grasses to establish themselves. Until 1975, local cowboys ran their cattle here in winter, leaving behind line camps in shady overhangs such as Cave Creek.

After the visitor center, the scenic drive passes **Roadside Ruin G**, a small Ancestral Pueblo dwelling, and **Wooden Shoe Overlook H**, which has views of a clog-shaped rock formation to the east. **Pothole Point I** is named for the

BELOW: whitewater jostles a party of rafters on the Green River.

The Chesler Park Trail provides sweeping views of the Needles district.

BELOW: Mesa Arch.

depressions in the rock that trap rainwater for thousands of microorganisms, such as miraculous tadpole shrimp, which can survive even when water isn't present. The road ends at **Big Spring Canyon Overlook**, where a trail to **Confluence Overlook ❶** begins.

From **Squaw Flat Campground**, a 3-mile (5-km) unpaved spur leads to **Elephant Hill ❸**, and thence a dirt road takes you to the collapsing fins of the **Grabens** near the river. The 5-mile (8-km), round-trip **Chesler Park Trail**, which eventually passes through a meadow surrounded by eroded rocks, makes a good hike from Elephant Hill. The canyons and meadows of The Needles support many wood rats, chipmunks, squirrels, kangaroo rats and other rodents, as well as horned larks and black-throated sparrows.

There are a number of places along the scenic drive to turn off and explore. One four-wheel-drive road, beginning at the **Needles Visitor Center ❶** (daily 8am–4.30pm,), takes you north to the **Colorado River Overlook ❶**. The sandy road is decent until the last 1½ miles, when stair-step rocks and tight turns make for some nerve-wracking moments. Farther down, a short, unpaved spur south of the pavement leads to **Cave Spring Trail**, which preserves a historic cowboy camp beside a spring. The camp is a reminder that much of Canyonlands was grazed by cattle and sheep from the late 1800s until well into the 20th century.

From Cave Spring, you will need a four-wheel-drive vehicle or sturdy legs to explore sandy-bottomed **Salt Creek**, the only year-round riparian area in Canyonlands beside the Colorado and Green Rivers. Salt Creek's main tributary, **Horse Canyon ❶**, has hidden Indian dwellings. Salt Creek Road is now closed beyond Peekaboo (the site of a rock art panel) in order to protect park resources.

Salt Creek has more cultural remains of Ancestral Pueblo people, who lived

here between about AD 1 and 1300, than anywhere else in the park. **Horse Canyon** contains the masonry structures of **Tower** and **Keyhole** ruins, as well as the **Thirteen Faces**, red-and-white pictographs painted on the sandstone walls. Pueblo families farmed along ephemeral washes, now overgrown with willow, tamarisk and cottonwood, but they continued to hunt small game and supplement meals with seeds, nuts and edible plants. Surplus grain was stored in granaries built into hard-to-reach ledges. About 100 families lived in this area, probably using these cliff-side homes seasonally and farming atop the mesas in summer.

Rock paintings found in these canyons portray large, mysterious, anthropomorphs, both shield-shaped and triangular, bejeweled and brightly painted in red, white and sometimes blue. Images were also pecked into the walls. Here as elsewhere, you may look but not touch rock art. Disturbing artifacts is strictly prohibited. Archaeologists speculate that when life here became too tough sometime in the 1200s, the Ancestral Puebloans moved to farmlands along the Rio Grande and the Little Colorado, where their descendants still live.

Map on page 266

The Maze

An even earlier culture has also been identified in Canyonlands: the Archaic people who hunted and gathered here between 10,000 and 2,000 years ago. Signs of their passage are preserved in ghostly, 3,000-year-old, Barrier Canyon-style pictographs found along the 6½-mile (10-km) hike to the **Great Gallery ⓞ** in Horseshoe Canyon. This canyon is a non-contiguous section of the Maze District, an area that has been kept primitive and hard to reach by overland routes. (Robber's Roost, where Butch Cassidy and his cattle-rustling cohorts hid, is nearby.) You can go as far as **Hans Flat Ranger Station ⓟ** (daily 8am– 4.30pm), reached along a 46-mile (74 km) unpaved road. After that, you'll need a four-wheel-drive to get around this incredibly tangled landscape, much of which can only be hiked.

Several long unpaved roads traverse wild country dotted with strangely named landmarks, which, in true western style, arose from differing perspectives of native people, early adventurers and poetic travelers. A road leads north to Horseshoe Canyon, south to **Bagpipe Butte Overlook ⓠ**, then east along the Flint Trail to Ernies Country and the Land of Standing Rocks. From here you can hike through the **Doll House** above the river confluence and down into Spanish Bottom. For a look into The Maze, backtrack to the Golden Stairs, then drive northeast to the **Maze Overlook ⓡ** or hike the 14-mile (23-km) **North Trail Canyon** to the overlook. A 3-mile (5-km) trail leads into The Maze itself, where Archaic pictographs known as the **Harvest Scene ⓢ** reward your efforts.

The Maze is the park's most pristine experience – a place where quiet desert residents, such as kit foxes, coyotes and mountain lions, are bolder, and unexpected seeps deep in the canyons nourish throngs of maidenhair ferns, mosses, monkeyflowers and columbines. It is rugged, beautiful country, but it can be treacherous. You need to be an experienced and well-prepared hiker or four-wheel-driver (towing fees in Canyonlands can cost you up to $1,000). Err on the side of caution, and talk to park rangers before attempting a trip.   ❑

BELOW: known as the All-American Man, this red-white-and-blue pictograph was made by ancient Puebloans about 650 years ago.

ARCHES NATIONAL PARK AND THE MOAB AREA

Mountain bikers, river runners, rock climbers and other adventurers come to play at a hip desert town surrounded by a beguiling sandstone wilderness

Writer Ed Abbey, one of the Southwest's most passionate advocates, marveled: "This is a landscape that has to be seen to be believed – and even then, confronted directly by the senses, it strains credulity." Indeed. Yet, one of the pleasures of a trip across the Colorado Plateau is the way its ever-changing topography pushes us to understand our surroundings according to different rules, to change our sense of what is normal. **Arches National Park ❷**, with its world-renowned population of carved, salmon-colored arches, fins, spires, pinnacles and balanced rocks, is a case in point. Here, the very landmarks for which this park is famous are windows through which we experience the natural world in a new way.

This 120-sq-mile (310-sq-km) desert park, 5 miles (8 km) north of Moab, is home to more than 2,000 natural arches and many other strangely eroded redrock giants. Unlike neighboring Canyonlands, which requires many visits to appreciate, Arches is small enough to experience in a day by way of its paved scenic drive, pullouts and many short trails, yet large enough to warrant longer explorations into the backcountry, where its wild nature becomes apparent.

Arches has the largest number of natural sandstone arches in the world, with many more being formed all the time – the fortuitous result of location, geology and water erosion. You might think that the explanation for the large number of shape-shifting rocks in this place is complicated, but you would be wrong. The key to this odd convention of geologic landmarks is salt – a common enough commodity, which here has given rise (quite literally) to this high-relief landscape.

LEFT: camping near Moab.
BELOW: a backpacker meditates on the scenery.

Pass the salt

The salt that lies below Arches was deposited 300 million years ago, when a succession of large, shallow seas lay landlocked by the Uncompahgre Uplift, the highlands to the east where the La Sal Mountains are today. As the climate gradually dried, the seawater evaporated, leaving behind salt deposits thousands of feet thick in an enormous depression known as the Paradox Basin. Eventually, the highlands began shedding debris into the basin, which compacted there, cemented by calcium carbonate and other minerals. Its tremendous weight bore down on the underlying Paradox deposits, causing the salt, which is somewhat "plastic," to flow west, away from the burden. The movement stalled when the salt ran up against ancient fault blocks.

One of the most obvious of these faults can be seen in rocks opposite the visitor center, where a 2,500-ft (760-meter) displacement along the Moab Fault has

exposed the fossiliferous strata of the ancient Honaker Trail Formation – a rare glimpse of the rocks that make up the park's basement. Unable to move farther, the salt layer domed up through the 12 layers of rocks lying on top of it, cracking the rocks and weakening the strata. Joints appeared along these fault lines, giving groundwater a chance to enter and dissolve the salt. Undermined by this erosion, the salt domes began to collapse. The low-lying Salt and Cache Valleys and the parallel lines of formations sweeping across them (most evident from overlooks in the nearby La Sal Mountains) are testimony to this ongoing weakening of loosely cemented sedimentary rocks.

It's not difficult to understand what happened next. The evidence can be found everywhere in Arches. Once water, ice and snow went to work on the rock, deepening and widening joints, all manner of oddly carved stones gradually emerged, of which the delicate spans of reddish-brown sandstone, known as natural arches, are some of the most interesting.

Exploring Arches

The entrance to Arches adjoins US 191, beyond the bridge over the Colorado River, which forms the southeastern boundary of the park. In 2004, a new entrance road was unveiled and ground was broken on a large, new visitor center, replacing the 1960s building that had become cramped and out of date. The new visitor center is due for completion in July 2005 and will include a large outdoor plaza for after-hours information, a 150-seat auditorium, interactive educational kiosks, extensive new exhibits and a bookstore. The old visitor center will be "recycled" for administrative office space.

The visitor center is the place to pick up information, purchase books and

"I come more and more to the conclusion that wilderness, in America or anywhere else, is the only thing left that is worth saving."

— EDWARD ABBEY

BELOW: a park ranger discusses the ecology of "potholes," pools of water that collect in depressions in the rock.

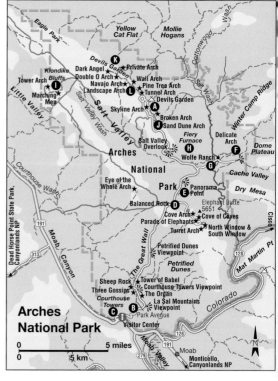

Map
on page
274

maps, and watch a film on the park (every half hour). You can also sign up for ranger-led walks and private trip permits for the Fiery Furnace, a maze of convoluted rock fins just beyond Salt Valley, offered daily between April and October. Top off your water bottles here; water is only available at the visitor center and Devil's Garden Campground, 18 miles (29 km) north of the park entrance, at the end of the scenic drive.

Many travelers have their hearts set on staying in **Devil's Garden Campground Ⓐ**, an attractive 52-site area set amid the most popular arches in the park. Inquire at the visitor center about available campsites. Because these are usually snapped up early in the morning during peak season, a better idea is to reserve your campsite ahead of time through the new reservation system serving all federal campgrounds. For online reservations, log on to www.ReserveUSA.com or call 877-444-6777 or 518-885-3639. Reservations must be made at least four days ahead of your arrival. For current information, visit the park's website at www.nps.gov/arch or call the park information line at 435-719-2299.

For a look at the many different types of arches and geologic phenomena in the park, take the scenic drive from the visitor center to **Devils Garden**, stopping to hike along the short trails that wind through this oversized Zen garden of standing stones. The first weathered rocks you encounter are the skyscraper-like monoliths in **Park Avenue Ⓑ**, so named because of the way their sheer walls jostle the skyline. Nearby, in the **Courthouse Towers Ⓒ**, are Sheep Rock, the Organ, the Tower of Babel and the Three Gossips, soaring giants composed of iron-rich Entrada sandstone, the principal rock layer in the park. Different rates of erosion in the three "members" of Entrada sandstone are responsible for the majority of

BELOW:
North Window
Arch frames a
view of Turret Arch.

A primitive cabin is all that remains of the Wolfe Ranch.

BELOW: mountain bikers follow a precarious stretch of Portal Trail outside Moab.

features, with the lower Dewey Bridge Member crumbling easily beneath the harder Slick Rock Member. The uppermost layer, the white Moab Member, can be seen capping some of the higher landmarks. Underlying the Entrada are the swirling beds of cream-colored Navajo sandstone, whose ancient Sahara-like origins can easily be seen just beyond Courthouse Towers in the humped shapes of "petrified" sand dunes. In this open landscape, you get a great view of the 12,000-ft (3,600-meter) snowcapped La Sal Mountains, great laccoliths with hearts of lava, exposed by erosion in forested crags and peaks that dominate the eastern sky.

Even if you don't have much time, park rangers recommend that you drive at least as far as the **Windows Section**, for it is here that you can see single and double arches, buttes, windows and the gravity-defying **Balanced Rock ⓓ**, sitting beside the 2-mile (3.5-km) paved spur road. Between May and August, Indian paintbrush, larkspur, sand verbena and other wildflowers blooming in front of the rocks are at their most photogenic. In 1956 and 1957, seasonal ranger Ed Abbey lived in a trailer next to Balanced Rock. He welcomed visitors who entered Arches from the highway on what is now a bumpy four-wheel-drive road across from the newer paved park road. The erudite but curmudgeonly Abbey fell in love with Arches and kept a journal of his time here, which he published to wide acclaim in 1968 as *Desert Solitaire: A Season in the Wilderness*. Although he went on to write many other books, *Desert Solitaire* is a sentimental favorite: a love letter to the desert and a rallying cry to stop the growth of "industrial tourism" in our national parks before it is too late.

Just beyond The Windows, you can stop and take in much of the park at **Panorama Point ⓔ**. The canyon of the Colorado River is visible on the park's southeast border. The green belt of willows, tamarisks and cottonwoods that grows

Map
on page
274

along the waterway seems like a mirage at the edge of this sparsely vegetated salt valley, where only salt-tolerant plants like pickleweed and seepweed grow.

After Panorama Point, a road turns northeast for 3 miles (5 km), crossing an area of collapsed rocks of the more recent Dakota, Morrison and Mancos Formations. The road ends at a wheelchair-accessible trail that leads to a viewpoint of **Delicate Arch** Ⓕ, the world-famous symbol of Utah's red-rock country. Delicate Arch is actually not very tall – only 45 ft (14 meters) – but its location on the lip of a slickrock bowl gives it a dramatic bearing. For a close-up look, climb the steep trail to the arch – one of the most rewarding hikes in the park.

The trail begins at a rudimentary cabin, the 1906 **Wolfe Ranch** Ⓖ, which was home to Civil War veteran John Wesley Wolfe and his son. Wolfe came here for his health in 1888, but it's hard to understand why he settled in such a remote outpost so far from society. Maybe that was exactly the point. Canyon country seems to attract loners who value silence and the harmony of the desert. Near the cabin is an important rock art panel, containing pictographs depicting horses drawn by Ute Indians, the only place in the park with clear signs of their presence.

Desert fire

A few miles farther along the scenic drive, you reach the flaming rock fins known as **Fiery Furnace** Ⓗ, which explode with vibrant color at sunset. If time permits, sign up at the visitor center for this three-hour hike; it's one of the most spectacular backcountry hikes in the park but not a good idea to do alone. There is no marked trail through the radiating rocks, so it is quite easy to lose your way. The Fiery Furnace is popular with seasoned rock climbers who may enter (with permit) in a private group or with local outfitters.

Beyond Fiery Furnace, a left turn onto a gravel road leads 9 miles (14 km) across Salt Valley to **Klondike Bluffs** Ⓘ, whose Marching Men and Tower Arch formations so impressed prospector Alexander Ringhoffer that he persuaded the railroad to conduct tours to the spot in 1923. Arches was named a national monument just six years later, though it did not become a national park until 1971. Klondike is now one of the least visited places in the park. A moderate 3½-mile (5.5-km) trail leads to Tower Arch from a parking lot. Look for fresh deer tracks and occasional mountain lion tracks. Whistle loudly if you see the latter, to avoid any unexpected encounters.

Temperatures at this elevation reach 110°F (43°C) in summer, and thunderstorms and torrential rain are apt to swoop in suddenly. In winter, it is surprisingly frigid, with sub-freezing nighttime temperatures. The dry-rock landscape is occasionally transformed under a glittering white blanket of snow, making colors seem deeper and more intense – a great time to experience Arches with almost no other visitors. The area is subject to dramatic changes in temperature, which can fluctuate by 50°F (28°C) in a 24-hour period. Check the weather forecast before heading out, and take cover in your car if a thunderstorm blows in. Most of Arches is very exposed. On all hikes, bring plenty of water, wear sunscreen, a hat and sturdy hiking boots, and cover exposed skin in summer. The best time of

BELOW: a gopher snake warms itself on a rock.

day to hike is before 9am or in the evening. Night hikes are particularly beautiful. Naturally dark, unpolluted skies make star gazing a popular activity at Arches. The contrast of rock and sky makes this park an ideal location for viewing celestial events such as comets and eclipses.

Head back to the road to visit **Sand Dune Arch** , which shelters a large sand dune at its base – a fun place for the family to romp. Nearby **Skyline Arch** demonstrates how quickly the rocks here can change. A major rockfall in November 1940 doubled its size overnight. The scenic drive ends at **Devils Garden** **K**, where the park's densest array of arches and fins makes a fitting climax to any visit. Several easy trails meander among its soaring spans. A 1-mile (1.6-km) trail from the road leads to **Landscape Arch** **L**, a 306-ft (93-meter) span of "desert varnished" beige rock, one of the longest natural arches in the world (the longest is in Zion National Park). You may continue from Landscape Arch to two other formations – **Double O Arch** and **Dark Angel**. A short side trail leads to massive **Navajo Arch** and the twin openings of **Partition Arch**.

The secret of survival

While out hiking, stay on the trails. The desert floor is dotted with dark patches of cryptobiotic soil, composed of mosses, lichen, fungi and algae that retain moisture, protect against erosion, and provide nitrogen and other nutrients in which plants can grow. Once stepped on, this fragile, new soil, on which so much new life depends, is destroyed for centuries.

Plants and animals must be very choosy about where they live in this difficult environment, jealously guarding their special places in an ongoing bid for survival. Desert creatures are generally nocturnal, venturing out only when the

A climber reaches the pinnacle of Fisher Towers, a popular rock climbing site outside Moab.

desert cools down. You are likely to hear the yip of coyotes at night, as they and gray foxes trot great distances in search of jackrabbits, cottontails, ground squirrels and the smaller rodents you may hear investigating your campsite at night.

Rattlesnakes, collared lizards and other reptiles, which are unable to control body temperatures, doze beneath rocks and bushes at midday (so watch where you put your hands). The sheerest cliffs make good perches for lazy-winged golden eagles and red-tailed hawks, while the joyous song of the tiny canyon wren bounces off seeping sandstone walls decorated with colorful water-loving plants.

Maps:
Area: 288
Park: 274

Moab and environs

Travelers on the Spanish Trail in the 1830s and 1840s forded the Colorado River just north of modern-day **Moab ❸**. Few towns in the Southwest have as beautiful and dramatic a setting as this bustling small town. Sheer sandstone cliffs form fortress-like walls on all sides, enclosing the town in a private world of red rock, verdant riverbanks and tidy houses fronted by ditches irrigating cottage gardens of hollyhocks and other colorful flowers. Moab has a typically Mormon, grid-like layout in its quaint historic downtown but has burst its confines to the south, spilling into Spanish Valley near the southern turnoff for the La Sal Mountain Loop.

The town's history is unusual. Members of the Elk Mountain Mission – one of many colonizing efforts in southern Utah in the 1850s and 1860s by the LDS Church – built a settlement here in 1855 near the Colorado River but were driven out by hostile Utes. By the time another group of Mormons succeeded in founding the town in the 1870s, a motley crew of homesteaders, rustlers, drifters and grifters had settled in, hoping to find their fortune at the end of the Civil War.

Until well into the 20th century, Moab was a sleepy hamlet, miles from

BELOW:
the slender span of
Landscape Arch is
more than 300 ft
(91 meters) long,
making it one of
the world's longest
natural arches.

Jeeps parade down Main Street in Moab. Backcountry driving is popular among visitors and residents.

BELOW: downtown Moab has a variety of eating places.

nowhere. And it might have stayed that way if it hadn't been for the atomic bomb. At the onset of the Cold War, the former U.S. Atomic Energy Commission (AEC), as part of a nationwide search for uranium, established a generous fixed price for uranium as an incentive to miners. Charlie Steen was the first to make a big strike. In an area south of Moab that the AEC had deemed "barren of possibilities," Steen discovered his Mi Vida mine, from which he shipped $100 million of uranium-235. Overnight Moab became the "Uranium Capital of the World."

Mining today takes a very different form: that of mining for tourist dollars. Following the huge recreational boom of the postwar years, surplus army rafts were converted to river-running boats, four-wheel-drive Jeeps were used as recreational vehicles, and then, in the 1980s, the mounting popularity of mountain biking on slickrock trails put Moab on the outdoor recreation map. This boom appears to be here to stay. Between 1995 and 1999, the resident population of Moab doubled – to more than 5,000 – with thousands more descending on the town from Spring Break all the way through October.

Moabites, a frisky, independent bunch who are always free with their opinions, grouse that with real estate prices and property taxes what they now are, they can barely afford to live here anymore. And the growing number of motels, fast-food outlets, overpriced eateries, brew pubs, espresso joints and T-shirt boutiques that have sprung up along Main Street certainly signals major changes. But one can't argue with success. Pretty little Moab is perfectly located for trips to Canyonlands and Arches National Parks, the Manti-La Sal Forest and other public lands nearby. It has become a bona-fide destination, complete with all the attendant headaches when a small rural town is "discovered" by outsiders.

Your first stop in town should be the multi-agency **Moab Information Cen-**

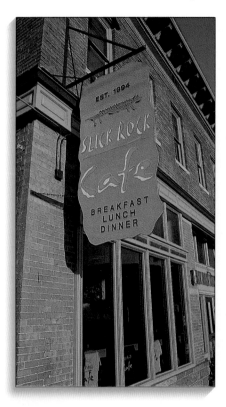

THE SCRIBE OF THE DESERT

In 1956–57, iconoclastic writer Edward Abbey worked as a seasonal ranger in Arches National Monument. A native of the Appalachian community of Home, Pennsylvania, Abbey had fallen in love with the Southwest while riding the rails and, after a stint in the army in Europe, moved west to attend the University of New Mexico.

While working at Arches, Abbey explored the backcountry and kept a journal. Ten years later, he transformed this material into a popular memoir, *Desert Solitaire: A Season in the Wilderness*. Although he wrote 20 other books, including *The Monkey Wrench Gang*, a humorous eco-thriller, *Desert Solitaire* remains Abbey's masterpiece.

"I see myself as an entertainer," he once said. "I'm trying to write good books... make people laugh, make them cry. Provoke them, make them angry. Make them think, if possible."

Friends and admirers delighted in Ed's humor, word play, penchant for philosophical debate, camaraderie and spirit of adventure, and felt a huge loss when he died in 1989. At his request, he was buried under a pile of rocks in the Sonoran Desert at an undisclosed location. His fondest wish was that he would be reborn as a buzzard and haunt the skies above the desert.

ter (MIC) on Center and Main Streets (daily 8am–9pm in summer, shorter hours the rest of the year; tel: 435-259-6111; www.discovermoab.com), where you can discuss your trip with rangers and choose books and maps from a large selection in the attractive bookstore. Afterward, consider strolling a half-block east to the enjoyable little **Dan O'Laurie Museum** (summer Mon–Sat 1pm–8pm, winter Mon–Thurs 3pm–7pm, Fri–Sat 1pm–7pm; 118 E. Center, tel: 435-259-7985; admission), a good place to learn more about the history of the area. You can continue your walk farther by following the Downtown Moab Historic Walking Tour brochure, available at the MIC.

Map on page 288

On the trail

There is so much for outdoor lovers to do in Moab that they could easily spend weeks here and never tire of the possibilities. Immediately adjoining the town is the infamous **Slickrock Trail**, a 9½-mile (15-km) mountain bike loop that begins about 2 miles (3 km) from the junction of Sand Flats Road and Mill Creek Drive in Moab and continues over surrounding sandstone mesas. This is Moab's most difficult mountain biking route, a Class IV. If you're new to the area, you should ride the 2-mile (3-km) practice loop first to test your skills (note: even this route isn't for novices). The Slickrock Trail is located in the **Sand Flats Recreation Area ❹**, adjoining the La Sal Mountains, and has 110 primitive campsites. Bring water; none is available here.

Exposed sandstone in summer gets as hot as an oven. Heat exhaustion and stroke are common problems for hikers and mountain bikers, and there are deaths every year from people who misjudge their heat tolerance. Stay safe. Don't head out in the middle of the day. Stay in a group, wear a helmet, make

BELOW: reddened by sunset, sandstone cliffs along Scenic Byway 128 are reflected in the Colorado River.

The Slickrock Trail is one of the most demanding bike routes in southern Utah.

BELOW: rafters on the Colorado River take in a view of the snowcapped La Sal Mountains.

sure your brakes are in good working order, and carry a first-aid kit. Anyone exercising in the desert in summer should drink at least a gallon (4 liters) of water a day, eat high-energy snacks, and keep skin covered and cool.

Drivers and mountain bikers share the road on several scenic byways around Moab. **Utah Scenic Byway 128**, which begins 2 miles (3 km) north of Moab at the bridge over the Colorado River, winds for 44 miles (71 km) below 1,000-ft-high (300-km) red rocks carved by the river and includes a hiking trail, an old ranch used in the movies, and the historic Dewey Bridge at the confluence with the Dolores River. The BLM manages small campgrounds between the road and the riverbank. These sites in the thick tamarisk, or salt cedar, get hot and buggy in summer, a bit smelly, and suffer from road noise, but are a reasonable alternative to crowded national park campgrounds, at least for one night.

Three miles (5 km) from the bridge is **Negro Bill Trail**, which may be one of Moab's most pleasant day hikes. The moderately difficult 3½-mile (5.5-km) trail, named for a 19th-century African-American named William Granstaff who ran a ranch here, parallels a pretty creek beneath high cliffs and ends up at Morning Glory Arch, in the northern end of the Sand Flats Recreation Area.

At Mile Marker 14 is **Red Cliffs Ranch Film Museum** (Mon–Sun 8am–10pm; tel: 866-812-2002; free), which is packed with movie memorabilia. The museum is located on a guest resort that, beginning in the John Ford era of the 1940s, has been a popular film location. *Wagon Master*, *Rio Grande*, *Son of Cochise*, *Warlock*, *Comancheros*, *Cheyenne Autumn* and, more recently, *Geronimo*, *City Slickers* and *Thelma and Louise*, have all used the magnificent scenery surrounding the ranch as a backdrop. There are numerous other movie loca-

tions in the Moab area, including many in Arches and Canyonlands National Parks. Ask at the MIC for the Movie Tour brochure.

Two famous geological landmarks that have appeared in movies – **Castle Rock** and 1,500-ft-high (450-meter) **Fisher Towers** – can be seen at the start of the **La Sal Mountain Loop**, a paved scenic drive that begins 11 miles (18 km) from the Moab bridge in Castle Valley and continues high into the La Sal Mountains. The scenic drive makes for a truly spectacular four-hour tour around Moab and is highly recommended. From high in the La Sals, there are several viewpoints with breathtaking vistas of the unique geology of southeastern Utah. You can see all the way to the **Canyon Rims Recreation Area**, adjoining the Needles District of Canyonlands, historically used by ranchers and increasingly popular with the thousands of four-wheel-drive, backpacking, rock climbing and camping enthusiasts that flood into southeast Utah each year. When Moab hits the 100°F (39°C) mark, there may be no more pleasant place than the La Sal Mountains, where you'll find picnic sites, lakes and several idyllic campgrounds set among the cool aspens and conifers. The loop exits onto US 191 just south of Moab.

Map on page 288

TIP

Dinosaur tracks are abundant in the Moab area, but particularly accessible around Utah Scenic Highway 279.

Dinosaurs and rock art

The BLM also manages many lesser-known natural and cultural sites. Closest to Moab is **Utah Scenic Byway 279**, also known as Potash Road, which begins 3 miles (5 km) north of Moab, off US 191, and parallels the Colorado River for 17 miles (27 km). All along Potash Road are Indian rock art panels and several three-toed dinosaur tracks. Petroglyphs scratched into the dark mineralized "desert varnish" date to Archaic times, more than 3,000 years ago. There are also rare etchings by Fremont Indians, whose homeland adjoined that of the Ancestral Pueblo people along the Colorado River about a thousand years ago.

Just past the petroglyphs and dinosaur tracks are several natural arches carved out of the sandstone. A 1½-mile (2.5-km) hiking trail leads to **Corona** and **Bow Tie Arches**. Farther on is the aptly named **Jug Handle Arch**. The paved road ends at the Moab Potash Plant, which produces fertilizer from salt deposits below the earth's surface, and continues on a very rough road through **Behind the Rocks Recreation Area**. This high-clearance road emerges on the southwest side of Moab near Kane Creek Road, which leads to the **Matheson Wetland Preserve** (daily sunrise–sunset, guided walks Sat 8am Mar–Oct; tel: 435-259-4629), managed by The Nature Conservancy. This little-known gem is Utah's only Colorado River wetland and harbors some 175 species of birds.

At the end of Potash Road is the main put-in for river trips below the Island in the Sky district of Canyonlands National Park. Outfitters offer day trips on the river, and if you have time, this is one of the most enjoyable ways to visit the sprawling, wild park. In just a day, you can float past the 2,000-ft-high (600-meter) cliffs below the "goosenecks" of the Colorado River. Outfitters usually offer lunch on the riverbank, then a bumpy Jeep ride back up to the mesa top, stopping at sites along the famous Shafer Trail before returning to Moab. ❏

BELOW: a hiker descends the Fisher Towers Trail.

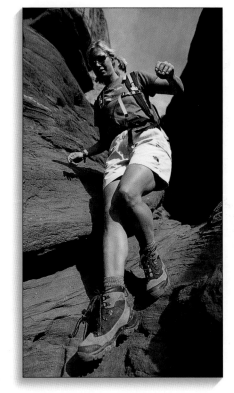

SAN JUAN COUNTY

Mormon, Navajo and ancient Pueblo cultures intersect
in Utah's southeast corner, a rough-hewn land of red-rock
monuments, salmon-colored dunes and a gentle desert river

Map on page 288

Salt Lake City

High in southeastern Utah's La Sal Mountains, in the shadow of 12,721-ft-high (3,877-meter) Mount Peale, rancher Hardy Redd stops the truck at a rocky overlook, gets out, and stretches out the kinks from the rough road. Tipping back his hat, he places one dusty boot on a granite boulder, the other on smooth slickrock, and points out the landmarks of the Redds' backyard.

To the south, about 1,000 ft (300 meters) below, electric-green hayfields butt up against the tidy Redd Ranch, a cluster of refurbished pioneer log cabins and stuccoed houses surrounding a low-slung ranch house, sheds and corrals. An expanse of sagebrush and pale grass undulates past the tackle of a uranium mine to the Abajo Mountains near Monticello and beyond to the San Juan River and the Navajo Nation. To the east, the snaggle-toothed Rockies wall the horizon, rearing above the reddish earth of pinto bean fields near the famous Four Corners, where Utah, Arizona, New Mexico and Colorado meet.

But it's the land immediately in front of him that boggles the mind. Stacked sandstone planes, plateaus and plunging abysses tilt and fall away into the convoluted canyons of the Green and Colorado Rivers, then climb out the other side into fantastically sculpted rock gardens and glowing orange cliffs in Canyonlands National Park, one of the world's most spectacular desert parks. To the southwest are Lake Powell, the Henry Mountains and the San Rafael Swell, and beyond are Capitol Reef and Grand Staircase-Escalante National Monument. Remarkably, it's nearly all public land; only 8 percent of it is privately owned. Some backyard, some view!

Hardy Redd's great-grandfather Lemuel arrived with southeastern Utah's earliest Mormon pioneers in 1880 and helped found Bluff City, on the San Juan River. It wasn't an easy mission. The party crossed 180 miles (290 km) of dangerous, unexplored canyon country, blasting a wagon route through rocks above the Colorado River now known as the Hole in the Rock. The Redds and a number of Hole in the Rockers farmed and ranched in Bluff for 30 years, continuing through floods and other disasters to build a foothold in one of the most remote regions of the United States. In 1887, some Bluff pioneers moved north and founded Monticello. When Blanding was founded in 1910, Bluff was abandoned.

PRECEDING PAGES: the Redd family at the Dugout Ranch. **LEFT:** ancient Pueblo kiva. **BELOW:** a young rafter on the San Juan River.

Pueblos and pioneers

Southeast Utah's tangled topography delayed European settlement of the region compared with other areas of the United States, but it has had a much longer human occupation than you might imagine. As early as 6,000 years ago, nomadic Desert Archaic hunter-gatherers wandered these canyons, living off the seasonal bounty of the desert and leaving behind

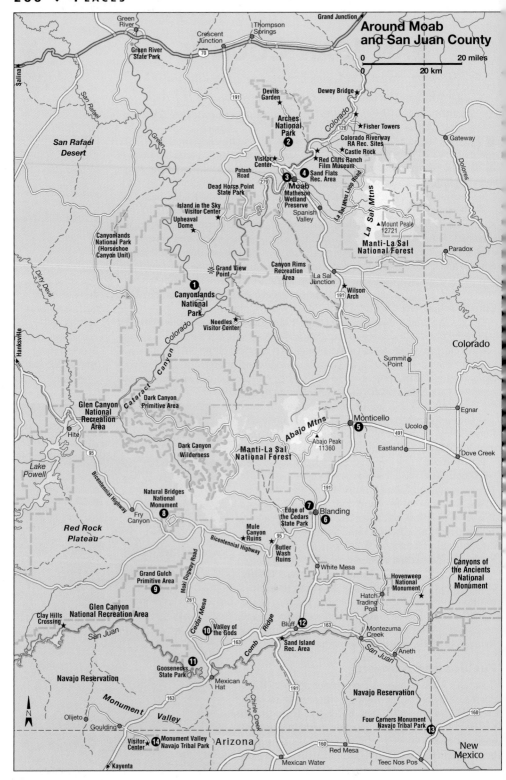

Around Moab
and San Juan County

0   20 miles
0   20 km

their haunting paintings deep within the pale-walled canyons of Cedar Mesa Sandstone that is a hallmark of southeastern Utah. About 2,000 years ago, they were replaced by the region's first farmers. These early agriculturists built cool pithouses near washes and raised corn, squash and beans. They gathered their harvest in baskets, which has led archaeologists to dub them the Basketmakers.

With the help of technologies from Mexico, such as agriculture, building with stone, making pottery, and ceremonies to ensure a good harvest, the ancestors of the modern Hopi and other Pueblo people became successful farmers. By the eighth century, people throughout the Four Corners were living in extended clans in small stone villages, or pueblos, built around a plaza. Even though they now lived above ground, they retained their strong spiritual connection to the earth by using underground rooms called kivas to plan ceremonies. They, too, left rock art on sandstone walls, depicting what was most important in their daily lives: game animals, water, corn, deities, fertility and the patterns of their travels across the land.

In the 1200s, Pueblo people from near Mesa Verde in southwestern Colorado began moving west into Utah, perhaps displaced by crowding and friction among neighbors, scarce natural resources due to a long drought, and a desire to seek safety amid the canyons of the Colorado River and its tributaries. At **Hovenweep** and **Canyons of the Ancients National Monuments** (daily; tel: 970-562-4282, www.nps.gov/hove), on the Utah–Colorado border, they built unusual defensive villages of D- and C-shaped buildings with tower kivas, where unobstructed views could keep the people safe.

Other clans pushed farther into Canyon Country and constructed single family units and granaries under overhangs that blended into the rocks. By 1300, for reasons known only to themselves, the people had left these homes, sealed their granaries, and moved south to Hopi, Zuni, Acoma and the Rio Grande pueblos, where their descendants remain today. Southeastern Utah is now home to Navajo and Ute Indians who have lived in the area for centuries, possibly arriving before the departure of the Pueblos, according to new evidence.

BELOW: Ancestral Puebloan ruin.

Europeans arrive

In 1776, two friars from Santa Fe named Dominguez and Escalante were the first Spaniards to travel through the Colorado River country, searching unsuccessfully for a route to California. Spaniards named the Abajo ("low") and La Sal ("the salt") Mountains in southeastern Utah, as well as the Colorado River, during a visit to the Grand Canyon. In 1869 and 1871, geologist John Wesley Powell became the first to run the length of the Colorado River in wooden dories, thrilling Americans back east with his account of a landscape he called "The Great Unknown."

Several years later, soldiers who had first visited the area as part of Kit Carson's roundup of Navajos during the 1864–68 Long Walk period returned, hoping to find rumored Navajo gold and silver deposits. They were killed by a party of local Indians. Soon afterward, prospector Cass Hite arrived in Monument Valley, determined to learn the secrets of the Navajo.

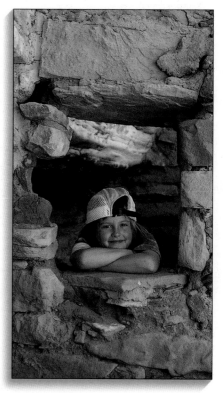

Map on page 288

Fortunately for him, chief Hoskannini took a liking to him and showed him where gold could be found on the Colorado River. By the 1880s, Hite's was among a number of gold-mining operations on the Colorado, San Juan and other rivers that boomed briefly, then were abandoned due to the difficult terrain.

Last stop for java at Monticello.

Other settlers, such as John Wetherill and his wife Louisa and Harry and "Mike" Goulding, were attracted by the Navajo themselves. They, and other adventurous entrepreneurs, built trading posts in remote areas on the new Navajo reservation and began trading flour, sugar, cloth, hardware and other necessities for Navajo crafts like silver jewelry and wool rugs. Acting as a bridge between Indian people and the world beyond the reservation, they introduced visitors to Indian culture, even offering food and lodging in the early days, when roads through this area did not exist. Although Indian people no longer need to shop at trading posts, most maintain close bonds with traders, whose support continues to open new and lucrative markets for Indian arts and crafts.

BELOW: San Juan River trips range in length from a few hours to several days.

After World War II, mining again became big news in the region, after huge deposits of uranium were found in the Four Corners region. Recreation, too, began to take off. Enterprising locals like Mexican Hat resident Norm Nevills and other river runners used wooden rowboat dories and government-surplus rubber rafts to transport paying visitors through previously inaccessible canyons. In Monticello, a young rancher's son named Kent Frost and his wife Fern bought army Jeeps and almost single-handedly invented the craze for four-wheel-driving in Canyonlands National Park, a park they were instrumental in helping create in 1964.

Down by the river

All of southeastern Utah is contained within **San Juan County**, which takes its name from the nearby San Juan River, a major tributary of the Colorado. At 7,884 sq miles (20,420 sq km), San Juan County is the state's second largest county. Its 13,830 residents are spread out across the whole region and still make a living from ranching and farming in traditional Mormon communities founded by their forefathers. About an hour south of Moab, at the junction of US 191 and 491, the small town of Monticello is the county seat and a good place to begin your trip. It has clean motels, a mix of down-home restaurants and cafés, and tourist facilities.

Your first stop in **Monticello ❺** should be the **San Juan County Multi-Agency Visitor Center** (Apr–Oct daily 8am–5pm, Nov–Mar Mon–Fri; 117 S. Main, tel: 800-574-4386) in the heart of downtown. Run by the U.S. Forest Service and the county, this building (the old San Juan Courthouse) has exhibits on the history of San Juan County and information on planning a trip to the area. Outfitters offer tours. You can also hire Jeeps for the day and explore the area yourself.

If you're planning on rafting the **San Juan River** or hiking on the 2.1 million acres (850,000 hectares) of land managed by the Bureau of Land Management (41 percent of the land base), be sure to stop at the **BLM Field Office** in Monticello (Mon–Fri 8am–5pm; 435 N. Main St, tel: 435-587-1500, www.blm.gov/utah/monticello). A permit is required to hike into 52-mile-long (84-km) Grand Gulch Primitive Area or any of the other canyons above the San Juan River. Inexpensive day-hiking permits are available at the on-site Kane Gulch Ranger Station and trailheads; overnight backpackers must reserve in advance through the Monticello office.

Map on page 288

BELOW: playing in the mud on the San Juan River.

A fairly restrictive lottery system is in place for private trips on the San Juan River. You must submit your requested dates by February of the year you wish to go or hope for a cancellation. Check with the Monticello River Office (Mon–Fri 8am–noon; tel: 435-587-1510). It's easier to arrange a trip of two to six days with an approved commercial outfitter. The BLM can give you a list of approved companies. In addition, if you plan to hike or camp on the south side of the river, on the Navajo Nation, you will need a permit from Navajo Parks and Recreation (PO Box 9000, Window Rock, AZ 86515, tel: 928-871-6647). Allow 6 to 8 weeks for processing.

Back road to Blanding

The **Harts Draw Scenic Backway** through the Abajos (locally called the Blues) offers a little-known but spectacular shortcut into the Needles District of Canyonlands National Park. Look for County Road 285, in downtown Monticello. This paved road quickly turns to dirt and winds up to Abajo Peak, passing through part of the 1.4-million-acre (570,000-hectare) **Manti-La Sal National Forest**, which contrasts dramatically with the desert vistas below.

Spanish explorers were fooled into thinking the Abajos are low. In fact, they are quite high – more than 9,000 ft (2,700 meters) – and snow-covered in winter. They offer wonderful hiking and camping at two primitive campgrounds between May and October. If you're visiting the area at that time of year, you may come upon cattle being rounded up in these parts. Cattle ranchers trail their cows and calves into the cool mountains to fatten up all summer in high-country pastures, then bring them down to corrals at lower elevations in September to ready them for market. The Harts Draw route also allows

A freeze-and-thaw process of erosion gradually deepens cross-hatched furrows in a sandstone formation on Cedar Mesa.

BELOW:
the Goosenecks of
the San Juan River.

Map on page 288

you to take a scenic backway to **Blanding** ❻, 30 miles (48 km) to the south – a good alternative to US 191.

Like Monticello, Blanding has lodgings, restaurants and other visitor facilities. The whole town is built atop six large pueblos that were occupied between AD 770 and 1200. An excavated pueblo and rare great kiva can be viewed at the excellent **Edge of the Cedars State Park** ❼ (daily 8am–8pm; tel: 435-678-2238; admission), named for a clearing in the junipers, or "cedars," on the west side of town used as a cowboy camp. The modern museum has thoughtful exhibits that explore the links among the area's Ancestral Puebloan, Ute, Navajo and modern white residents. Also noteworthy are a large Ancestral Pueblo pottery collection donated by an early Blanding pioneer; a garden containing such native plants as beeweed and yucca used by early Indians; and whimsical iron sculptures by Bluff artist Joe Pachak evoking early Pueblo rock art.

Blanding was the scene of the West's last gun battle, in 1923, when a couple of Ute Indian rustlers broke out of jail with the help of a Paiute named Old Posey. A posse chased them for two days before Posey was fatally wounded. A band of Utes, whose homeland originally was in southwestern Colorado, inhabits the White Mesa Ute Reservation south of Blanding.

Ruins and bridges

The highlight of this area is UT 95, which begins just south of Blanding and links that community with the tiny Mormon settlement of **Hanksville**, a gateway to Capitol Reef National Park and Grand Staircase-Escalante National Monument, the Maze district of Canyonlands, and the San Rafael Swell. Dubbed the Bicentennial Highway because it was completed in 1976, this 140-mile-long (225-km),

BELOW: erosion of the Raplee Anticline reveals folds in the Earth's crust.

A rock climber scales a distinctive formation known as Mexican Hat.

paved scenic byway figured prominently in Edward Abbey's eco-terrorism novel *The Monkey Wrench Gang* and traverses rough topography above the San Juan River. It has plenty of attractions, from scenery and unusual geological formations to one of the Southwest's largest concentrations of Indian ruins, and several early pioneer communities. This route is part of the larger **Trail of the Ancients** scenic loop, highlighting natural and cultural sites throughout the Four Corners. Ask for a brochure at the Monticello Multi-Agency Visitor Center.

Just west of Blanding, the highway cuts through one of the major topographical features of this region, **Comb Ridge**. This geological monocline was pushed up 1,000 ft (300 meters) in elevation by volcanic forces deep below the thick sedimentary rocks of Canyon Country. It runs 80 miles (130 km) north to south, from the Abajo Mountains to Kayenta, Arizona, and can be seen from miles away, domed up above the San Juan River. Its high ramparts provided plenty of headaches for the Hole in the Rock pioneers who tried to cross it in 1880. Stop at a viewpoint and take a closer look, instead of quickly driving on. You'll gain new respect for the wagon pioneers of the 19th century whose faith spurred them through some of the toughest country imaginable.

There are numerous places to get out and explore the area around Comb Ridge. Two of the most interesting are roadside archaeological sites managed by the BLM preserving Pueblo cliff dwellings from the 13th century. Just before Comb Ridge, you'll pass **Butler Wash Ruins**, which are notable for their circular and rectangular kivas, showing influences from both the Mesa Verde area to the east and the Kayenta area to the south. You can see another set of ruins from the same era a few miles farther on at **Mule Canyon Ruins**. This small archaeological site has a partially reconstructed kiva and a residence unit. They can be

BELOW: taking in the view from the edge of Comb Ridge.

HOLE-IN-THE-ROCK EXPEDITION

In 1879, a party of Mormons answered a call from their Church to establish a mission in Utah's unpopulated southeastern corner. Setting out from Escalante, 250 men, women and children, 80 wagons and a thousand head of cattle traveled overland across the rugged Escalante Canyons, searching for a route across the Colorado River, as winter approached.

Spirits remained high until the settlers reached the 1,200-ft-deep (365-meter) Colorado River gorge, where, for six weeks, men were forced to construct a wagon road down the vertical cliffs. Inch by inch, the wagons were lowered down the "road" using ropes, then taken across the 300-ft-wide (90-meter) river at a ford used in 1776 by the Dominguez-Escalante expedition.

On April 6, 1880, after enduring frigid winter conditions, the settlers reached the San Juan River, where they established Bluff City. The journey took six months, two babies were born, and no one died. Today, you can drive part of the Hole-in-the-Rock road in Grand Staircase-Escalante National Monument, passing landmarks like Dance Hall Rock, a natural amphitheater used for dancing by the pioneers. A four-wheel-drive vehicle is required for the final couple of miles to the Hole in the Rock itself.

viewed from a wheelchair-accessible trail. There are picnic tables at this site. Both are open year-round.

A few miles on is the turnoff for **Natural Bridges National Monument** ❽ (daily 8am–6pm; tel: 435-692-1234; admission), which preserves three natural bridges carved by a tributary of the Colorado River through White Canyon. Each of the three bridges in the monument – Sipapu, Kachina and Owachomo – can be seen along the 9-mile-long (15-km) **Bridge View Scenic Drive**, which starts at the small, solar-powered visitor center and loops around White Canyon. You can hike to the base of all three bridges from trailheads or all the way along the bottom of the canyon to visit each one. Watch for mountain lions in the thick brush; they and other animals are frequent visitors to this park. Natural Bridges has one of the nicest little campgrounds in the area. In summer, rangers offer interesting campfire talks on subjects ranging from herpetology to archaeoastronomy.

If you continue driving northwest on UT 95, you'll pass over the Colorado River in Glen Canyon National Recreation Area and eventually reach Hanksville, where you'll find gas, food and lodging. The nearby Henry Mountains have plenty of primitive camping and hiking far from other people; there is also a buffalo herd here. For more information, stop at the BLM Hanksville Field Office (Mon–Fri 8am–5pm; tel: 435-542-3461).

Valley of the Gods

To the south of Natural Bridges, just off UT 261 in an area known as Cedar Mesa, is the **Grand Gulch Primitive Area** ❾, a world-class archaeological site. Hundreds of Basketmaker and Ancestral Pueblo dwellings and rock art

Map on page 288

BELOW: making camp in the Valley of the Gods.

sites, dating back 700 to 2,000 years, can be found beneath overhangs throughout this 52-mile (84-km) canyon, making it very special indeed. Some people hike the entire canyon one way and arrange a pickup on the San Juan River; most, however, explore for several days, staying in designated campsites near some of the best Pueblo ruins, then hike back out.

If you take the detour to Grand Gulch, don't miss a white-knuckle ride down the **Moki Dugway**, a mining road that switchbacks 1,100 ft (335 meters) down Cedar Mesa. At the bottom is the **Valley of the Gods ⑩**, a miniature and lesser-known version of Monument Valley, complete with a rough 17-mile (27-km) drive past hoodoo rocks weathered out of sandstone. A number of formations here have spiritual meaning for the Navajo. Hogan-shaped Lime Ridge, just to the north, for example, is said to have served as a prison for disobedient children placed there by the Sun Bearer. When they did not repent after four days, the Sun Bearer turned the hogan to solid rock. One can still hear crying near the rock, or so the locals say.

Before reaching **Mexican Hat**, take a detour to tiny **Goosenecks State Park ⑪** for an eye-popping view of the entrenched meanders, or Goosenecks, of the San Juan River in the dark gray Halgaito Shale below. There are no facilities or water here, but you can make camp on the headland. If you look carefully, you'll see river runners winding through the Goosenecks on their rafts. River access is either at **Sand Island Recreation Area**, 3 miles (5 km) east of Bluff, or at Mexican Hat, 26 miles (42 km) downriver, just before the Goosenecks. You can raft 84 miles (135 km) to **Clay Hills Crossing**, camping on beaches below **Johns Canyon**, **Grand Gulch** and **Slickhorn Gulch**, before the river flows into Lake Powell. The stretch between Sand Island and Mexi-

can Hat is popular for its Pueblo ruins, rock art and leisurely river running. The best time to go is during spring runoff in May; by late summer, the river is usually too low for rafting.

Pretty little **Bluff ⓬**, to the east via UT 163, has been reborn as an artist haven. The old fort built by Hole in the Rock pioneers to defend themselves against Indian incursions is still visible. Pick up the historic walking-tour brochure in town and take a look at the refurbished brick homes. Those belonging to Hardy Redd's great-grandfather Lemuel Redd and Al Scorup, a young cattleman who eventually ran stock on millions of acres of what is now Canyonlands National Park, have been restored and are now residences.

End the day at **Cow Canyon Trading Post**, which occupies a cool, stone building and offers delicious dinners based on Navajo family recipes. Owners Liza Doran and Jim Ostler are knowledgeable traders with a passion for the area. The trading post has an excellent bookstore in addition to high-quality Navajo arts and crafts. Call for hours.

Navajo Nation

Bluff and Mexican Hat are on the edge of the 29,000-sq-mile (75,000-sq-km) **Navajo Nation**, or Dineh Bikeyah. Some Navajos live at **Montezuma Creek**, just east of Bluff, off US 191, which heads south across the river and joins US 160, the main east-west route across the northern reservation. A few miles east of the junction is **Teec Nos Pos**, which has a nice little trading post run by members of the Foutz family. Turn north here to visit **Four Corners Monument Navajo Tribal Park ⓭** (May–Aug 7am–8pm, 8am–5pm in winter; admission), the only place in the United States where four states –

Map on page 288

BELOW: tending sheep at the family homestead on the Navajo Reservation.

Map on page 288

Navajo guides offer tours of Monument Valley.

BELOW: wind ripples the dunes of Monument Valley.
PAGE 300: highway near Cannonville.

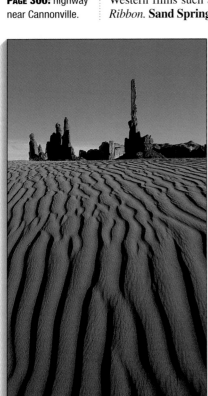

Utah, Colorado, Arizona and New Mexico – join. There is a modest visitor center but no water. Vendors from local Navajo and Ute families sell fry bread and arts and crafts.

Heart of the nation

Many travelers head south on UT 163, going through homely Mexican Hat and crossing the river into the Big Rez just north of Monument Valley, which sits astride the Utah–Arizona line. **Monument Valley Navajo Tribal Park** ❶ (visitor center open daily May–Sept 8am–7pm, winter 8am–5pm; tel: 435-727-3287; admission) is one of those places everyone should see at least once, especially at sunrise or sunset, when the wind-carved red De Chelly Sandstone monoliths, scattered Ancestral Pueblo ruins, and traditional Navajo who live among them are at their most photogenic.

Begin at the visitor center, which has exhibits about the Dineh as well as water and restrooms. The View Restaurant has good food and great views of the park through enormous picture windows. Navajo Park Trading Post sells Navajo arts and crafts, books and other gifts. The 17-mile-long (27-km), unpaved scenic drive into the valley takes about two hours. The dusty, rutted road may be driven by passenger cars but becomes impassable after rain. Inquire before setting out. Be sure to bring plenty of water and food with you. These are not available along the tour route.

A tour booklet for the scenic drive is available in the store. It has information on 11 overlooks, including **John Ford Point**, made famous by the director of Western films such as *Stagecoach, Cheyenne Autumn* and *She Wore a Yellow Ribbon*. **Sand Springs**, Monument Valley's only water source, offers glimpses of a hogan, corrals, sheep and goats, and local residents dressed in traditional velveteen blouses, broomstick skirts and silver-and-turquoise jewelry. Off-road hiking, biking, camping, horseback riding and driving are allowed only with a registered Navajo guide. A number of companies offer reasonably priced two-hour, five-hour and overnight Jeep and van tours. Sign-up booths are located at the visitor center and nearby **Gouldings Lodge**. If you want to meet Monument Valley residents, this is your best bet. You'll also see some of the 100 small ruins built by ancient Pueblo people, known to the Navajo as the Anasazi, or Enemy Ancestors.

You'll find an ATM, supermarket, gas station, convenience store, campground, restaurant and gift shop at Gouldings Lodge, west of UT 163, at the foot of Oljato Mesa. In 1923, Colorado-raised Harry Goulding and his wife "Mike" bought a patch of former Paiute land, pitched a tent, and began trading with the Navajo out of the back of a horse-drawn wagon. In the 1930s, they built a stone trading post and began publicizing the area to famous Hollywood directors like John Ford. Goulding's original trading post, adjoining the modern Gouldings motel, is now a museum. The first floor is much as Mike Goulding left it when she died in the 1990s. The second floor displays movie stills and memorabilia from films shot in Monument Valley. A cabin used by John Wayne in *She Tied a Yellow Ribbon* can be seen behind the post.   ❏

Navajo Art

Historic trading posts abound on and around the Navajo Nation, many built soon after the Navajo reservation was established in 1868. The reservation's most famous trading post is Hubbell Trading Post in Ganado, Arizona. Now a national historic site, it was established in 1878 by Lorenzo Hubbell. With partner C. N. Cotton, Hubbell reinvigorated arts and crafts among the Navajos. He hired Mexican silversmiths to teach Navajo men how to work silver and encouraged women to switch from weaving blankets to more saleable rugs.

By the early 1900s, catalogs selling various grades of weavings marketed Hubbell's Ganado rugs as far as New York City. His biggest buyer was hotelier Fred Harvey who furnished his hotels along the railroad line with Indian art and popularized Indian tourism in the Southwest.

Hubbell Trading Post has changed little over the years. Visitors enter a low, cool, brick building into the "bullpen," where Bluebird flour, coffee, tobacco, canned fruit, calico and other goods are still prized items among the Navajo. Women continue to bring in rugs they have painstakingly woven to trade for necessities. Surrounded by textiles in the famed rug room, the traders work closely with families, urging women to continue weaving and developing new talent.

Hubbell wasn't the only trader to develop a unique style of weaving associated with his trading post. Other traders also got in on the act, and today you'll find a range of regional styles, including Ganado, Teec Nos Pos, Wide Ruins, Two Grey Hills and Burntwater styles. In Monument Valley, you'll find pictorial rugs featuring Yei or Yeibichei dancers and scenes from daily Navajo life. Rugs by well-known weavers cost thousands of dollars. The biggest prize of all are rare historic rugs, such as Navajo Slave rugs, Eye Dazzlers and other patterns dating back to the 18th and 19th centuries.

Turquoise, sacred to the Navajo, ranges in color from robin's-egg blue to blue-green and can be found throughout the reservation. The stones are shaped by jewelers into disks, nuggets, pendants and other forms and set into silver to make squash blossom necklaces, bracelets, earrings, watch bands and belt buckles. In the 1800s, silver coins were sewn onto clothing or melted down to make jewelry. Concha belts, originally made from coins and now made from stamped silver, harken back to that time.

Round woven baskets made from sumac are used in Navajo ceremonies and are prized by every family. Baskets are traditionally woven by Navajos and Southern Paiutes on the Shonto Plateau area, just south of Lake Powell. A tightly woven basket starts at about $100. The best baskets on the reservation can be found at Blue Mountain Trading Post in Blanding and Twin Rocks Trading Post in Bluff, both run by the Simpson family, experts on basketmaking. The Simpsons champion the work of Mexican Hat basketmaker Mary Black, whose award-winning basketry is now nationally known. These two trading posts also specialize in contemporary pictorial and mosaic rugs developed with Navajo artists. ❏

RIGHT: Navajo rug and concha belt.

TRAVEL TIPS

TRANSPORT

GETTING THERE AND GETTING AROUND

GETTING THERE

By Air

The only major airport in Utah is Salt Lake City International Airport, 5 miles (8km) northwest of downtown Salt Lake City. Commercial and charter air service is available in Provo, Cedar City, St. George, and Moab.

The following major carriers serve Salt Lake City International Airport:

Air Canada. Tel: 888-247-2262
America West. Tel: 800-235-9292
American. Tel: 800-433-7300
Continental. Tel: 800-525-0280
Delta. Tel: 800-221-1212
Frontier. Tel: 800-432-1359
JetBlue. Tel: 800-538-2583
Northwest. Tel: 800-225-2525
SkyWest. Tel. 800-453-9417
Southwest. Tel: 800-435-9792
United. Tel: 800-241-6522

Stricter airport security is expected to continue indefinitely and will impose some constraints on passengers and visitors, so keep the following guidelines in mind as you prepare for your flight:

Check directly with your airline before going to the airport. Make absolutely sure your flight has not been cancelled, rescheduled or delayed.

Allow plenty of time for check-in prior to your scheduled departure time. As much as two hours may be required. Anticipate longer lines at airline ticket counters, increased security screening and other potential delays. Your airline can advise you how much extra time to

allow. Call your airline in advance for a recommendation.

Picture ID (such as a driver's license or passport) is absolutely essential for flight check-in at the ticket counter and other locations prior to boarding your aircraft. Please be prepared to present your ID at the security checkpoint and at the gate area.

Only passengers with tickets or passengers who can produce airline-approved documentation will be allowed beyond the security checkpoint. If you are utilizing e-tickets or ticketless travel, please confirm with your airline what you will need at the checkpoint.

Exceptions to this rule may be made for special circumstances such as parents escorting children or a need to accompany an elderly individual to the gate. Please check with your airline prior to reaching the security checkpoint for advice on how to best handle this situation so you avoid any unnecessary delays once you reach the checkpoint.

Family members, friends and others waiting for arriving passengers or accompanying departing passengers will have to stay outside the security checkpoint area. Meeters and greeters are no longer allowed access to the gate areas.

Sharp objects of any description, composition or length are strictly prohibited beyond the security checkpoint. This includes knives and scissors of any kind. Cutting objects such as box cutters and straight razors are not allowed past the checkpoint. Metal nail files, corkscrews, ice picks, letter openers, nail clippers with a comb knife, and screwdrivers are among other restricted items.

If you happen to be carrying a

restricted item and it is detected at the security checkpoint, you will be given the option of taking the item back to your vehicle or checking it at your airline ticket counter. If you choose neither of these options, the item will be collected by security screening personnel and cannot be returned.

The Transportation Security Administration (TSA) is responsible for the passenger screening at the security checkpoint. For more information about screening policies, see www.tsa.dot.gov.

New carry-on baggage restrictions allow only one carry-on bag and one personal item such as a purse, briefcase or laptop computer per passenger. If you have more items than allowed, you will be asked to go back and check the extra items at the ticket counter.

By Rail

Amtrak offers more than 500 destinations across the U.S. The trains are comfortable and reliable, with lounges, dining cars, snack bars and, in some cases, movies and live entertainment. Most routes offer sleeper cars with private cabins in addition to regular seating.

Three Amtrak trains serve Salt Lake City. The east-west *California Zephyr* runs from Chicago to San Francisco. The *Desert Wind* goes southwest from Salt Lake City to Las Vegas and Los Angeles. And the *Pioneer* heads northwest from Salt Lake City to Portland and Seattle.

Ask about two- or three-stopover discounts, senior citizens' and children's discounts, and Amtrak's package tours. International travelers can buy a USA Railpass, good for 15 to 30 days of unlimited travel on

Amtrak throughout the United States.

Contact Amtrak (tel: 800-872-7245, www.amtrak.com) for detailed scheduling.

In addition, the Wasatch Front has a light rail system called TRAX, operated by Utah Transit Authority (UTA), which currently runs from downtown Salt Lake City to the south end of Salt Lake Valley (1000 South in Sandy) and eastward to the University of Utah. Passenger service operates from 5.30am to midnight, Monday through Saturday. TRAX trains are wheelchair-accessible and accommodate bicycles. Contact www.rideuta.com/trax.

By Bus

One of the least expensive ways to travel in America is by interstate bus. The largest national bus company is Greyhound, tel: 800-231-2222; www.greyhound.com. The company routinely offers discounts such as go-anywhere fares. An Ameripass offers unlimited travel for 7, 15, 30 or 60 days. Greyhound offers a transcontinental route across Utah, via Salt Lake City, and the north-south Interstate 15 route. Local bus service includes Beaver, Brigham City, Cedar City, Duchesne, Echo, Fillmore, Green River, Heber City, Hurricane, Logan, Myton, Nephi, Ogden, Park City, Price, Provo, Roosevelt, Salina, Salt Lake City, St. George, Tremonton, Vernal, and Wendover. The Salt Lake City terminal is at 160 West Temple, near Temple Square.

In northern Utah, UTA operates buses between Provo and North Ogden, including express service between cities. UTA operates the main metro bus service in Salt Lake City and also offers seasonal transportation to the Big and Little Cottonwood Canyons ski resorts as well as Park City resorts. UTA also offers a once-daily van from the Salt Lake International Airport to Moab and other towns in southeastern Utah. Contact 801-287-4636; www.rideuta.com.

By Car

Driving is the most convenient way to travel in Utah, especially outside the major cities. Major roads are well maintained, but many backcountry roads, particularly in southern Utah, are either graveled or unmaintained. If you plan on driving into remote areas or in heavy snow, mud or severe weather, it's best to use a four-wheel-drive vehicle with high clearance.

Car Rentals

Auto rental agencies are located at Salt Lake City International Airport. Jeeps are available for rent in Moab and Monticello for exploring southeastern Utah's rugged Canyon Country. In most places, you must be at least 21 years old (25 at some locations) to rent a car and you must have a valid driver's license and at least one major credit card. Drivers under 25 may have to pay an extra fee, as will additional drivers. Foreign drivers must have an international driver's license. Be sure that you are properly insured for both collision and personal liability. Insurance won't be included in the base rental fee. Insurance cost varies depending on the car and the type of coverage, but it is usually $15–35 per day. You may already be covered by your own auto insurance or credit card company, so check with them first.

Many companies offer unlimited mileage. If not, you may be charged an extra 10–25¢ or more per mile over a given maximum. Rental fees vary depending on the time of year, location, how far in advance you book your rental, and if you travel on weekdays or weekends. Inquire about discounts or benefits for which you may be eligible, including corporate, credit-card or frequent-flyer programs. Auto rental is available at Salt Lake City International Airport. For a full listing of auto and RV rental agencies, log on to www.utah.com/tranportation or contact the following:

Advantage	505-247-1066
Alamo	800-327-9633
Avis	800-331-1212
Budget	800-527-0700
Dollar	800-800-4000
Enterprise	800-325-8007
Hertz	800-654-3131
National	800-227-7368
Thrifty	800-367-2277

RV Rentals

No special license is necessary to operate a motor home (or recreational vehicle – RV for short), but they aren't cheap. When you add up the cost of rental fees, insurance, gas and campsites, renting a car and staying in motels or camping may be less expensive.

Keep in mind, too, that RVs are large and slow and may be difficult to handle on narrow mountain roads. If you plan on driving through the 1.1-mile Zion-Mt. Carmel Tunnel in Zion National Park in a large RV, for example, you must call ahead to make arrangements for an escort. If

parking space is tight, driving an RV may be extremely inconvenient. Still, RVs are very popular, and some travelers swear by them. For additional information about RV rentals, call the Recreational Vehicle Rental Association, tel: 800-336-0355; www.rvra.org.

Maps and Information

Your greatest asset as a driver is a good road map. Maps can be obtained from state tourism offices, filling stations, supermarkets and convenience stores. Although all roads are maintained even in remote areas, it is advisable to listen to local radio stations and to check with highway officials or police officers for the latest information on weather and road conditions, especially in winter or if planning to leave paved roads. Mountain passes are often closed by heavy snowfall in winter.

Driving in Remote Areas

Utah has many uninhabited areas. If you plan on driving there, make sure someone knows your route and approximate arrival time. Always carry a spare tire, extra water – at least 1 gallon (4 liters) per person per day – and nutritious food. A cell phone is a good idea, too, but be aware that many areas are out of range of the nearest communications tower. This is also true of GPS satellite systems.

Service stations can be few and far between in remote areas. Not every town will have one, and many close early. It's always better to have more fuel than you think you will need. Note: many businesses in the Capitol Reef and Grand Staircase-Escalante National Monument areas of southern Utah close in winter. Be extra careful to have everything you need with you if you're traveling then.

A word of caution: If your car breaks down on a back road, do not attempt to strike out on foot, even with water. A car is easier to spot than a person and provides shelter from the elements. If you don't have a cell phone or your phone doesn't work, sit tight and wait to be found.

A CCOMMODATIONS

HOTELS, YOUTH HOSTELS, BED & BREAKFAST

Choosing Accommodations

Utah is somewhat schizophrenic in its hospitality options. If you're visiting anywhere with large numbers of tourists, such as Salt Lake City and the surrounding canyon ski resorts or the better-known national parks in southern Utah, such as Zion, Arches and Bryce, you'll generally find plenty of expensive boutique hotels, cozy inns, chain motels, family-run bed-and-breakfasts, all-inclusive resorts and spas, and self-catering condominiums and house rentals. In between, it can often feel like a wasteland, with lodgings tending toward bare-bones family-owned motels, out-of-the-way bed-and-breakfast operations in historic homes, and dude and working ranches where you'll often sit down with a Mormon family at breakfast. It's always advisable to make reservations well in advance, especially in the summer in southern Utah and the winter ski season in northern Utah's canyon resorts.

Chain Motels. Chains are reliable and convenient but tend to lack character and are often located next to highways and, therefore, suffer from road noise. You can usually depend on a clean, comfortable, air-conditioned room with cable TV and phone for a reasonable cost. In general, prices range from $50 to $150, depending on location and additional amenities such as a pool, exercise room, restaurant, kitchenettes, coffeemakers, microwave ovens, and ironing boards and hair dryers. In rural Utah, most chain motels are owned by Best Western.

Moderate to Expensive

Best Western	800-528-1234
Hilton	800-HILTONS
Holiday Inn	800-HOLIDAY
Hyatt	800-228-9000
Sheraton	800-325-3535
La Quinta	800-531-5900
Marriott	800-228-9290
Radisson	800-333-3333
Ramada	800-2-RAMADA
Westin	800-228-3000

Budget

Comfort Inn	800-228-5150
Days Inn	800-325-2525
Econo Lodge	800-553-2666
Howard Johnson	800-654-2000
Motel 6	800-466-8356
Quality Inn	800-228-5151
Red Lion Inn	800-733-5466
Super 8	800-800-8000
Travelodge	800-578-7878

Hotels. Larger and generally more comfortable than motels, hotels are designed for upscale business travelers and tourists, and are usually situated in a central area with easy access to attractions and public transportation. Nearly all have at least one restaurant and such amenities as a pool, fitness center, hot tub, meeting facilities, room service, in-room data ports, gift shop, and an extensive lobby. Some hotels in larger Utah towns offer private on-premises clubs that, for a small temporary membership fee, allow guests to drink alcohol at the bar or in the restaurant. Suites hotels, growing in popularity, such as Embassy Suites and AmeriSuites offer one- or two-bedroom suites (some with kitchenettes) that are suited for long stays or families. Always look for new or newly renovated properties, as these will be in the best condition and have the

most up-to-date facilities. Log on to the property's website, if possible, to view photographs of the rooms, so that there are no surprises.

Resorts. Luxury, relaxation and recreation are emphasized at resort properties, most of which have large, sumptuous rooms, suites or log cabins, fine dining, extensive grounds with manicured landscaping and such recreational facilities as ski slopes, hiking trails, golf courses, tennis courts and elaborate pools as well as health and beauty spas. A minimum stay of two to three nights is often required. In southern Utah, some dude ranch resorts are American Plan, meaning that lodging, meals and many activities are all included in the price. In Utah, you'll find quite a few rustic resorts, where rooms and cabins do not have phones and TVs. In the St. George area, two popular desert spas have programs to encourage lasting lifestyle changes, including fitness classes, bodywork treatments, spa food and workshops.

Bed and Breakfasts. B&Bs tend to be more homey and personal than hotels. In many cases, you're a guest at the innkeeper's home. Some are historic houses or inns decorated with antiques, quilts, art and various period furnishings; others offer simple but comfortable accommodations. Before booking, ask if rooms have telephones or televisions (your room will actually be quieter if the home doesn't have these) and whether bathrooms are private or shared. Ask about breakfast, too. The meals are included in the price but may be anything from continental (croissants, muffins and pastries) to a multicourse feast. Guests may be served at a common table or private tables in a dining room or in their rooms. For more information, contact:

Bed and Breakfast Inns of Utah
Box 3066, Park City, UT 84060;
www.bbiu.org

BB Getaways
www.bbgetaways.com

BNB Finder
www.bnbfinder.com

Guest Ranches. Guest, or dude, ranches range from working cattle

operations with basic lodging to full-fledged "resorts with horses" that have swimming pools, hot tubs, tennis courts, massage treatments, ATV and hiking trails and other amenities. Most ranches offer horseback riding lessons, guided pack trips, hearty western cowboy and chuckwagon cookouts with spontaneous cowboy poetry and storytelling around a campfire, and entertainment like rodeos and square dancing. If traveling with a family, be sure to ask about a children's program. As you'd expect, family-oriented Utah is very kid-friendly, and many resorts have

children's playgrounds, basketball hoops and other sports facilities. For more information and extensive list of dude ranches, contact:

Dude Ranchers Association
112 12th St, P.O. Box 2307, Cody, WY 82414; tel. 307-587-2339;
www.dudranch.org

Guest Ranches of North America
P.O. Box 191625, Dallas, TX 75219;
tel. 214-912-1100;
www.guestranches.com

SALT LAKE CITY, OGDEN AND ENVIRONS

Ogden

Alaskan Inn
435 Ogden Canyon Rd, Ogden, UT 84401
Tel: 821-621-8600
www.alaskaninn.com
The quiet open beauty of Alaska is recalled at this upscale rural B&B in Ogden Canyon. 23 backwoods-themed suites in the lodge and cabins featuring lodgepole pine furniture offer guests their own private *Northern Exposure* environment. $$–$$$

Best Western High Country Inn
1335 W. 12th St, Ogden, UT 84404
Tel: 800-594-8979
www.bestwestern.com
A comfortable, friendly chain hotel near Eccles Dinosaur Park. 111 rooms have refrigerators, cable TV with movies and video games. Pool, gym, hot tub, laundry facilities. $

Snowberry Inn
1315 N. Rte. 158, Box 795; Eden, UT 84310
Tel: 888-334-3466
www.snowberryinn.com
A rustic and cozy B&B at the upper end of Ogden Canyon, central to all three Ogden ski areas. 5 view rooms, 2 suites. Hot tub, laundry facilities and vegetarian breakfasts. No air conditioning or room phones. $–$$

Heber Valley

Blue Boar Inn
1235 Warm Springs Rd, Midway, UT 84049
Tel: 888 650-1400
www.blueboarinn.com
Voted top B&B in the state in 2004, the Bavarian-styled Blue Boar Inn sits on the edge of peaceful Heber Valley, adjacent to two spectacular golf courses. The 14 modern rooms are attractively decorated in varied styles and all have fireplaces, private baths, TVs and phones. Onsite pub. The vaulted dining room serves award-winning European cuisine.
$$$–$$$$

Logan

Providence B&B
10 S. Main, Providence, UT
Tel: 435-752-3432
This pretty, three-story stone inn in Providence, 3 miles (5 km) south of Logan, includes part of the 1889 Old Rock Church and is listed on the National Register of Historic Places. Its 15 rooms are decorated in Victorian, Georgian and Colonial styles. All have private baths, TV/VCRs and phone. A full breakfast is served in the dining room or in-room, if you overnight in a suite. $$ –$$$$

Zanavoo Lodge
4880 East, Hwy 89, Logan, UT 84321

Tel: 435-752-0085
This 1948 former rancher's home in Logan Canyon will appeal to champagne tastes on lemonade budgets. Its 11 inexpensive rooms are basic with TVs and little else, but it's the killer views and fresh, tasty food that people come here to enjoy. Breakfast is brought right to the door. Nicely presented Western-styled dinners served in the rustic lodge restaurant bring people from miles around. $

Logan House Inn
168 N. 100 East, Logan, UT 84321
Tel: 800-478-7459
www.loganhouseinn.com
Located a block from downtown, this 1890 mansion is attractive, convenient and upscale. The 6 rooms are furnished differently; all have TV/VCRs, in-room data ports. Full breakfast is served in the dining room with white linen and silverware. Laundry and business services. $–$$$

Sherwood Hills Resort
US 89/91, 14 miles (23 km) southwest of Logan, Wellsville, UT 84339
Tel: 800-532-5066
Golfers, hikers and those aiming to get away from it all will enjoy this isolated mountain resort halfway between Logan and Brigham City. All rooms have great views, cable TV, VCRs, microwaves,

refrigerators; some have hot tubs. The onsite Italian restaurant has an excellent wine list and desserts; no lunch on weekdays, no dinner on Sun. 100 rooms, 5 themed rooms and 2 suites. Spa, meeting rooms, hiking trails, 2 golf courses, cross-country skiing. $–$$.

Salt Lake City

Anton Boxrud Bed and Breakfast
57 S. 600 East, Salt Lake City, UT 84102
Tel: 800-524-5511
www.antonboxrud.com
This unusual B&B, located a half-block from the Governor's Mansion, was designed in 1901 by Walter Ware, one of Salt Lake City's best-known architects. It is filled with unusual details, including dark woods, stained glass, hardwood floors and pocket doors, a type of door that disappears into side walls. Decor in the 6 rooms and 1 suite is International Eclectic. Breakfasts here are particularly good. Evening snacks and drinks served in an attractive parlor. Outdoor hot tub. $–$$

Brigham Street Inn
1135 East South Temple, Salt Lake City, UT
Tel: 801-364-4461
Built in 1898 as the home of self-made businessman

Walter Cogswell Lynn, this elegant red-brick Victorian has been restored to its former glory. The 9 rooms each have a private bath. Continental breakfast served in the parlor. $$$

Chase Suite Hotel by Woodfin
765 E. 400 South St, Salt Lake City, UT 84102
Tel: 800-237-8811
www.woodfinsuitehotelscom
A pleasant all-suites hotel on the East Side with easy access to downtown or the University of Utah via the TRAX Light Rail Line. 128 suites with vaulted ceilings, fireplaces, kitchens, sitting rooms. Full dining room service also available. In-room data ports, cable TV, pool, gym, hot tub, spa, dry cleaning and laundry facilities, meeting rooms. $-$$

Grand America
555 S. Main St, Salt Lake City, UT 84111
Tel: 800-621-4505
www.grandamerica.com
Salt Lake's grandest accommodations can be found at this ritzy 24-story luxury hotel, which dominates its location three blocks south of downtown. Inside it's all glass and marble, European chandeliers and antiques. Each of its 775 guest rooms average 700 square feet in size and many have views and balconies. All rooms have cable TV with movies and video games, in-room data ports, safes and minibars. On-site spa and restaurant are both very popular. Other amenities include an indoor and outdoor pool, sauna, hot tub, hair salon, shops, convention center, meeting rooms and health club. $$$$

Hotel Monaco Salt Lake City
15 West 200 South, Salt Lake City, UT 84101
Tel: 877-294-9710
www.monaco-saltlakecity.com
A plush boutique hotel just two blocks from Temple Square, the Monaco has transformed a former bank into a delightful hostelry, with such unusual special features as a pet floor (for travelers who can't bear the thought of leaving Fido or Fluffy behind), two newspapers (The *New York Times* and *Salt Lake Tribune*) at your door every morning, extra long beds for extra tall guests, a wine gathering in the lobby every afternoon, and a goldfish swimming happily in its own bowl in every room. The lobby's classically inspired architecture befits the building's former life as a bank, but the guest rooms are sheer whimsy, with a pleasantly offbeat, though never tiresome, mixture of stripes, stars, dots and plaids. Beds are made up with downy duvets and mounds of pillows. Rooms are furnished with upholstered armchairs and ottomans, linen drapes and contemporary art. This is decidedly not a chain hotel. Bambara, a hip bistro on the ground floor, is one of Salt Lake's favorite upscale restaurants. 187 rooms, 38 suites. Restaurant, health club, massage, bar, meeting room. All rooms have in-room data ports, safes, and minibars, cable TV with movies and video games. $$$-$$$$

Inn on Capitol Hill
225 North State, Capitol Hill, UT 84103
Tel: 888-884-3466
www.utahinn.com
Another leftover from Salt Lake's own Victorian "Nob Hill" district, this early 20th-century Renaissance Revivial mansion is both aesthetically beautiful and comfortable. The exterior is hewn from redrock and painted with a bright trim. The 14 rooms all have themes drawn from Utah history and include private baths and fireplaces, in-room data ports, cable TV and VCRs. Larger parties may prefer to rent the adjoining carriage house. $-$$$$

Inn at Temple Square
71 W. South Temple, Salt Lake City, UT 84101
Tel: 800-843-4668
www.theinn.com
Across the street from Temple Square, this seven-story brick hotel will appeal to those looking for quiet, old-fashioned lodgings while they take in Salt Lake's downtown attractions. 80 rooms and 10 suites have a chintzy 1930s feel with fussy wallpaper and chaise longues. Restaurant, in-room data ports, refrigerators, cable TV, business services and meeting space. $$-$$$$

La Europa Royale
1135 E. Vine St, Murray, UT 8121
www.laeuropa.com
With easy access to Big and Little Cottonwood Canyons, this small resort hotel in southern Salt Lake offers a chance to get away from it all close to town. 8 rooms with in-room data ports, gas fireplaces, Jacuzzis and gleaming dark wood decor. Attractive grounds for strolling. Large breakfasts served in an airy atrium. Other amenities include an on-site gym, laundry and dry cleaning service, and airport shuttle. $$$-$$$$

Little America Hotel
500 S. Main St, Salt Lake City, UT 84101
Tel: 800-453-9450
www.littleamerica.com
This conservative hotel chain has reliably good inns across the West. Salt Lake's Little America is typically large, with 850 rooms, located in a 17-story tower or a garden setting with private entrances. Excellent amenities include large comfortable rooms with luxurious furniture and fixtures, in-room data ports and cable TV with movies and video games. Restaurant, coffee shop, pool, health club, hair salon, hot tub, sauna, piano bar, laundry facilities, business services. Located on a TRAX light rail stop. $-$$$

Peery Hotel
110 W. Broadway, Salt Lake City, UT 84101
Tel: 800-331-0073
www.peeryhotel.com
The Peery was constructed in 1910 as a luxury hotel for visitors arriving at the nearby Rio Grande Railroad station. Today, after a careful renovation, it's one of Salt Lake's most delightful boutique hotels. The lobby has marble floors, chandeliers and a grand piano. The 73 pleasant rooms feature canopied beds, in-room data ports and cable TV. Prices here are surprisingly reasonable. Amenities include 2 restaurants, health club, bar, meeting rooms, nonsmoking rooms. $$-$$$

Pinecrest Bed and Breakfast Inn
6211 Emigration Canyon Rd, Salt Lake City, UT
Tel: 800-359-6663
Located about 10 miles (16 km) from downtown Salt Lake City, in historic Emigration Canyon, this attractively landscaped inn is spread out across 6 acres of gardens, ponds, and streams. The 6 rooms have private baths; some have fireplaces, kitchens and Jacuzzi tubs. $$-$$$

Saltair Bed and Breakfast
164 S. 900 East St, Salt Lake City, UT 8184
www.saltlakebandb.com
Named after the old-fashioned pavilion that once graced Salt Lake, this 1920s Mission Revival home is on the National Register of Historic Places and is Utah's oldest continuously operated B&B. Rooms feature lots of wood paneling, antiques and beds with down comforters. Suites have fireplaces and some have kitchenettes. Separate bungalows are a good bet for families. Full breakfasts in the dining room. This is a good budget choice close to the University of Utah. 7 rooms, 9 suites. Cable TV, outdoor hot tub. $-$$$

Wildflowers Bed and Breakfast
936 E. 1700 South, Salt Lake City, UT 84105
Tel: 800-569-0009
A favorite with literary visitors to nearby Westminster College, this 1891 "Painted Lady" is in the old Perkins Addition,

one of Salt Lake's first streetcar suburbs, which was designed to allow the city's affluent population a chance to live a "pure, healthful" life in the country. It is well known for its English-style garden, filled with columbine,

foxglove and other wildflowers. The 5 rooms are light and airy with period furnishings; the "bird's nest" suite has a kitchen and dining room. $-$$

Wolfe Krest Suites
273 NE Capitol Blvd, Capitol Hill,

UT 84103
Tel: 800-669-4525; www.wolfekrestcom
Set on a hill close to Memory Grove, one of Salt Lake's most attractive small parks, this Georgian mansion is the epitome of elegance. Its 13 rooms have wonderful views of

the Wasatch Mountains, fireplaces and Jacuzzis. Many also have four-poster beds and window seats. Expensive but worth it. In-room VCRs, Internet, meeting room. $$$-$$$$

PROVO, PARK CITY, AND ENVIRONS

Provo

Colony Inn Suites
1380 S. University Ave, Provo, UT
Tel: 800-524-9999.
All of the rooms in this inexpensive chain motel in downtown Provo are suites with kitchens, dining and sitting areas. Sauna, pool, and hot tub on the premises. $

Hines Mansion Bed and Breakfast
383 W. 100 South St, Provo, UT 84606
Tel: 801-428-5636
www.hinesmansion.com
This 1896 mansion was once owned by one of the wealthiest residents in Provo. Much of its old-world charm – stained glass windows, dark woods, and brick – remains. 9 rooms with antiques and Jacuzzis. Cable TV, in-room VCRs. Full breakfast in the dining room. No smoking. $-$$$

Provo Marriott Park Hotel
101 W. North, Provo, UT
Tel: 800-777-7144
Provo's most upscale hotel, mainly serving the business community, has large rooms with TVs, minibars and coffeemakers. Pool, spa and weight room. The hotel has its own private club, allowing you to purchase drinks. $$

Sundance Cottages
Sundance Resort, N. Fork Provo Canyon, RR 3, Box A-1, Provo, UT 84604
Tel: 800-892-1600
www.sundanceresort.com
The Western aesthetic reaches its zenith at Utah's famous Sundance Resort. 95 attractive cottages and 2- and 5-bedroom mountain homes are available, all linked by forested paths.

Cottages are beautifully furnished with warm woods and rich furnishings; suites have stone fireplaces or woodstoves, deck, and full kitchen and dining area or kitchenettes. Many rooms in the 13 mountain homes have private baths and hot tubs. Two excellent on-site restaurants, bar, spa, theater, shops, baby-sitting, laundry service, convention center, fitness classes. In-room VCRs. $$$$

Deer Valley

Stein Eriksen Lodge
7700 Stein Way, Deer Valley, UT 84060
Tel: 800-453-1302
www.steinlodge.com
Named after the famous Norwegian skier, this luxurious European-style ski lodge in Deer Valley has been voted one of the top hotels in the world by *Travel and Leisure* magazine. The 111 oversized rooms and 59 suites all have whirlpool tubs, steam showers, hot tubs on the deck, fireplaces, kitchens, in-room data ports, and cable TV with movies and video games. On-site spa, 2 restaurants, laundry and dry cleaning facilities, 6,000 square feet of convention and business meeting services. Tip: Rates in the shoulder or summer seasons are quite affordable, with a number of reasonable overnight packages to choose from. Ask about the Culinary Pleasures room, cooking class and dinner package. The hotel offers Utah's best Sunday Brunch. $$-$$$

Park City

1904 Imperial Hotel
221 Main St, Box 1628, Park City, UT 84060
Tel: 800-669-8824
www.1904imperial.com.
A former boardinghouse for miners that has been renovated to neo-Victorian glory. The 8 rooms and 2 suites are named after local mines and have antiques, and down quilts on the beds. Cable TV in the rooms. No smoking. $$-$$$$

Old Town Guest House
1011 Empire Ave, Park City, UT 84060
Tel: 800-290-6423
www.oldtownguesthouse.com
Listed on the National Register of Historic Places, this small B&B is comfortable, with lodgepole pine furniture and country decor. 4 rooms. Cable TV, hot tub, dining room. No smoking. $-$$

Washington School Inn
543 Park Ave, Box 536, Park City, UT 84060
Tel: 800-824-1672
www.washingtonschoolinn.com
This inn occupies an 1880s schoolhouse and has loads of atmosphere. The 12 rooms and 3 suites have quaint country furnishings, including four-poster beds and claw-foot tubs. Gym, hot tub, sauna, laundry facilities, dining room, cable TV in rooms and data ports. $$-$$$$

Solitude

Silver Fork Lodge
SR 1, Big Cottonwood Canyon, UT
Tel: 888-649-9551
A quaint, old-fashioned ski lodge with plenty of character, reasonable rates

and good home cooking. Guest rooms are rustic, with no phones or TVs, but homey touches such as down quilts and feather beds. 5 rooms with queen beds and baths; 1 family suite with a queen bed and bunk beds. The family room has satellite TV, a sauna and workout room. Breakfast is included with room. Off-season rates are reasonable. $$-$$$

Alta

Alta's Rustler's Lodge
P.O. Box 8030, Alta, UT 84092; 888-532-2582
This large slopeside lodge is one of the top-rated ski lodges in North America: 85 rooms, ranging from luxury suites with sofa beds to 3- and 6-bed dorm rooms, a gym, outdoor heated pool, hot tub, spa, massage therapy, fine dining, business services, ski shop, children's activities, shuttle. A good splurge option. $$-$$$$+

Snow Pine Lodge
P.O. Box 8062, Ata, UT 84092
Tel: 801-742-2000
Built in 1938 by the Civilian Conservation Corps, this classic stone lodge is the best deal in pricy Alta. Guests can choose from suites, rooms or dormitory beds. Rate includes full breakfast and four-course dinner. $$-$$$

PRICE CATEGORIES

Price categories are for a double room without breakfast:
€ = $50 or less
€€ = $50–150
€€€ = $150–250
€€€€ = $250 or more

FLAMING GORGE, DINOSAUR, AND THE HIGH UINTAS

Vernal

Best Western Antlers Inn
423 W. Main St, Vernal, UT 84078
Tel: 888-791-2929
www.bestwestern.com
This Best Western has a few more amenities than its Vernal neighbor, including in-room refrigerators, some microwaves and an on-site gym. Breakfast at a neighboring restaurant is included in the price. $

Best Western Dinosaur Inn
251 E. Main St, Vernal, UT 84078
Tel: 800-780-7234
www.bestwestern.com
This basic motel is conveniently located close to downtown museums. The 60 rooms have the usual Best Western features, including cable TV, queen beds, hairdryers, irons, ironing boards and coffeemakers. Kids will enjoy the dinosaur motif throughout. Cable TV, pool, hot tub, shop, playground, business services. $

Landmark Inn Bed and Breakfast
288 E. 100 South St, Vernal, UT 84078
Tel: 888-738-1800
www.landmark-inn.com
Housed in a former Baptist church building, this friendly inn is one of Vernal's top lodgings. 7 rooms and 3 suites are decorated in Western motifs and have quilts on the beds. Suites have fireplaces and jet tubs. Cable TV. No smoking. $–$$$

Dutch John

Flaming Gorge Lodge
155 Greendale, US 191, Dutch John, UT 84023
Tel: 435-889-3773
www.fglodge.com
A favorite with outdoorsmen, the lodge is conveniently located close to Flaming Gorge Lake in Flaming Gorge National Recreation Area, and offers raft, boat and bike rentals as well as fishing guide service. The lodge is nothing fancy, but rooms have cable TV and VCRs, and some have kitchens. One-bedroom condominiums with twin and queen beds, kitchens and sitting rooms are available. The restaurant is friendly and serves reasonably priced American food. 21 rooms, 24 condos. Gas station. Large convenience store with outdoor supplies. Guide service. $

Red Canyon Lodge
790 Red Canyon Rd, Dutch John, UT 84023
Tel: 435-889-3759
www.redcanyonlodge.com
A forested backcountry retreat off US 44 with its own stocked lakes, cabins, restaurant, recreation and resident wildlife. The 18 new lakeside log cabins are pretty as a picture, with wood-burning stoves, bathrooms and kitchenettes. The restaurant has views of the lakes and the busy birdfeeders on the deck. Dining here is particularly good, with dinner specials featuring local game or fish. Breakfast, lunch and dinner are served from April to mid-October; weekend dinners only the rest of the year. Boat and bike rentals, horseback riding, snowshoeing, hiking, boating. Gift shop. No air conditioning or in-room phones. Campgrounds, hiking trails, views and Red Canyon Visitor Center are nearby. $–$$

Kamas

Bear River Lodge
Milemarker 49 on Mirror Lake Highway (Rte. 150)
Tel: 800-559-1121
www.bearriverlodge.com
A log cabin resort in the forest on the busier west side of the High Uintas. The 15 log cabins are simply furnished but comfortable and have cable TV; some have kitchens, microwaves and refrigerators. Use the lodge as a base for scenic drives and hikes on Mirror Lake Scenic Byway. The restaurant serves up the usual burgers and sandwiches on weekends only. Open year-round. US 150 from Kamas is closed in winter but access from Evanston, Wyoming, remains open. Good rates available in fall. 2 hot tubs, fishing gear, mountain bike and snowmobile rentals, horseback riding, hiking. Guided tours available. No in-room phones. $$–$$$$

Whiterocks

J/L Ranch
Box 129, Whiterocks, UT 84085
Tel: 435-4181
www.jlranch.com
This small working ranch offers multiday guided horseback and fishing tours of the High Uintas and Ashley National Forest. Overnight lodgings are comfortable and nicely furnished. A cabin sleeps four people. The ranch's "bunkhouse" suite, located on the second floor of the horse barn, sleeps six. Both rooms are nonsmoking and have fully equipped kitchens and VCRs. Some rooms have phones. No credit cards. $$.

Altamont

Falcon's Ledge Lodge
Rte. 87, Box 67, Altamont, UT 84001
Tel: 877-879-3737
www.falconsledge.com
Sportsmen enjoy the fly fishing, falconry, shooting and upscale amenities at this exclusive rustic lodge. None of the 9 nonsmoking rooms has phones or TVs, allowing guests to disconnect from the outside world. The popular lodge restaurant is by far the best dining in the region, serving up five- to seven-course banquets, and attracting locals as well as visitors for special-occasion meals. Make reservations well ahead of time. Children under 12 not permitted. Other amenities include an outdoor hot tub, meeting room and kennel. Expert guides available. $$$

Roosevelt

Frontier Grill and Motel
75 S. 200 East St, Roosevelt, UT 84066
Tel: 435-722-2201
A good bet for basic Western food and lodging in Roosevelt while exploring the High Uintas and Uinta Basin. The 54 rooms are simply furnished but adequate. All have cable TV; some have kitchenettes. Restaurant, pool, hot tub, business services, meeting room. $

BELOW: the alternative to a hotel room.

CASTLE COUNTRY

Helper

The Helper Emporium-Kenyon Hotel
124 S. Main, Helper, UT
Tel: 877-472-3070
This luxurious new bed-and-breakfast is located in the heart of Helper's downtown historic district. $–$$

Nine Mile Canyon

Price Canyon Ranch
Nine Mile Canyon Rd, Box 212, Wellington, UT 84542
Tel: 435-637-2572
www.ninemilecanyon.com
This working ranch is the only accommodation in remote Nine Mile Canyon. The Meads run a reasonably priced, no-frills "bunk and breakfast" operation, which includes rustic log cabins, two rooms in the ranch house and a basic campground with flush toilets. If you rent a room in the house, breakfast is included. The 3 cabins and the 20-site campground are self-catering, but you can arrange a cowboy breakfast or Dutch oven dinner if you call ahead. Open year-round but call ahead for reservations. A store is open in summer. $

Price

Best Western Carriage House Inn
590 E. Main St, Price, UT 84501
Tel: 435-637-5660
www.bestwestern.com
A small inexpensive motel in downtown Price with standard rooms equipped with in-room data ports, some microwaves, some refrigerators, cable TV, irons, hairdryers and coffeemakers. Complimentary newspaper. 41 rooms. Pool and hot tub. $
Greenwell Inn and Convention Center
655 E. Main, Price, UT 84501
Tel: 800-666-3520
www.greenwellinn.com
A good value in rather humdrum downtown Price, this inn offers lots of

extras, including in-room refrigerators and hairdryers, free continental breakfast and membership in the hotel's private club, which allows guests to purchase drinks. 125 rooms, some with kitchenettes. The 3 suites have waterfall tubs and remote-control fireplaces. Cable TV, restaurant, indoor pool, gym, hot tub, sports bar, video game room, laundry and business facilities, convention center. Nonsmoking rooms available. $
Holiday Inn and Suites
838 Westwood Blvd, Price, UT 84501
Tel: 800-465-4329
www.ichotelsgroup.com
An attractive, airy hotel with a glassed-in nightclub, restaurant and pool. The 136 rooms have in-room data ports, cable TV with movies, Jacuzzi tubs, kitchenettes, hairdryers, irons and coffeemakers. The restaurant is open on Sundays. A good base for exploring the area. $–$$

Castle Dale

San Rafael Bed & Breakfast
15 E. 100 North, Castle Dale, UT
Tel: 435-381-5689
A restored Victorian 3-bedroom home on the National Register of Historic Places in pretty little Castle Dale. The inn has 2 honeymoon suites, hot tub and garden. $$

Ferron

Sky Haven Lodge
Ferror Reservoir, Ferron, UT 84523
(USFS Ranger Station
Tel: 435-384-2372)
One of the few non-campground options on the Wasatch Plateau, this lodge is located at an elevation of 9,400-ft (3,130 meters) at Ferron Reservoir, just east of Skyline Drive. Basic accommodations are in cabins. A small cafe serves breakfast, lunch and dinner daily in summer. Store, boat rentals and guided

horseback rides and pack trips available. $

Emery

Castle Valley Outdoors
Castle Valley Ranch, Emery, UT
tel: 435-749-0508
"Cowboy up" at this secluded working cattle ranch in the San Rafael Desert. Accommodations are in two far-flung ranch houses. Muddy Creek Lodge has four comfortable rooms sharing two bathrooms. Even more secluded is the Johnson Ranch, nestled at the base of Thousand Lake Mountain, on the northern edge of Capitol Reef National Park. Meals range from self-catering to cowboy cookouts and fancy steak and fowl dinners. All-inclusive, multiday packages offer a variety of activities, including horseback riding, fishing, game hunting, wildlife viewing, cattle roundups and four-wheel-driving. $$$$

Green River

Best Western River Terrace Motel
880 East Main, Green River, UT
Tel: 435-564-3401
This attractively landscaped, three-story motel on the banks of the Green River is the town's top motel lodging and conveniently located opposite the John Wesley Powell River History Museum and visitor center. Spacious rooms all have queen and king beds, cable TV, irons, ironing boards, hairdryers and coffeemakers. The adjoining Tamarisk Restaurant is a favorite with river runners for hearty breakfasts and dinners. Relaxing views of the river from rooms, pool and restaurant. $$
The Bankurz Hatt Bed and Breakfast
214 Farrer St, Green River, UT 84525
Tel: 435-564-3382

www.bankurzhatt.com
An unexpected find in dusty Green River, this elegant 1890s Victorian home was built by an immigrant Englishman who, among other things, served as Green River's first banker. The house has been in the Coomer family since the 1930s. They have carefully restored the home and furnished it with antiques, canopy beds, old photographs and other period details. One deluxe downstairs room has a private bath; the two upstairs rooms share a bath and sitting room. Full breakfast; dinner by reservation. $$.

Tavaputs Plateau

Tavaputs Ranch
P.O. Box 1736, Price, UT
Tel: 435-637-1236 or 435-636-5008
www.tavaputsranch.com
A top-rated backcountry lodge on a ranch in the high country above Desolation Canyon. Horseback riding, wildlife tours and hiking. Breakfast, lunch and dinner served cowboy style in the 4,000-square-foot lodge, which can accommodate up to 25 people. The ranch can be reached overland via a rough four-wheel-drive road, but most visitors arrive by plane from Green River. Contact Redtail Aviation (888-745-6949) for day trips featuring lunch at the lodge and multiday fly-float packages. $$$

SANPETE AND SEVIER VALLEYS

Ephraim

Ephraim Homestead Bed and Breakfast
135 W. 100 North St, Ephraim, UT 84627
Tel: 435-238-6367
www.sanpete.com
A touch of Scandinavia reigns in this old Mormon homestead, which includes a converted log granary, barn and 1860s cottage. The 2 rooms and 1 suite have wood- and coal-burning stoves and private baths. No phones or TVs. The suite has a full kitchen. Breakfast is served in the main house. Gardens. No smoking. $–$$

W. Pherson House Bed and Breakfast
244 S. Main St, Ephraim, UT 84627
Tel: 435-283-4197
Groups and families will enjoy this 1895 Victorian home, which once belonged to a banker. Its three rooms all share a bathroom. $

Manti

Manti House Inn Bed and Breakfast
401 N. Main St, Manti, UT 84642
Tel: 800-835-0161
www.mantihouse.com
This restored 1880 home once housed workers on the Manti Temple. It is now a state historic site and one of the best inns in Manti. The 6 rooms are furnished with antiques and have cable TV and VCRs. Some rooms have hot tubs. Bountiful breakfasts feature crepes, French toast and egg dishes, fresh fruit and tea or coffee. On Friday and Saturday nights in summer, dinner is available in the dining room or in your bedroom for an extra charge. No smoking. $$

Temple View Lodge
269 E. 400 North St, Manti, UT 84642
Tel: 888-505-7566
Cheap and cheerful, this motel is a good bet if you're traveling with kids on a budget. It's opposite the Manti Temple and has 12 rooms with cable TV. It is located next to a grassy park and has a playground, volleyball and basketball. $

Legacy Inn
337 N. 100 East St, Manti, UT 84642
Tel: 435-835-8352
www.legacyinn.com
This pretty Victorian-style home, a half-block from the Manti Temple, is new but has many luxury touches, including substantial evening snacks and chocolate truffles in your room. 3 rooms and one family suite sleeping six. No TVs. $

Marysvale

Big Rock Candy Mountain
4479 N. US 89, Marysvale, UT 84750
Tel: 888-560-7625
www.marysvale.org/brcm
This old-fashioned resort was built in the 1940s next to the Sevier River at the base of the legendary Big Rock Candy Mountain. Its basic motel rooms and rustic cabins sit amid a nicely landscaped property. The 9 large rooms have cable TV and big bathrooms. The 7 cabins have attractive porches. Hot tub, horseback riding. Cafe across the street. ATV trail. River rafting. A sentimental favorite. $–$$

Richfield

Richfield Travelodge
647 S. Main St, Richfield, UT 84701
Tel: 800-549-8208
Locals often refer visitors to this reasonably priced, comfortable chain hotel adjacent to I-70 and US 89. The 58 motel rooms are airy and have cable TV. Restaurant and pleasant indoor pool and hot tub. $

Salina

The Victorian Inn B&B
190 W. Main St, Salina, UT
Tel: 800-972-7183
A charming historic home with many period features. The 3 guest rooms have private baths. $

Spring City

Wind Walker Guest Ranch
11550 Pigeon Hollow Rd, Spring City, UT 84662
Tel: 888-606-9463
www.windwalker.org
A working ranch outside historic Spring City that combines horseback riding with massage and other pampering. American Plan includes lodging, activities and meals. 23 rooms. Pool, hot tub, biking, archery, hiking, fishing, children's programs. $$$$

The Garden Bed and Breakfast Inn
11650 Canal Canyon Rd, Spring City, UT 84662
Tel: 877-537-2337
www.bedsandroses.com
The place to get away from it all, this comfortable B&B sits at the base of Horseshoe Mountain and has great views. The 3 rooms are luxuriously appointed. Some have Jacuzzis, kitchenettes, VCRs and cable TV. $$

THE GREAT BASIN

Beaver

Sleepy Lagoon Motel
882 S. Main, Beaver, UT 84713
Tel: 435-438-5681
A sweet little place on the outskirts of historic Beaver with a pond and large rooms. 20 rooms with air conditioning, cable TV. Pool. $

Delta

Rancher Motel
171 W. Main, Delta, UT 84624
Tel: 435-864-2741.
Desert rats will love this classic dusty 1960s motel built by an ex-miner one piece at a time. Handmade jewelry for sale in lobby. 16 no-frills rooms and lots of personality. $

Fillmore

Inn at Apple Creek
940 Rte 99, Fillmore, UT 84631
Tel: 435-743-4334
This pleasant inn has more personality than anywhere else in conservative Fillmore. The 48 rooms and 6 suites feature data ports and cable TV. Some rooms have Jacuzzi tubs. Indoor pool, hot tub and laundry facilities. $

Hampton Inn
461 N. Main St, Tooele, UT 84074
Tel: 800-426-7866
An attractive, reasonably priced hotel with views of the Oquirrh Mountains and Great Salt Lake and a pleasant sitting area with stone fireplace. The 51 rooms have cable television. Indoor pool and gym. $

Nephi

Whitmore Mansion Bed and Breakfast
110 S. Main, Nephi, UT
Tel: 435-623-2047
Built in 1898, this gingerbread-laden inn in downtown Nephi is filled with antiques. It has five rooms, all with private baths. $

Tooele

Best Western Tooele
365 N. Main St, Tooele, UT 84074
Tel: 435-882-5010
A small, friendly motel with 31 rooms. Air conditioning, microwaves, refrigerators, cable TV. The Arts and Crafts bungalow next door has rooms with antiques

and jetted tubs. Outdoor pool. The gift shop sells items related to the Goshute Indian Reservation next door. $

Wendover, Nevada

Montego Bay Hotel and Casino
100 Wendover Blvd, Wendover, NV 49883
Tel: 775-664-9100
This modern casino hotel is just over the border in Nevada with views of the Bonneville Salt Flats. 240 rooms with all amenities. Outdoor pool, tennis courts, hot tub, spa, two good restaurants. $

ZION NATIONAL PARK AND THE ST. GEORGE AREA

Hurricane

Motel Park Villa
650 W. State, Hurricane
Tel: 435-635-4010
One of the Zion area's best-kept secrets, this clean, nicely landscaped motel is located in quaint Hurricane, about a half-hour from Zion. The owners are world travelers, and it is popular with Europeans and families. 17 of the 23 pleasant rooms have kitchens. Barbecue pits and playground. Weekly rates available. $

Kanab

Parry Lodge
89 E. Center St, Kanab, UT 84741
Tel: 888-289-1722
www.parrylodge.com
Constructed in 1929, this faded gem is filled with photos of Hollywood stars like Barbara Stanwyck and Ronald Reagan, who stayed here while making movies in the area. Its 88 rooms, some non-smoking, have cable TV and air conditioning. Pool,

hot tub, laundry facilities, playhouse. Restaurant open for breakfast. By reservation only between November and March. $$.

Mount Carmel

Zion Ponderosa Ranch Resort
P.O. Box 5547, Mt. Carmel, UT 84755
Tel: 435-648-2700
This large family-oriented resort on an 8,000-acre ranch on Zion's quieter East Rim has a variety of accommodations, from camping to log cabins and huge mountain homes. All meals included in the flat-fee American Plan. Many activities including horseback riding, ATV riding, tennis, basketball, volleyball, climbing wall and hiking. Pool. $$$

St. George

Green Valley Spa and Tennis Courts
1871 W. Canyon View Dr, St. George, UT 84770
Tel: 800-237-1068
Nestled in an idyllic canyon setting just a few minutes

west of St George, this elaborate resort offers scenic hikes, a variety of exercise classes, the latest massage and bodywork therapies and delicious spa cuisine. 35 well-appointed rooms have refrigerators, air conditioning, in-room safes. 19 tennis courts, 4 pools, 2 gyms, spa, laundry service, airport shuttle. Restaurant. No smoking. $$$$

Seven Wives Inn
217 N. 100 West, St. George, UT 84770
Tel: 435-628-3737
Brigham Young is said to have stayed in this historic home of a former polygamist in downtown St George. The 13 romantically furnished rooms have antiques, flowers, air conditioning, TVs, VCRs and private baths. One room has a Jacuzzi installed in a Model T Ford. Pool. Breakfast $–$$$$.

Green Gate Village Historic Inn
76 W. Tabernacle St, St. George, UT 84770
Tel: 800-350-6999
www.greengatevillage.com
A complex of 9 restored pioneer homes from the 1860s. 14 rooms with antiques and modern amenities, such as private baths, air conditioning, cable TV, VCRs and data ports. Restaurant, snack bar, pool, meeting rooms. Children allowed with prior approval. No smoking. $–$$$

Springdale

Best Western Zion Park Inn
1215 Zion Park Blvd, Springdale
Tel: 435-772-3200.
A large, well-appointed motel with 120 rooms. Gift

shop, pool, good restaurant. $$
Cliffrose Lodge & Gardens
281 Zion Park, Springdale
Tel: 435-772-3234.
A pretty, modern lodge at the eastern end of Springdale set on extensive landscaped grounds. $$
Desert Pearl Inn
707 Zion Park
Tel: 888-828-0898
www.desertpearl.com
Gorgeous Pueblo-style timber-and-stone inn partially constructed from old railroad timbers rescued from Promontory Summit near Salt Lake City. 61 artsy Southwestern rooms have vaulted ceilings, air conditioning, huge bathrooms, cable TV, and balconies or patios with views of the river or the beautifully landscaped pool. A real standout! $$–$$$
Zion Lodge
Zion Canyon
Tel: 303-297-2757
www.amfac.com
Inside the national park in Zion Canyon, the lodge offers motel-style rooms and historic cabins. The latter are survivors of the original lodge, the rest of which burned down in the 1960s. Reserve early: The lodge tends to fill up, even in early fall. Registered guests may bypass the shuttle and drive to the lodge in summer. Check in at the visitor center. $$–$$$.

BELOW: Main Street, Park City.

BRYCE CANYON NATIONAL PARK AND THE CEDAR CITY AREA

Bryce Canyon

Best Western Ruby's Inn, Bryce Canyon
Hwy 63, 1 mile south of Hwy 12, Bryce Canyon, UT 84764
Tel: 800-468-8660
The largest and most popular motel in the Bryce area, historic Ruby's Inn is conveniently located on the park boundary. Its 368 rooms are comfortable though unremarkable, and all have cable TV. Two restaurants, two pools, gift shop, laundry facilities. The inn hosts a nightly rodeo in summer at the rodeo grounds opposite. Free bus system to tour the park begins here. $–$$

Bryce Canyon Lodge
Amfac Parks and Resorts, 14001 East Iliff, Aurora, CO 80014
Tel: 303-297-2757
This 1924 lodge, situated off the scenic drive in Bryce Canyon National

Park, was designed by Gilbert Stanley Underwood to harmonize with the natural landscape. It has 114 rooms, including 40 cabins. Very popular. Make reservations a year in advance. Open Apr–Oct. Restaurant. $$–$$$

Bryce Canyon Resort
13500 E. Rte. 12, Bryce Canyon, UT 84764
Tel: 800-834-0043
Located 3 miles (5 km) from the park entrance, on Highway 12, this resort has cabins and cottages as well as rooms and suites. All have cable TV and data ports. Indoor pool, laundry facilities. $

Tropic

Francisco's Farm Bed and Breakfast
51 Francisco Lane, Tropic, UT 84776
Tel: 800-642-4136

www.franciscofarm.com
Charley and Evadean Francisco, otherwise known as Grandma and Grandpa, have run a B&B operation at their 10-acre farm for over 15 years. Guests enjoy a friendly, rural atmosphere, homegrown breakfasts and the farm's many animals. $$

Brian Head

Cedar Breaks Lodge
223 Hunter Ridge Rd, Brian Head, UT 84719
Tel: 888-282-3327
www.cedarbreakslodge.com
On the west end of the ski resort town, this pleasant lodge among the pines is upscale but laid back and family oriented. Large studio-style rooms. Suites have sleeper sofas. 120 units, some nonsmoking with kitchenettes, microwaves, cable TV, pool,

gym, hot tub, sauna, video game room, Internet, business services, no air conditioning. $–$$

Cedar City

Bard's Inn Bed and Breakfast
150 S. 100 West, Cedar City, UT 84720
Tel: 435-586-6612
Each of the 7 rooms in this early 20th-century historic home is named after Shakespearean heroines, making it the sentimental choice for those attending the Utah Shakespearean Festival. Rooms have antiques, handmade quilts on beds, cable TV, Internet, but no phones. No smoking. Open Nov–May by advance reservation. $

GRAND STAIRCASE-ESCALANTE NATIONAL MONUMENT

Boulder

Boulder Mountain Lodge
P.O. Box 1397, Boulder, UT 84716
Tel: 800-556-3446
www.boulder-utah.com
Eleven of this attractive lodge's 15 acres are a peaceful waterfowl sanctuary. Three main buildings hold a Great Room and 20 Southwestern-furnished rooms; those on the top

floors have balconies and views of the Burr Trail. Two rooms have kitchenettes. Superb organic restaurant on the premises. $$–$$$

Boulder Mountain Ranch
Tel: 435-335-7480
www.boulderutah.com/bmr
Not your average working ranch, this spread at the base of the Hell's Backbone Road is run by a surf-mad family who periodically head to Mexico

to ride waves. Three cabins and a ranch house with five rooms. Backcountry horseback riding available for the adventurous. Open year-round; call for dates. $$

Escalante

Escalante Outfitters
310 West Main, P.O. Box 570, Escalante, UT 84726
Tel: 435-826-4266

Seven mini log cabins each accommodate two people; guests share bath facilities. Escalante Outfitters sells topo maps, guidebooks, backpacking food and other camping supplies, as well as good coffee and food in the on-site restaurant. $

GLEN CANYON NATIONAL RECREATION AREA

Bullfrog Marina, Utah

Defiance House Lodge
P.O. Box 4055, Lake Powell, UT 84533
Tel: 800-528-6154
www.visitlakepowell.com
Most people sleep in the campground or aboard their boats, but this clifftop lodge next to Bullfrog Marina on the Utah side of Lake Powell offers a good

alternative, if you just want a room for the night on the quieter side of the lake. 48 rooms and 8 suites, including three-bedroom units with kitchens. Air conditioning, cable TV, restaurant. $–$$.

Hanksville

Desert Inn Motel
107 E. 100 North, Hanksville, UT
Tel: 435-542-3241

The rooms here are clean and basic. The grounds are decorated with found-object metal sculptures. $

Page, Arizona

Wahweap Lodge
Lake Powell Resorts and Marinas, P.O. Box 1597, Phoenix, AZ 85079
Tel: 800-528-6154
www.visitlakepowell.com
This huge complex of motel rooms, restaurants and

public facilities is next to Wahweap Marina, just west of Page, Arizona, headquarters for Glen Canyon NRA. Always busy, the lodge has a large selection of rooms, none of them cheap. If you're looking for a cheaper room, the concessionaire also offers **Lake Powell Motel**, a few miles northwest of Glen Canyon Dam ($$).
$$$–$$$$

CAPITOL REEF NATIONAL PARK

Torrey

Austin's Chuckwagon Lodge
12 W. Main, Torrey, UT 84775
Tel: 800-863-3288
Western writer Zane Grey used to rent the 1892 cabin on the grounds of this lovingly tended lodge. Some of its 25 rooms and 3 cabins have kitchens. Cable TV with movies. Air conditioning, pool, hair salon, hot tub, shops, laundry facilities. Closed Nov–Feb. $
Capitol Reef Inn
360 W. Main St, Torrey, UT 84775
Tel: 435-425-3271
Redrock-mad Southey Swede's family-oriented inn has 10 basic motel rooms with hand-carved furniture, small refrigerators and TVs. He and his brother also built the Pueblo-style kiva, waterfall, trails and children's play area. The restaurant serves healthy

organic road food at reasonable prices. A great place to meet the locals. $
Skyridge Bed and Breakfast
950 E. Rte. 24, Torrey, UT 84775
Tel: 435-425-3222
Artist-built and filled with unique touches, this award-winning B&B on pinyon-juniper-clad hills adjacent to Capitol Reef has new owners who continue to improve it. Breakfasts are a standout, in a sunny dining room next to a cozy library filled with art, games and bird-watching through big windows. 6 rooms, some with balcony hot tubs. Happy hour mixer features local trout. $$–$$$

Teasdale

Lodge at Red River Ranch
2900 W. Rte. 24, Box 69, Teasdale, UT 84773
Tel: 800-205-6343
A classic Western lodge

with a great room complete with chandeliers, Native American rugs and Remington sculptures. 15 rooms each have a fireplace, patio or balcony overlooking the grounds. Restaurant has a toy train. No air conditioning. No smoking. $–$$.

Fish Lake

Fish Lake Lodge
Fish Lake Resorts, 10 E.Center, Hwy. 25, Richfield, UT 84701
Tel: 435-638-1000
Built in 1932, this old log lodge is full of character, with lake views and breakfast and dinner available in the dining room. Both rustic and newer cabins are available for overnight lodging. The newer cabins are available year-round; older cabins only in summer. The old lodge has a dance hall, a small store, and offers

showers to non-guests for a fee. Fish Lake Resorts also operates neighboring Lakeside Resort, which offers cabins. $–$$

Loa

Road Creek Inn
90 S. Main, Loa, UT
Tel: 800-338-7688
Housed in a former mercantile, this unusual inn is operated by the family of former Utah Governor Mike Leavitt and offers 12 chintz-filled guest rooms in the converted main building and an old barn. The surprisingly low-key restaurant specializes in one thing: trout raised in the ranch's commercial hatchery. Horseback riding, cattle drives, cookouts, convention and meeting facilities. $$

ARCHES NATIONAL PARK AND THE MOAB AREA

Moab

The Gonzo Inn
100 W. 200 South, Moab, UT 84530
Tel: 435-259-2515
www.gonzoinn.com
A new luxury hotel appealing to mountain bike nuts and Abbey-style Monkey Wrench types. An off-center desert mind-set infuses this place, from the "Fear and Loathing in Las Vegas"-style lizard sculpture to touches like bike wash and repair. Luxurious rooms have all amenities. Outdoor pool, hot tub, meeting rooms, air conditioning. Complimentary breakfast and espresso bar. $$$–$$$$
Red Stone Inn
535 S. Main, Moab, UT 84532
Tel: 800-722-1972
www.moabredstone.com
Moab's best deal, this attractive motel on the main drag has 50 small, air-conditioned rooms. All exude a surprising amount of character, with pine

panel walls, Southwestern-patterned curtains and log furniture; all have data ports, TVs, refrigerators and kitchenettes. Guests mingle in the cookout area. The more modern Big Horn Lodge across the street is under the same ownership and has a pool and restaurant. Room rates in both motels include a voucher for breakfast at the restaurant. Note: this place attracts groups. If that's not your bag, request a quieter room in the back. Pets allowed. Laundry facilities. Ask about AAA discounts. $

La Sal

Pack Creek Ranch
P.O. Box 1270, Moab, UT 84532
Tel: 435-259-5505
A sophisticated yet rustic retreat on La Sal Loop Road, this well-known working ranch has 12 attractive guest cabins, all named after writer Ed

Abbey. Abbey often enjoyed the hospitality of owner Ken Sleight, who eventually popped up as Seldom Seen in Abbey's famous novel *The Monkey Wrench Gang*. There are no TVs or phones in the cabins, but you won't be roughing it. There's a lovely lodge, where Jane Sleight serves up tasty meals, a huge outdoor pool, a hot tub, on-call massage, and lots of hiking and horseback riding on the agenda. $$$
La Sal Mountain Guest Ranch
P.O. Box 247, La Sal, UT 84530
Tel: 888-870-1088 or 435-686-2223
Guests enjoy bed and breakfast comfort on a family's working ranch in the La Sal foothills. Eleven historic buildings, including a 19th-century log cabin and old miners' homes, accommodate up to 70 people. A favorite for family reunions. $$

Highway 128

Castle Valley Inn
HC 64, Box 2602, Castle Valley, UT 84532
Tel: 435-259-6012
This peaceful, stone-and-wood inn on La Sal Loop Road is surrounded by soaring redrock cliffs in Castle Valley, a secluded valley near Moab that is home to well-known writers, mountaineers and other creative types. The inn has five guest rooms with private baths in the main building. For an extra measure of privacy, ask for one of the cabins. Each is a modern unit with high ceilings, tile bathrooms,

PRICE CATEGORIES

Price categories are for a double room without breakfast:
€ = $50 or less
€€ = $50–150
€€€ = $150–250
€€€€ = $250 or more

wood floors, kitchenettes, barbecue grills and, in some cases, extra bedrooms – perfect for family accommodations. When the weather is fine, which is almost always in summer and fall, a full breakfast is served on a deck brimming with flowerpots. Expect Belgian waffles topped with homegrown fruit and other hearty fare, while hummingbirds buzz around feeders. Soak in the hot tub, stroll the grounds, nap in a hammock, or watch the variety of bird life that is attracted to this desert oasis. A good base for exploring the backcountry. $$–$$$$

Red Cliffs Lodge
Rte. 128, Moab, UT 84532
Tel: 800-325-6171
www.redcliffslodge.com

The surrounding redrock scenery has inspired movie makers who have been coming to this old ranch on the Colorado River for decades. The 69 rooms and 1 suite are classically southwestern, with lots of lodgepole pine furniture, saltillo tile and desert hues. The resort offers a pool, hot tub, gym, volleyball court, winery, a movie museum, clay-pigeon shooting, guided horseback rides, river rafting, hiking and mountain biking. All rooms have data ports, kitchenettes, cable TV and VCRs. A restaurant offers views and good food. $$$

Sorrel River Ranch Resort
Rte. 128, Box K, Moab, UT 84532
Tel: 877-359-2715
www.sorrelriver.com
It doesn't get much more luxurious than this elegant

ranch on the Colorado River Scenic Byway, 17 miles (28 km) from Moab. Views are spectacular amid the redrocks, and the comfortable, oversized rooms are beautifully furnished with big lodgepole pine beds and other furniture, Navajo rugs and Western art. Activities include river rafting, mountain biking, Jeep tours and horseback riding. The on-site spa offers a full array of bodywork options. The restaurant is one of the top dining spots in the Moab area. 32 rooms, 27 suites, some with kitchenettes and hot tubs. Other amenities include a basketball court, playground, babysitting service, laundry facilities, meeting rooms. $$$$

Los Vados Canyon House
Tel: 435-971-3325
www.losvados.com
Located in the backcountry, about 15 miles (26 km) from Moab, this beautiful retreat on 40 acres is one of the area's best-kept secrets. The solar-powered home is owned by a filmmaker and was designed by an architect to highlight the surrounding redrocks and adjoining creek. There are two small guest rooms, Japanese tubs, spacious kitchens and porches. VCRs, hiking trails, archaeological sites, pool. Self-catering. Available year-round, 3-night minimum. Reserve through the Web site. $$$–$$$$

SAN JUAN COUNTY

Bluff

Desert Rose Inn
701 W. Main St, Bluff, UT 84512
www.desertroseinn.com
You'll see a big billboard advertising this new log inn on US 191, south of Moab. The newer lodge is as lovely as pictured, with rooms that are decorated tastefully with Southwest-style log furniture, quilts and art. $$

Recapture Lodge
Highway 191, Bluff, UT 84512
Tel: 435-672-2281
A longtime favorite with river runners, the lodge offers rustic accommodations with air conditioning, TV, slide shows and interpretive talks; some rooms have kitchenettes. The owners are longtime river outfitters and can set you up for river

trips and other tours, such as nearby Monument Valley. Groups can reserve rooms in the 1898 Decker Pioneer House. The pool and playground make it a good family option. $–$$

Fry Canyon

Fry Canyon Lodge
Rte. 95, Fry Canyon, UT 84533
Tel: 435-259-5334
www.frycanyon.com
The only building on Highway 95 between Blanding and Hanksville, Fry Canyon Lodge was built in 1955 to serve the uranium-mining community at Lake Powell. Attractively renovated in the mid-1990s, the 10 rooms have Southwest furnishings and balconies that take advantage of desert views. Restaurant and gift shop. $.

Mexican Hat

Valley of the Gods Bed and Breakfast
Off UT 261, Mexican Hat, UT 84531
Tel: 435-749-1164
Set at the entrance to the Valley of the Gods scenic

drive, at the base of Cedar Mesa, this may well be the most unusual B&B in Utah. Originally built as a ranch by the descendants of infamous Mormon elder John D. Lee, the homestead has been converted to an inn with two suites and endless views from the spacious porch. It's all solar powered. The ideal place to get away from it all. $$$

San Juan Inn
US 163, Mexican Hat, UT 84532
Tel: 435-683-2220
The ideal place after a river trip, the San Juan Inn is set right above the takeout on the San Juan River, just beyond the river bridge into Monument Valley. You'll find everything you need to clean up and relax, including rustic but clean rooms, a gym, hot tub, groceries in the old trading post, laundry facilities and a terrific restaurant and bar overlooking the river. The largely Navajo staff is friendly and welcoming. $$

Monticello

Dalton Gang Adventures
P.O. Box 8, Monticello, UT 84535
Tel: 435-587-2416
Val Dalton and family run cattle just outside the Needles district of Canyonlands. Adventurous guests can join them on spring and fall drives and other genuine cowboy activities at any time of year. Restricted to one family at a time, with children 12 or older. Three-day minimum. All meals included. $$$

Monument Valley

Goulding's Monument Valley Lodge
P.O. Box 1, Monument Valley, UT 84536
Tel: 435-727-3231
Standard rooms with great views of Monument Valley. Amenities include air conditioning, TV, restaurant, pool, Indian souvenir shop. Nearby supermarket, gas station and ATM. Reserve well ahead in summer. $$–$$$

PRICE CATEGORIES

Price categories are for a double room without breakfast:
€ = $50 or less
€€ = $50–150
€€€ = $150–250
€€€€ = $250 or more

EATING OUT

RECOMMENDED RESTAURANTS, CAFES & BARS

Local Cuisine

There are so many great places to eat in the Salt Lake City metro area, you'll be spoiled for choices, whether you want authentic Mexican chile verde, Italian osso bucco, organic coffee and tea, traditional American diner food, or nouvelle Southwestern novelty. The development of ritzy, high-end ski resorts has brought culinary excellence to a new level, and guests at many B&Bs can expect excellent breakfasts as well as, increasingly, gourmet dinners. In rural Utah, dining-out options almost completely disappear once you leave larger towns that attract tourists, so plan on having food and drink with you at all times. Folks in traditional Mormon agricultural and ranching communities emphasize simple family meals at home and rarely eat out.

When you do find a good hometown cafe, it will usually be jammed with locals enjoying American food your Grandma used to make: big eggy breakfasts, meat-and-potatoes dishes, biscuits and gravy, canned vegetables, homemade pies, and watery or burnt-tasting coffee. One exception is former mining towns that have attracted a lot of immigrants, where you'll enjoy terrific ethnic food. Price's best restaurants, for example, are Greek and Mexican.

In Tooele and Delta, in the lonesome Great Basin, look for good Thai, Chinese and Mexican food. Pioneer Dutch-oven cooking is popular at family reunions and cowboy-style cookouts in ranch country for its connection to the state's pioneer past, but even locals are catching on to Texas-style barbecue, a fast-growing trend in Utah.

Visitors to Utah's internationally famous national parks represent a huge in-season market for would-be restaurateurs, and world-class cuisine can now be found in even the remotest desert towns in canyon country, such as Boulder, Torrey and Moab. At its best, this is food with heart, inspired by world cuisine, the Indian, Pueblo and Mormon cultures that have called Utah home, and the chefs' love of the desert.

RESTAURANT LISTINGS

OGDEN, LOGAN AND ENVIRONS

Brigham City

Maddox Ranch House
1900 US 89, Perry, UT
Tel: 435-723-8545
Another roadside attraction in rural Utah, this 55-year-old burger joint is housed in a log structure that was built on skids in case the owners decided to move it to town. A friendly staff serves up huge portions of fried chicken, prime rib, bison steak and other western fare. Leave room for a slice of homemade pie so good it attracts customers from other states. Gift shop. **$–$$**

Heber City

Snake Creek Grill
650 W. 100 South, Heber City, UT
An award-winning restaurant cooking up above-average meat dishes, including Belle Isle baby back ribs, Angus beef ribeye and other favorites. **$$$**

Huntsville

Shooting Star Saloon
7345 East 200 South, Huntsville, UT
Tel: 801-745-2002
The Shooting Star is a legend. It's been around for nearly 125 years and is the oldest bar in continuous operation in Utah. The dilapidated wooden building is rather dingy, smoky and creaky now, but if it's beer and burgers you crave, with a shot of pool on the side, this is your place. *USA Today* has called the Shooting Star's burgers the "best in the West." No self-respecting lover of road houses should miss this tough-as-nails honky tonk. **$**

Logan

Bluebird Restaurant
19 N. Main St, Logan, UT
Tel: 435-752-3155
Utah's oldest continuously operated restaurant was established in 1914 and has many old-fashioned details, including a marble soda fountain and a multiwall mural depicting scenes from Cache Valley history. Home cooking and ice cream are the big draws. **$–$$**

Zanavoo
4880 E. US 89, Logan, UT 84321
Tel: 435-752-0085
This 1948 log cabin lodge

next to the river is an old rancher's home that has been converted into one of northern Utah's best budget lodgings and restaurants. Western dinners consisting of trout, steak and other meats are well prepared and presented. Breakfast "ain't too shabby, neither" (and brought to your door if you spend the night). Not open for lunch. **$**

Bistro 258
258 25th St, Ogden, UT
Tel: 801-394-1595
Enjoy top-notch meat and vegetarian dishes at this sophisticated restaurant on historic 25th Street. Dine inside or on a pleasant patio. Try the wild mushroom penne or oven-roasted lemon bistro chicken. Wines are

available. **$$–$$$**
The Greenery
1875 Valley Dr, Ogden, UT
Tel: 801-392-1777
This popular riverside cafe is located in Rainbow Gardens, a defunct spa turned curio emporium at the mouth of Ogden Canyon. Dishes are as weird and wonderful as the setting, including a Mormon Muffin and a homemade caramel apple pie. **$**

Union Grill
2501 Wall Ave, Ogden, UT
Tel: 801-621-2830
Situated in the old Union Pacific Railroad Depot, this casual restaurant is a good lunch spot for museum goers. Substantial meat dishes and sandwiches available. Desserts are homemade and delicious.
$$–$$$

SALT LAKE CITY

Bambara
202 S. Main St, downtown Salt Lake City
Tel: 801-363-5454
On the ground floor of the ritzy Hotel Monaco, wildly popular Bambara is located in a beautiful former bank building. It excels in international-flavored American cuisine infused with the chef's own herbs, grown on the roof garden. Try the tea-cured duck or the grilled prawn salad. The adjoining private club allows you to purchase drinks. **$–$$$**

Cafe Trio
680 S. 900 East St, Salt Lake City
Tel: 801-533-8746
An eastside gem near the University of Utah, this down-to-earth Italian restaurant excels with

dishes such as Tuscan-style chicken, perfect thin-crust pizza and a delectable kahlua-flavored chocolate pudding. Wine list. Closed Sundays. **$–$$**
Cucina Toscana
307 W. Pierpont Ave, downtown Salt Lake City
Tel: 801-328-3463
Frequently cited as Salt Lake's favorite Italian restaurant, this busy trattoria is in a renovated Firestone Tire Shop and has red-brick walls, pressed-tin ceilings, an open kitchen and banquette seating. Owner Valter Nassi's constant presence creates a Little Italy atmosphere, fragrant with osso bucco, Tuscan-style trout and homemade pastas like mamma *use-ta* make. Wine list Closed Sunday. **$–$$$$**
Log Haven
Millcreek Canyon, 3800 South St,

Salt Lake City
Tel: 801-272-8255
The Salt Lake area's premier dining spot, this converted log home boasts a killer combination: spectacular scenery, a cozy rustic atmosphere and memorable east-meets-west food. Set in the mountains, the forested setting is romantic and perfect for a special night out. Try the coriander-rubbed ahi tuna with guava-lemon sauce. **$$–$$$$**
Oasis
151 S. 500 East St, downtown Salt Lake City
Tel: 801-322-0404
As the name suggests, this is a peaceful haven in the midst of busy Salt Lake, serving substantial vegetarian and seafood dishes at modest prices. Also a great spot for morning coffee and either cooked breakfasts or

homemade pastries. An adjoining bookstore, the Golden Braid, and gift shop make this a popular meeting place and good general hangout. **$–$$**
Market Street Grill
48 Market St, downtown Salt Lake City
Tel: 801-322-4668
This lively steak and seafood place is set in the former New York Hotel, built in 1906. Reliably good, the restaurant is open for breakfast, lunch, and dinner. **$$–$$$$**
Martine
22 E. 100 South St, downtown Salt Lake City
Tel: 801-363-9328
Downtown's favorite romantic restaurant is the perfect place to sample many extraordinary tastebud treats on the inventive American tapas menu. Try the mustard-and-lavender seared lamb loin with mission fig chutney. Entrees include marjoram halibut with French rose wine. Leave room for dessert. **$$$**
Q4U
4655 S. 4800 West St, West Valley City, UT
"Call the dogs in, put the fire out, the hunt's over" says the sign over the door to the best barbecue in the city. Well worth the drive to the increasingly international west side for the owners' lip-smacking beef brisket, baby back ribs, pulled pork and other barby treats as well as authentic sweet potato pie and cobblers. **$**

BELOW: an outdoor cafe in Salt Lake City.

Red Iguana
W. North Temple, downtown Salt Lake City
Tel: 801-322-1489
With a growing Mexican population, authentic Mexican *comida* is increasingly easy to find in Salt Lake. But this hugely popular spot continues to win "best of" awards and draw celebrities like Los Lobos, Carlos Santana and other musicians playing in town. The mole and chile verde dishes are *muy sabroso*, and the margaritas are strong. A good stop en route to the airport. There may be a wait on weekends. **$**

Ruth's Diner
2100 Emigration Canyon, Salt Lake City, UT 84108
Tel: 801-582-5807
No doubt about it: this 70-year-old diner housed in an old trolley car in scenic Emigration Canyon is unique. A longtime favorite for breakfast, the down-home ambiance, good home cooking and friendly service keep bringing back locals and visitors alike. The pretty patio backs onto Emigration Canyon. Barbecue is served on Thursday nights, and there's always plenty of biscuits and gravy and coffee. The curmudgeonly Ruth – now serving at the great diner in the sky – would approve. Convenient to museums and the national forest. **$**

Spencers for Steak and Chops
Hilton Hotel, 255 South St on West Temple, Salt Lake City
Tel: 801-238-4748
Frequently cited as Salt Lake's best steak and seafood restaurant, this relative newcomer has a gentleman's club atmosphere with dark wood paneling and booths. The filet mignon is perfect. The restaurant also functions as a members-only club where you can buy drinks at the bar. **$$$–$$$$**

Salt Lake Roasting Co.
320 East 400 South, Salt Lake City
Tel: 801-363-7572
Salt Lake's longtime premier coffee purveyors brew a mean cup of joe in this large two-story brick building. Relax with the morning paper, surf the Internet, and enjoy tasty quiches, salads and sandwiches at lunchtime. Closed Sunday. **$**

Squatters Pub Brewery
147 W. Broadway, downtown Salt Lake City
Tel: 801-363-2739
Utah is getting quite a rep for good microbrewed beer. This lively brewpub, located in the 1906 Boston Hotel building, is one of the best. Not only is the ale top-notch but so is the food. An extensive menu includes grilled meats, fish and chips, and tasty buffalo burgers. A convenient place for "a quick one" before or after a game at the nearby Delta Center or shows at the Rose Wagner Performing Arts Center. **$–$$**

Tiburon
8256 S. 700 East St, Sandy, UT
Tel: 801-255-1200
Sandy's best restaurant by far, Tiburon ("shark" in Spanish) excels with contemporary seasonal dishes ranging from duck, mussels and lamb to salmon and daily pastas. Try the New Zealand elk tenderloin with green peppercorn demi-glace or scallops in chipotle cream sauce. There's something here to appeal to everyone. **$$**

PROVO, PARK CITY AND ENVIRONS

Alta

The Shallow Shaft
Alta
www.shallowshaft.com
This funky place highlights Alta's former incarnation as a mining town and serves outstanding southwestern food. **$$**

Park City

Chez Betty
1637 Short Line Dr, Park City, UT
Tel: 435-649-8181
www.chezbetty.com
Set in the Copper Bottom Inn, this award-winning restaurant is in a bright room with a big central fireplace. Dishes here lean toward gourmet meat and seafood specialties, such as wild salmon, grilled beef tenderloin on a crispy potato pancake with sautéed spinach and smoked onion demi-glace, and New Zealand rack of lamb marinated in garlic and herbs with roast potatoes, braised mushrooms and spinach, finished with green peppercorn demi-glace. **$$–$$$$**

Chimayo
368 Main St, Park City, UT
Tel: 435-649-6222
Named for the famous shrine in northern New Mexico, this popular restaurant serves excellent contemporary Southwestern and Mexican food. Dishes like the adobe chicken, piñon crab cakes and seared elk burritos showcase the chef's way with spices. **$$**

Riverhorse Cafe
540 Main St, Park City, UT
Tel: 435-649-8424
The leader of the pack in a competitive field, the Riverhorse is a favorite steak-and-seafood joint for celebrities, who arrive via their own entrance and eat in a private dining area. The upstairs loft setting is open and happening. Live jazz and piano music contributes to the urban ambiance. The signature dish is macadamia-encrusted Alaskan halibut; the mashed potatoes are a particular favorite. **$$–$$$$**

Wasatch Brew Pub
250 Main St, Park City, UT
Tel: 435-649-0900
Established in 1986, this Park City staple is a favorite for fresh rainbow trout as well as suds. It was Utah's first brewpub and still attracts a loyal following. **$$**

Zoom
660 Main Street, Park City, UT
Tel: 435-649-9108
A magnet for celebrity watchers during the Sundance Film Festival every January, Robert Redford's roadhouse-style restaurant in Park City serves all-American fare at upmarket prices in an old train depot. Specials like pumpkin-seed-encrusted trout fillet, buffalo and the osso bucco please this crowd. Vegetarians will enjoy the oversized portobello mushroom burger. **$$–$$$**

Provo

La Dolce Vita
61 North 100 East St, Provo, UT
Tel: 435-373-8482
Italian food prepared and served by an immigrant family from Naples in downtown Provo. **$$**

Snowbird Resort

The Aerie at Cliff Lodge
Cliff Lodge, Snowbird Resort
Tel: 801-933-2160
This rooftop restaurant at Snowbird specializes in seafood, sushi and wild game. Diners enjoy great views and top-notch cuisine. **$$**

PRICE CATEGORIES
Price categories are for one dinner, excluding beverages, tax and tip:
€ = $20 or less
€€ = $20–40
€€€ = $40–60
€€€€ = $60 and up

Solitude Resort

Silver Fork Lodge
SR 1, Big Cottonwood Canyon, UT
Tel: 888-649-9551
An old-fashioned lodge that also serves hearty fare to keep you going on the slopes all day. Sit at the old soda-fountain counter or in a booth to enjoy your morning eggs and sturdy caffeine jolt courtesy of Salt Lake Roasting Company. **$**

Sundance Resort

The Tree Room at Sundance
Sundance Resort, Upper Ogden Canyon
Tel: 801-223-4200
The place in northern Utah to push the boat out, the Tree Room has it all: cutting-edge cuisine; a rustic but elegant ambiance set off by rugs, artwork and photographs from proprietor Robert Redford's personal collection; and a remarkable attention to detail, from the sustainably grown food to the once-living but still-standing tree that remains the heart and soul of the restaurant. Among the stars on the menu are seared foie gras on zucchini bread with blood orange sauce and Pacific striped marlin "borracho" served with Tongue of Fire beans, watercress, Anaheim chili marmalade and wild game demi-glace. **$$$$**

FLAMING GORGE, DINOSAUR AND THE HIGH UINTAS

Altamont

Falcon's Ledge Lodge
Rte. 87, Box 67, Altamont, UT
Tel: 877-879-3737
www.falconsledge.com
The five- to seven-course meals served at this upscale, rustic lodge are legendary in these parts. Main dishes include whiskey-grilled fillet mignon, bacon-wrapped ahi tuna and other gourmet dishes. Bring your own wine. Advance reservations necessary. No smoking. **$$$$**

Flaming Gorge NRA

Red Canyon Lodge
790 Red Canyon Rd, Dutch John,
UT 84023
Tel: 435-889-3759
Some of the best dining for miles around can be had in this airy dining room overlooking a lake in the middle of Flaming Gorge National Recreation Area. Breakfast, lunch and dinner are served from April to November, then dinner is served on the weekend only in winter. Dinner specialties include wild game and fish. Breakfast and lunch lean toward mainstream egg dishes, pastas, sandwiches, soup and salad. **$–$$**

Flaming Gorge Lodge
155 Greendale, US 191, Dutch John, UT 84023
Tel: 435-889-3773
The lodge's diner is cozy, reliable and popular with outdoorsmen. You can sit at the counter to enjoy coffee, eggs and bacon, and other American fare or sit at a booth or table and dine family style. The wait staff is friendly and efficient. **$**

Vernal

Betty's Cafe
416 Main St, Vernal, UT
Tel: 435-781-2728
This friendly little down-home cafe on Main Street in Vernal serves good home cooking. Try the catfish or burger, followed by a slice of homemade pie. **$**

Niki's Restaurant and Steak House
2750 W. US 40, Vernal, UT
Tel: 435-781-8239
A good place to enjoy locally reared steaks and prime rib. You can also find homemade soups, salads and pies in this hometown restaurant. **$–$$$**

Reader's Roost
25 W. Main St, Vernal, UT
Tel: 435-789-8400
This colorful, little cafe is a good stop-off for espresso and sandwiches in downtown Vernal. It's also open Friday and Saturday evenings in summer. Closed Sundays. Look for the used-book exchange. **$**

CASTLE COUNTRY

Price

El Salto
19 S. Carbon Ave, Price, UT
Tel: 435-637-6545
Price's other large immigrant population rivals the Greek community for cheap, tasty ethnic food. Tamales, burritos and other authentic Mexican food spice up a traditional menu. One of the best Mexican restaurants in the area. **$**

Farlaino's
87 W. Main St, Price, UT
Tel: 435-637-9217
A downtown favorite, this Italian restaurant serves decent American breakfasts and lunches and popular Italian dishes for dinner. Closed for dinner on Monday and Tuesday. Nice atmosphere in a renovated historic building. **$**

Greek Streak
84 S. Carbon, Price, UT
Tel: 435-637-1930
Named for the owner's athlete son, the Greek Streak is a Price institution. Delectable Hellenic treats include dolmades, lemon-rice soup, moussaka and gyros. Leave room for dessert. The restaurant's honey-drenched baklava, kataifi and koulorakia have fans all over the state. A great place to connect with one of Price's largest immigrant communities. **$**

Helper

Balance Rock Eatery
148 S. Main, Helper, UT
Tel: 435-472-0403
Shop for antiques and curios while you wait for lunch at this fun place in Helper's historic downtown district. The food runs to burgers and fries, pasta and other American fare, but it's all pretty good. **$**

Green River

Ray's Tavern
25 S. Broadway, Green River, UT
Tel: 435-564-3511
Renowned for its juicy, old-fashioned burgers, Ray's is popular with river runners putting in or taking out on the Green River. The burgers live up to their name. This is the place to end up after working up an appetite on the river or exploring the surrounding San Rafael Swell backcountry. A lively night out. **$**

Tamarisk Restaurant
870 E. Main St, Green River, UT
Tel: 435-564-8109
The airy dining room overlooks the Green River at this restaurant adjoining the Best Western Hotel. Steaks and Mexican dishes are a specialty, along with homemade pies and fudge. Expect a short wait for breakfast on weekends and holidays. **$–$$**

SANPETE AND SEVIER VALLEYS

Ephraim

The Satisfied Ewe
350 N. Main St, Ephraim, UT
Tel: 435-283-6364
With an irresistible name and pleasant hometown ambiance, this diner scores by doing traditional things well: bacon and eggs at breakfast, fish and chips and roast beef at dinner. The specialty is – what else? – lamb. **$–$$$**

Manti

Don's Gallery Cafe
115 N. Main St, Manti, UT
Tel: 435-835-3663
An artsy cafe in downtown Manti with the kind of small flourishes that add up to good eating. Homemade scones are particularly good. **$–$$**

Mount Pleasant

Horseshoe Mountain Resort
850 S. US 89, Mount Pleasant, UT 84647

Tel: 435-462-9330
Decent steaks, seafood and pasta are served at this reliable restaurant in little Mount Pleasant, set in a lodge opposite the downtown park. Both the restaurant and inn are reasonably priced. **$**

Richfield

El Mexicano
499 S. Main St, Richfield, UT
Tel: 435-896-9358
Never mind the unremarkable exterior, this Mexican restaurant serves excellent, fresh-cooked *platos*, ensuring it is always full of appreciative customers. You'll find the usual list of burritos, tacos, tostados and enchiladas as well as some tasty specials, including shrimp enchiladas and chiles rellenos. **$**

The Little Wonder Cafe
101 N. Main St, Richfield, UT
Tel: 435-896-8960
A local favorite, this is the best place in Richfield for

traditional breakfasts and mainstream but reliable cooking served up in ample quantities. Dinners include interesting "surf 'n turf" specials such as tempura cod and steak. Desserts are homemade and delicious. **$**

Salina

John's Mad House Cafe
430 W. Main St, Salina, UT
Tel: 435-529-4123
A local hangout, specializing in comfort food, the Wasatch Cafe (affectionately known as the Mad House) satisfies the crowd with daily burgers, sandwiches, soup and salad. On weekends, prime rib, filet mignon and fish specials hit the menu. Pace yourself; portions are huge. **$**

Mom's Cafe
10 East Main St, Salina, UT
Tel: 435-529-3921
If you tend to be suspicious of any eatery called "Mom's" or

"Grandma's" (of which there are plenty in Utah), make an exception for Mom's Cafe located in a vintage storefront in downtown Salina. A succession of Moms have been serving great home cooking at this location since 1898 and, from the chrome stools and Formica counter to the uniformed waitresses, you won't find a more authentic diner in Utah. Choose from classics like liver and onions, turkey, roast beef, spare ribs and a very retro salad bar, but leave room for a slice of pie that would make grandma proud. This is the kind of cozy hometown spot where the staff knows all the customers by name and squeeze your arm and call you "hon" when you ask for more biscuits. A classic road trip experience. **$–$$**

THE GREAT BASIN

Beaver

Garden of Eat'n
324 W. 1425 North St, Beaver, UT
Tel: 435-438-5464
An attractive restaurant in a garden setting at the Paradise Inn, the Garden of Eat'n serves up tasty sandwiches, salads, burgers and steaks. **$–$$**

Arshel's Cafe
711 N. Main St, Beaver, UT
Tel: 435-438-2438
No visit to Beaver is complete without a meal at Arshel's, which has been a Utah tradition for over 60 years. As you'd expect, good home cooking is the draw. Heaping plates full of pancakes, chicken-fried steak and gravy, and other favorites keep people coming back. If nothing else, enjoy a good cup of coffee and homemade cobbler or pie. **$**

Delta

The Rancher
171 W. Main St, Delta, UT
Tel: 435-864-2741
The American and Mexican food won't win any awards for taste or freshness but this popular local hangout and the adjoining motel offer a priceless opportunity to rub elbows with one of the many characters drawn to remote desert locales. Proprietor Ted Harris is a classic desert rat. He built his place from recycled materials and owns the only working beryl mine in the United States. You can buy his handmade jewelry at the checkout as a souvenir. A classic backroad encounter. **$**

Tooele

Jim's Family Restaurant
281 N. Main St, Tooele, UT
Tel: 435-833-0111
The homemade pies are the big draw at this hometown favorite serving up big quantities of American standards. **$**

The Thai House
297 N. Main St, Tooele, UT
Tel: 435-882-7579
Some of the best food in Tooele is ethnic. That is certainly true at this excellent Thai restaurant in the Tri Peak mall. An extensive Thai menu includes the popular kao pad sup-pa rod, made with Chinese sausage, pineapple, cashews, cilantro, curry spices and rice. Closed Sundays. **$**

Tracks
1641 N. Main St, Tooele, UT
Tel: 435-882-4040

This surprisingly urban brewpub serves ale and cooks up the best American food in Tooele. Good for watching the game on TV or grooving to live music on weekends. **$**

Wendover

Salt Flats Cafe
off I-80, at Bonneville Salt Flats exit, east of Wendover, NV
Tel: 435-665-7550
This truck stop serves carne asada, chiles rellenos and other Mexican dishes. Cheap, fast, good. **$**

PRICE CATEGORIES

Price categories are for one dinner, excluding beverages, tax and tip:
€ = $20 or less
€€ = $20–40
€€€ = $40–60
€€€€ = $60 and up

Montego Bay Hotel and Casino
100 Wendover Blvd, Wendover, NV
Tel: 775-664-9100
Wendover's best deal, this hotel has two good restaurants with the kind of reasonable prices that casinos offer to lure

customers. The Oceano Buffet has seafood specials and the Paradise Grill is a mainstream American coffee shop. **$–$$**
Peppermill Hotel and Casino
680 Wendover Blvd, Wendover, NV

Tel: 800-648-9660
Under the same ownership as the Montego Bay Hotel and Casino, the Peppermill has two restaurants that offer a change of pace for diners. The international fare at the Coco Palms Restaurant is above

average, as is the Texas-style barbecue served up at the Texas Barbeque Grand Buffet. Seafood is offered at the latter on Friday nights, and brunch is served on Sundays. **$**

ZION NATIONAL PARK AND THE ST. GEORGE AREA

Hurricane

Main Street Cafe
138 S. Main St, Hurricane, UT
Tel: 435-635-9080
This pretty garden cafe is tiny Hurricane's best-kept secret. Situated next to the Chums eye-glass retainer factory and clothing outlet, it used to be the staff restaurant. Now under new ownership, the place still attracts loyal employees, locals and visitors for some of the best coffee and vegetarian food in southwestern Utah. Try one of the excellent salads with homemade dressing, burritos and homemade breads and desserts. A great place away from busy St George or Springdale, where you can while away an afternoon after a long, hot morning hike. The cafe has art on the walls, a friendly staff and a relaxing atmosphere. **$**

BELOW: homegrown chiles give a spicy kick to traditional Mexican dishes.

St. George

Bear Paw Coffee Company
75 North Main St, St. George, UT
Tel: 435-634-0126
Whatever you're in the mood to eat, you can probably get it at this friendly downtown coffeehouse. The big attraction, though, is the excellent coffee and loose-leaf tea, fresh-squeezed juice drinks, and all-day breakfast. A good place to start a day of exploring southwestern Utah. **$**
Painted Pony
2 West St George Blvd, St. George
Tel: 435-634-1700
Voted St. George's best restaurant, the Painted Pony has legions of fans who flock here for the restaurant's signature cilantro-ginger escolar, a fish dish that arrives as pretty as a picture and tastes as good. Located in Ancestor Square, in the heart of historic downtown St. George, a haven for eating and shopping. **$–$$$**
Sullivan's Rococo Inn and Steak House
511 Airport Rd, St. George, UT
Tel: 435-628-3671
The views are spectacular at this formal restaurant on the lava mesa near the airport overlooking St. George. A good place to put on the dog, specials include excellent meat dishes, such as prime rib and rib-eye steak, as well as seafood. **$–$$$**

Springdale

Bit & Spur Mexican Restaurant and Saloon
1212 Zion Park
Tel: 435-772-3498
The Bit and Spur is

Springdale's most consistently happening restaurant. You'll find a relaxed, hip ambiance and excellent Southwestern food that keeps people coming back night after night. Try the New Mexican rabbit enchilada or sweet potato tamales. **$**
Spotted Dog Cafe
428 Zion Park
Tel: 772-3244 or (800) 765-7787
The food at this restaurant inside popular Flanigan's Inn is always reliable. A good place for lunch, you'll find sandwiches, salads, steaks and local trout on the menu. The restaurant is named after the dog of the original pioneer family. **$–$$**
Switchback Grille
1149 Zion Park
Tel: 435-772-3700.
Located in the Best Western Zion Park, the Switchback Grille is a large, airy dining room with an attractive stone-and-timber western motif. The trout, sea bass and other fish specials are good, as are the pasta dishes and wood-fired oven pizzas. **$–$$**
Watchman Cafe
445 Zion Park
Tel: 435-772-3678
Locals rendezvous at this favorite morning hangout in midtown Springdale. Coffee and homemade pastries are excellent, but it's also a good lunch option, with a selection of tasty sandwiches on the chalkboard. **$**
Zion Pizza and Noodle Company
868 Zion Park
Tel: 435-772-3815
Consistently tasty Italian food draws the crowds in this old church next to the

gallery of landscape photographer Michael Fatali. Expect a wait in summer. **$–$$**

Kanab

Fernando's Hideaway
332 N. 300 West St, Kanab, UT
Tel: 435-644-3222
Slightly off the main drag in Kanab, this quiet neighborhood Mexican restaurant serves unexpectedly good Mexican and American Southwest food. Dine on the patio or inside, where there's a fresh southwestern ambiance, with tile floors, whitewashed walls and Mexican folk art on the walls. The consistently good food, killer margaritas, and inexpensive prices make this a restaurant that locals recommend to visitors again and again. **$**
Rocking V Cafe
97 W. Center St, Kanab, UT
Tel: 435-644-8001
Kanab's most sophisticated restaurant serves up some unexpected gems in the heart of red-rock country, including wild Alaskan salmon, which is flown to Kanab four times a week in season. Filet mignon and rib-eye steaks are on the menu, but there are also lots of vegetarian and vegan items as well. Save room for the dessert specialty: creme brulee. Lunchtime dining is more casual, consisting of soups, salads, sandwiches and burgers. Closed Jan and Feb. Mon and Tues in March, November and December. **$–$$$**

BRYCE CANYON NATIONAL PARK AND THE CEDAR CITY AREA

Bryce Canyon Lodge
2 mi. south of the park entrance
Tel: 435-834-5361
If the lodge is full, you can always soak up some of the historic ambiance in the lodge's rustic dining room, which looks out into the ponderosa forest. The young, friendly, international staff make dining here fun, but don't expect more than standard national park concession food. Homemade soups and chef salads are a good bet for a light lunch. Mexican-style entrees with homemade tomatillo sauce lead the more substantial dishes. Reservations are recommended for dinner. **$$**

Bryce Canyon Pines
6 miles northwest of the park entrance on US 12
Tel: 435-834-5441
The restaurant adjoining this woodsy motel serves good home cooking. Try the made-from-scratch soups, simple meat entrees and homemade pies. **$**

Cedar City

Milt's Stage Stop
Cedar Canyon, 5 miles east of Cedar City on Hwy 14
Tel: 435-586-9344

This rustic restaurant is a popular dining spot in beautiful Cedar Canyon. Specialties include 12-ounce rib-eye steak, prime rib, fresh crab, lobster and other seafood dishes. Open for dinner year-round, it's particularly cozy in winter, when deer graze outside the window and a roaring fire is going inside. **$$–$$$$**

The Pastry Pub
86 W. Center St, Cedar City, UT
Tel: 435-867-1400
Despite the fanciful name, there's no ale on tap here; it's all espresso drinks, pastries and desserts. Sandwiches on your choice of croissant, bread, or flavored tortilla wrap head the lunchtime offerings. The coffee is the best in Cedar City. **$**

Boomer's and Boomer's Pasta Garden
5 N. Main St, Cedar City, UT
Tel: 435-865-9665
This attractive, casual restaurant has good standard American fare, such as burgers and fries, salads, and sandwiches. As the name implies, the sister restaurant upstairs specializes in pasta dishes. Popular with downtown business people. **$**

Panguitch

Buffalo Java
47 N. Main St, Panguitch, UT
Tel: 435-676-8030
You'll find some of the best espresso and coffee drinks in the area at this great little coffee shop and outdoor clothing store housed in a renovated brick mercantile in downtown Panguitch. The coffee is from the Salt Lake Roasting Company and the bagels and pastries are homemade. The bookstore has a nice selection of titles on Utah. Closed in winter. **$**

Cowboy's Smokehouse Cafe
95 N. Main St, Panguitch, UT
Tel: 435-676-8030
This authentic Texas barbecue joint is high on many fans' lists for best BBQ in the state. Beef, chicken, turkey and pork are smoked dry over mesquite, then covered with the owners' (a rancher's son from southern Colorado and two transplanted Texans) secret recipe barbecue sauce. A large selection of homemade cobblers make a good finale. One wall is

dedicated to signed photographs and business cards from satisfied customers. Live music six nights a week. **$$**

Grandma Tina's Italian and Vegetarian Restaurant
523 N. Main St, Panguitch, UT
Tel: 435-676-2377
This authentic Italian restaurant is a real standout in meat-mad ranch country. Try the spaghetti with vegetable sauce and the excellent homemade cannolis and strawberry pie. Closed Nov–Mar. **$–$$**

Tropic

Doug's Place
141 N. Main St (US 12), Tropic, UT
Tel: 800-993-6847
This friendly small-town inn and adjoining restaurant is one of Tropic's best deals. The restaurant specializes in meat dishes, such as Texas-style barbecue and steak Milanesa a la Neapolitana, breaded with ham and swiss cheese. The Friday and Saturday night prime rib dinners are justly famous in these parts. Save room for good homemade pie. **$**

GRAND STAIRCASE-ESCALANTE NATIONAL MONUMENT

Boulder

Hell's Backbone Grill
20 Hwy 12, Boulder, UT
Tel: 435-335-7464
www.hellsbackbone.com
This unique Buddhist-inspired restaurant in Boulder has received nationwide acclaim. Blake Spalding, a backcountry gourmet cook, and business partner Jen Castle, an award-winning dessert maker and restaurateur, moved here from Flagstaff, Arizona, seven years ago, with a dream of building community and pursuing "right livelihood," and have received strong local

support as well as regular diners from Salt Lake City. The small revolving menu riffs creatively on Pueblo, Southwest, Ranch and Mormon Dutch oven cooking traditions and showcases organic beef, buffalo, chicken and Loa trout raised in the area. All the produce and herbs are grown organically on-site. Save room for Jen's famous lemon chiffon cake or any of the other spectacular desserts made fresh everyday. The restaurant has the town's only wine and liquor license. Note: Hell's Backbone Grill is on the grounds of the equally

fabulous Boulder Mountain Lodge. You may want to reserve ahead and make a weekend of it. Open for breakfast, lunch and dinner. Closed Nov–April. **$$–$$$**

Escalante

Cowboy Blues
530 W. Main St, Escalante, UT
Tel: 435-826-4577
Good western American food is served at this ranch-style eatery on the west side of town. The menu features local trout, steaks, ribs, burgers, salads and sandwiches. The restaurant has a wine and liquor license. **$–$$**

Esca-latte Coffee Shop and Pizza Parlor
310 W. Main St, Escalante, UT
Tel: 435-826-4266
You'll find excellent coffee, sandwiches, pizza, salad bar and microbrews in this friendly restaurant in the back of Escalante Outfitters. Pore over a map while enjoying the outdoorsy ambiance. On-

PRICE CATEGORIES

Price categories are for one dinner, excluding beverages, tax and tip:
€ = $20 or less
€€ = $20–40
€€€ = $40–60
€€€€ = $60 and up

site Internet is available, and there's a patio. Tiny log cabins with shared bath facilities can be rented, too. **$**

Kiva Koffee House
Highway 12, mile marker 73.86
Tel: 435-826-4550
Lovingly constructed by the late California architect Brad Bowman, Kiva Koffee House is another unique Grand Staircase-Escalante National Monument eating-out experience you shouldn't miss, if you're in the area between May and October. The kiva-style old log-and-stone building is built on a hillside above Highway 12, just south of the Escalante River, and has breathtaking 360-degree views of the Escalante Canyons through huge glass windows. The patio is the perfect place to sip an espresso or enjoy a casual meal of sandwich, soup and pastry. Closed Mon and Tues. **$**

Paria, Arizona

Paria Outpost and Outfitters
US 89, mile marker 22, 43 miles east of Kanab; 928-691-1047
www.paria.cm
About halfway between Kanab and Big Water, in the Grand Staircase section of Grand Staircase-Escalante National Monument, this Texas-smoked barbecue buffet is worth the long drive. Pizza and Mexican food are also served on weekends. The couple who built the outpost know this country like the back of their hands and are willing to offer tours. Tip: bed-and-breakfast is offered in the outpost's single room, a good idea if you are traveling between Page and Kanab or cutting through to US 89 on the dirt Cottonwood Road from US 12. Not open for lunch. **$**

CAPITOL REEF NATIONAL PARK

Torrey

Cafe Diablo
599 W. Main St, Torrey, UT
Tel: 435-425-3070
This artistic nouvelle Southwestern cafe is right up there with the best restaurants in southern Utah. The chef/owner demonstrates artistic flair with everything he does, attracting foodies from far away. Signature dishes include lime-and-honey-glazed chicken with tomatillo salsa, local trout encrusted with pumpkin seeds accompanied by cilantro lime sauce, and rattlesnake cakes, a rare delicacy, served with ancho-rosemary aioli. The cozy dining room features saltillo floors, white-washed walls and Southwest art, and has the happy buzz of contented diners. Wine and beer served. No lunch. Closed mid-Oct to mid-April. **$$–$$$$**

Capitol Reef Cafe
360 W. Main St, Torrey, UT
Tel: 435-425-3271
"Road food" mavens Jan and Michael Stern loved this bright cafe, which has had a loyal local following for years. Owner Southey Swede is a former Berkeley professor and possesses a wealth of knowledge about Torrey. He buys locally raised meat and fish and organic veggies grown in Caineville and concocts healthy fare that will win smiles from everyone in the family. Try the popular 10-vegetable salad, the local trout or one of the wholesome veggie stir fry and pasta offerings. Attached motel, children's playground and gift shop. Wine and beer served. Closed Nov-April. **$–$$**

Rim Rock Inn
2523 E. Route 24, Torrey, UT
Tel: 435-425-3398
www.therimrock.com
This 19-room inn has spectacular views of Capitol Reef Country from its airy bluff-top location. The restaurant has quite a creative way with beef, fish and game. Try the mixed grill. Closed Nov–Mar. **$–$$**

Robber's Roost Books and Beverages
185 W. Main St, Torrey, UT
Tel: 435-425-3256
Headquarters for the Entrada Institute, which offers author readings, art workshops and educational events throughout the summer, Robber's Roost is an essential stop for book lovers, outdoor enthusiasts and coffeehouse aficionados. Housed in the unusual former home of one of Torrey's most important environmentalists, Robber's Roost is the perfect place to sit beneath the huge old cottonwood trees and enjoy an espresso drink, lulled by the soothing sounds of water burbling next to the patio. The book selection here is one of the best-chosen and interesting in southern Utah. Open year-round. **$**

GLEN CANYON NATIONAL RECREATION AREA

Bullfrog Marina, Utah

Defiance House Lodge
Bullfrog Marina, Box 4055, Lake Powell, UT 84533
Tel: 800-528-6154
This cliff-top lodge overlooks the marina. The pleasant Anasazi Restaurant serves three meals a day. It's standard American food, but the views are good. **$**

Hanksville

Stan's Burger Shack
140 S. Route 95, Hanksville, UT
Tel: 435-542-3330
A favorite with lake-goers, this unpretentious burger joint is the only eatery on this section of US 95, between Lake Powell and Capitol Reef. The burgers and fries, milk shakes and homemade onion rings are first rate. **$**

Page, Arizona

Stromboli's Pizza
711 N. Navajo Drive, Page, AZ
Tel: 928-645-2455
A branch of the popular Flagstaff pizzeria, Stromboli's serves excellent thin-crust pizza. Diners can either sit inside or out on the patio. A popular boater's gathering place. Closed in winter. **$**

Bella Napoli
810 N. Navajo Dr, Page, AZ
Tel: 928-645-2706
A good place for upscale Italian dining. Open daily for dinner in summer and Monday to Saturday the rest of the year; closed late Dec to mid-Feb. **$$**

Butterfield Stage Co. Restaurant
704 Rim View Dr, Page, AZ
Tel: 928-645-2467
Mainstream American fare is served at this diner next to the Best Western Arizona Inn. Dinner includes steak, seafood and prime rib. **$**

TRANSPORT

ARCHES AND CANYONLANDS NATIONAL PARKS

Moab

Buck's Grill
1393 N. Main St, Moab, UT
Tel: 435-259-5201
Don't be put off by the rather pedestrian surroundings of this log restaurant on the north end of town. As soon as you walk through the door, you'll love the combination of white tablecloth-and-silverware elegance mixed in with Western-style hospitality and beautiful views to the meadows beyond. It's all the vision of the chef-owner, a local boy who trained in cordon bleu, then returned home to open a restaurant that rates as one of Moab's best-kept secrets for a fabulous meal at good prices. Buck does amazing things with wild game meats, such as buffalo and elk, as well as duck, steak and vegetables. Try the duck tamales, buffalo chorizo tacos or the elk stew, and order a glass of wine off the extensive wine list. **$–$$$**

Center Cafe
60 N. 100 West St, Moab, UT
Tel: 435-259-4295
It started in 1996, on Center Street, near the Moab Information Center, but the hugely popular Center Cafe really came into its own when it moved into a renovated home in a quiet side street, where the chef-owners, Zee and Paul McCarroll, have created a cozy Spanish-style hacienda, complete with flower-decked courtyard. Regularly voted southern Utah's best restaurant, the Center Cafe is memorable for its beautifully plated, creative contemporary American and Mediterranean-influenced dishes. Try the pan-seared lamb with port-balsamic reduction and roasted garlic flan or roasted eggplant lasagna with feta cheese and olive marinara. Even on a budget, the Center Cafe has options. A bowl of homemade soup, such as autumn butternut infused with apples, a house salad, homemade

bread and a glass of wine will leave you change from $20. Don't miss the Center's signature dessert: baked-to-order chocolate molten cake. The accolades are deserved.
$–$$$

Eddie McStiff's
57 S. Main St, Moab, UT
Tel: 435-259-2337
One of two microbreweries that are always packed with fat-tire enthusiasts after a hot, sweaty day of riding the slickrock. A laid-back atmosphere, filling food for the whole family that won't break the bank, and a huge selection of brews. Try the raspberry wheat beer or IPA. **$**

Eklekticafe
352 N. Main St, Moab, UT
Tel: 435-259-6896
You can tell by its name that Eklekticafe is going to be fun. Savvy locals bring visitors here to enjoy owner Michelle's organic coffee, healthy pastries and unusual dishes such as satay kebabs, stir fries, salads and wraps. The funky interior is a cozy

space where you can also buy collectibles. But the real reason to eat here is to sit on the patio in the midst of a fantastic cottage garden made up of colorful flowers gently irrigated by water from the community ditch. An inspiring place to read, write and meet or make friends. **$**

Fat City Smokehouse
2 S. 100 West St, Moab, UT
Tel: 435-259-4302
A popular BBQ rib place just south of Center Cafe with plenty of beef, chicken, garlic sausage and other meats to keep carnivores happy. Vegetarians will enjoy the Portobello mushroom sandwich. **$–$$**

Jail House Cafe
101 N. Main St, Moab, UT
Tel: 435-259-3900
Breakfast is all they do at this hugely popular restaurant in the old county jail on Main, but they do it brilliantly. You can't go wrong with anything on the menu, including the range of excellent omelettes, eggs Benedict and waffles. For a bit extra, you can also order a cup of Jamaican Blue Mountain coffee, one of the best coffees in the world, to accompany your morning repast – a rare treat. Expect a line and allow plenty of time to eat. Sadly, this place is closed on Sundays. **$**

Miguel's Baja Cantina
51 N. Main St, Moab, UT
Tel: 435-259-6546
www.miguelsbajagrill.com
Mexican-born Miguel Valdes no longer co-owns this haven of Baja cooking in the desert. A pity because his remaining American partners seem to have lost some of the relaxed South-of-the-border approach to

BELOW: chefs at top restaurants make use of fresh produce and local ingredients.

ACCOMMODATIONS

EATING OUT

ACTIVITIES

PRICE CATEGORIES

Price categories are for one dinner, excluding beverages, tax and tip:
€ = $20 or less
€€ = $20–40
€€€ = $40–60
€€€€ = $60 and up

A – Z

dining that made this tiny eatery on Main Street stand out from its competitors. Still, you won't go wrong if you order the grilled fish tacos, excellent ceviche or mole dishes. With a cold beer in hand, you can almost imagine you're sitting under a *palapa* on the Sea of Cortez. *Sabroso!* Closed Nov–Feb. **$–$$**

Peace Tree Juice Cafe
20 S. Main St, Moab, UT
Tel: 435-259-8503
A Moab favorite for fresh smoothies and juices, wrap sandwiches and organic espresso. There's a branch in Monticello. **$**

Red Rock Bakery and Net Cafe
75 S. Main St, Moab, UT
Tel: 435-259-5941
A local favorite for its

excellent homemade bread, bagel sandwiches, pastries, and piping-hot Fair Trade coffee. The friendly Scottish owner knows everyone, and you can check your email in the cool dark Internet room in back for a small charge. **$**

Sorrel River Ranch
Rte. 128, Box K, mile marker 17.5, Moab, UT 84532
The food is top notch at

this elegant ranch, east of Moab, along the Colorado River Scenic Byway. It's a great place for a spiffy evening out when what you want is to get away from busy Moab and relax amid the red rocks on the riverside patio. **$–$$$**

SAN JUAN COUNTY

Blanding

Old Tymer
733 S. Main St, Blanding, UT
Tel: 435-678-2122
A favorite with local ranchers for its big, stick-to-the-ribs breakfasts and meaty lunch and dinner items, this family restaurant is one of the few decent restaurants in Blanding. **$**

Bluff

Cow Canyon Trading Post
Intersection of US 191 and 163, Bluff, UT
Tel: 435-672-2208
People drive here from miles around to enjoy superb dining in the pretty dining room adjoining the creaky old trading post. The creative dishes draw heavily on family recipes developed by the Navajo women cooks. The menu is kept small – three entrees daily – and each one

shines. The friendly and knowledgeable owners work closely with the local Navajo population and sell highly collectible folk art and a good selection of art books in the trading post. Occasional poetry readings and art openings. Not open for lunch. Closed Nov.-Mar. **$–$$**

Fry Canyon

Fry Canyon Lodge
Rte. 95, mile marker 71, Fry Canyon, UT 84533
Tel: 435-259-5334
The only building in the 120 miles between Blanding and Hanksville, Fry Canyon seems to jump out of nowhere – a welcoming symbol of humanity in an unpopulated sea of red rock. The inn is a great overnight option, and the restaurant is surprisingly good. Meat dishes shine, including a slab of roast

pork loin with apple-chile chutney. Open all year. **$**

Mexican Hat

San Juan Inn and Trading Post
US 163, Mexican Hat, UT; 435-683-2220
Set on the banks of the San Juan River next to a popular takeout, this is the best place in Mexican Hat to relax, watch the river currents, and enjoy decent food and lodging. The woodsy Old Bridge Bar and Restaurant has the only liquor license in the area and is a popular stop-off for a cold beer after a long day on the river. The Navajo cooks do a good job with steak and burgers, fresh trout and reservation staples such as Navajo tacos on piping hot frybread. The adjoining 39-room inn is a good value. It has a gym, hot tub and laundry facilities. The

trading post sells Indian arts and crafts and groceries. **$–$$**

Monticello

Peace Tree Juice Cafe
516 N. Main St, Monticello
no phone
A second location of the popular Moab vegetarian restaurant, the Peace Tree in Monticello serves the best smoothies, wrap sandwiches and coffee in town. The restaurant, on the north side of town, doubles as an art gallery, selling jewelry and other arts and crafts made by local Navajo people. Closed in winter. **$**

Monument Valley

Gouldings' Lodge
off US 163, Monument Valley, UT
Tel: 435-727-3231
The main lodging in the Monument Valley area has a decent restaurant (the Stagecoach, named for John Ford's classic western film, shot in Monument Valley). The food is standard American with the ubiquitous Navajo taco thrown in. Nothing fancy, but a good place for breakfast before taking a tour. **$–$$**

BELOW: artfully prepared dishes please the eye as well as the taste buds.

ACTIVITIES

FESTIVALS, THE ARTS, NIGHTLIFE, SHOPPING AND SPECTATOR SPORTS

PERFORMING ARTS

Northern Utah

Park City

Egyptian Theatre
tel: 435-649-9371
Music and drama productions
throughout the year and movies
during the Sundance Film Festival.
St Mary of the Assumption Church
1505 White Pine Canyon Rd, Park
City, UT; tel: 801-355-ARTS;
www.arttix.org
Chamber and classical music
concerts are held at this church in
Park City.
The Canyons Resort
tel: 435-649-5400
The Summer Outdoor Concert Series
features international performers.
Deer Valley
2250 Deer Valley Dr, Park City, UT;
tel: 801-355-ARTS or 888-451-2787;
www.arttix.org
The Utah Symphony performs at this
popular ski resort in summer.
Eccles Center for the Performing Arts
1750 Kearns Blvd, Park City, UT
A beautiful new performing arts
center in Park City.

Provo

Sundance Theatre
North Fork, Provo Canyon, Provo, UT;
tel: 801-225-4107
Performances by the Utah Symphony
and Opera and other groups, along
with theater and outdoor cinema. The
world-famous **Sundance Film Festival**
(tel: 801-328-FILM) is held at the
theater and at venues around Park
City, Salt Lake City and Ogden in late
January.
Brigham Young University
Provo, UT 84602; tel: 801-378-7447;

www.byu.edu
A wide variety of productions is
featured through Brigham Young
University's Theatre department.

Salt Lake City and Environs

Mormon Tabernacle
Temple Square, Salt Lake City, UT;
tel: 801-240-3318
The world-renowned Mormon
Tabernacle Choir performs weekly
Sunday television and radio
broadcasts at the Mormon Tabernacle
at 9.30am (audience must be seated
by 9.15am). The public is also
welcome at rehearsals every
Thursday at 8pm. Organ recitals are
held in the Tabernacle at noon
Mon–Sat and at 2pm Sunday.
Assembly Hall
Temple Square, Salt Lake City, UT;
tel: 801-240-3318
Free LDS-sponsored Temple Square
Concerts are held at the hall every
Friday and Saturday evening.
Capitol Theatre
50 West 200 South, Salt Lake City,
UT; tel: 801-35-ARTS; www.arttix.org
Opened in 1913, this beautifully
renovated venue offers a variety of
performance events, including **Ballet
West** (tel: 801-355-2787) and the
Ririe-Woodbury Dance Company (tel:
801-328-1062). RDC is one of
America's premier modern dance
companies. When not touring
nationally, the company performs
locally and puts on community
workshops. Other companies
performing here include Repertory
Dance Theatre, which specializes in
classical American and contemporary
dance, and **Utah Opera Company,**
which performs four operas at the
theater between October and May.
Promised Valley Playhouse
132 South State, Salt Lake City, UT;
tel: 801-364-5677

Musicals and dramas are performed
at this old vaudeville venue in
summer and at Christmas.
Abravanel Hall
123 West South Temple, Salt Lake
City, UT; tel: 801-355-ARTS or 888-451-2787; www.arttix.org
Part of Salt Lake County Center for
the Arts, Abravanel Hall is home to
the Utah Symphony and Opera for
year-round symphonic concerts. Each
June, top pianists from around the
world compete in the Gina Bachauer
International Piano Competition.
Rose Wagner Performing Arts Center
138 West Broadway, Salt Lake City;
tel: 801-355-ARTS; www.arttix.org
A favorite venue for contemporary
theater, the center is part of Salt
Lake County Center for the Arts and
includes the Jeanne Wagner Theatre,
Leona Wagner Black Box Theater and
Rose Wagner Studio.
Symphony Hall
123 West South Temple, Salt Lake
City, UT; tel: 801-533-6407
Each year, the Utah Symphony plays
15 concerts at Symphony Hall at the
Salt Palace in downtown Salt Lake,
eight concerts in Orem, three
concerts in Provo, three concerts in
Logan, and other cities.
Delta Center
301 West South Temple, Salt Lake
City, UT 84101; tel: 801-325-SEAT;
www.delta.com or www.ticketmaster.com
Home to Utah's famed basketball
team, the Utah Jazz, the Delta Center
is also Salt Lake's premier music
venue, featuring big acts like Cher,
Sting and others; the Mountain
Bluegrass Gathering; and national
touring shows.
Off Broadway Theatre
272 South Main St, Salt Lake
City,UT; tel: 801-355-4628
Home to Utah's longest-running
improv comedy theater troupe,

ACCOMMODATIONS

EATING OUT

ACTIVITIES

A – Z

Laughing Stock.

D. R. Puppets' Theatre
602 East 500 South, Salt Lake City, UT; tel: 801-363-1441
Live puppet shows for children by an acclaimed Russian pupeteer on the south side of Trolley Square.

Salt Lake Acting Company
168 West 500 North, Salt Lake City, UT; tel: 801-363-SLAC or 801-355-ARTS; www.arttix.org
In the heart of Salt Lake City's quaint Marmalade district, the Acting Company is the place to see award-winning local works, and cutting edge performances. Located in the historic Marmalade Ward House, the company's hysterical take on Utah life, *Saturday's Voyeur*, has become an annual tradition.

Salt Lake Community College
4600 S. Redwood Rd, Salt Lake City, UT 84130-0808; tel: 801-957-4111; www.slcc.edu
Home to the Grand Theatre, the community college's performing art company.

Lab Theatre
240 South 1500 East, University of Utah, Salt Lake City, UT; tel: 801-355-ARTS; www.arttix.org
Experimental theater is the focus of this venue on campus.

Babcock Theatre
300 South 1400 East, University of Utah, Salt Lake City, UT; tel: 801-355-ARTS; www.arttix.org
Another beautiful theater space at the University of Utah.

Kingsbury Hall
1395 East President's Circle, University of Utah, Salt Lake City, UT
A 2,000-seat theater in a grand building on campus.

Alice Sheets Marriott Center for Dance
330 South 1500 East, University of Utah, Salt Lake City, UT; tel: 801-355ARTS; www.arttix.org

The university's premier dance performance space.

Libby Gardner Concert Hall
1375 East President's Circle, University of Utah, Salt Lake City, UT; tel: 801-355-ARTS; www.arttix.org
Symphonic and chamber music, jazz and classical concerts.

Westminster College
1840 South 1300 East, Salt Lake City, UT 84105; tel: 801-484-7651; www.wcslc.edu
This small private college is in the Sugarhouse district of Salt Lake City and is strong in the arts. A variety performance events are held here.

Pioneer Theatre Company
300 South 1400 East, Salt Lake City, UT 84112; tel: 801-581-6961; www.pioneertheatre.org
Affiliated with the University of Utah, this fully professional, 900-seat theater presents a seven-play season from September to May. The schedule includes popular Broadway-quality comedies, dramas, classics and musicals as well as work by such contemporary playwrights as Tom Stoppard, August Wilson and Wendy Wasserstein.

Bountiful

Bountiful Performing Arts Center
745 S. Main St, Bountiful, UT 84010; tel: 801-294-7469
Theater and other events at Bountiful's premier venue for the performing arts.

Midvale

Hispanic Center for the Arts
7677 Main St, Midvale, UT 84047; tel: 801-567-9090
Contemporary Hispanic culture is celebrated at this venue in Midvale.

Logan and Environs

Ellen Eccles Theatre
43 S. Main, Logan; 435-752-0026

Part of an arts complex and a fixture in Cache Valley since 1923, this attractive theater is home to the Utah Festival Opera each summer.

American West Heritage Center
Wellsville, UT; tel: 800-225-FEST
This western cultural center has year-round exhibits and programs but is best known for its popular annual Festival of the American West the last week in July and first week in August. Events include the Great West Fair, featuring a mountain man encampment, arts and crafts demonstrators, Shoshone village, Dutch oven cookoff, cowboy poetry gathering, art show and quilt show. The highlight is a multimedia outdoor show entitled *The West: American Odyssey* with 200 performers and taped narration by Jimmy Stewart.

Pickleville Playhouse Summer Theatre
Garden City, UT;
Family entertainment on summer evenings.

Ogden

Weber State University
3750 Harrison Blvd, Ogden, UT 84408; tel: 801-626-8500; www.weber.edu/culturalaffairs/
Live theater, dance and music are performed in several theaters on campus, about 35 miles north of Salt Lake City. Venues include **Browning Center for the Arts** and **Eccles Theater. Peery's Egyptian Theater** (tel: 801-626-6437; 800-337-2690) is home to the Utah Musical Theater. Ballet West and the Utah Symphony also perform here.

Utah Valley State College
800 West University Parkway, Orem, UT 84058-5999; tel: 801-222-8000
The on-campus David O. McKay Events Center hosts athletic programs and major concerts.

Orem

Hale Center Theater, Orem
tel: 801-984-9000
The Hale Center Theater Company plays at this theater in Orem.

Vernal

Outlaw Trail Festival
tel: 800-477-5558
An original musical production based on the area's colorful past is performed in Vernal, June through August each year. Uintah Arts Council and Uinta Basin Continuing Education Center in Vernal sponsor touring performers and local music and theater productions. For more information, call 435-789-6932.

BELOW: outdoor concert in Park City.

Central Utah

Ephraim

Snow College
tel: 435-283-7000
This college in the Sanpete Valley offers concerts, theater and other productions by students and touring performers during much of the year.

Huntington

Castle Valley Pageant
tel: 435-381-5505
Held on a hill overlooking the San Rafael Desert in Emery County, this pioneer pageant celebrating the settling of Castle Valley is one of Utah's most impressive outdoor productions.

Southern Utah

Cedar City

Southern Utah University
tel: 435-586-7878
Utah's premier theatrical event each year is the nationally acclaimed **Utah Shakespearean Festival**, held at a replica of London's Globe Theatre on the SUU campus in downtown Cedar City. Events include a Renaissance Faire, three Shakespearean plays rotated nightly throughout the summer, and modern plays. Free "Green Shows" include puppet shows, strolling vendors, musicians, and dancers preceding the evening play performances. A fall season has just been added. SUU also sponsors the **Thunderbird International Film Festival**, a film fest showcasing family-friendly student and independent films during the first weekend of June. For more information, call 435-586-7861.

St George

Dixie College
St George, UT; tel: 800-746-9882
Set on the downtown campus of Dixie College, the Celebrity Concert Series features dance, music and other productions from October to May.
Tucahn Amphitheater
10 miles north of St George; tel: 800-746-9882
Southwestern Utah's premier performance space, this desert amphitheater offers a season of concerts from October to May by the Southwest Symphony and a colorful extravaganza featuring hundreds of performers reenacting the Mormon pioneer history of southwestern Utah.

Torrey

Robber's Roost Books and Beverages
185 W. Main St, Torrey, UT; tel: 435-425-3265
Entrada Institute, headquartered at this coffeehouse, bookstore and community center sponsors weekend readings, one-person shows, workshops and other events throughout the summer. The three-day September Art from the Land Workshop is the highlight of the year.

Springdale

O. C. Tanner Auditorium
Downtown Springdale, outside Zion National Park; tel: 435-652-7994
The multimedia presentation *The Grand Circle: A National Park Odyssey*, highlighting the history and beauty of several national parks, is presented here nightly from June through September. The amphitheater also hosts summer concert series ranging from symphony to a popular folklife festival.
Bumbleberry Inn Playhouse
Springdale, UT
Adjoining Bumbleberry Restaurant, this playhouse is home to *Twist the Night Away*, a 1950s family musical featuring Doo Wop music, rock 'n' roll and other fifties fun.

Moab

Moab Arts Center
Moab, UT; tel: 435-259-8825
Home to the Moab Community Theater and Moab Community Chorus. Each fall, the center hosts the Canyonlands Arts and Performance Festival.

Blanding

Kagilia Fine Arts Center
Blanding, UT; tel: 435-587-3235
Live performances throughout the year take place at this theater. "Edge of the Seaters," a theater company, performs melodramas during Blanding's Fourth of July celebration.

Monticello

Blue Mountain Entertainment
Monticello, UT; tel: 435-587-3235
Presents five concerts a year in Monticello.

THE GREAT OUTDOORS

Parks and Historic Sites

Northern Utah

Antelope Island State Park
4528 West 1700 South, Syracuse, UT 84075; tel: 801-773-2941
Bear Lake State Park
P.O. Box 184, Garden City, UT 84028-0184; tel: 435-946-3343
Camp Floyd-Stagecoach Inn State Park
P.O. Box 446, Riverton, UT 84065-0448; tel: 801-768-8932
Deer Creek State Park
P.O. Box 257, Midway, U 84049-0257; tel: 435-654-0171
Dinosaur National Monument
P.O. Box 4545, Dinosaur, CO 81610; 970-374-3000; Quarry Visitor Center, P.O. Box 128, Jensen, UT 84035; tel: 435-789-2115
East Canyon State Park
5535 Hwy 66, Morgan, UT 84050-9694; tel: 801-829-6866
Flaming Gorge National Recreation Area
Flaming Gorge Ranger District, P.O. Box 279, Manila, UT 84046; tel: 435-784-3445
Fort Buenaventura State Park
2450 A Ave, Ogden, UT 84401-2203; tel: 801-621-4808
Golden Spike National Historic Site
P.O. Box 897, Brigham City, UT 84032; tel: 435-471-2209
Great Salt Lake State Marina
P.O. Box 16658, Salt Lake City, UT 84116-0648; tel: 801-250-1898
Historic UP Rail Trail State Park
P.O. Box 754, Park City, UT 84060-0754; tel: 435-649-6839
Hyrum State Park
405 West 300 South, Hyrum, UT 84319-1547; tel: 435-245-6866
Jordan River State Park
1084 N. Redwood Rd, P.O. Box 16658, Salt Lake City, UT 84116-0658; tel: 801-533-4496; golf: tel: 801-533-4527
Jordonelle State Park
SR 319, #515, Box 4, Heber City, UT 84032-0001; Hailstone: tel: 435-649-9540; Rock Cliff: tel: 435-783-3030
Palisade State Park
2200 Palisade Rd, P.O. Box 650070, Sterling, UT 84665-0070; tel: 435-835-7275
Piute State Park
P.O. Box 43, Antimony, UT 84712-0043; tel: 435-624-3268
Red Fleet State Park
8750 Hwy 191, Vernal, UT 84078-7801; tel: 435-789-4432
Rockport State Park
9040, Hwy 302, Peoa, UT 84061-9702; tel: 435-336-2241
Starvation State Park
P.O. Box 584, Duchesne, UT 84021-0584; tel: 435-738-2326
Steinaker State Park
4335 Hwy 191, Vernal, UT 84078-7800; tel: 435-789-4432
This is the Place Heritage Park
2601 Sunnyside Ave, Salt Lake City, UT 84108-1453; tel: 801-584-8391
Timpanagos Cave National Monument
Rte. 3, Box 200, American Fork, UT 84003; tel: 801-756-5238
Utah Field House of Natural History State Park Museum

235 E. Main St, Vernal, UT 84078-
2605; tel: 435-789-3799
Utah Lake State Park
4400 W. Center St, Provo, UT 84601-
8238; tel: 801-375-0731
Veterans Memorial Cemetery
17111 Camp Williams Rd, P.O. Box
446, Riverton, UT 84065-0446; tel:
801-254-9036
Wasatch Mountain State Park
P.O. Box 10, Midway, UT 8404449-
0010; tel: 435-654-1791; golf: tel:
435-654-0532; Salt Lake: tel: 801-
266-0268
Willard Bay State Park
900 W. 650 North #A, Willard, UT
84340-9999; tel: 435-734-9494
Yuba Lake State Park
P.O. Box 159, Levan, UT 84639-
0159; tel: 435-758-2611

Central Utah

Fremont Indian State Park
11550 W. Clear Creek Canyon Rd,
Sevier, UT 84766-9999; tel: 435-
527-4631
Huntington State Park
P.O. Box 1343, Huntington, UT
84528-1343; tel: 435-687-2491
Millsite State Park
P.O. Box 1343, Huntington, UT
84528-1343; tel: 435-687-2491
Minersville State Park
P.O. Box 1531, Beaver, UT 84713-
1531; tel: 435-438-5472
Otter Creek State Park
P.O. Box 43, Antimony, UT 84712-
0043; tel: 435-624-3268
Scofield State Park
P.O. Box 166, Price, UT 84501-0166;
summer: tel: 435-448-9449; winter:
tel: 435-637-2732
Territorial Statehouse State Park
50 W. Capitol Ave, Fillmore, UT
84631-5556; tel: 435-743-5316

Southern Utah

Anasazi State Park
P.O. Box 1429, Boulder, UT 84716;
tel: 435-335-7308
Arches National Park
P.O. Box 907, Moab, UT 84532-
0907; tel: 435-719-2299;
www.nps.gov/arch
Bryce Canyon National Park
Bryce Canyon, UT 84717; tel: 435-
834-5322; www.nps.gov/brca
**Canyons of the Ancients National
Monument**
c/o Anasazi Heritage Center, 10
miles north of Cortez, off CO 184;
tel: 970-882-4811;
www.co.blm.gov/ahc/hmepge.htm
Canyonlands National Park
2282 S. West Resource Blvd, Moab,
UT 84532; tel: 435-259-7164;
www.nps.gov/cany
Capitol Reef National Park
Torrey, UT 84775; tel: 435-425-
3791; www.nps.gov/care

Cedar Breaks National Monument
2390 Hwy 56, Suite 11, Cedar City,
UT 84720; tel: 435-586-9451;
www.nps.gov/cebr
Coral Pink Sand Dunes State Park
P.O. Box 95, Kanab, UT 84741; tel:
435-648-2800
Dead Horse Point State Park
P.O. Box 609, Moab, UT 84532-
0609; tel: 435-259-2614
Edge of the Cedars State Park
660 West 400 North, Blanding, UT
84511-4000; tel: 435-678-2238
Escalante State Park
710 N. Reservoir Rd, Escalante, UT
84726-4466; tel: 435-826-4466
Glen Canyon National Recreation Area
P.O. Box 1507, Page, AZ 86040; tel:
928-608-6404; www.nps.gov/glca
Goblin Valley State Park
P.O. Box 637, Green River, UT
84525-0637; tel: 435-564-3633
Gooseneck State Park
c/o Edge of the Cedars State Park,
660 West 400 North, Blanding, UT
84511-4000; tel: 435-678-2238
**Grand Staircase-Escalante National
Monument**
P.O. Box 246, Escalante, UT 84726;
tel: 435-826-5499;
www.ut.blm.gov/monument
Gunlock Lake State Park
P.O. Box 140, Santa Clara, UT
84765-0140; tel: 435-628-2255
Hovenweep National Monument
McElmo Route, Cortez, CO 81321;
tel: 970-562-4282; nps.gov/hove
Kodachrome Basin State Park
P.O. Box 238, Cannonville, UT
84718-0238; tel: 435-679-8562
Natural Bridges National Monument
P.O. Box 1, Lake Powell, UT 84533;
tel: 435-692-1234; www.nps.gov/nabr
Pipe Spring National Monument
HC 65, Box 5, Fredonia, AZ 86022;
tel: 928-643-7105; www.nps.gov/pisp
Quail Creek State Park
P.O. Box 1943, St. George, UT
84771-1943; tel: 435-879-2378
Rainbow Bridge National Monument
P.O. Box 1507, Page, AZ 86040; tel:
520-608-6200; www.nps.gov/rabr
Snow Canyon State Park
P.O. Box 140, Santa Clara, UT
84765-0140; tel: 435-628-2255
Zion National Park
Springdale, UT 84767; tel: 435-772-
3256; nps.gov/zion

Tour Operators

All Seasons Adventures
P.O. Box 680547, Park City, UT
84068; tel: 435-649-9619;
www.allseasonsadventures.com
Summer and winter guide service.
Castle Valley Outdoors
P.O. Box 770, Emery, UT 84537; tel:
435-748-5559;
www.castlevalleyranch.com
Horseback riding, cattle drives,

rafting, fishing, wildlife watching and
bed-and-breakfast at two remote
ranches in the San Rafael Swell and
Capitol Reef Country.
Crawdads and Yoo Hoos
1071 East 740 North, St George,
UT; tel: 435-673-9810;
www.crawdadstours.com
Specialty tours with mountain men,
Dutch oven cooking and storytelling.
Escalante Outfitters and Bunkhouse
210 W. Main, Escalante, UT 84726;
tel: 435-826-4266;
www.escalanteoutfitters.com
Rentals and tours in many
southwestern Utah locations.
Hondoo Rivers and Trails
90 E. Main St, Torrey, UT; tel: 800-
332-2696; www.hondoo.com
Guided backpacking, hiking,
horsepacking, trail rides and Jeep
tours around Capitol Reef.
Pleasant Valley Hunting Preserve
Rt. 3, Box 3736, Myton, UT 84052;
tel: 435-646-3194;
www.hickenschickens.com
Guided pheasant hunting trips in the
Uinta Basin.
Recapture Lodge
P.O. Box 309, Bluff, UT 84512; tel:
435-672-2281;
www.bluffutah.org/recapturelodge
Guided tours of San Juan River,
Monument Valley and the Navajo
Reservation. Ideal for river runners,
hikers, llama packers and bicyclists.
Southern Utah Scenic Tours
115 N. Main St, #202, Cedar City,
UT; tel: 888-404-8687;
www.utahscenictours.com
Guided expeditions to southern
Utah's national parks and
monuments, movie sets and more.
Sorrel River Ranch Resort
P.O. Box K, Moab, UT 84532; tel:
877-359-2715; www.sorrelriver.com
Rafting, biking, horseback rides, four-
wheeling and more on a working
ranch on the Colorado River.
Tavaputs Ranch
P.O. Box 1736, Price, UT 84501; tel:
435-637-1236; www.tavaputsranch.com
Horseback riding, hiking, biking on a
historic working family ranch on the
remote Tavaputs Plateau.
The Homestead Resort
700 N. Homestead Dr, Midway, UT
84049-0099; tel: 800-327-7220;
www.homesteadresort.com
Golf course, fishing, horseback
riding,, cross-country skiing, and
scuba diving in a volcanic crater.
The Lodge at Red River Ranch
2900 Hwy 24, Teasdale, UT 84773;
tel: 800-205-6343; www.redriverranch.com
Guided hiking, biking, scenic drives
and fishing in Capitol Reef Country.
**Zion Ponderosa Resort/Zion
Excursions, Inc.**
P.O. Box 521436, Salt Lake City, UT;

tel: 800-293-5444;
www.zionponderosa.com
Backpacking, hiking, horsepacking,
trail rides, bicycle touring, cabin
rentals and more.
Zion Adventure Company
36 Lion Blvd, Springdale, UT 84767;
tel: 435-772-1001;
www.zionadventures.com
Outfitters for Zion Narrows hikers
providing dry suits, camping rentals
and backcountry planning.

***Outdoor Adventure Outfitters
and Guides***
Bear River Lodge
Highway 50, Kamas, UT; tel: 800-
559-1121; www.bearriverlodge.com
Trail riding in Wasatch National
Forest on the west side of the High
Uinta Mountains.
Boulder Mountain Ranch
Hells Backbone Rd, Salt Gulch,
Boulder, UT; tel: 435-335-7840
Adventurous horseback riding, pack
trips, camping, full-service or drop
camp fishing, and bed and breakfast
on an unusual family ranch.
Boulder Outdoor Survival School
P.O. Box 1590, Boulder, UT 80306;
tel: 800-335-7404; http://boss-inc.com
Unique desert wilderness survival
courses in Grand Staircase-Escalante
National Monument.
Bunk 'n Breakfast
P.O. Box 212, Wellington, UT 84542;
tel: 435-637-2572;
www.ninemilecanyon.com
Guided rock art/history tours,
working cattle ranch, bed-and-
breakfast, camping.
Canyonlands Field Institute
1320 Hwy 191, Moab, UT; tel: 800-
860-5262;
www.canyonlandsfieldinstitute.org
Field camping and river study
programs for youths and adults.
Canyonlands Needles Outpost
Hwy 211, Canyonlands National Park,
Needles District; tel: 435-259-8545
The only outfitter on the border with
the national park offers scenic flights
over Canyonlands, jeep and four-
wheel-drive rentals.
Chapoose Canyon Adventures
7237 East 500 North, Fort Duchesne,
UT 84026; tel: 877-722-4072
Native American outfitter offering
authorized Uintah-Ouray Ute Indian
Reservation camping.
Colorado Plateau Field Institute
P.O. Box 517, Price, UT 84501; tel:
435-637-1248; www.cpfieldinstitute.org
Geology, paleontology, archaeology
and outdoors education.
Dinosaur River Expeditions
P.O. Box 3387, Park City, UT 84068;
tel: 800-345-RAFT; www.dinoadv.com
River or river/bicycling trips on the
Green River.

**Ed Black's Monument Valley Trail
Rides**
P.O. Box 310155, Monument Valley,
UT 84536; tel: 435-739-4285
Navajo-guided Monument Valley
horseback expeditions.
Escalante Canyon Outfitters, Inc.
842 Hwy 12, Boulder, UT 84716; tel:
888-326-4453; www.ecohike.com
Multi-day hiking and horse packing
trips in the Escalante Canyons.
Falcon's Ledge
P.O. Box 67, Altamont, UT 84001;
tel: 877-879-3737; www.falconsledge.com
Fly fishing and falconry with expert
guides at an upscale lodge.
Flaming Gorge Lodge
155 Greendale, US 191, Dutch John,
UT 84023; tel: 435-889-3773;
www.fglodge.com
Fly fishing, rafting, snowmobiling and
camping in Flaming Gorge.
Four Corners Outdoor School
P.O. Box 1029, Monticello, UT
84535; tel: 800-525-4456;
www.fourcornersschool.org
Environmental and natural history
educational programs.
Hatch River Expeditions
55 E. Main, Vernal, UT; tel: 800-342-
8243; www.hatchriver.com
River trips on the Yampa, Green and
Colorado Rivers.
Heber Valley Historic Railroad
450 South 600 West, Heber City, UT
84032; tel: 801-581-9980;
www.hebervalleyrr.org
Specialty train rides on a historic
railroad throughout the year. On
winter weekends a special Polar
Express steam train.
Holiday Expeditions
544 East 3900 South, Salt Lake City,
UT; tel: 800-624-6323;
www.bikeraft.com
Biking, rafting, kayaking on the
Green, Yampa and Colorado Rivers.
Kayak Powell/Grand Circle Tours
tel: 888-854-7862; www.kayakpowell.com
Boat-supported kayaking trips in the
vicinity of the Grand Circle parks.
L. C. Ranch
P.O. Box 63, Altamont, UT 84001;
tel: 435-454-3750; www.lcranch.com
Fly fishing at a resort.
Moab Cyclery and Escape Adventures
391 S. Main, Moab, UT 84532; tel:
800-559-1978; www.escapeadventures.com
Rentals, repairs, trail advice and
tours for mountain bikers.
Moki Mac River Expeditions
6006 South 1300 East, Salt Lake
City, UT; tel: 800-284-7280;
www.mokimac.com
River rafting through the canyons of
the Green and Colorado Rivers.
Moki Treks
P.O. Box 162, Moab, UT 84532; tel:
435-259-8033; www.mokitreks.com
Navajo-guided hiking in Monument

Valley and Canyon de Chelly.
Morning Star Balloons
5300 South 625 West, Ste A-133,
Murray, UT 84123; tel: 435-645-
RIDE; www.morningstarballoons.com
Park City hot air balloon adventures.
**O.A.R.S. (Outdoor Adventure River
Specialists)**
543 N. Main, Moab, UT 84532; tel:
800-342-5938; www.moab-
utah.com/oarsutah
Rafting and lodge-based adventures.
Outlaw Trails
129 Raindance Ranch, Hanksville,
UT; tel: 435-542-3421
Unique overnight trail rides into
Robbers Roost country and other
southern Utah areas where Butch
Cassidy and the Wild Bunch hid out.
Red Rock 'n Llamas
P. O. Box 1304, Boulder, UT 84716;
www.redrocknllamas.com
Family-run guided hiking trips into
Grand Staircase-Escalante and
environs as well as jeep tours,
specialty trips and friendly llamas.
Redtail Aviation
30995 E. Airport Rd, Price, UT
84501; tel: 435-637-9556
Aircraft charter rental, instruction,
tours of the Tavaputs Plateau.
Sherri Griffiths Expeditions
2231 Hwy 191, Moab, UT; tel: 800-
626-7335; www.griffithexp.com
Guided river journeys on the Green,
Colorado and Dolores Rivers.
Slickrock Air Guides
P.O. Box 901, Moab, UT; tel: 435-
259-6216
"Flightseeing" transportation service
to Moab, Canyonlands and Southern
Utah.
Tag-a-Long Expeditions
452 N. Main St, Moab, UT; tel: 800-
453-3292; www.tagalong.com
Whitewater and flatwater rafting,
kayaking, canoeing, jetboating, hiking
and jeeping in the Canyonlands area.

SPORT

Spectator Sports
Basketball
Utah Jazz
Delta Center, 301 West South
Temple, Salt Lake City, UT 84101;
tel: 801-355-DUNK
Utah's premier pro basketball team
plays at the Delta Center. Bring your
ear plugs. This huge center gets *loud*.
Utah Starzz
301 West South Temple, Salt Lake
City, UT; tel: 801-325-STAR;
www.wnba.com/starzz
From May through August, Utah's
WNBA pro women's basketball team
plays at the Delta Center.

Baseball

The Stingers
77 West 1300 South, Salt Lake City,
UT; tel: 801-485-3800;
www.stingersbaseball.com
The Salt Lake Stingers, the AAA
affiliate of the Anaheim Angels, play
baseball in the Pacific Coast League.
Home games are held April to
September at Franklin Covey Field,
which has the majestic Wasatch
Mountains as its eastern backdrop.

Ice Hockey

Utah Grizzlies
E Center, 3200 South Decker Lake
Dr, West Valley City, UT; tel: 801-988-
8000 or 801-988-PUCK;
www.utahgrizz.com
The former Denver Grizzlies moved to
Salt Lake City in 1995. The AHL team
now plays games at the E Center,
one of Salt Lake's newest venues, in
West Valley City.

Rodeo

Traditional cowboy skills – riding,
roping and bronco busting – are on
display at these genuine Western
competitions. There are rodeos
somewhere in the state every
weekend in summer.

June
Moab Rodeo, www.prorodeo.com
Deseret Peak Rodeo, Tooele,
www.prorodeo.com
Strawberry Days Rodeo, Pleasant
Grove; tel: 801-785-6128
Delta Rodeo, 435-783-5753
American West Rodeo, Logan, tel:
435-245-6867
Lehi Round-Up, www.prorodeo.com

July
Oakley 4th of July Rodeo, tel: 435-
783-5753
Western Stampede, West Jordan;
tel: 801-561-0418
Dinosaur Roundup, Vernal, tel: 435-
789-1352
Ute Stampede, Nephi, 435-623-0761
Days of 47 Rodeo, Salt Lake City,
www.daysof47.com
Fiesta Days, Spanish Fork, tel: 801-
798-5041
Ogden Pioneer Days, 801-629-8125
San Rafael Pro Rodeo, Castle Dale,
tel: 435-381-2108

August
Mountain Valley Stampede, Heber
City, tel: 435-654-3666
Cache County Fair Rodeo, Logan,
tel: 435-716-7150
Summit County Fair Rodeo, Coalville,
tel: 435-336-3221 or 435-615-3221
Davis County Fair Rodeo,
Farmington, tel: 801-451-4080

Golden Spike Rodeo, Tremonton, tel:
435-279-0307

September
Utah State Fair Rodeo, Salt Lake
City, tel: 801-538-3247
Dixie Lions Round-Up, St George, tel:
435-632-3802

December
Wilderness Circuit Finals, Ogden,
tel: 800-442-7362

Participant Sports

Bicycling

Mountain biking has been one of
Utah's major outdoor sports since
fat-tire cyclists first discovered the
slickrock trails around Moab in the
1980s. Today, Moab hosts popular
fat-tire festivals each year and
provides a variety of specialized
facilities geared toward bikeheads,
from specialist bike repair shops and
area tours to a bike wash and
espresso bar at one local inn. The
most popular rides in the area are
the **Slickrock Bike Trail,**
internationally known for its
challenges; the multiday **Kokopelli
Trail**, a red-rock adventure between
Moab and Grand Junction, Colorado;
and **White Rim Trail**, a 100-mile
(160 km) backcountry route
encircling the Island in the Sky
District of Canyonlands National
Park. All of southern Utah's national
parks have good paved scenic roads
suited to bicycling, especially **Zion**,
where bicyclists can ride into Zion
Canyon in summer, when the scenic
drive is closed to auto traffic. In the
Salt Lake City area, the **Bonneville
Shoreline Trail** around Great Salt
Lake offers miles of bike riding and
outstanding birding, while the many
scenic canyons of the Wasatch
Mountains offer some uphill
challenges for the extremely fit.
Bicyclists are also discovering **Goblin
Valley State Park** in the **San Rafael
Swell**, where you can set up camp in
the state park and ride for miles
amid breathtaking scenery, old
mining camps and ancient Indian
rock art sites. For more information,
contact the **Utah Travel Council** at tel:
800-200-1160 or www.utah.com/bike/trails
or www.bicycleutah.com.

Fishing

Fly fishing in Utah's high mountain
streams is hugely popular. There are
over 1,000 fishable lakes in the
state and numerous fishing streams,
supporting a variety of fish species,
from stocked rainbow and cutthroat
trout, large mackinaw, brown trout
and striped bass to walleye, bluegill,

whitefish, Bonneville cisco and other
sport fish. The Provo and Green
Rivers draw fly fishers from all over
the West to their blue-ribbon waters.
Flaming Gorge Lake in northern Utah
offers some of the best fishing in the
country while southeastern Utah's
Lake Powell is popular with desert
fishers. Guided fishing is available at
Flaming Gorge and other towns
adjoining the High Uinta Mountains
as well as other rivers and lakes
throughout Utah. You can purchase
fishing licenses at tackle shops and
other stores as well as online. You will
need a special license to fish on
Indian reservation lands. For more
information, contact **Utah Division of
Wildlife Resources**, 1596 W. North
Temple, Salt Lake City, UT 84116, tel:
801-538-4700, www.nr.utah.gov/dwr.htm;
Utah Travel Council, tel: 800-200-
1160, www. utah.com/fish; and **Utah Fish
Finder**, www.utahfishfinder.com.

Golf

There are scores of public and private
golf courses as well as full-fledged
golf resorts throughout Utah. St
George in southwestern Utah, where
the desert weather is pleasant for
golfing year-round, now offers eight
golf courses. Both hotels and tee
times can be reserved through a
central reservation system, **Red Rock
Golf Trail**, a marketing cooperative of
the St George Area Convention and
Visitors Bureau, tel: 888-401-PLAY.
Some of the better courses around
the state are listed below.

Southern Utah
Cedar Ridge
100 East 800 North, Cedar City, UT
84720; tel: 435-586-2970, 18/72,
6,650 yards, public/
Coral Cliffs
700 E. Highway 89, Kanab, UT
84741; tel: 435-644-5005, 9/36,
3,300 yards, public.
Entrada at Snow Canyon
2511 West Entrada Trail, St George,
UT 84770; tel: 435-674-7500.
18/72, 7,262 yards, public.
The Hideout Golf Club
549 S. Main, Monticello, UT 84535;
tel: 435-587-2200. 18/72, 6,900
yards, public.
Moab Golf Course
2705 S.E. Bench Rd, Moab, UT
84532; tel: 435-259-6488. 18/72,
6,819 yards, public.
St George Golf Club
2190 South 1400 East, St George,
UT 84790; tel: 435-634-5854.
18/73, 6,712 yards, public.
Thunderbird Resort
Junction Highway 9/89, Mt. Carmel,
UT 84755; tel: 435-648-2503. 9/31,
1771 yards, public.

Central Utah
Canyon Hills Park
East Canyon Rd, Nephi, UT 84648;
tel: 435-623-9930. 9/36, 3,452
yards, public.
Millsite State Park Golf Course
Canyon Rd, Ferron, UT 84523; tel:
435-384-2887. 9/36, 3,202 yards,
public.
Paradise Golf Resort
905 N. Main, Fillmore, UT 84631;
tel: 435-743-4439. 9/36, 3,293
yards, public.
Green River State Park Golf Course
P.O. Box 637, Green River, UT
84525; tel: 435-564-8882. 9/36,
3,435 yards, public.
Carbon County Golf Course
Hwy 6, Helper, UT 84526; tel: 435-
637-2388. 18/70, 6,186 yards,
public.
Palisade State Park
Palisade State Park, Manti, UT
84642; tel: 435-835-4653. 18/72,
6,360 yards, public.

Northern Utah
Alpine Country Club
4994 W. Country Club Dr, Highland,
UT 84003; tel: 801-322-3971.
18/72, 7,200 yards, private.
Ben Lomond Golf Course
1600 North 500 West, Ogden, UT
84404; tel: 801-782-7320. 9/35,
6,176 yards, public.
Cascade Fairways Golf Course
1313 East 800 North, Orem, UT
84057; tel: 801-225-6677. 9/35,
3,000 yards, public.
Central Valley Golf Course
600 West 330 South, Salt Lake City,
UT 84119; tel: 801-973-6271. 9/33,
2,500 yards, public.
Dinaland Golf Course
675 South 2000 East, Vernal, UT
84078; tel: 435-781-1428. 18/72,
6,773 yards, public.
Homestead Resort
700 N. Homestead Dr, Midway, UT

84049; tel: 800-327-7220. 18/72,
6,967 yards, public.
Mountain View Golf Course
2400 West 8660 South, West
Jordan, UT 84088; tel: 801-255-
9211. 18/72, 6,748 yards, public.
Oquirrh Hills Golf Course
7th and Edgemont, Tooele, UT
84074; tel: 435-882-4220. 9/35,
3,200 yards, public.
Park City Golf Course
P.O. Box 2067, Park City, UT 84060;
tel: 801-521-2135. 18/72, 6,800
yards, public.
Seven Peaks Resort
1450 East 500 North, Provo, UT
84606; tel: 801-375-5155. 18/59,
3,328 yards, public.
Stonebridge
2400 S. Bangerter Hwy, West Valley
City, UT 84120; tel: 801-966-4653.
27/72-36, 7,1080-3,500 yards, public.
Sun Hills Golf Course
3185 N. Northhills Drive, Layton, UT
84041; tel: 801-771-4814. 18/71,
6,500 yards, public.
Tri-City Golf Course
1400 North 200 East, American
Fork, UT 84003; tel: 801-756-3594.
18/72, 6,710 yards, public.

Kayaking, Canoeing, and Rafting
Whitewater and flatwater paddling
are popular activities on Utah's
scenic rivers and lakes, especially in
southern Utah. For information on
routes and conditions, consult the
agency that manages the river or
lake. Other sources of information
are paddling clubs and outdoor-gear
retailers. The most popular rivers for
rafting are the Green, Colorado,
Yampa and San Juan Rivers, where
you will find places of flat and white
water. The San Juan River is largely
flat water and well suited for families,
whereas the whitewater rapids along
the Green River within Dinosaur
National Monument and Cataract

Canyon in Canyonlands National Park
are mainly suited to experienced
oarsmen. Private trips on these rivers
are by lottery permit only at the
beginning of the season. You can
avoid the lottery by signing on with
one of the many outfitters operating
as concessionaires. Numerous lakes
offer boating. By far the most popular
is Lake Powell in southeastern Utah.
Here you can find budget and luxury
houseboats, kayaks and other water
vehicles for rent by the week at
Bullfrog Marina. For more information,
log on to www.utah.com/raft.

Skiing
"The Greatest Snow on Earth" is the
way the State of Utah describes the
deep, fluffy powder that makes Utah
one of North America's premier ski
destinations and led to the selection of
Salt Lake City as host of the 2002
Winter Olympics. Utah has 13 downhill
ski resorts, seven of them less than
an hour's drive from Salt Lake City.
Less well known is Brian Head Ski
Resort east of Cedar City in southern
Utah. Snowboarding is allowed at all
but two resorts – **Alta** and **Deer Valley;**
enthusiasts will now find special
terrain parks featuring state-of-the-art
sound and lighting systems, jumps and
rails at many resorts. The downhill ski
season generally begins statewide
around mid-November and continues
through April with some after-season
opportunities available at selected
resorts. For advanced skiers, the **Ski
Utah Interconnect Adventure Tour** is a
backcountry route linking Park City,
Brighton, Solitude, Alta and Snowbird
resorts along the spine of the Wasatch
Mountains. A discount **Ski Salt Lake
Super Pass** is available to destination
skiers through hotels and travel
agents. For information and
reservations, contact Ski Utah, 150
West 500 South St, Salt Lake City, UT
84101; tel: 801-534-1907;
www.skiutah.com. General ski information
is available at www.utah.com/ski.
Alta
tel: 801-359-1078; www.alta.com
Beaver Mountain
tel: 435-753-0921; www.skithebeav.com
Brian Head
tel: 435-677-2035; www.brianhead.com
Brighton
tel: 800-873-5512;
www.brightonresort.com
The Canyons
tel: 435-649-5400; www.thecanyons.com
Deer Valley
tel: 800-424-3337; www.deervalley.com
Nordic Valley
tel: 801-392-0900
Park City Mountain Resort
tel: 800-222-PARK;
www.parkcitymountain.com

BELOW: a San Juan River guide takes a well-deserved rest.

Powder Mountain
tel: 801-745-3772;
www.powdermountain.net
Snowbasin
tel: 800-620-1000; www.snowbasin.com
Snowbird
tel: 800-232-9542; www.snowbird.com
Solitude Mountain Resort
tel: 801-534-1400; www.skisolitude.com
Sundance
tel: 801-225-4107;
www.sundanceresort.com
Nordic Skiing
Utah's premier cross-country skiing
(as well as tubing) can be found at
Soldier Hollow in the beautiful Heber
Valley of northern Utah, site of the
Nordic skiing venue at the 2002
Olympic Winter Games. For more
information, call 435-654-1791 or log
on to www.soldierhollow.org. Cross-
country skiers will find plenty of good
powder on hundreds of roads and
trails in national forests and on BLM
lands. Higher-elevation plateaus
throughout southern Utah's canyon
country, including those surrounding
Bryce Canyon, are open to nordic
skiers in winter and become magical
after a snowfall. The following nordic
ski centers offer groomed trails,
lessons, rentals and in some cases
tours and hut-to-hut rentals:

Northern Utah
Homestead Cross-Country Ski Center
tel: 800-327-7220
Located near Midway-Park City. 12
km of groomed trails, lessons and
rentals available.
Solitude Nordic Center
tel: 800-748-4SKI
Big Cottonwood Canyon near Salt
Lake City. 20 km of groomed trails,
lessons, rentals and tours offered.
Sherwood Hills
tel: 800-532-5066
Near Logan. 20 km of trails, 5 km
groomed. Lessons by prior
arrangement, rentals and night skiing
available.
Park City Yurts
tel: 435-615-YURT
Park City, near the Canyons Resort.
Sundance Nordic Center
tel: 800-892-1600
Provo Canyon, east of Provo. 15 km
of groomed trails, lessons, rentals
available, night skiing.
White Pine Touring Center
tel: 435-649-8710
Park City. 18 km of groomed trails,
lessons, rentals and tours available.
Rocking C Ranch
68 High Country Rd, Riverton, UT
84065; tel: 801-249-1742

Central Utah
Scofield State Park
Scofield Reservoir, on the Wasatch

Plateau, is a 2,800-acre lake just east
of the city of Scofield near the
northern edge of the Manti-La Sal
National Forest. Park facilities close in
late autumn, but in winter the area
functions as a base camp for cross-
country skiing and snowmobiling, and
is a popular ice fishing area.

Southern Utah
Brian Head Resort
tel: 800-27-BRIAN
Near Cedar City. 42 km of trails, 10
km groomed. Lessons, rentals and
night skiing.
Best Western Ruby's Inn
tel: 800-468-8660
Bryce Canyon National Park. 50 km
of groomed trails, with lessons,
rentals, tours, night skiing. Note:
cross-country skiing and
snowshoeing is allowed anywhere in
Bryce Canyon National Park in winter,
although skiing on the steep, winding
trails below the rim is not
recommended due to hazardous
snow conditions. A ski trail brochure
is available at the visitor center. The
visitor center offers free snowshoes
on a first-come, first-served basis.
Duck Creek Village
30 miles east of Cedar City, near
Strawberry Point, on UT 14. The
facility has groomed cross-country
ski trails, ski and snowmobile
rentals, and ski instructors.
**West of Monticello or north of
Blanding**
tel: 435-259-SNOW
Trails for cross-country skiing and
snowmobiling lead into the Abajo
Mountains of Manti-La Sal National
Forest. Groomed trails and private
backcountry huts are available.

CALENDAR OF EVENTS

January
Sundance Film Festival, Park City
North America's big Indie film fest
swoops down on Park City, Salt Lake
City and Sundance in late January,
tel: 801-328-3456
Utah Winterfest, Salt Lake City
Snow sports and activities. Various
venues around Salt Lake City, tel:
801-294-5887
**Annual Winter Storytelling Festival,
Blanding**
Storytellers from several cultures,
including Navajo, entertain with tall
tales. 700 West 200 South,
Blanding; tel: 435-678-2201(ext. 1)

February
**Annual World of the Wild Art Show,
Salt Lake City (Feb–Apr)**
Art exhibition held at the Hogle Zoo

Auditorium, 2600 Sunnyside Ave,
Salt Lake City; tel: 801-584-1729
Bryce Canyon Winter Festival
Snow sports. Best Western Ruby's
Inn, Highway 63, Bryce Canyon; tel:
435-834-5341

March
Moab Skinny Tire Festival
Races, group rides and other
activities for road cyclists. tel: 435-
259-2698
**"Echoing Traditional Ways" Annual
Powwow at USU, Cedar City**
An event celebrating Utah's tribal
history at Utah State University Field
House, Logan, tel: 435-797-2891
**Annual Canyon Country Western
Arts Festival, Cedar City**
Arts and crafts at the Sharwan Smith
Center, 351 W. Center St, Cedar City;
tel: 435-586-5124
**Steve Young Celebrity Ski Classic
Challenge, Snowbird**
Celebrities compete for ski prizes at
Snowbird and Little Cottonwood
Canyon; tel: 801-933-2110

April
Annual Easter Jeep Safari, Moab
Moab's big four-wheel-drive jamboree
at various locations around Moab;
tel: 435-259-7625
**Tour of Canyonlands Annual
Mountain Bike Race, Moab**
Fat-tire fans compete for prizes in the
Moab area; tel: 303-432-1519
St George Arts Festival
Downtown St George comes alive
for this annual arts and crafts
extravaganza; tel: 800-88869-6635

May
Bear River Bird Festival (May–June)
Birders flock to Bear River Bird
Refuge to view a dazzling array of
bird life; tel: 435-723-5887
Great Salt Lake Bird Festival
A celebration of birds and bird-
watching at Antelope Island State
Park; tel: 801-451-3286
**Joining of the Rails–Golden Spike
Anniversary Celebration**
An event commemorating the
completion of the country's first
transcontinental railroad at Golden
Spike National Historic Site; tel: 435-
471-2209
**Old Ephraim's Mountain Man
Rendezvous, Ephraim**
Mountain men encampment and
traditional arts and crafts, Ephraim;
tel: 435-245-3778
Scandinavian Festival
A celebration of the Scandinavian
communities in the Sanpete Valley;
tel: 435-281-4346
**Living Traditions Folk and Ethnic
Arts Festival, Salt Lake City**
Salt Lake City's biggest cultural

celebration of the year features Mexican folkloric dancing, Scandinavian arts and storytelling, American Indian dancing, Greek food and more. At Washington Square; tel: 801-596-5000

Mother's Day 10K Run, Kanab
Running moms compete for prizes; tel: 435-644-2562

June
Utah Shakespearean Festival, Cedar City (through Sept)
Plays are performed at a replica of the Globe Theater at Southern Utah University throughout the summer; tel: 800-PLAYTIX

Paiute Restoration Gathering, Cedar City
The Southern Paiute tribe celebrates its reinstatement with a parade and other events.

Mormon Miracle Pageant, Manti
The annual reenactment of events from the Book of Mormon and other texts takes place at the Manti Temple over several nights.

Pony Express Days, Clarkston
Events commemorate the days of the Pony Express mail carriers through the Great Basin. In Clarkston; tel: 435-563-9090

Walleye Classic Tournament, Duchesne
Fishing tournament at Starvation State Park in Duchesne; tel: 800-477-5558

Outlaw Trail Ride, Vernal
A horseback ride along part of the Outlaw Trail from southern Utah to Brown's Park; tel: 800-477-5558

Utah Arts Festival, Salt Lake City
Downtown Salt Lake City, tel: 801-322-2488

Downtown Farmers Market, Salt Lake City (June–Oct)
Organic farmers sell in Historic Pioneer Park at 300 South 300 West, Salt Lake City; tel: 801-359-5118

July
Black Hawk Mountain Man Rendezvous, Mount Pleasant
A mountain man celebration at the Park and Rodeo Grounds, Heritage Hwy 89, Mount Pleasant; tel: 435-462-0152

Days of '47 Rodeo, Salt Lake City
Rodeo events commemorating Pioneer Day at Delta Center Arena, Salt Lake City; tel: 801-964-5325

Days of '47 Parade, Salt Lake City
Floats commemorate Pioneer Day in downtown Salt Lake City; tel: 801-254-4656

Annual Northern Ute 4th of July Powwow, Duchesne
Fancy dancing and other contests at the big gathering of the year at the Uintah and Ouray Ute Indian

Reservation powwow grounds on US 40; tel: 435-722-8541

Mondays in the Park Concert Series, Salt Lake City
Free concerts at the Chase Home Museum at Liberty Park, 1150 South 600 East; tel: 801-533-5760

International Film Festival, Bicknell
One of the world's smallest international film fests shows B movie classics at the Wayne Theatre in Bicknell, near Capitol Reef National Park; tel: 435-425-3554

Festival of the American West, Wellsville
A celebration of western living at the American West Heritage Center; tel: 800-255-3378

August
Park City Jazz Festival
Deer Valley and The Canyons Resorts; tel: 435-655-2621
Top jazz artists perform at this popular festival.

Moab Music Festival
Concerts in downtown Moab and along the Colorado River; tel: 435-259-7003

Bear Lake Raspberry Days, Garden City
Fruit harvest festival; tel: 800-448-2327

Labor Day Boat Parade and Fireworks Extravaganza and Dagget Daze, Manila and Lucerne Valley
Dagget County celebration at Flaming Gorge National Recreation Area; tel: 435-784-3483

Western Legends Roundup, Kanab
Kanab's biggest event of the year includes a cowboy poetry "rodeo" (poetry slam for cowboys), western arts, music, street vendors, a wild horse parade, a wagon-building display, mountain men, Indian dancing, daily stage shows, a fiddle contest and more; tel: 800-733-5263; www.westernlegendsroundup.com

September
Greek Festival, Salt Lake City
Food, dancing and other cultural activities at the Greek Orthodox Church; tel: 801-581-7989

World of Speed, Bonneville Salt Flats
Speedway exit, Wendover, Nevada; tel: 801-467-8628

Top of Utah Marathon, Hyrum
A cool run through Blacksmith Fork Canyon to Merlin Olsen Park; tel: 801-797-2636

Green River Watermelon Days
Celebrate the annual harvest of watermelons at Green River City Park; tel: 435-564-8225

Utah State Fair, Salt Lake City
Livestock, concerts, rides and other special events at the Utah State Fair

park, 155 North 1000 West; tel: 801-538-8400

October
St George Marathon
The popular desert run brings out a large crowd; tel: 435-634-5850

Bison Roundup
Antelope State Park; tel: 801-773-2941

Moab Fat Tire Festival
Mountain bikers converge on Moab; tel: 435-259-1182

November
Folk Music Festival, Moab
Moab, tel: 435-260-2488
A multiday celebration of folk music traditions with some of the best acts in the West.

Moab Bighorn Sheep Festival
Learn more about the reintroduction of this endangered animal in Canyon Country through talks at Moab Information Center. Main and Center Street; tel: 435-636-0266

Lighting of Temple Square, Salt Lake City
Temple Square is illuminated with thousands of Christmas lights for the holidays; tel: 801-240-1000

Northern Ute Thanksgiving Powwow, Fort Duchesne
The second powwow contest of the year at the powwow grounds on US 40; tel: 435-722-8541

WinterFest Christmas Parade, Provo
North on University Avenue to 100 South, Provo; tel: 801-852-6600

Heber Valley Historic Railroad Polar Express
SmithsTix, tel: 800-888-8499
Special train rides for the holidays.

December
Electric Light Parade, Helper
The old mining town comes alight; tel: 435-472-5391

Frontier Christmas Eve, Wellsville
Celebrating Christmas past in pioneer Utah; tel: 800-225-3378

Golden Spike Film Festival, Promontory
A film series dedicated to railroad movies; tel: 435-471-2209

First Night Celebrations, Salt Lake City, Ogden, Provo (Dec 31)
New Year's Eve celebrations; tel: 801-359-5118, 801-627-8288, and 801-852-6600

A – Z

A HANDY SUMMARY OF PRACTICAL INFORMATION, ARRANGED ALPHABETICALLY

Auto Club

If you intend to do a lot of driving, consider joining the American Automobile Association (AAA). Fees are reasonable and benefits many: emergency road service, maps, insurance, traveler's checks, bail bond protection and other services. AAA has reciprocity agreements with many foreign automobile clubs. AAA, 4100 E. Arkansas Drive, Denver CO 80222, tel: 800-222-4357; www.aaa.com

Business Hours

Standard hours for business offices are Monday–Friday 9am–5pm. Many banks open a little earlier, usually 8.30am. A few open on Saturday morning. Post offices are usually open Monday–Friday 8am–5pm and Saturday 8am–noon. Most stores and shopping centers are open weekends and evenings.

Climate

Utah spans a wide range of climate and life zones but is mostly a desert state with sunny skies, low humidity and limited precipitation. Climate varies widely with elevation. Climbing 1,000 feet (300 meters) is equivalent to traveling 300 miles (500 km) northwards. Conditions atop the highest peaks are akin to those in the Arctic.

Between the mountain ranges, Utah's climate is semiarid. Yearly precipitation ranges from 5–10 inches (13–26 cm) in the Great Basin and along the Colorado River, and an average 8–14 inches (20–37 cm) at elevations of 5,000–7,000 ft (1,500–2,100 meters). In the Wasatch and other mountain ranges rainfall totals climb to more than 50 inches (130 cm). These big variations allow for a wide choice of recreational activities in Utah, from pleasant desert hiking and river running during the winter months in the south to snowboarding and skiing in the north. Most rain falls in brief, intense thunderstorms during the summer season, when small streams, dry washes and narrow canyons are prone to flash floods. Violent electrical storms are common on desert peaks during summer afternoons. Nights in the mountains can be chilly even in July and August, and winds are often brisk, so bring a sweater or jacket. Snow, hale and sleet are possible at the highest elevations at any time of year.

The spring thaw usually begins in March, though snow lingers well into July on the highest peaks and mountain passes. Summer weather begins in late June or early July. Autumn begins in September, a lovely period of sunny days, chilly nights and spectacular colors on the forested slopes of the Wasatch Front, High Uintas and Colorado Plateau. Winter sets in by late November, though ski areas in northern Utah sometimes open as early as late October (with the aid of snow-making machines) and close in June.

Low elevations throughout this desert state sizzle under extremely hot temperatures in summer, hitting the 90s and 100s (32°–38°C) regularly and barely dropping to the 60s and 70s (15–21°C) at night. Many residents escape the heat by spending time at second homes in the mountains, where summer daytime temperatures are usually pleasant, dropping by roughly 5°F (3°C) for every 1,000 ft (330 meters) climbed, and hovering in the 40s and 50s (4°–10°C) at night.

With no moderating influences, desert winters are also very cold and

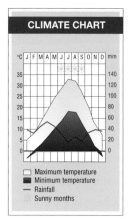

CLIMATE CHART

☐ Maximum temperature
■ Minimum temperature
— Rainfall
  Sunny months

often sunny, although the Salt Lake Valley often suffers from a winter inversion layer that brings smog to the Wasatch Front. Only the extreme southern part of the state, around St. George, has daytime temperatures averaging above freezing in winter; the Colorado Plateau and mountains frequently post sub-zero temperatures during the winter months and plummet even farther at night. Snowfall at lower elevations is sporadic and often dust redrocks briefly before melting during warm spells between storms. Annual snowfall in excess of 500 inches (1,270 cm) is common in the ski areas of the Wasatch Mountains, creating what Utah used to call "the greatest snow on earth." Winter storms roll into Utah from the Pacific, lose moisture over Great Salt Lake, and then dump piles of the light, dry powder for which the Wasatch Mountains are famous.

Clothing

With few exceptions, western dress is informal. A pair of jeans or slacks, a polo or button-down shirt, and boots or shoes are appropriate at all but the fanciest places and events. Shorts and light shirts are suitable for most situations in the warmer months, though it's always a good idea to have a sweater or jacket for evenings, high elevations or overly air-conditioned shops and restaurants.

Many destinations in Utah require some walking, often on rough ground, so be sure to bring good walking shoes or sandals as well as a sturdy pair of hiking shoes or boots for rugged trails. A thin, inner polypropylene sock and a thick, outer wool sock will help keep your feet dry and comfortable. If blisters or sore spots develop, quickly cover them

with moleskin or surgical tape, available at most pharmacies or camping supply stores. Good river sandals are important for river trips.

A high-factor sunblock, wide-brimmed hat and polarized sunglasses are advisable too, even if the day starts out cloudy. The sun is merciless in desert areas and at high elevations.

Customs & Entry

All people entering the country must go through U.S. Customs, often a time-consuming process. To speed things up, be prepared to open your luggage for inspection and keep the following restrictions in mind.
● You must declare cash in excess of $10,000.
● Anything for personal use may be brought in duty- and tax-free.
● Adults are allowed to bring in one liter of alcohol for personal use.
● You can bring in gifts worth less than $400 duty- and tax-free. Anything over the $400 limit is subject to duty charges and taxes.
● Agricultural products, meat and animals are subject to complex restrictions, especially if entering California. Leave these items at home if at all possible.

For more details contact a U.S. consulate or U.S. Customs, www.customs.gov/travel/travel.htm.

Passports & Visas

A passport, visa and evidence of intent to leave the U.S. after your visit are required for entry into the U.S. by most foreign nationals. Visitors from the United Kingdom and several other countries staying less than 90 days may not need a visa if entering as tourists. All other nationals must obtain a visa from a U.S. consulate or embassy. An international vaccination certificate may be required depending on your country of origin.

Canadians entering from the Western Hemisphere, Mexicans with border passes and British residents of Bermuda and Canada do not normally need a visa or passport, but it's best to confirm visa requirements before leaving home.

Once in the U.S. foreigners may visit Canada or Mexico for up to 30 days and re-enter the U.S. without a new visa. For additional information, contact a U.S. consulate or embassy or the U.S. State Department, tel: 202-663-1225.

Extensions of Stay

Tourist visas are usually granted for six months. If you wish to remain in

the country longer than six months, you must apply for an extension of stay at the Bureau of Citizenship and Immigration Services, Washington District Office, 4420 N. Fairfax Drive, Arlington, VA 22203; tel: 800-375-5283; www.bcis.gov

Electricity

Standard electricity in North America is 110–115 volts, 60 cycles A.C. An adapter is necessary for most appliances from overseas, with the exception of Japan.

Embassies

Australia: 1601 Massachusetts Ave NW, Washington, DC 20036, tel: 202-797-3000.
Canada: 501 Pennsylvania Ave NW, Washington, DC 20001, tel: 202-682-1740.
Great Britain: 3100 -Massachusetts Ave NW, Washington, DC 20008, tel: 202-462-1340.
India: 2536 Massachusetts Ave NW, Washington, DC 20008, tel: 202-939-7000.
Israel: 3514 International Drive NW, Washington, DC 20008, tel: 202-364-5500.
Mexico: 1911 Pennsylvania Ave NW, Washington, DC 20006, tel: 202-728-1600.
New Zealand: 37 Observatory Circle NW, Washington, DC 20008, tel: 202-328-4800.
Singapore: 3501 International Place NW, Washington, DC 20008, tel: 202-537-3100.
South Korea: 2600 Virginia Ave NW, Washington, DC 20037, tel: 202-939-5600.
Taiwan: 4201 Wisconsin Ave NW, Washington, DC 20016, tel: 202-895-1800.

Environmental Ethics

Remember the old saying: "Take nothing but pictures, leave nothing but footprints." The goal of low-impact/no-impact backpacking is to leave the area in the same condition as you found it, if not better. If you're camping in the backcountry, don't break branches, level the ground or alter the landscape in any way. Make fires in designated places only. Otherwise, use a portable camping stove. When nature calls, answer with a trowel: dig a hole 6 inches (15cm) deep and at least 200 ft (60m) from water, campsites and trails. Take away all trash, including toilet paper.

F ilm

All consumer formats of photographic films are available in most grocery stores, pharmacies and convenience stores. If you need professional-quality photographic equipment or film (especially transparency or black-and-white films), consult the local telephone directory for the nearest camera shop. If you don't have a camera, consider the relatively inexpensive disposable cameras available at many supermarkets, pharmacies and convenience stores. Disposable digital cameras are available, too.

H ealth

Insurance

It's vital to have medical insurance when traveling. Though hospitals are obligated to provide emergency treatment to anyone who needs it whether or not they have insurance, you may have to prove you can pay for treatment of anything less than a life-threatening condition. Know what your policy covers and have proof of the policy with you at all times or be prepared to pay at the time service is rendered.

Precautions

Flash floods: Sudden downpours – even those falling miles away from your location – can fill canyons and dry riverbeds with a roaring torrent of water and mud that will sweep away everything in its path. Travelers should be especially careful during the summer "monsoon" season. Avoid hiking or driving in arroyos or narrow canyons, and never try to wade or drive across a flooded

stream. If rain begins to fall or you see rain clouds in the distance, move to higher ground. It's impossible to outrun or even outdrive a flash flood. Take action before the water level begins to rise.

Sunburn: Even a short time in the desert or mountains can result in sunburn, so protect yourself with a high-SPF sunscreen and polarized sunglasses. The elderly and the ill, small children and people with fair skin should be especially careful. Excessive pain, redness, blistering or numbness mean you should seek professional medical attention. Minor sunburn can be soothed by taking a cool bath and using aloe vera gel.

Overheating: Heat exhaustion and heat stroke are very real possibilities when hiking in southern Utah's desert country in summer. Every year, several mountain bikers and hikers traveling on slickrock around Moab die of heat stroke within a few miles of town. Overheating often comes on insidiously. The body normally deals with excess heat by sending more blood closer to the skin's surface, causing reddening and sweating to bring body temperature down. That mechanism frequently gets overwhelmed when temperatures are high and conditions arid, so that sweat evaporates rapidly without your even realizing you're getting overheated. Eventually, the body loses its ability to control temperature. Initially, skin may become pale and clammy, then, as full-blown heat stroke begins, it gets red and dry and sweating stops. In

summer, keep skin cool and moist by keeping exposed skin covered in damp breathable cotton clothing. Wear a wet bandanna around the neck, mist your face and other exposed areas with a portable spray bottle, and, if you feel dizzy, unwell or shaky, immediately pour copious amounts of water over your head, or find a cool (but not cold) water source for full immersion, to prevent full-blown heat stroke. Be very conservative about outdoor recreation in hot summer conditions. Better to be safe than sorry.

Dehydration: Drink plenty of water (not sodas) and, if outdoors, carry liter bottles of water and something to eat. The rule of thumb in arid conditions is a gallon (4 liters) of water per person per day. Don't wait to get thirsty – start drinking as soon as you set out. Limit alcohol and caffeine at high elevation; they are very dehydrating.

Drinking water: All water from natural sources must be purified before drinking. Giardia is found throughout the West, even in crystal-clear water, and it can cause severe cramps and diarrhea. The most popular purification methods are tablets or filters (both available from camping supply stores) or by boiling water for at least 3 minutes. Some Neoprene water bottles now have built-in filters.

Cactus: To avoid being pricked, stay on trails and wear long pants and sturdy boots.

Hypothermia: This occurs when the core body temperature falls below 95°F (35°C). At altitude, combinations of alcohol, cold and thin air can produce hypothermia. Watch for drowsiness, disorientation and sometimes increased urination. If possible get to a hospital, otherwise blankets and extra clothing should be piled on for warmth. Don't use hot water or electric heaters and don't rub the skin. The elderly should be especially careful in extremely cold weather.

Frostbite: Symptoms of frostbite, which occurs when living tissue freezes, include numbness, pain, blistering and whitening of the skin. The most immediate remedy is to put frostbitten skin against warm skin. Simply holding your hands for several minutes over another person's frostbitten cheeks or nose may suffice. Otherwise, immerse frostbitten skin in warm (not hot!)

BELOW: skiers dress warmly for a day on the slopes.

water. Refreezing will cause even more damage, so get the victim into a warm environment as quickly as possible. Check other members of your party. If one person is hypothermic or frostbitten, others may be, too.

Altitude sickness: Even fit people traveling from sea level to Utah may feel uncharacteristically winded at elevations as low as 6,000 or 7,000 ft (1,800–2,100 meters). The sensation usually passes after a few days. Symptoms, including nausea, headache, vomiting, extreme fatigue, light-headedness and shortness of breath, intensify over 10,000 ft (3,000 meters). Although the symptoms may be mild at first, they can develop into a serious illness. Move to a lower elevation and try to acclimatize gradually.

Lightning: In Utah, lightning is the number one life-threatening weather hazard. Stay alert for fast-changing weather conditions. It doesn't have to be raining where you are for lightning to be a threat. Avoid being the tallest object in the area, and stay away from other tall objects such as a small group of trees. If hiking in the mountains, go early in the day, before thunderstorms develop. Above treeline, there are few places to take cover. If you are in the mountains when a storm is moving in, descend from high points. If you can't get away from an exposed area, make yourself as small as possible, crouching down or perching on a small rock with insulation such as a poncho or foam pad under you, your feet touching rock and your hands clasped around your knees. Never seek shelter under a lone tree, in a shallow cave, or under a rock overhang. Your car is the safest place to be if you are away from a building.

Wilderness Activities: Every year people underestimate remote desert backcountry areas in southern Utah, such as Grand Staircase-Escalante National Monument, where adventurous hikers regularly get lost in enchanting but mazelike slot canyons and jeopardize not only their own lives but those of search-and-rescue teams looking for them. Never enter wild areas without adequate planning and letting someone know your plans (if it's a last-minute trip, at least leave a note of your expected itinerary and travel time in your car). Know how to use a topographical map and compass, and don't rely on GPS satellite devices or cell phones;

ABOVE: one person's risk…

they rarely work in remote canyon country or the mountains. Protect yourself from the elements, depending on the season, and carry a backpack containing any necessary medicines and the so-called Ten Essentials: a gallon of water per person per day, adequate high-energy foods, matches or other fire starter, flashlight, mirror, topo map, compass, whistle, warm clothing and first-aid kit. Realistically assess your physical and emotional resilience before setting out, avoid traveling alone, and, it's worth reiterating: always let someone know where you are planning to go and when you plan to return. It may save your life.

Insects & Animals

Snakes: Sidewinder, Great Basin and other western rattlesnakes are the only venomous snake species in Utah and are usually seen in Upper Sonoran desert regions of the state, if at all. There are six basic ways to distinguish this venomous snake from its non-venomous relatives: 1) rattles at the end of the tail; 2) fangs in addition to their rows of teeth; 3) facial pits between the nostrils and eyes; 4) vertical and elliptical pupils that may look like thin lines in bright light (non-venomous snakes have round pupils); and 5) a broad triangular head and narrow neck. Only about 3 percent of people bitten by a rattlesnake die, and these are mainly small children. Walk in the open when possible, proceed with caution among rocks, sweep grassy areas with a long stick before entering, avoid dark or overgrown places where snakes might lurk, shake out bedding or clothing that has been lying on the ground, and

wear sturdy hiking boots. Snakes often lie on roads at night because of the residual heat radiating from the pavement, so use a flashlight if walking on a paved road after dark. Keep your hands and feet where you can see them, and don't let children poke under rocks or logs.

Snakebite kits are good psychological protection, but there is some question over how effective they really are. The most useful snakebite kit consists of car keys and coins for calling a hospital. If bitten, remain calm so as not to increase circulation and spread the venom faster, remove rings, watches, bracelets and other articles that may constrict swelling below the bite area, if possible, wash the wound with soap and water, immobilize the bite area and keep it below the heart, and get to a hospital immediately. Do not wait for the pain to become severe. The use of an approved anti-venom is the most effective treatment. Do not use a tourniquet, make an incision at the bite site, suck out the venom with your mouth, or pack the limb in ice.

Lizards: There are numerous lizard species in Utah but the only poisonous species is the Gila monster, a beautiful creature with a black-beaded skin patterned with black and yellow markings that is found only in the southwestern corner of the state. Gila monsters are slow moving and typically don't strike. When they do, they inject venom by gripping prey in powerful jaws and excreting a potentially lethal dose through a gland in the lower jaw.

Insects: Bees are abundant, which should concern only those allergic to the sting. Those with severe allergies should carry epinephrine in the form of an EpiPen or other form of emergency treatment, especially if hiking in remote areas. The bite of a black widow spider or tarantula and the sting of a scorpion's tail can pack a punch but are rarely a serious health threat to adults. The pale desert scorpion is nocturnal, so use flashlights if you walk barefoot at night. It often hides in recesses, dark corners and old wood piles and likes to crawl into protected places, so shake out clothes or sleeping bags that have been on the ground and check your shoes before slipping them on in the morning. Most annoying are mosquitoes, huge deer flies and clouds of cedar gnats, or no-see-ums, which begin hatching in May and June on the Colorado

Plateau and in river canyons, making life miserable for hikers, campers and river runners. If you can plan a trip in March or April, before these insects emerge, or fall, when they are gone for the year, you'll be much more comfortable. Insect repellents seem to have little effect, nor do most folk remedies, such as the herb pennyroyal or Avon's Skin-So-Soft. Your best bet is to carry and wear specially designed mesh headgear fine enough to keep out no-see-ums and be sure to keep tents tightly zipped.

Hitchhiking

Hitchhiking is illegal in many places and ill-advised everywhere. It's an inefficient and dangerous method of travel. Don't do it!

Insurance

Most visitors to the U.S. will have no health problems during their stay. Even so, you should never leave home without travel insurance to cover both yourself and your belongings. Your own insurance company or travel agent can advise you on policies, but shop around since rates vary. Consider coverage for accidental death, emergency medical care, trip cancellation and baggage or document loss.

Liquor Laws

It's not as difficult to get an alcoholic drink in Utah as you may have been led to believe. Two- week "visitor" memberships are available at private clubs, usually associated with hotels and bars, for a nominal $5 fee and are good for up to five people. Travelers can also find packaged liquors, beer and wine available for purchase at State Liquor Stores, located throughout Utah. Taverns, grocery stores and convenience stores sell "3.2 beer," which signifies the percentage of alcohol by weight. A more detailed explanation of Utah liquor regulations may be found at www.utah.com/visitor/state_facts/liquor_laws. htm.

Maps

Accurate maps are indispensable in Utah, especially when one is leaving paved roads. Road maps can be found at bookstores, convenience stores and gas stations. Free maps may be available by mail from state or regional tourism bureaus. Free city, state and regional maps as well

as up-to-date road conditions and other valuable services are also available to members of the Automobile Association of America (AAA). If you are driving any distance, the service is well worth the membership fee. AAA has reciprocity agreements with auto clubs in many countries. If you are an auto club member in your home country, you may be eligible for AAA benefits in the United States. Ask about AAA discounts at hotels.

Maps of national parks, forests and other public lands are usually offered by the managing governmental agency. Good topographical maps of national parks and forests are available from Trails Illustrated, PO Box 3610, Evergreen, CO 80439, tel: 303-670-3457 or toll-free 800-962-1643; these maps are often in bookstores. Extremely detailed topographical maps of the state are available from the U.S. Geological Survey (www.usgs.gov/sales.html). Topo maps are usually available in higher-end bookstores and shops that sell outdoor gear, such as REI in Salt Lake City and outfitters in southern Utah.

Media

Newspapers

Every city and most large towns have a local newspaper. For national and international news, along with local and regional events, check the papers listed below. Also available are *The New York Times, Los Angeles Times, Washington Post, USA Today* and *Wall Street Journal*. Overseas newspapers are not available except in a few large hotels and specialty bookstores.

Canyon Country Zephyr
P.O. Box 327, Moab, UT 84532; tel: 435-259-7773;
www.canyoncountryzephyr.com
Iconoclastic free bimonthly newspaper highlighting southern Utah and southern Colorado issues and proudly "clinging hopelessly to the past since 1989."

Catalyst
tel: 801-363-1505
A good all-round free monthly focusing on community, arts, health and the environment.
City Weekly
248 S. Main, Salt Lake City, UT 84101; tel: 801-575-7003
Salt Lake City's free alternative weekly covers the city's arts and entertainment.
Deseret News

tel: 801-237-2100;
www.deseretnews.com
The conservative, LDS-affiliated daily comes out in the afternoon.
Emery County Progress
410 East Main, Castle Dale, UT 84513; tel: 435-381-2431;
www.ecprogress.com
The Event
tel: 801-487-4556;
www.eventnewsweekly.com
A free newsweekly that covers arts, news and entertainment in the state.
Moab Times-Independent
35 East Center St, Moab, UT 84532; tel: 435-259-7525; www.moabtimes.com
Weekly hometown newspaper
Salt Lake Tribune
tel: 801-257-8742; www.sltrib.com
Salt Lake City's liberal-leaning morning daily newspaper.
Southern Utah News
26 N. Main St, Kanab, UT 84741; tel: 888-468-2900; www.sunews.net
The Spectrum
275 E St. George Blvd, St. George, UT 84770; tel: 435-674-6200;
www.thespectrum.com
Southwest Utah's daily newspaper.
Uintah Basin Standard
268 South 200 East, Roosevelt, UT 84066; tel: 435-722-5131;
www.ubstandard.com
The Web
Utah Society for Environmental Education, Salt Lake City, UT; tel: 801-328-4578; www.usee.org
A quarterly free newspaper educating people about the environment.
Wild Utah
Transcending Mundane, Inc., Park City, UT; tel: 435-615-9609;
www.wildutah.com
A lively free biweekly newspaper that takes a uniquely alternative look at life in Utah.

The following magazines feature profiles of interesting destinations and local people as well as restaurant listings and a calendar of events.

Salt Lake City Magazine
240 E. Morris Ave, Ste. 350, Salt Lake City, UT 84115; tel: 801-485-5100; www.saltlakemagazine.com
Published monthly.
St. George Magazine
275 E. St. George Blvd, St. George, UT 84770; tel: 435-674-6279
Everything you wanted to know about Utah's Dixie.
The Canyons Resort and Park City Magazines
Park City Publishing, Box 738, Park City, UT 84060; tel: 435-649-5806
Published annually and semiannually, respectively, and aimed at the ski resort communities.

Utah Business

tel: 801-568-0114;
www.utahbusiness.com
Focuses on what's happening in the Salt Lake City business community.

Money Matters

Currency

The basic unit of American currency, the dollar ($1), is equal to 100 cents. There are four coins, each worth less than a dollar: a penny or 1 cent (1¢), a nickel or 5 cents (5¢), a dime or 10 cents (10¢) and a quarter or 25 cents (25¢).

There are several denominations of paper money: $1, $5, $10, $20, $50 and $100. Each bill is the same color, size and shape; be sure to check the dollar amount on the face of the bill.

It is advisable to arrive with at least $100 in cash (in small bills) to pay for ground transportation and other incidentals.

Automatic Teller Machines (ATMs)

ATMs are the most convenient way to access cash and are widely available throughout the state. They are usually found at banks, shopping malls, supermarkets, service stations, convenience stores and hotels. ATM, or debit, cards may also be used at most grocery stores and gas stations, much as credit cards are.

Traveler's Checks

Foreign visitors are advised to take U.S. dollar traveler's checks since exchanging foreign currency – whether as cash or checks – can be problematic. A growing number of banks offer exchange facilities, but this practice is not universal.

Most shops, restaurants and other establishments accept traveler's checks in U.S. dollars and will give change in cash. Alternatively, checks can be converted into cash at a bank. With the advent of ATMs, traveler's checks are becoming less and less common.

Credit Cards

These are very much part of daily life in the U.S. They can be used to pay for pretty much anything, and it is common for car rental agencies and hotels to take an imprint of your card as a deposit. Rental companies may oblige you to pay a large deposit in cash if you do not have a card.

You can also use your credit card to withdraw cash from ATMs. Before you leave home, make sure you know your PIN (personal identification

number) and find out which ATM system will accept your card. The most widely accepted cards are Visa, MasterCard, American Express, Diners Club and Discovery.

Electronic Transfer

Money may be sent or received by wire at any Western Union office (tel: 800-325-6000) or American Express Money Gram office (tel: 800-543-4080).

N ational Park Passes

If you plan to visit several parks on your vacation, consider buying a 12-month National Park Pass. The pass costs $50 and covers entrance fees to all National Park Service areas but does not cover camping fees or other use fees, such as cave tours.

The Golden Age Passport is available to U.S. citizens who are age 62 or older. There is a one-time charge of $10, but the pass is good for life. It provides free entrance to

Public Holidays

On public holidays, post offices, banks, most government offices and a large number of shops and restaurants are closed. Public transport usually runs less frequently.
New Year's Day: January 1
Martin Luther King, Jr.'s Birthday: The third Monday in January
Presidents' Day: The third Monday in February
Good Friday: March/April – date varies
Easter Sunday: March/April – date varies
Memorial Day: Last Monday in May
Independence Day: July 4
Labor Day: First Monday in September
Columbus Day: Second Monday in October
Election Day: The Tuesday in the first full week of November during presidential-election years
Veterans Day: November 11
Thanksgiving Day: Fourth Thursday in November
Christmas Day: December 25

Utah celebrates Pioneer Day on July 24 to commemorate the arrival of Brigham Young and the first Mormon pioneers in the Salt Lake Valley. Many shops will be closed. Parades and other festivities are held in Salt Lake City and in towns and cities throughout the state.

most federal recreation areas and provides a 50% discount on use fees, such as camping fees.

The Golden Access Passport is available to U.S. citizens who have a permanent disability. The pass is free and is good for life. It provides free entrance to most federal recreation areas and provides a 50% discount on use fees.

Passes are available at parks that charge an entrance fee.

P ostal Services

Even the most remote towns are served by the U.S. Postal Service. Smaller post offices tend to be limited to business hours (Monday–Friday 9am–5pm), although central, big-city branches may have extended weekday and weekend hours.

Stamps are sold at all post offices. They are also sold at some convenience stores, filling stations, hotels and transportation terminals, usually from vending machines.

For reasonably quick delivery within the U.S. at a modest price, ask for priority mail, which usually gets there within two or three days.

For overnight deliveries, try U.S. Express Mail or one of several domestic and international courier services:
Fedex, tel: 800-238-5355
DHL, tel: 800-345-2727
United Parcel Service, tel: 800-742-5877

Poste Restante

Visitors can receive mail at post offices if it is addressed to them, care of "General Delivery," followed by the city name and (very important) the zip code. You must pick up this mail in person within a week or two of its arrival and will be asked to show a valid driver's license, passport or some other form of picture identification.

S ecurity & Crime

A few common-sense precautions will help keep you safe while traveling in Utah. For starters, know where you are and where you're going. Whether traveling on foot or by car, bring a map and plan your route in advance. Don't be shy about asking for directions. Most people are happy to help.

Don't carry large sums of cash or wear flashy or expensive jewelry. Lock unattended cars and keep your belongings in the trunk. If possible, travel with a companion, especially after dark.

If involved in a traffic accident, remain at the scene. It is illegal to leave the scene of an accident. Find a nearby telephone or ask a passing motorist to call the police, then wait for emergency vehicles to arrive.

Carry a cell phone. Few items are more useful if you're lost, in an accident, need to report an emergency, or your car has broken down.

Driving under the influence of alcohol carries stiff penalties, including fines and jail. Wearing seat belts is required. Children under four must be in a child's safety seat.

Dial 911 for police, medical or fire emergencies.

Telecommunications

Public telephones are located at many highway rest areas, service stations, convenience stores, bars, motels and restaurants, although, with the advent of cell phones, they are less common than they once were.

To call from one area to another, dial 1 before the three-digit area code, then the local seven-digit number. If you want to pay for the call with coins, a recorded voice will tell you how many to insert. Unless you have a calling card, your only other option is to call your party "collect" (reversing the charges) by dialing 0 before the number. Rates vary for long-distance calls, though you can often take advantage of lower long-distance rates on weekends and after 5pm on weekdays.

Prepaid calling cards are sold at convenience stores and some filling stations. Essentially, customers pay in advance for a specific number of minutes of calling time. Not all cards work for international calls. Be sure to inquire before purchasing.

Many businesses have toll-free (no charge) telephone numbers; these are always prefaced with 800, 888 or 887 rather than an area code. Note that if you dial a toll-free number from abroad, you will be charged the normal international rate for the call.

The quickest way to get information is to dial 0 for the operator. Directory Assistance calls from pay telephones are free. However, to be connected to some of them you must first insert a coin, but as soon as you are connected with the operator it will be returned to you. To get the information operator dial 411, but to get an information operator in another city, dial 1-(area code of the city)-555-1212.

Dialing Abroad

To dial abroad (Canada follows the U.S. system), first dial the international access code 011, then the country code. If using a U.S. phone credit card, dial the company's access number below, then 01, then the country code.
Sprint, tel: 10333
AT&T, tel: 10288.
Some country codes:

Australia	61
Hong Kong	852
Israel	972
New Zealand	64
Singapore	65
South Africa	27
Switzerland	41
United Kingdom	44

Western Union (tel: 800-325-6000) can arrange money transfers and telegrams. Check the Web (www.westernunion.com) or phone directory or call information for local offices.

Fax machines are available at most hotels and motels. Printers, copy shops, stationers and office-supply shops may also have them, as well as some convenience stores.

Dataports for laptop computers and Palm Pilots are available at most business hotels. E-mail and Internet access is also available at public libraries, Internet cafes and copy shops like Kinkos.

Time Zones

The continental U.S. is divided into four time zones. From east to west, later to earlier, they are eastern, central, mountain and Pacific, each separated by one hour. Utah is on mountain standard time, seven hours behind Greenwich mean time. On the first Sunday in April, Utahns set the clock ahead one hour in observation of daylight savings time. On the last Sunday in October, the clock is moved back one hour to return to standard time. Neighboring states are also in the mountain time zone except Nevada, which, like California, is in the Pacific time zone. Note: Arizona does not observe daylight savings time and, during the summer, is in the same time zone as California. Glen Canyon National Recreation Area, which spans the Utah-Arizona line but is headquartered in Page, Arizona, is one hour behind Utah in summer.

Tipping

Service workers in restaurants and hotels depend on tips for a significant portion of their income. With few exceptions, tipping is left to your discretion and gratuities are not automatically added to the bill. In most cases, 15–20 percent is typical for tipping waiters, taxi drivers, bartenders, barbers and hairdressers. Porters and bellmen usually get $1–$2 per bag.

Tourist Information

Statewide

Utah Travel Council
300 North State St, Salt Lake City, UT 84114; tel: 800-200-1160; www.utah.com
Utah Hotel and Lodging Association
150 West 500 South, Salt Lake City, UT 84101; tel: 866-SEE-UTAH

Northern Utah

Bear Lake Convention and Visitors Bureau
P.O. Box 55, Garden City, UT 84028; tel: 800-448-2327; www.bearlake.org
Box Elder County Tourism and Community Development
1 South Main St, Brigham City, UT 84302; tel: 435-734-3315; www.boxelder.org
Cache Valley/Bear Lake Tourist Council
160 North Main St, Logan, UT 84321; tel: 800-882-4433; www.tourcachevalley.com
Tourism Davis County
28 East State St, Farmington, UT 84025; tel: 801-451-3286; www.co.davis.ut.us/discoverdavis
Dinosaurland Travel Region
25 East Main St, Vernal, UT 84078; tel: 800-477-5558; www.dinoland.com
Duchesne County Area Chamber of Commerce
50 East 200 South, Roosevelt, UT 84066; tel: 435-722-4598; www.duchesne.net
Heber Valley Chamber of Commerce
4754 North Main St, Heber City, UT 84032; tel: 435-654-3666; www.hebervalleycc.org
Mountainland Travel Region
586 800 North, Orem, UT 84097; tel: 801-229-3800; www.mountainland.org
Ogden/Weber Convention Visitors Bureau
2501 Wall Ave, Ste. 201, Ogden, UT 84401; tel: 801-627-8288; www.ogdencvb.org
Park City Chamber/Bureau
1910 Prospector Ave, Park City, UT 84060-1630; tel: 800-453-1360; www.parkcityinfo.com
Salt Lake Convention and Visitors Bureau
90 South West Temple, Salt Lake City, UT 84101; tel: 800-541-4955; www.visitsaltlake.com
Tooele County Tourism
47 South Main St, Tooele, UT 84074; tel: 800-378-0690; www.co.tooele.ut.us

Utah Valley Convention and Visitors Bureau
51 South University Ave, Ste. 111, Provo, UT 84601; tel: 800-370-3893; www.utahvalley.org/cvb

Vernal Convention and Visitors Bureau
147 East Main St, Vernal, UT 84078; tel: 435-781-6730; www.utahconvention.org

Central Utah

Castle Country Travel Region
90 North 100 East, #2, Price, UT 84501; tel: 800-842-0789; www.castlecountry.com

Millard County Tourism
460 N. Main St, Fillmore, UT 84631; tel: 800-441-4288; www.millardcounty.com

Mt. Pleasant Chamber of Commerce
115 W. Main St, Mt. Pleasant, UT 84647; tel: 435-462-2456

Panoramaland Travel Region
4 S. Main St, Nephi, UT 84648; tel: 800-281-4346; www.sanpetecounty.org

Sevier County Travel Council
250 N. Main St, Richfield, UT 84701; tel: 800-662-8898; www.sevierutah.net

Southern Utah

Beaver County Travel Council
40 S. Main St, Beaver, UT 84713; tel: 866-891-6655; www.beavercountyutah.com

Capitol Reef Country/Wayne County Travel Council
Junction Hwy 12 and 24, Torrey, UT 84775; tel: 800-858-7951; www.capitolreef.org

Emery County Travel Bureau
48 Farrer St, Green River, UT 84525;

tel: 435-564-3600; www.emerycounty.com

Garfield County Travel Council
55 S. Main St, Panguitch, UT 84759; tel: 800-444-6689; www.brycecanyoncountry.com

Grand County Travel Council
40 North 100 East, Moab, UT 84532; tel: 435-644-5033; www.discovermoab.com

Iron County Travel Council
581 N. Main St, Cedar City, UT 84720; tel: 800-354-4849; www.scenicsouthernutah.com

Kane County Travel Council
78 South 100 East, Kanab, UT 84741; tel: 800-733-5263; www.kaneutah.com

Piute County Tourism
550 N. Main St, Junction, UT 84740; tel: 435-577-2949; www.piute.org

San Juan County Visitor Services
117 S. Main St, Monticello, UT 84535; tel: 800-574-4386; www.southeasutah.com

St. George Area Convention and Visitors Bureau
1835 Convention Center Dr, St. George, UT 84790; tel: 800-869-6635; www.utahstgeorge.com

Parks and Wilderness Areas

Bureau of Land Management
324 S. State St, Ste. 301, Salt Lake City, UT 84145-0155; tel: 801-539-4001; www.ut.blm.gov

National Park Service Southwest Region
P.O. Box 728, Santa Fe, NM 87504-0728; tel: 505-988-6016; www.nps.gov

Utah State Park and Recreation Division

1594 West North Temple, Ste. 116, Salt Lake City, UT 84114-5610; tel: 801-538-7220; www.stateparks.utah.gov

U.S. Forest Service
125 S. State St, Rm. 8301, Salt Lake City, UT 84138; tel: 877-444-6777; www.fs.fed.us

Weights & Measures

Despite efforts to convert to metric, the U.S. still uses the Imperial System of weights and measures.

1 inch	=	2.54 cm
1 foot	=	30.48 cm
1 yard	=	0.9144 meter
1 mile	=	1.609 km
1 pint	=	0.473 liter
1 quart	=	0.946 liter
1 ounce	=	28.4 grams
1 pound	=	0.453 kg
1 acre	=	0.405 hectare
1 sq mile	=	259 hectares
1 centimeter	=	0.394 inch
1 meter	=	39.37 inches
1 kilometer	=	0.621 mile
1 liter	=	1.057 quarts
1 gram	=	0.035 ounce
1 kilogram	=	2.205 pounds
1 hectare	=	2.471 acres
1 sq km	=	0.386 sq. mile

Wildlife

Never approach wild animals. Use binoculars, a spotting scope or a camera with telephoto lens. Don't try to feed or touch wildlife, not even the "cute" ones like chipmunks, squirrels and prairie dogs (they may carry diseases). Don't try to move animals by calling or herding them.

BELOW: a bobcat on the prowl. Never approach wildlife; use a telephoto lens or binoculars to get a better view.

FURTHER READING

Nonfiction

History

Arrington, Leonard and Davis Bitton. *The Mormon Experience: a History of the Latter-day Saints.* Urbana : University of Illinois Press, 1992.

Brodie, Fawn. *No Man Knows My History: The Life of Joseph Smith.* New York, NY: Vintage Books, 1995.

Brooks, Juanita. *The Mountain Meadows Massacre.* Salt Lake City, UT: Howe Brothers. 1950

Inskip, Eleanor. *The Colorado River Through Glen Canyon Before Lake Powell: Historic Photo Journal 1872 to 1964.* Moab, UT: Inskip Ink, 1995.

Powell, Allen Kent, editor. *Utah History Encyclopedia.* Salt Lake City, UT: University of Utah Press, 1994.

Woodbury, Angus. *A History of Southern Utah and its National Parks.* Springdale, UT: Zion Natural History Association, 1997.

Culture

Adams, William Jenson. *Sanpete Tales: Humorous Folklore from Central Utah.* New York, NY: Signature Books, 1999.

Brooks, Juanita. *Quicksand and Cactus. A Memoir of the Southern Mormon Frontier.* Salt Lake City, UT: Howe Brothers, 1982.

Cuch, Forrest S., editor. *A History of Utah's Native Americans.* Salt Lake City, UT: Division of Indian Affairs/Utah Division of State History, 2000.

Frost, Kent with Rosalie Goldman. *My Canyonlands.* Monticello, UT: Canyon Country Publications, 1997.

Krakauer, Jon. *Under the Banner of Heaven : a Story of Violent Faith.* New York: Doubleday, 2003.

Locke, Raymond Friday. *The Book of the Navajo, Fifth Edition.* Los Angeles, CA: Mankind Publishing, 1976.

Morrow, Baker H. and Price, V. B., editors. *Anasazi Architecture and American Design.* Albuquerque, NM: University of New Mexico Press, 1997.

Murray, John. *An Illustrated Guide to the Movies and their Locations.* Flagstaff, AZ: Northland Publishing, 2000.

Negri, Richard F., editor. *Tales of Canyonlands Cowboys.* UT: Utah

State University Press, 1997.

O'Neil Floyd A. and Kathryn L. McKay. "A History of the Uintah-Ouray Ute Lands." American West Occasional Papers No. 10, 1979.

Ostling Richard N. and Joan K. Ostling. *Mormon America: The Power and the Promise.* San Francisco: Harper San Francisco, 1999.

Papanikolas, Helen Zeese, editor. *The Peoples of Utah.* Salt Lake City: Utah State Historical Society, 1976.

Quinn, D. Michael. *Early Mormonism and the Magic World View.* New York, NY: Signature Books. 1998.

Rutter, Michael. *Outlaw Tales of Utah: True Stories of Utah's Most Famous Robbers, Rustlers, and Bandits.* Guilford, CT: Twodot Press, 2003.

Sorensen, Virginia. *Where Nothing is Long Ago: Memories of a Mormon Childhood.* Signature Mormon Classics. New York, NY: Signature Books, 1999.

Stanton, Bette. *Where God Put the West: Movie Making in the Desert.* Moab, UT: Moab to Monument Valley Film Commission, 1994.

Stegner, Wallace. *Mormon Country.* Lincoln, NE: University of Nebraska Press, 1970.

Trimble, Stephen. *The People: Indians of the American Southwest.* Santa Fe, NM: School of American Research Press, 1993.

Wharton, Tom and Gayen. *It Happened in Utah.* Guilford, CT: Twodot Press, 1998

Essays

Abbey, Edward. *Desert Solitaire: A Season in the Wilderness.* New York, NY: Ballantine Books, 1971.

Melloy, Ellen. *Raven's Exile: A Season on the Green River.* New York, NY: Henry Holt, 1994.

Trimble, Stephen and Gary Nabhan. *The Geography of Childhood: Why Children Need Wild Places.* Boston, MA: Beacon Press, 1994.

Williams, Terry Tempest. *Refuge: An Unnatural History of Place.* New York: Vintage Books, 1992.

Williams, Terry Tempest. *Red: Passion and Patience in the Desert.* New York: Vintage Books, 2002.

Nature

Baars, Donald L. *The Colorado*

Plateau: A Geologic History. Revised Edition. Albuquerque, NM: University of New Mexico Press, 2000.

Buchanan, Hayle. *Wildflowers of Southwestern Utah: A Field Guide to Bryce Canyon, Cedar Breaks, and Surrounding Plant Communities.* Bryce Canyon, UT: Bryce Canyon Natural History Association, 1992.

Chesher, Greer. *Grand Staircase-Escalante National Monument: Heart of the Desert Wild.* UT: Bryce Canyon Natural History Association, 2000.

Cole, Jim. *Utah Wildlife Viewing Guide.* Helena, MT: Falcon Press, 1990.

De Buys, William. *Seeing Things Whole: The Essential John Wesley Powell.* San Francisco, CA: Island Press, 2001.

Hafen, Lyman. *Mukuntuweap: Landscape and Story in Zion Canyon.* St. George, UT: Tonquint Press, 1996.

Williams, David. *A Naturalist's Guide to Canyon Country.* Helena, MT: Falcon Press in cooperation with Canyonlands Natural History Association, 2000.

Travel

Brenchley, Julius and Jules Remy. *Journey to the Great Salt Lake City* (1861). Salt Lake City, UT: Red Butte Press, University of Utah Libraries, 1984

Burton, Sir Richard F. *The City of the Saints: Among the Mormons and Across the Rocky Mountains to California* (1861). New York, NY: Narrative Press, 2003.

Hinchman, Sandra. *Hiking the Southwest's Canyon Country.* Seattle, WA: The Mountaineers Books, 1997.

Houk, Rose and Nicky Leach. *The Guide to National Parks of the Southwest,* Revised Edition. Tucson, AZ: Western Parks Association, 2005.

Leach, Nicky. *National Parks of Utah.* Mariposa, CA: Sierra Press, 2002.

Roylance, Ward. *The Enchanted Wilderness: A Redrock Odyssey.* Torrey, UT: Four Corners West Publishing, 1986.

Rusho, W. L. *Everett Reuss: A Vagabond for Beauty.* Salt Lake City,

UT: Gibbs Smith Publishers, 1983.
Spangler, Jerry D. and Donna K.
*Horned Snakes and Axle Grease: A
Roadside Guide to the Archaeology,
History, and Rock Art of Nine Mile
Canyon*. Salt Lake City, UT: Uinta
Publishing, 2003.
Twain, Mark. *Roughing It* (1871). New
York, NY: Signet Classics, 1994.
Powell, Allan Kent. *The Utah Guide*.
Golden, CO: Fulcrum Publishing,
1995.

Fiction and Poetry

Cannon, Blanche. *Nothing Ever
Happens Sunday Morning*. New York,
NY: Putnam Publishers, 1948.
Fisher, Vardis. *Childen of God: An
American Epic*. New York, NY: Harper
and Brothers, 1939.
Freeman, Judith. *The Chinchilla Farm.
A Novel*. New York, NY: W.W. Norton
and Company, 2003.
Sillitoe, Linda. *Sideways to the Sun*.
New York, NY: Signature Books,
1987.
Sillitoe, Linda. *Windows on the Sea
and Other Stories*. New York, NY:
Signature Books, 1990.
Stegner, Wallace. *The Big Rock
Candy Mountain* (1943). New York,
NY: Penguin Books, 1995.
Whipple, Maurine. *The Giant Joshua*
(1941). Western Epics Publishing,
1982.

Movies and Videos

Hundreds of movies have been made
in Utah, particularly the scenic
southern part of the state, where
dramatic redrock country has drawn
filmmakers since John Ford filmed
westerns in Monument Valley in the
late 1930s and 40s.
Back to the Future 3, 1990
Goblin Valley is one of the backdrops
for this futuristic fantasy starring
Michael J. Fox.
*Butch Cassidy and the Sundance Kid,
1968*
Paul Newman and Robert Redford
play lovable outlaws in this sweet
buddy film, shot partly in the ghost
town of Grafton, near Zion National
Park.
Cheyenne Autumn, 1964
Parts of John Ford's last western
about the fate of the Cheyenne
Indians was shot in Professor Valley,
east of Moab.
City Slickers II, 1994
Billy Crystal and cohorts reprised
their roles in this comedy about
innocent dudes from the city caught
up in hilarious western intrigues.
Deadwood Coach, 1924
Veteran cowboy actor Tom Mix
starred in this early western shot in

picturesque Kanab Canyon, near
Kanab's "Little Hollywood." The
location was also featured in the
1960s television series *Gunsmoke*.
Easy Rider, 1969
Anti-heroes Peter Fonda and Dennis
Hopper rumbled through Utah, among
other places, in this counterculture
classic.
Footloose, 1984
Much of this movie about a young
man who dances his way into a
conservative town was filmed in
Provo, south of Salt Lake City. Provo
Flour Mill, visible at the Lehi exit of
Interstate 15, is featured in the
movie.
Forrest Gump, 1994
Tom Hanks starred in this huge hit
about a simple man who finds
himself at the center of major world
events. A pivotal scene was shot at
John Ford Point in Monument Valley.
Geronimo, 1993
White Ranch, near Canyonlands
National Park, was the backdrop for
this biopic about the famous Apache
leader starring Wes Studi, Gene
Hackman and Robert Duvall.
*Indiana Jones and the Temple of
Doom, 1989*

Feedback

We do our best to ensure that the
information in our books is as
accurate and up-to-date as possible. The books are updated on a
regular basis, using local
contacts, who painstakingly add,
amend and correct as required.
However, some mistakes and
omissions are inevitable and we
are ultimately reliant on our
readers to put us in the picture.
We welcome your feedback on any
details related to your experiences
using the book "on the road."
Maybe we recommended a hotel
that you liked (or another that you
didn't), as well as interesting new
attractions, or facts and figures you
have found out about the country
itself. The more details you can
give us (particularly with regard to
addresses, e-mails and telephone
numbers), the better.
We will acknowledge all contribu-
tions, and we'll offer an Insight
Guide to the best letters received.

Please write to us at:
Insight Guides
PO Box 7910
London SE1 1WE
United Kingdom
Or send e-mail to:
insight@apaguide.co.uk

Steven Spielberg's adventurous
archaeologist, played by Harrison
Ford, pops up in Arches National
Park, near Moab.
Jeremiah Johnson, 1972
Robert Redford starred in this
unusual story, based on Vardis
Fisher's novel *Mountain Man*, about
a man in the mid-1800s who
becomes disenchanted by civilization
and moves to the wilderness.
Redford fell in love with the area and
purchased land that would eventually
become Sundance Ski Resort and
Sundance Institute.
The Outlaw Josey Wales, 1976
Based on the Forrest Carter novel
set during the Civil War era, this
movie starred Clint Eastwood as a
Confederate guerilla raider out to
revenge the deaths of his family at
Union hands. Much of the film was
shot at Old Pariah, near Kanab, Utah.
Heritage of the Desert, 1932
Western writer Zane Grey's classic
penny western about Mormon
ranchers was shot at Old Pariah in
the Grand Staircase section of what
is now Grand Staircase-Escalante
National Monument.
Rio Grande, 1950
Another John Ford classic shot at the
White Ranch near Canyonlands
National Park.
Stagecoach, 1939
John Ford's classic western about
cross-country travelers thrown
together on a stagecoach journey
was shot in Monument Valley.
Thelma and Louise, 1991
This women's buddy road movie
starring Susan Sarandon and Geena
Davis as gals on the lam scored big
with movie goers. Scenes were shot in
Arches National Park, and the final
suicide scene was shot at Dead Horse
Point State Park next to Canyonlands
National Park.
The Greatest Story Ever Told, 1965
The Sermon on the Mount Scene of
this Biblical classic starring Max Von
Sydow was shot at the Green River
Overlook in the Island in the Sky
district of Canyonlands National Park.
Wagonmaster, 1949
This western directed by John Ford
was the first Hollywood movie to deal
with Mormon history in Utah. Much of
it was shot in Professor Valley along
the Colorado River and in Spanish
Valley, southeast of Moab.

ART & PHOTO CREDITS

Daughters of Utah Pioneers 38, 42, 44, 46
Denver Public Library 31
Steve Greenwood back cover right, 124 bottom, 127, 130–131, 137, 138 bottom left, 138 bottom right, 140, 184 bottom, 189
Blaine Harrington 16, 60, 121, 296 top, 300, 302
George H. H. Huey back flap top & bottom, 6 top, 7 middle, 23, 26, 72–73, 86, 129, 148 top, 159, 160 top, 162 top, 163, 185, 198–199, 201, 207, 217, 219, 220 top, 220–221, 222, 234, 235, 242 top, 249, 267, 282 top, 294 top, 341
Kerrick James front flap top, 55, 78 right, 92, 166, 231, 238–239, 240, 268 bottom, 269, 270 top, 275, 278–279, 282 bottom, 292 bottom, 315, 331
Library of Congress 27, 32, 48, 49, 50
Scott Markewitz 1, 4–5, 8 top, 8 bottom, 14–15, 93, 99, 101, 104–105, 196, 272, 278 top, 283
Mark Maziarz front flap bottom, 2–3, 95, 96, 100, 102, 103, 142–143, 144, 145, 146 top, 146 bottom, 152, 273, 308, 311, 325, 326, 334, 336, 337
Museum of Church History and Art 18–19 (*Handcart Pioneers* by C. A. A. Christensen © by

Intellectual Reserve, Inc.), 40 (*Joseph Smith Preaching to the Indians* by William Armitage © by Intellectual Reserve, Inc.), 41 (*Mormon Panorama Four, The First Latter-day Settlement in Missouri* by C. A. A. Christensen © by Intellectual Reserve, Inc.), 43 (*Brigham Young* by George M. Ottinger © by Intellectual Reserve, Inc.), 45 (*Brigham Young and His Family* by William Warner Major © by Intellectual Reserve, Inc.)
Nick Nacca/Photophile 276 bottom
Dale O'Dell/Photophile 248
Jack Parsons 64, 280 bottom, 298 top, 298 bottom, 320
Louie Psihoyos 75, 77, 81, 156, 173
Tom Till back cover bottom, 7 top, 7 bottom, 9 top, 9 bottom, 12–13, 20, 24–25, 34, 37, 61, 74, 76, 78 left, 79, 84, 106–107, 108–109, 110, 114–115, 118–119, 120, 132, 148 bottom, 154–155, 160 bottom, 162 bottom, 168–169, 174 bottom, 176 bottom, 177, 178–179, 181, 186–187, 188, 192 bottom, 200, 203, 206, 208, 209, 210 bottom, 212, 214–215, 216, 223, 224–225, 233, 242–243, 247, 260, 264, 271, 277, 280 top, 281, 284–285, 286

Stephen Trimble back cover center, 6 bottom, 10–11, 28, 29, 30, 33, 36, 54, 56–57, 58, 59, 62, 63, 65, 66, 67, 68, 69, 70, 71, 80, 82, 83, 85, 87, 90, 91, 97, 98, 116, 123, 124 top, 125, 126 top, 126 bottom, 128, 133, 135, 136 top, 136 bottom, 138 top, 139, 141, 147, 150 top, 150 bottom, 149, 151, 153, 161, 164–165, 170, 171, 174 top, 175, 176 top, 180, 183, 184 top, 191, 192 top, 193, 194–195, 204 top, 204 bottom, 210 top, 213, 227, 229, 230 top, 232, 236, 237, 241, 244 top, 245, 246, 250–251, 252, 253, 255, 256 top, 256 bottom, 257, 258, 259, 261, 268 top, 270 bottom, 274, 276 top, 289, 290 top, 290 bottom, 292 top, 294 bottom, 295, 296 bottom, 297, 299, 304, 316, 323
Utah State Historical Society 21, 22, 35, 39, 47, 51, 52, 53
Wiley/Wales spine, back cover left, 88, 94, 157, 205, 226, 230 bottom, 244 bottom, 262–263, 265, 287, 291, 293

Cartographic Editor: Zoë Goodwin
Map Production: Stephen Ramsay
©2005 Apa Publications GmbH & Co. Verlag KG, Singapore Branch

INDEX

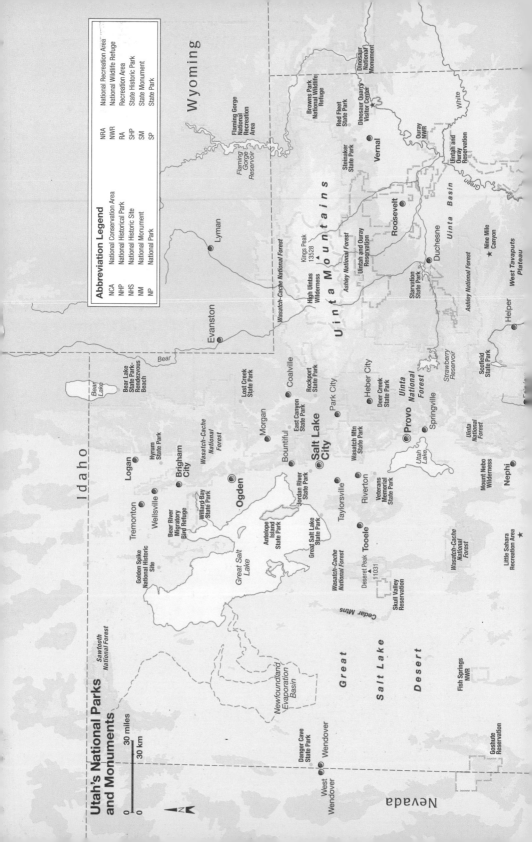

Utah's National Parks and Monuments

Idaho

Wyoming

Nevada

Abbreviation Legend

NCA	National Conservation Area	NRA	National Recreation Area
NHP	National Historical Park	NWR	National Wildlife Refuge
NHS	National Historic Site	RA	Recreation Area
NM	National Monument	SHP	State Historic Park
NP	National Park	SM	State Monument
		SP	State Park

Sawtooth National Forest

Bear Lake State Park–Rendezvous Beach

Bear Lake

Lyman

Evanston

Bear

Flaming Gorge National Recreation Area

Flaming Gorge Reservoir

Wasatch-Cache National Forest

Browns Park National Wildlife Refuge

Red Fleet State Park

Dinosaur National Monument

Dinosaur Quarry Visitor Center

Steinaker State Park

Vernal

White

Uintah and Ouray Reservation

Green

Uinta Mountains

Kings Peak 13528

High Uintas Wilderness

Ashley National Forest

Uintah and Ouray Reservation

Roosevelt

Uinta Basin

Duchesne

Starvation State Park

Ashley National Forest

Nine Mile Canyon

West Tavaputs Plateau

Helper

Scofield State Park

Strawberry Reservoir

Lost Creek State Park

Coalville

Rockport State Park

Park City

Heber City

Deer Creek State Park

Uinta National Forest

Springville

Provo

Uinta National Forest

Mount Nebo Wilderness

Nephi

Logan

Tremonton

Wellsville

Hyrum State Park

Brigham City

Wasatch-Cache National Forest

Morgan

East Canyon State Park

Bountiful

Salt Lake City

Ogden

Willard Bay State Park

Bear River Migratory Bird Refuge

Golden Spike National Historic Site

Great Salt Lake

Antelope Island State Park

Jordan River State Park

Great Salt Lake State Park

Wasatch-Cache National Forest

Desert Peak 11031

Cedar Mtns

Skull Valley Reservation

Taylorsville

Riverton

Veterans Memorial State Park

Wasatch Mtn State Park

Utah Lake

Wasatch-Cache National Forest

Little Sahara Recreation Area

Newfoundland Evaporation Basin

Great

Salt Lake

Desert

Tooele

Fish Springs NWR

Danger Cave State Park

Wendover

West Wendover

Goshute Reservation

N

0		30 miles
0		30 km